the argument of ulysses

the argument of ulysses

by stanley sultan

ohio state university press

All selections from *Ulysses*, by James Joyce, Copyright 1914, 1918
and renewed 1942, 1946 by Nora Joseph Joyce. Reprinted by permission of Random House, Inc., New York, and The Bodley Head
Ltd., London.

All selections from *A Portrait of the Artist as a Young Man*, by James
Joyce, are used by permission of The Viking Press, Inc., Publishers,
New York; the Executors of the James Joyce Estate; and Jonathan
Cape Ltd., London.

"Who Goes with Fergus?" reprinted with permission of Mrs. W. B.
Yeats; the Macmillan Company, New York; the Macmillan Com-
pany of Canada; Messrs. Macmillan and Company Ltd.; and Messrs.
A. P. Watt and Son, London, from *Collected Poems of W. B. Yeats*,
Copyright 1906 by The Macmillan Company, Renewed 1934 by
William Butler Yeats.

Portions of "Joyce's Irish Politics: The Seventh Chapter of *Ulys-
ses*," by Stanley Sultan, reprinted from the *Massachusetts Review*,
Vol. II, No. 3 (Spring, 1961), by permission of the publishers.
Copyright © 1961 by Stanley Sultan.

Portions of "The Sirens at the Ormond Bar: *Ulysses*," by Stanley
Sultan, reprinted from the *University of Kansas City Review*, Vol.
XXVI, No. 2 (Winter, 1959), by permission of the editors.

this book is dedicated to **Jamie and Sonia**

acknowledgments

I wish to thank: the Shell Oil Company and Deans H. Donaldson Jordan and Robert F. Campbell of Clark University for grants that met the bulk of the expenses for typing, editorial assistance, and permissions fees; the rare book librarians and Donald Wing of the Yale University Library; Ethel Mahue Delaney and Betty Hill Place, for help of various kinds; Alfred Young Fisher, George Gibian, Gordon S. Haight, Wendell Stacy Johnson, and Martin Price (among others), for their interest in the book and their encouragement.

For assistance in the preparation of the manuscript, I am indebted to Cynthia Forman Johanson, Dona Luongo Stein, and Florence Lehman Sultan.

To the late Newton Arvin, to Harold Bloom, Cleanth Brooks, Malcolm Cowley, Robert Gorham Davis, Charles Feidelson, Richard M. Kain, Thomas E. Sheahan, and Robert A. Stein, I owe certain virtues of the book and the diminution of certain defects.

I have saved my first and greatest indebtedness for last. The major part of *The Argument of Ulysses* is based on a Yale University doctoral dissertation, which originated in Professor Cleanth Brooks's seminar on certain modern writers, was tested and tempered by the critical intelligence of my fellow student Thomas M. Greene, and benefited above all from the counsel of Professor Eugene M. Waith. He gave me guidance and encouragement beyond my deserts; but the debt that I owe him for determined, eloquent battle with my stubborn will only he and I know.

STANLEY SULTAN

contents

abbreviations *used for works cited*

First references are given full citation in the footnotes; subsequent references in the footnotes and text employ, for the sake of brevity, the abbreviations listed alphabetically below.

Beebe Maurice Beebe, "Joyce and Stephen Dedalus: The Problem of Autobiography," *A James Joyce Miscellany: Second Series*, ed. Marvin Magalaner (Carbondale, Ind., 1959), pp. 67-77.

Blackmur R. P. Blackmur, "The Jew in Search of a Son," *Virginia Quarterly Review*, XXIV (1948), 96–116.

Budgen Frank Budgen, *James Joyce and the Making of Ulysses* (New York, 1934).

Butcher and Lang S. H. Butcher and A. Lang, *The Odyssey of Homer Done into English Prose* (4th ed.; London, 1883).

Byrne J. F. Byrne, *Silent Years: An Autobiography with Memoirs of James Joyce and Our Ireland* (New York, 1953).

Critical Writings *The Critical Writings of James Joyce*, ed. Ellsworth Mason and Richard Ellmann (London, 1959).

Daiches David Daiches, *The Novel in the Modern World* (Chicago, 1939).

Damon S. Foster Damon, "The Odyssey in Dublin," *Hound & Horn*, III (1929–30), 7-44. (Reprinted in Givens, pp. 203–42.)

Duff   Charles Duff, *James Joyce and the Plain Reader* (London, 1932).

Dummelow   *A Commentary on the Holy Bible by Various Writers*, ed. J. R. Dummelow (London, 1910).

Finnegans   James Joyce, *Finnegans Wake* (London, 1950).
  Wake

Gilbert   Stuart Gilbert, *James Joyce's Ulysses* (New York, 1930).

Givens   *James Joyce: Two Decades of Criticism*, ed. Seon Givens (New York, 1948).

Goldberg   S. L. Goldberg, *The Classical Temper: A Study of James Joyce's Ulysses* (London, 1961).

Golding   Louis Golding, *James Joyce* (London, 1933).

Hutchins   Patricia Hutchins, *James Joyce's Dublin* (London, 1950).

James Joyce Richard Ellmann, *James Joyce* (New York, 1959).

Joyce   Marvin Magalaner and Richard M. Kain, *Joyce: The Man, the Work, the Reputation* (New York, 1956).

Jung   C. G. Jung, "Ulysses—A Monologue," tr. W. Stanley Dell, *Nimbus*, II (1953), 7–20.

Kain   Richard M. Kain, *Fabulous Voyager: James Joyce's Ulysses* (Chicago, 1947).

Kenner, "The   Hugh Kenner, "The *Portrait* in Perspective," in Givens, pp. 132–74.
  Portrait in
  Perspective"

Kenner,   Hugh Kenner, *Dublin's Joyce* (Bloomington, Ind., 1956).
  Dublin's
  Joyce

Larbaud   Valery Larbaud, "The 'Ulysses' of James Joyce," *Criterion*, I (1922), 94–103.

Letters   *Letters of James Joyce,* ed. Stuart Gilbert (New York, 1957).

Levin   Harry Levin, *James Joyce: A Critical Introduction* (Norfolk, Va., 1941).

Lewis   Wyndham Lewis, *Time and Western Man* (New York, 1928).

Noon   William T. Noon, S.J., "James Joyce: Unfacts, Fiction, and Facts," *PMLA,* LXXVI (1961), 254–76.

Portrait   James Joyce, *A Portrait of the Artist as a Young Man* (New York, 1956).

Schutte   William M. Schutte, *Joyce and Shakespeare: A Study in the Meaning of Ulysses* (New Haven, 1957).

Stanislaus Joyce   Stanislaus Joyce, *My Brother's Keeper: James Joyce's Early Years,* ed. Richard Ellmann (New York, 1958).

Stanislaus Joyce, "Memoir"   Stanislaus Joyce, "James Joyce: A Memoir," tr. Felix Giovanelli, *Hudson Review,* II (1950), 485-514.

Strong   L. A. G. Strong, *The Sacred River* (London, 1949).

Tindall   William York Tindall, *James Joyce: His Way of Interpreting the Modern World* (New York, 1950).

Tindall, Reader's Guide   William York Tindall, *A Reader's Guide to James Joyce* (New York, 1959).

Ulysses   James Joyce, *Ulysses* (New York, 1934).

Von Abele   Rudolph Von Abele, "*Ulysses:* The Myth of Myth," *PMLA,* LXIX (1954), 358–64.

Wilson   Edmund Wilson, *Axel's Castle* (New York, 1931).

the argument of ulysses

introduction

Ulysses was officially published on February 2, 1922, its
author's fortieth birthday, when the first printed copy of the
book was put into Joyce's hands by his publisher, Sylvia
Beach. It was available in Paris very soon thereafter, and
duly reported on in the press of the English-speaking countries. A review printed in a number of provincial British
newspapers on April 6 said:

> Only a few have seen, but everyone is saying how
> wonderful it is. If a single sentence were quoted in the
> presence of these fashionable dilettante they would run
> in horror. I have seen a copy. It is inconceivable how
> any man outside a lunatic asylum could produce such
> unadulterated filth and claim that it was literature.[1]

The legal and spiritual guardians of Anglo-Saxon society
had expressed themselves a year earlier in New York, when
they placed the two well-bred spinsters who printed the
first chapters serially in the *Little Review* under criminal
indictment on a morals charge; and the book was soon
banned in every country whose language was its own. The
literary establishment passed judgment in October, when
Alfred Noyes, England's "unofficial poet laureate," spoke
on *Ulysses* before the Royal Society of Literature. "There
is no foulness conceivable to the mind of madman or ape
that has not been poured into its imbecile pages," he said,[2]
and asserted sarcastically that the *Sporting Times or the*

Pink 'Un, London's organ of bookmaking and burlesque, had "the only sound analysis of the book in this country."

The *Pink 'Un* had accompanied its issue of April 1 with a broadside announcing a special article, "The Scandal of *Ulysses.*" Given a banner headline, but deferred to page four in favor of "Sportive Notes" and a poem, "The Kissers," the article had a subhead, "Europe's Most Notorious Book Disgustingly Dull," which reveals the essence of the *Pink 'Un's* criticism—the word "scandal" in the title is a clever ambiguity suggesting that Joyce is a fraud, that the real scandal of *Ulysses* is not its salaciousness, which the vehicle of "The Kissers" also deplores, but the fact that the salacious book is "sordid" and "dull" rather than erotically rewarding. In *Finnegans Wake,* in answer to the question "in Sam Hill, how?" Shem the Penman could have been boycotted by Anglo-Saxon society and forced to write in exile, the author explains:

> Let manner and matter of this for these our sporting times be cloaked up in the language of blushfed porporates that an Anglican ordinal, not reading his own rude dunsky tunga, may ever behold the brand of scarlet on the brow of her of Babylon and feel not the pink one in his own damned cheek. (p. 185)

The provocations to anger were not to cease, of course. The prohibitions, the destruction by the British customs of a whole edition (less one copy), the vice-squad raids, pulpit attacks, newspaper snickering, even the inaccurate and unjust obituary and "appreciation" in the London *Times* following Joyce's death on January 13, 1941, all are part of the cultural history of our century.

Practically speaking, however, the causes for anger were unimportant. Despite their power and zeal, all the bigoted enemies of *Ulysses* could affect little more than its accessibility. Once it became legally available, they may have deterred some prospective readers, but they could mislead none. And their effort was more than counterbalanced by sympathetic attention from the very beginning. Although Joyce's hope that his book would appeal to a large audience was quixotic (despite what was said about him, he very

much wanted to be read), and although such impressive
literary artists and critics as Arnold Bennett, John Gals-
worthy, D. H. Lawrence, F. R. Leavis, Paul Elmer More,
and Virginia Woolf found themselves unable to assimilate
his radical innovation, *Ulysses* was reviewed seriously by
most of the literary and liberal political journals in London
and New York, favorably in many cases, and its author
became the most famous and respected figure in English-
speaking literary and expatriate circles in Paris. Within
five years after its appearance, Joyce and his work, which
consisted of only a slight volume of verse, a collection of
short stories, and two longer narratives, had inspired three
books and dozens of articles; they were the first items in a
corpus that grew with the subject's fame until today more
than a score of books and hundreds of articles have been
written wholly or largely about *Ulysses* alone.

Nevertheless, while one student of Joyce declares in his
recent book:

> I do not propose at this late date to say anything
> general about *Ulysses*. Accounts of the book have been
> given by Mr. Stuart Gilbert, Mr. Frank Budgen, Mr.
> Louis Golding, and many others. It has been charted
> and mapped, and no reader nowadays need experience
> any difficulty with it . . . ,[3]

another, in his more recent book, says:

> The enigma of *Ulysses* continues to invite and repel,
> to tantalize by suggesting one interpretation only to ridi-
> cule it.[4]

There is a great deal of incidental fun in *Ulysses*, a great
deal of ingenuity that is either impressive as tour de force
or annoying, depending upon one's tolerance for gratuitous
pyrotechnics and networks of correspondence, and some
writing that is admirable simply in its own right (the portrait of Mr. Deasy, the representation of Shakespeare's
environment, the depiction of Bloom beleaguered in the
funeral car). A number of the critics who were gratified
by the book's varied attractions and tantalized by their

meaning have helped its other readers, and the present study would have been impossible if their work had not been available for the guidance and instruction of its author. Even the line of criticism that has become progressively more ingenious in its articulation and defense of networks of correspondence—some esoteric and trivial, but proven to be intentional by the various caches of Joyce's papers, some integral and relevant, some trumped up—has been indirectly useful when it has not been directly so.

However, the "enigma" remains. And the difficulty is far more fundamental than the considerable amount of material written about *Ulysses* would suggest. From the beginning, books and articles have discussed stylistic singularities, patterns of allusion, and various complexes of symbolic meaning; but there exists no general agreement about that which would ordinarily be regarded as an antecedent, even a primary, consideration: what happens in the book. The book clearly has a protagonist, yet there has been no generally accepted account of what he experiences or of what he does. No one has demonstrated conclusively how Mr. Bloom's odyssey has ended, or even if it has ended. The development of his relations with the two other major characters is unclear; and thus, the fate the narrative indicates for all three principals is unclear. If there is a scandal connected with *Ulysses*, it relates to this striking fact.

The critical interpretations of the book reflect the situation: they are numerous and extend over the whole range of possibilities. One, and it is argued well only by Edmund Wilson,[5] is that *Ulysses* ends happily, and therefore expresses an affirmative philosophy of life; another is that the author holds out hope for his protagonists although their condition is miserable, and therefore shows the human condition to be potentially positive;[6] a third is that he presents with deep sympathy a pathetic world.[7] In addition to affirmation, optimism, and commiseration, the book is thought to assert pessimism—a simple despair about life[8]— and even nihilism—the author's attempt to discredit or destroy all traditional values of life and art.[9]

These are the interpretations of critics who regard the book as fundamentally serious. Those who think it quite the opposite differ from one another in a corresponding way, with the determining consideration whether Joyce is seen to be: (a) involved with the characters and world of his comedy; or (b) outside that world ("the indifferent artist" "paring his fingernails") and mocking it. The more substantial interpretation in the first category is that the book is essentially positive because its heroic and mythic allusions ennoble rather than denigrate its commonplace modern world.[10] The other considers it to be simply "genial and comic," the work of a "humorous writer of the traditional English school—in temper, at his best, very like Sterne."[11] One interpretation in the second category represents the book as comic pessimism—pessimistic and not nihilistic because it asserts spiritual and moral values which its characters fail to live up to, comic because "To be able to laugh with others at the recognized absurdity of a common tangential position ["all men's sundering"] may be a first step in the direction of a reconciliation."[12] Mostly, however, critics of this persuasion are among the many who find it nihilistic, even when they do not draw the conclusion themselves. Its essence "is God laughing at the world from which (as the Cabala tells us) he has withdrawn,"[13] its comic principle, "the hard cerebral ridicule of the ironist who has smashed through all the paper-walls of his environment and, turning suddenly, observed the essential filth of life. . . ."[14]

Thus, the lack of general agreement about what happens in *Ulysses* is naturally reflected in a lack of general agreement about the nature and ultimate meaning of the book: it is called both comic and serious, both affirmative and negatory. Ironically, however, the disagreements on both levels are largely the result of a subtle consensus—a cluster of untested critical suppositions about characters, literary devices, tone, and action; a few critics accept all of those suppositions, every critic seems to accept some of them, and each supposition alone is a serious obstacle to reading the book.

The general acceptance of them has obscured the relationship, but those prior conclusions all in their turn derive directly and logically from one basic presumption about the philosophy of the author and the meaning of his book.

The influential presumption is itself unimportant except
as literary history, but exposing it will implicate the corollary
judgments which have so dominated treatment of *Ulysses;*
and the exposition can be done without reviewing forty
years of criticism, for an almost complete descriptive bibliography already exists. In the recent book, *Joyce: The Man,
the Work, the Reputation,* Richard M. Kain describes
chronologically: the comments (including letters to the
editor) on the installments published in *The Little Review*
beginning March, 1918; the scores of reviews of the first
edition; the early books and articles on *Ulysses;* and "Three
Decades of Interpretation, 1925-1955."[15]

Professor Kain says of the hostile reviewers, "It was the
alleged obscenity that most enraged these reviewers, together with what they felt to be the nihilistic tendencies
of the work."[16] But while they ranted against the "nihilism"
in Joyce's "queer new" "imbecile pages" of "literary
Bolshevism," [17] responsible reviewers calmly or exultantly
found in *Ulysses* precisely that same treatment of traditional
artistic and human values.   What J. Middleton Murry's
laudatory review said of Joyce:

> He is the man with the bomb who would blow what
> is left of Europe into the sky,

and of *Ulysses* itself:

> For just as Mr. Joyce is in rebellion against the social
> morality of civilization, he is in rebellion against the
> lucidity and comprehensibility of civilized art,[18]

was generally either declared or implied by the serious
reviewers.[19] And the subsequent canonization of Joyce as
"the grand archetype of literary genius"[20] by the young
writers and readers of one of the most experimental periods
in English literature reinforced an unfortunate initial impression. The extremist Paris magazine *transition,* "after
the excitement of the publication of *Ulysses,* declared 'The
Revolution of the Word' and implicated the innocent Joyce
in outlandish literary excesses."[21] This magazine published

the early work of many of the now distinguished figures of American literature and European painting.[22] But it began and ended its twelve-point "Proclamation" with "The revolution in the English language is an accomplished fact" and "The plain reader be damned";[23] it made Joyce its household god; it was attempting the destruction that so many considered Joyce's aim; and it had among its editors and contributors a number of people who wrote influential criticism of *Ulysses*.[24]

The prior assumption that it is the first great expression of nihilism in literature has been the dominant direct and indirect influence on the criticism of *Ulysses* during its forty-year history. Professor Kain's bibliography will confirm that, although the range of interpretations of the book is as broad as possible, the actual number of critics who consider its outcome or viewpoint positive is relatively small. A more important fact (for short studies can be neither so thorough nor so influential) is that while his own book *Fabulous Voyager* treats *Ulysses* as pessimistic but compassionate (see note 7), almost every other whole book devoted to it or to the corpus of Joyce's work gives the ultimate impression of either grim (see note 9) or mocking (see notes 13 and 14) nihilism.[25]

Some of the specific corollaries to this assumption about *Ulysses* that have made the assumption important for readers of the novel were derived by earlier critics,[26] but the first extrapolation of them all accompanied the first full statement of the nihilism thesis itself. There is no way of assessing the influence of "Ulysses," the essay published by Carl Jung in 1932,[27] although almost every book about *Ulysses* or Joyce's work which was published after that date mentions it explicitly;[28] but whatever its influence, Jung appropriately created the archetype.

The essay begins with a description:

> *Ulysses* is a book which pours along for seven hundred and thirty-five pages, a stream of time of seven hundred and thirty-five days which all consist in one single and senseless every day of Everyman, the completely irrelevant 16th day of June, 1904, in Dublin—a day on which, in all truth, nothing happens[29]

and then links it to the general view of *Ulysses* from which it derives:

> It thus gives cruellest [sic] expression to that emptiness which is both breath-taking and stifling, which is under such tension, or is so filled to bursting, as to grow unbearable. This thoroughly hopeless emptiness is the dominant note of the whole book. It not only begins and ends in nothingness, but it consists of nothing but nothingness.

The interpretation is reasserted on the next page:

> Every sentence raises an expectation which is not fulfilled; finally, out of sheer resignation, you come to expect nothing any longer. Then bit by bit, again to your horror, it dawns upon you that in all truth you have hit the nail on the head. It is actual fact that nothing happens and nothing comes of it . . .

and again and again thereafter.

The observations that *Ulysses* "pours along," that it is about the "irrelevant" and "senseless every day of Everyman," that "nothing happens" in it, can be found even in the early reviews, and are ubiquitous in the criticism, but Jung anchors them firmly in the general assumption which is their source. And he praises Joyce, not only for his social and moral nihilism:

> Strange as it may sound, it is nevertheless true that the world of *Ulysses* is undeniably *better* than the world of those who are hopelessly bound to the darkness of their spiritual birthplaces. Even though the evil and destructive elements predominate, still they thrive . . . at the cost of . . . that "good" which has come down from the past and which shows itself actually to be a ruthless tyrant . . . ,

but also for having realized—as distinguished from merely asserting—that philosophy in his art:

We can ascribe a positive, creative value and meaning not only to *Ulysses,* but also to that art in general to which it is spiritually related. In its attempt to destroy the criteria of beauty and meaning that have held until today, *Ulysses* accomplishes wonders. It . . . brutally disappoints one's expectation of sense and content, it turns all synthesis to ridicule. . . . Everything abusive we can say about *Ulysses* bears testimony to its peculiar quality, for our abusiveness springs from the resentment of the unmodern man. . . .

The passage just above provides the key to the critical suppositions about the characters, literary devices, action, and form of *Ulysses* which derive from the assumption of nihilism because it explicates the bridge between a general interpretation of a difficult literary work and a conception of or way of dealing with that work's specific refractory elements. To the fundamental question, "What happens in *Ulysses?*", an early critic faced with the apparently narrative work which was uniquely difficult to read (in the simplest sense, as a construct of literal sentences) was disposed by a presumption based on the cultural conditions of a *transition* era, personal sympathies, precedent, or any combination of the three to say, "Nothing happens, that's the point." And to questions about form, patterns of allusion, stylistic devices, to the whole question of the place of *function* in the aesthetic of *Ulysses* ("Why newspaper headlines, style parodies, correspondences to Homer, intricate allusions to a bourgeois opera?"), the same assumption indicated the answer: "In its attempt to destroy the criteria of beauty and meaning that have held until today, *Ulysses* accomplishes wonders."

Jung himself say nothing more concrete than what has been quoted about the nature and function of the book's style and various literary devices (beyond blandly remarking "a way of presenting thing which takes no account of the reader"), although other critics have made extensive defenses and scholastic studies of these elements of it on the grounds that they are the work of the high priest of the experimental -ism. His analysis of the action as actionless has been noted. His conception of the one character he mentions as a type ("Everyman") is qualified only by the observation that Bloom is "inactive," "in strongest contrast to his Greek namesake"; and Stephen is presented implicitly as the direct projection of the author. Finally, Jung says of form: "*Ulysses* is the roaring, chaotic, nonsensical cataract of psychic or physical happenings . . . ," and, "The book can be read from the end, for it has no forwards and backwards, no top and no bottom."

The reader acquainted with criticism of *Ulysses* will recognize that the most familiar critical observation about each of the respective elements of the book is that which Jung derives from its supposed nihilistic nature. Even critics who disagree with the basic assumption say that the book has no significant action ("this indecisive day," "the day is hardly even a normal day"), or that Bloom is unchanging ("static," "passive," "frozen," "merely revealed") and an allegorical type ("Bloom or mankind," "Bloom, or Everyman"), or that Stephen is the author's alter ego, or that the tone is derisive when it seems sympathetic and caustic when it seems chaffing, or that any question about the function of a device or allusive pattern is irrelevant (a claim for indulgence which no work deserves and *Ulysses* does not need).

As one concrete example of the popularity of these products of the nihilism thesis, the comments on the form of *Ulysses* in the books written about it or Joyce's work as a whole include: two citations of Jung's "The book can be read from the end, for it has no forwards and backwards, no top and no bottom";[30] the derivation, "Tomorrow will be another day and, for Bloom, a similar Odyssey";[31] a repetition of both these points and the suggestion that

> it is by the isolation and segregation of eighteen hours of human history in one small locality that Joyce imposes an arbitrary unity upon his investigation . . .;[32]

a slight variation of this with the observation that "all epic narratives" are "episodic";[33] and ultimately:

> The final s of Mrs. Bloom's acceptance ["Yes."], meeting the initial S of the first chapter ["Stately"] leads us in a circle to Stephen and back to Mr. Bloom.[34]

Equally important, no meaningful formal pattern is suggested to challenge this prevailing representation of *Ulysses* as a large naturalistic slice of life (with symbols), oozing "flux" at both sides. The critical situation does not signify a failure to see any lineal progression in the narrative, of course, but it does suggest that there has been insufficient recognition of the validity of that progression. The dominant assumption that nothing of importance "happens" in the book quite naturally inhibits the perception of the organic form, chapter upon chapter, in which the development, climax, and resolution of that which in fact does happen is realized.

The prejudgment of theme and tone inherent in the nihilism thesis itself, and the preconceptions of action, characters, literary devices, and form that derive from it, all are implemented by the difficulties of reading *Ulysses*, a book whose discourse has no simple surface which the reader may once skim lightly over before plunging. They are also implemented by the touch of special pleading which the nihilism thesis rationalizes; for special pleading appears not only in the treatment of the book's allusive patterns and other devices but in an equivocation, which is occasionally even expressed, about the very need for comprehending what is read. Thus, again in the book-length studies, while one author speaks only of Joyce's "hope that this man-made chaos would synthesize in the reader's mind,"[35] another himself hopes that Joyce will make sense of the book for the reader:

> No amount of talk about expressionism, dadaism, or the subconscious mind, can reconcile ["the average reader"] to the unintelligibility of Joyce's unpunctuated pages. . . . And I am afraid that he cannot be touched by the plea that Joyce has achieved a masterpiece of modern subjective fiction. . . .
>
> But there are always a few who . . . are willing to give more serious effort to the understanding of way-breakers. . . . I cannot pretend to understand all of *Ulysses;* it is to Joyce himself that one must look for a complete guide, a sure key to unlock the mysteries of this unique volume,[36]

and a third says,

> The meaning of *Ulysses* . . . is not to be sought in any
> analysis of the acts of the protagonist or the mental
> make-up of the characters. . . .[37]

In view of this attitude and of the subtly pervading influence
of its inspiration, the statement made in 1949 that *Ulysses*
"has been charted and mapped, and no reader nowadays
need experience any difficulty with it," which was quoted
at the beginning of this Introduction, is understandable.

The precise extent of that influence cannot be fixed; even
some of the most fully committed adherents of the nihilism
viewpoint speak of contradictory impulses in Joyce or contradictory qualities in the book. Furthermore, with the
recession of the *transition* era, critics such as William
Empson, Hugh Kenner, and Douglas Knight have openly
challenged the characterizing of *Ulysses* by what Mr. Empson
calls "the intensely snooty gloom that [critics] evidently
thought smart."[38] However, the recent objections confirm
my point: that the assumption of its nihilism, a prior interpretation whose genesis coincides with the very publication
of the book, has been more general than is commonly
recognized, and is apparently the source, and certainly the
common denominator, of all the most familiar and popular
judgments made about the fundamental elements of *Ulysses*.
While my own borrowings from a number of books and
short studies testify to their value (and to my awareness
of it), I have tried to suggest that a preconception of the
philosophy, morality, or aesthetic of *Ulysses* can impede
the reading of the book, and that a most important set of
impediments already exists. The following pages should
indicate the error of the popular critical judgments of
formal qualities, plot, principal characters, and the rest,
but my obvious disagreement with the nihilism view and
all its works is secondary. This study is not concerned with
refutation nor with premature counter-interpretation, but
with that humbler and more vital job of criticism—providing a bridge to the book. And in order to clear the
approaches, an existing closed circle must be broken and
the proper sequence of specific perception and general
conclusion restored.

IN A SENSE this Introduction is a defense of a question about *Ulysses* which I have called fundamental—in its full form: "What happens in the novel?"—against the accusation that it begs two other questions. A pervasive influence in the criticism suggests that the familiar first part of this question begs the question of whether or not anything does happen; a sophisticated view of the book's possibilities suggests that the second part, suppressed until now for that very reason, begs the question of what its genre actually is.

Of course, a belief that the events of Bloomsday are pointedly insignificant, or a conception of the form of *Ulysses* as pointedly formless, expands those possibilities spuriously. However, this is not the case with two of the book's special qualities, at least. The first of them is the elaborate network of systems of reference and correspondence that Joyce implanted and insisted upon, not only literary, operatic, and historical allusions, but verbal symbolizations in successive chapters of (as his own notes list them) the organs of the human body, the arts of man, the colors of the spectrum, each chapter with its own "symbol," "relations" (e.g. "incest compared with journalism"), and (!) hour of the day, to make the whole a kind of compound allegory of all things. The second is the different levels of discourse: natural occurrence, mythical analogy, symbolic, parodic and allusive effects, even metaphysical and theological statement. Qualities such as these not only make interpretation difficult but also suggest that a conception of *Ulysses* as narrative fiction, primarily concerned with a developing action and historically valid figures in their own social milieu, is a conception fixed by blinders to the book's most superficial and uninteresting level:

> Thus *Ulysses* is written on three main levels. . . . Bloom and Stephen and their Dublin environment constitute the particular; they are expanded into the universal by their being linked, first, to the story of *Ulysses* as told by Homer in the *Odyssey* . . . and, second, to various mystical motifs (both occidental and oriental). . . . The relating of each episode in the book to an organ of the body and to an art as well as to a separate incident in the *Odyssey* is a further means of adding universal implications to the particular. . . .[39]

Dante's influence on Joyce is now established,[40] and a number of critics have remarked an affinity between the *Commedia* and *Ulysses* or Joyce's work in general.[41] The similarities between *Ulysses* and the *Commedia* (or, for example, Spenser's *Faerie Queene*) are striking, and readily suggest that Dante's description of the four levels of his work, corresponding to the four levels in medieval interpretation of the Bible, is also applicable to *Ulysses*. The levels—literal, allegorical (symbolical, what the letter represents), moral (didactical, what it teaches, "theme"), and anagogical (mystical, what it reveals that is, as Dante says in the *Convivio* [ii 1], "beyond sense")—are discussed in Dante's famous letter to his patron, Can Grande della Scala, with the specific illustration of an incident in the *Purgatorio;* and Joyce alludes to that same incident for his own purpose in the next to last chapter of *Ulysses*. Actually, he must have been long familiar with the letter to Can Grande simply as a student of Dante and almost undoubtedly knew of the fourfold interpretation of the Bible. Furthermore, *Ulysses* works precisely by the interaction of naturalistic, symbolical, and philosophical meaning; and there may be, if not a mystical revelation, the assertion of a truth "beyond sense."

Even if Dante could not be so nicely invoked for support, it would be both easy and prudent to take the apparently more sophisticated position that *Ulysses* is no one thing, that it is story and allegory, wisdom and revelation, and that where the lowest level—story—seems to contradict, for example, the highest—revelation—Joyce has represented the ultimate paradox at the center of existence, or the difference between appearance and reality. But as equivocal as the novel may be in method, it is, in my opinion, a novel; all the voices harmonize to one register—the story of what happens, to whom, how, and why.[42] Its method is the fullest instance of "the spatialization of form in a novel,"[43] that modern development in what was formerly a purely temporal art which so distinguishes the work of Woolf and Proust as well as *Ulysses* from earlier fiction, and which has now been fully assimilated by writers. In the novel which has spatial form, some elements relate to each other, indeed some can only be apprehended, reflexively, by juxtaposition, no matter where they occur in temporal sequence; the method is that of the short poem. And all the devices of *Ulysses* which had previously been alien to fiction, and which make it appear other or more than fiction, are enabled by its "spatial" form to be, to a unique extent (even until today), *bent to the service of fiction.*

In Dante and Spenser, what happens to the poet or to Saint George, Sir Guyon, or Artegall, what he sees, and even what he does, points to and serves in a context that is abstracted from the literal events themselves. In allegory, the literal is the vehicle, not only for the moral ("theme") as in most literature, but also for the symbolical, which in fact gives it its primary reason for being—the action is simply the conventional agent of a symbolic discourse. In *Moby-Dick, Nostromo,* or *Nana,* on the other hand, in symbolic fiction, the action is first fully important in itself and then important again in a new context abstracted from it. But *Ulysses* not only is unlike the former of these, it is in its *method* at least, and I think in its essence, unlike the latter as well, and is most akin to literal fiction. It is a story, with the important, novel, and confusing difference that its many refrains ("verbal motifs"), elaborate literary correspondences, bizarre stylistic devices, historical and mythical analogues, and all the rest work (symbolically for the most part) to implement its unfolding. Virginia Woolf's *To the Lighthouse* is a less flamboyant specimen of the same fictional method—the use of verbal motifs, allusion, symbolism, to tell the story.

One critic says of the upset in the Ascot Cup race on Bloomsday, an actual historical event that becomes significant in *Ulysses*: "Sceptre, the phallic favorite, loses to Throwaway, the outsider, who represents infertility."[44] My thesis does not dispute his calling attention to the event, or his invoking symbolism to connect the two horses with Blazes Boylan and Bloom—the treatment of Boylan is as a stallion and nothing else, Bloom's onanism on the beach in the thirteenth chapter is very important in the novel, and in many other ways the race is symbolically related to the story of *Ulysses;* the question is one of the terms of that relationship. The answer I would give is clear. The

Ascot Cup race is a symbolic indication of a specific action, but it does not have the value of *establishing* anything about that action: it can neither contradict a "literal level" nor substitute for it. The action is a central one, if not the central one, of the novel—the outcome of Bloom's contention with Molly's lover for his wife—and although the race indicates a fact of the story, suggests the meaning of the fact even, it cannot of itself do more, for there are characters to think, move, and speak: to act or pointedly fail to act. The race tells us what is to happen, that *service to the story* is its reason for being, but Bloom beats Boylan himself.

That they exist to serve the story of Bloomsday as no other story in literature has ever been served does not diminish the value of the special elements of *Ulysses,* but is the source of their beauty. The novel has some baroque embellishment; for example, the sets of correspondence to the organs of the body and the rest, created probably as a gesture of belief in the ultimate order of the real and verbal worlds, do not prove that order; and where they accomplish nothing else, those critics[45] who have attacked the prevailing assumption of the correspondence hunters that correspondences in *Ulysses* are good because they are in *Ulysses* have done readers a service. However, the details of such patterns of correspondence are so inconspicuous as to be almost unnoticed unless the attention is drawn to them—and indeed the author himself actually had to first do so. Those special elements of the novel that call attention to themselves, on the other hand—the Homeric correspondences; the allusions to other works: Shakespeare, the Bible, a grand opera, a bourgeois opera, a cheap novel, a perverted novel, ballads, popular songs; the changing styles of the chapters after a certain point; the symbolic effects; the many kinds of parody—are not embellishment but functional devices of fiction in the terms discussed above.

This book is not just a "reading" of *Ulysses* accompanied by an interpretation but a study of the way in which the novel works to unfold its story, chapter by chapter. My fundamental conception of *Ulysses* as a novel—of its action as rising to a climax and proceeding to a resolution, of its chief characters as constituting, like all proper principals in fiction, the Siamese twin to its developing plot, and of the dedication of virtually all its special qualities to the telling of the story—has been asserted in this Introduction with no support beyond circumstantial evidence of a negative kind based on a historical survey of the work of others, to many of whom I am indebted. The proof of the conception depends not only on the validity of my particular observations but also on the extent to which that conception assimilates what is in *Ulysses*. Maurice Beebe speaks of a traditional "Selective Fallacy"[46] in dealing with Joyce, of finding what one is looking for. My own principle of selection has been confessed, but I try to show that almost everything is implicated, all the Homeric, Biblical, and other literary correspondences; all the different chapter styles; all the parodies; almost all the allusions and symbolism.

If my view of *Ulysses* is wrong and the action is only the lowest and most trivial level of meaning in a *sui generis* "book," then understanding that action is not a primary necessity; yet it is certainly a preliminary necessity, if only for the negative reason that the action must be known before it can be discounted. And so the following pages can still contribute to the fuller appreciation of *Ulysses* in a modest way.

While my discussion follows the sequence of *Ulysses* itself, to do so slavishly would be more than pointless, for it would violate the nature of the novel. Therefore, the reader will find various important motifs and other cumulative effects reviewed when the discussion concerns those points in the novel where their import is felt; and the general critical topics listed in the Table of Contents are disposed at places in the book where they seem to me relevant and helpful.

Joyce himself prescribed quasi-Homeric tags for the unnamed and unnumbered chapters of *Ulysses*, and the critical convention has been to use them. However, they seem to me both to misrepresent the chapters to which they refer and to make the correspondences to the *Odyssey* a bit grotesque. The Table of Contents reflects my alternative practice, which is slightly clumsy but more consistent with the nature of the novel: reference to the chapters by their place in the sequence ("the first chapter," "the second chapter," etc.), accompanied where necessary by a parenthetical indication of the principal locale of each. The chapters, with their usual Homeric tags, are:

(1) tower—Telemachus
(2) school—Nestor
(3) strand-Stephen—Proteus
(4) kitchen—Calypso
(5) post office—The Lotus-eaters
(6) cemetery—Hades
(7) newspaper—Aeolus
(8) Byrne's—The Laestrygonians
(9) library—Scylla and Charybdis
(10) city—The Wandering Rocks
(11) Ormond—The Sirens
(12) Kiernan's—The Cyclops
(13) strand-Bloom—Nausicaa
(14) hospital—The Oxen of the Sun
(15) nighttown—Circe
(16) shelter—Eumaeus
(17) house—Ithaca
(18) bed—Penelope

Most important, the Table of Contents indicates that this Introduction is followed by eleven chapters discussing the eighteen chapters of *Ulysses,* and one concluding chapter of a more general nature. I have not devoted a chapter to each chapter of the novel, have not even taken up the same number of chapters, or of pages, in each of my chapters, and have actually treated part of Joyce's seventeenth (house) chapter in Chapter Ten and the rest in Chapter Eleven. The reason is that the chapters of *Ulysses* (like those of *A Portrait of the Artist as a Young Man*) are shaped primarily to perform special narrative functions; Joyce totally ignores formal consideration in his chapter divisions only in the case of the seventeenth, but the true parts of the novel—the phases in the development of its action—comprise varying numbers of its chapters. My eleven chapters reflect that essential form.

Any sketch of the form of *Ulysses* would have to reconcile, not only the eighteen chapters, but also its overt structural arrangement in three sections, labelled I, II, and III, with the divisions following the third (strand-Stephen) and fifteenth (nighttown) chapters. This roughly corresponds to the pattern of the *Odyssey*, but only roughly. The first four of the twenty-four books of the poem concern Telemachus, and the same proportion of the chapters of Ulysses (three of eighteen) parallel this "Telemachia"; however, the next section, in which Odysseus relates his wanderings to Alcinous' court, occupies only eight books or one-third of the twenty-four, while II, the corresponding section of *Ulysses*, is the subject of twelve chapters, or two-thirds of the eighteen; and a more obvious indication of a different emphasis is the contrast between III, which nicely balances I with just three chapters, and the corresponding "Nostos" (literally "return home") of the *Odyssey*, which occupies the last half of the poem.

Despite its loose quality, Joyce seems to have insisted on the structural correspondence strongly during the early years of composition. But his apparent attitude might really have been nothing more than another public effort to stress the parallel with the *Odyssey*, for the tripartite scheme is not a very rewarding index of the structure of *Ulysses*, even if the disproportions of the correspondence are allowed. In the first place, Stephen is involved in Bloom's wanderings; he appears in six of the twelve chapters of II, and is the main figure in two of those chapters, so that the parallel with the "wanderings of Odysseus" part of the epic is not very close. Furthermore, the three initial chapters of II (devoted to Bloom) precisely correspond to I (Stephen's three initial chapters) in the structure of the novel. Finally, as both these points suggest, Stephen is an independent protagonist, with an origin and destiny unrelated to those of Bloom and a prominence much greater than that of the son of Odysseus. The tri-partite scheme seems arbitrary at best for the first fifteen of the novel's eighteen chapters; only III, Joyce's abbreviated "Nostos," has formal relevance.

Nevertheless, three is an important number in the structure of the novel. The first three chapters (I or the "Telemachia") constitute a group because they are all devoted to the representation of Stephen: his character, his circumstances, and his problems. The next three form a similar group with respect to Bloom. There are no such trios between the first two and the final one (III), but the nine intervening chapters do have a pattern of climaxes at every third: the ninth (library), the twelfth (Kiernan's), and the fifteenth (nighttown).[47] In the first two instances, the climax occurs at the very end of the chapter, as a sudden final dramatic heightening and revelation. The case in the fifteenth chapter is a special one.

Although it sounds schematic when described abstractly, the form of the novel is that of a dramatic action with exposition, development, climax, and conclusion. Past a certain point, June 16, 1904, becomes very different from the ordinary day it has been in the life of Leopold Bloom— with the eleventh chapter (Ormond) the diurnal nature of the action of *Ulysses* begins to change; and the form of the novel is directly related to this fact. The following sketch is offered with the knowledge that it must be tentative until the narrative itself has been discussed, but it discloses the general conception of the novel behind this study and the reason for the particular organization that the study has. A parenthetical reference indicates the chapter in this book in which each chapter of *Ulysses* is discussed.

In the opening chapter of the novel, Stephen Dedalus is introduced in what passes for his home. His alienation from Mulligan and the latter's domination of their common residence share the chapter with a depiction of Stephen's remorse and self-reproach in connection with his mother's death. The two subsequent chapters elaborate in different respects the characterization of Stephen. (Chapter One.)

The fourth chapter of the novel (kitchen) introduces Leopold Bloom in what turns out to be his deteriorating home. His alienation from Molly is shown, and also its imminent intensification by an adulterous liaison she has arranged. Completing the situation, Bloom's daughter is away, and his son is dead. The two subsequent chapters function as do the corresponding chapters in the "Telemachia." (Chapter Two.)

The seventh chapter (newspaper) places Stephen and Bloom in the same public situation, and reveals certain things about the public attitude toward them both and about the Irish public in general. (Chapter Three.)

The eighth chapter (Byrne's) is devoted to Bloom's predicament respecting his wife and family. His preoccupation with it and suffering from it intensify in this chapter. (Chapter Four.)

The ninth chapter (library) presents Stephen's attempt to escape from his predicament, which ends in failure. At the very end of the chapter, however, Bloom and Stephen come face to face, and there is a symbolic foreshadowing of the outcome of Stephen's story. (Chapter Five.)

The tenth chapter (city) in no way advances the action and is not even especially concerned with either of the protagonists. As a number of critics have pointed out, it is a kind of portrait gallery of Dubliners, flanked by representatives of the two "pillars" of the society, Church and State. Although Joyce's public comments on his work must generally be mistrusted, the notation "End of first part of *Ulysses*, New Year's Eve, 1918," which is at the end of the ninth chapter of the manuscript Joyce sold to the collector John Quinn,[48] corroborates a statement he made to Frank Budgen in a letter written on October 24, 1920, while he was working on the fifteenth (nighttown) chapter:

P.S. Last night I thought of an *Entr'acte* for *Ulysses* in middle of book after 9th episode Scylla and Charybdis. Short with absolutely no relation to what precedes or follows like a pause in the action of a play.[49]

And the action confirms that the tenth chapter is an interlude between the true first part of the novel, which ends with the ninth chapter, and second part, which extends from the eleventh chapter (Ormond) through the eighteenth. (Chapter Six.)

It is in keeping with this scheme that the principal characters of the first nine chapters "Exeunt" in the dramatic sense at the end of the ninth:

> A dark back went before them. Step of a pard, down, out by the gateway, under portcullis barbs.
> They followed (215) *

and that the last word of the "overture" which opens the "musical" eleventh, the only word that is not an anticipation of a phrase in the chapter, is the imperative "Begin!" The eleventh chapter quite definitely begins a new part of the novel. The significant difference in the action is the change in Bloom's behavior from what it had been earlier in the day, and, obviously, on previous days. For example, the first time he saw Boylan, in the sixth chapter (cemetery), he intensely studied his fingernails. The second time the rake crossed his path, in the eighth chapter (Byrne's), he rushed into the museum. Near the beginning of the present chapter he sees Boylan in the distance:

> He eyed and saw afar on Essex bridge a gay hat riding on a jauntingcar. It is. Third time. Coincidence.
> Jingling on supple rubbers it jaunted from the bridge to Ormond quay. Follow. Risk it. Go quick. At four. Near now. Out. (259)

And this third time he proceeds to follow to the Ormond Hotel the man he had formerly so assiduously avoided. At the hotel he meets Richie Goulding, whom he accompanies into the dining room ("Diningroom. Sit tight there. See, not be seen," 261). From his vantage point he watches Boylan at the adjacent bar preen himself, flirt with Miss Douce, the barmaid, and depart for his assignation with Molly.

It is no coincidence that this same chapter is the first in which the narrative manner changes. Although the seventh chapter (newspaper) has interspersed boldface phrases simulating newspaper headlines, the narrative manner of that and all the other chapters preceding the present one

---

* Arabic numerals in parentheses indicate pages in the Modern Library edition of *Ulysses* (New York, 1934).

is the same. It does not differ too greatly, in fact, from that of the *Portrait,* although subjective revelation is made through "interior monologue" rather than in the author's voice. However, neither the present chapter nor any one following it is written like any other chapter in the book! In this, at least, the eleventh to eighteenth chapters are alike, and different from all that precede them.

They are also alike in the fact, suggested by Bloom's surprising audacity, that with the eleventh chapter a great difference in the rate with which things happen begins to manifest itself. The action is largely normal, diurnal, in nature, free of any new or unusual experience or situation, before it—throughout the first part of the novel and the interlude, "nothing happens." In this chapter Boylan makes his departure for the purpose of superseding Bloom; and Bloom's reaction is the beginning of the unique occurrences of the day which are the substance of what he thinks, does, and thus becomes, and which constitute the significant action of the novel.

The next chapter, the twelfth (Kiernan's), reveals a formerly unsuspected and crucial aspect of Bloom's nature and relationship to those about him which reinforces the intimation at the preceding minor climax, the end of the ninth chapter (library) and first part of the novel. (Chapter Seven.)

The thirteenth chapter (strand-Bloom) depicts Bloom committing an act symbolic of the complete denial of the wife and family he covets and recognizes as necessary to him. The fourteenth (hospital) is devoted to Bloom's recognition of this fact and to the reconfirming of his desire for reunion with Molly and for a son. The latter part of that desire causes him to decide to follow Stephen. (Chapter Eight.)

The fifteenth chapter (nighttown) contains the major climax of the novel. Both Stephen and Bloom undergo psychological experiences based on their respective predicaments. For each, the experience takes the form of a series of fantasies, and results in a definite change of character. (Chapter Nine.)

The sixteenth chapter (shelter) and the seventeenth (house) are concerned with both the relationship between

Bloom and Stephen and that between Bloom and Molly. In the sixteenth, the significance for Bloom of his relationship with Stephen is revealed to the reader; and Stephen himself, partly as a result of his experience in nighttown, understands what was intimated to the reader at the end of the first part of the novel—the significance of his meeting with Bloom. The seventeenth confirms Stephen in his understanding, with a result that completes the story of Stephen Dedalus. (Chapter Ten.)

The relationship between Bloom and Molly is more fully treated in the seventeenth chapter than in the sixteenth. As a result of his experience in nighttown, Bloom's attitude toward Molly undergoes a significant change, and this is expressed in his behavior to her. The final chapter (bed) is concerned with Molly's reaction to her brief exposure to Bloom's new attitude. It depicts Molly's attitude toward Bloom and indicates the nature of Bloom's destiny. (Chapter Eleven.)

The above sketch is necessarily inadequate, but it does suggest a clear development to a climax and a resolution and a tentative conception of the essential form of the novel. The first part contains half the chapters and yet somewhat less than one-third of the pages. It contains half the chapters for the simple reason, apparently, that it is the first of two parts, the chapter which follows it being an "Entr'Acte." It has a much smaller proportion of the actual text because its function prescribes this. Its function is to depict in a relatively conventional narrative manner relatively conventional conditions—not merely what Stephen and Bloom ordinarily do, but what they ordinarily think, whom they ordinarily see, how they ordinarily act with others, how they are regarded by them. The action of the first part is typical action; its function, the sheer presentation of these characters and of their situation (with all that this implies of "stasis" and "futility"). Thus, its pattern is one of parallel arrangement (three chapters for Stephen, three for Bloom, three in which both appear, and a joint "exit') rather than lineal development. The action of the second part is far different. There is an organic development from Bloom's surveillance of Boylan in the eleventh chapter to the very end of the book, with the dramatic climax in the latter part of the fifteenth (nighttown) chapter and the resolution of the action in III, the concluding trio of chapters.

The novel, then, has the presentation or exposition of an everyday situation ending in the intimation of a future development; a short interlude; and that development, a unique action, to its dramatic climax and resolution. *Ulysses* is, as Joyce's brother described it, "a cathedral in prose, as simple in design as a cross."[50]

1. Taken from the *Nottingham Journal and Express*. See also, e.g., *Liverpool Daily Courier*.

2. Taken from Noyes' article based on the lecture, published in the *Manchester Sunday Chronicle* on October 29.

3. L. A. G. Strong, *The Sacred River* (London, 1949), pp. 26–27.

4. Richard M. Kain, in Marvin Magalaner and Richard M. Kain, *Joyce: The Man, the Work, the Reputation* (New York, 1956), p. 192.

5. In his excellent chapter on *Ulysses* in *Axel's Castle*. See *Axel's Castle* (New York, 1931), pp. 201–2. See also, e.g. William York Tindall, *James Joyce: His Way of Interpreting the Modern World* (New York, 1950), pp. 36–37; A. J. A. Waldock, "Experiment in the Novel," in *Some Recent Developments in English Literature* (Sydney, 1935), pp. 8–17; and Richard Ellmann, "The Backgrounds of Ulysses," *Kenyon Review*, XVI (1954), 337–86, especially 377, 386; or *James Joyce* (New York, 1959), pp. 367–90, especially pp. 383, 390. These three critics and others regard Molly's soliloquy because of its rhapsodic conclusion ("and yes I said yes I will Yes"), as a counterbalance to the apparently negative action of the preceding chapters. But David Daiches' comment on this proposition in *The Novel in the Modern World* (Chicago, 1939), p. 142 ([Rev. ed., 1960], pp. 119–20), which is the sharpest, is also the most just: "It is amazingly crude criticism to suppose that, in a work so elaborately organized as *Ulysses*, the last sentence of the last speaker represents the author's view of life."

6. See, e.g., William M. Schutte, *Joyce and Shakespeare: A Study in the Meaning of Ulysses* (New Haven, 1957), pp. 151–52. S. L. Goldberg's *The Classical Temper: A Study of James Joyce's Ulysses* (London, 1961) presents an intelligent variation on this view, which is the one most characteristic of recent criticism. Mr. Goldberg says that *Ulysses* asserts the importance of positive values, above all "vitality of spirit," "in the patient scrutiny of Bloom and Stephen . . . in the disentangling of what makes for sanity and growth . . . " (pp. 314–15).

7. See, e.g., Richard M. Kain, *Fabulous Voyager: James Joyce's Ulysses* (Chicago, 1947), pp. 238–41.

8. See, e.g., E. M. Forster, "The Book of the Age?", *New Leader*, March 12, 1926, pp. 13–14; Horace Reynolds, "A Note on Ulysses,"

Irish Review, I (1934), 21, 28–29, 29; and W. H. Auden, "James Joyce and Richard Wagner," *Common Sense*, X (1941), 89–90.

9. The first elaborate presentation of this view is Carl Jung's essay "Ulysses." First published in the *Europäische Revue*, IX (1932), 547–68, it was reprinted in his *Wirklichkeit der Seele* (Leipzig, 1934), 132–69. Translated by W. Stanley Dell, it appeared under the title "Ulysses—A Monologue," in *Nimbus*, II (1953), 7–20. See also, Ernst Robert Curtius, *James Joyce und Sein Ulysses (Verlag der Neuen Schweizer Rundschau*, Zurich, 1929), pp. 61–62; Stuart Gilbert, *James Joyce's Ulysses* (New York, 1930), p. 222; Louis Golding, *James Joyce* (London, 1933), p. 98; Paul Elmer More, "James Joyce," *American Review*, V (1935), 129–58, 154–55; R. Miller-Budnitskaya, "James Joyce's 'Ulysses,'" tr. N. J. Nelson, *Dialectics*, No. 5 (1938), 6–26, 25–26; Harry Levin, *James Joyce: A Critical Introduction* (Norfolk, 1941), pp. 74, 122–23, 134–35.

10. Apparently first offered by Rudolph Von Abele in *"Ulysses: The Myth of Myth,"* *PMLA*, LXIX (1954), 358–64. See also, *James Joyce*, pp. 3–5, and Denis Donoghue, "Joyce and the Finite Order," *Sewanee Review*, LXVIII (1960), 256–73. Mr. Donoghue speaks of "weighing the spurious of one kind against the spurious of another, related kind" (268).

11. Wyndham Lewis, *Time and Western Man* (New York, 1928), p. 76. See also, e.g., Edwin Muir, *Transition* (London, 1926), p. 39; and Ellsworth Mason, "Joyce's Categories," *Sewanee Review*, LXI (1953), 427–32, 431–32.

12. William T. Noon, S.J., *Joyce and Aquinas* (New Haven, 1957), pp. 102–4. The quotation is on p. 103.

13. Daiches, p. 105. Mr. Daiches also says (p. 80) (Rev. ed., p. 63): "There are many definitions of comedy, but the definition that is most relevant to a consideration of such a work as *Ulysses* as comedy is that which identifies the comic spirit with the author's renunciation of any share in the world he portrays."

14. Herbert S. Gorman, *James Joyce: His First Forty Years* (New York, 1924), p. 204. See also, e.g., Charles Duff, *James Joyce and the Plain Reader* (London, 1932), p. 65, and Frank Budgen, *James Joyce and the Making of Ulysses* (New York, 1934), pp. 71–72.

15. Marvin Magalaner and Richard M. Kain, *Joyce: The Man, the Work, the Reputation* (New York, 1956), pp. 162–215.

16. *Ibid.*, p. 170.

17. The *London Daily Mail*, April 17, the April 6 review (see note 1), the Noyes article (see note 2), Shane Leslie, "Ulysses," *Quarterly Review*, CCXXXVIII (1922), 219–34, 225–26.

18. *Nation and Athenaeum*, XXXI (1922), 124–25.

19. One notable exception was T.S. Eliot, in his famous *Dial* review, "Ulysses, Order and Myth," *Dial* LXXV (1923), 480–84, reprinted in *James Joyce: Two Decades of Criticism*, ed. Seon Givens, (New York, 1948), pp. 198–202. Valery Larbaud's lecture introducing Joyce and his book, given at Adrienne Monnier's bookshop in Paris on December 7, 1921, two months before the first edition, also opposed the general opinion. It was printed as "James Joyce" in his magazine, *La Nouvelle revue française*, XXIV (1922), 385–409, and the portion dealing with *Ulysses* was reprinted in English by Eliot in *Criterion*, I (1922), 94–103.

20. William Troy, "To So Little Space," *Partisan Review*, XIV (1947), 424–27, 425. Mr. Kain says that upon publication *Ulysses* "gave the *avant-garde* a hero and a sacred book" (*Joyce*, p. 314). See also, "The Paris Joyce as Alter-Ego," pp. 359–62 of Hugh Kenner's *Dublin's Joyce* (Bloomington, Ind., 1956).

21. *Joyce*, p. 24.

22. E.g.: Malcolm Cowley, Hart Crane, E.E. Cummings, Ernest Hemingway, Archibald MacLeish, Allen Tate, William Carlos Williams, Yvor Winters, Georges Braque, Paul Klee, Joan Miro, Pablo Picasso.

23. The "Proclamation" opens the important dual number 16–17 (1929).

24. Most important were Eugene Jolas (the chief editor), Stuart Gilbert, Philippe Soupault, Ernest Robert Curtius, Valery Larbaud, Frank Budgen, and Carl Jung.

25. The impression is sometimes qualified; for example, Harry Levin speaks on p. 124 of "ironic pathos" and Frank Budgen moves toward what he calls (p. 73) "humane skepticism."

26. Especially Gilbert Seldes, in *The Nation* (New York), CXV (August 30, 1922), 211–12. The review is generally impressive.

27. See note 9.

28. Four exceptions are: Rolf R. Loehrich, *The Secret of Ulysses* (McHenry, Ill., 1953); Schutte; Tindall; and Mr. Tindall's *A Reader's Guide to James Joyce* (New York, 1959). However, Doctor Loehrich is a practicing psychoanalyst, and Mr. Tindall's two books reveal considerable familiarity with Jung's writings.

29. The quotations are taken from the *Nimbus* translation (see note 9), principally pp. 7, 8, 12, and 14.

30. Strong, p. 36; Levin, p. 95.

31. Levin, p. 132.

32. Kain, pp. 216–17.

33. Gilbert, p. 17.

34. Tindall, p. 37.

35. Levin, p. 95.

36. Paul Jordan Smith, *A Key to the Ulysses of James Joyce* (New York, 1927), pp. 15–16.

37. Gilbert, p. 22.

38. William Empson, "The Theme of *Ulysses*," *Kenyon Review*, XVIII (1956), 26–52, 43. See also, Hugh Kenner, "A Communication," *Hudson Review*, III (1950), 157–60; Douglas Knight, "The Reading of *Ulysses*," *ELH: A Journal of English Literary History*, XIX (1952), 64–80.

39. Daiches, pp. 122–23 (Rev. ed., pp. 101–2).

40. See references to Dante in *James Joyce*. Mr. Ellmann says, on p. 2, "Dante was perhaps Joyces' favorite author."

41. For some of these, see *Joyce*, pp. 210–11.

42. Mr. Goldberg makes precisely the same point in the "Introductory" to his book: "In short, it is not 'Romance,' not a joke, not a spiritual guide, not even an encyclopaedia of social disintegration or a re-creation of Myth or a symbolist poem; it is a

novel, and what is of permanent interest about it is what always interests us with the novel: its imaginative illumination of the moral —and ultimately, spiritual—experience of representative human beings" (p. 30).

43. Joseph Frank, "Spatial Form in the Modern Novel," *Critiques and Essays on Modern Fiction: 1920–1951*, ed. John W. Aldridge (New York, 1952), pp. 43–66, 44. Originally sections 2 and 3 of "Spatial Form in Modern Literature," *Sewanee Review*, Spring, Summer and Autumn, 1945.

44. William York Tindall; quoted from *Joyce*, p. 206.

45. Chiefly Joseph Frank, Richard M. Kain, Harry Levin, Ezra Pound, and Edmund Wilson. Chapter VII of Goldberg, "Structure and Values," is an extensive general examination of the narrative strategy of the novel. Mr. Goldberg does not recognize the function of some of its special elements; but he too insists on functional justification, and his critical standard helps him to achieve a highly rewarding discussion, especially of the limitations of the vision of life expressed in the novel and the reasons for them.

46. Maurice Beebe, "Joyce and Stephen Dedalus: The Problem of Autobiography," *A James Joyce Miscellany: Second Series*, ed. Marvin Magalaner (Carbondale, Ill., 1959), pp. 67–77, 67.

47. This conception is partly indebted to one offered three decades ago. See S. Foster Damon's classic essay on *Ulysses*, "The Odyssey in Dublin," *Hound & Horn*, III (1929–30), 7–44, 16, n. 13.

48. *James Joyce*, p. 456 n.

49. *The Letters of James Joyce*, ed. Stuart Gilbert (New York, 1957), p. 149.

50. Stanislaus Joyce "James Joyce: A Memoir," tr. Felix Giovanelli, *Hudson Review*, II (1950), 485–514, 500. This essay was translated by Ellsworth Mason and published by the James Joyce Society in the same year, under the title, *Recollections of James Joyce*.

chapter one

The subject of the novel's first three chapters is Stephen Dedalus, whose life from infantile sense perception to rebellion and presumed expatriation was the subject of Joyce's first novel. Hugh Kenner's excellent study of the *Portrait* describes in detail the manner in which "each ·chapter . . . gathers up the thematic material of the preceding ones and entwines them [sic] with a dominant theme of its own."[1] This very same practice informs the two groups of three chapters which, I have said, are devoted to the representation of Stephen and of Bloom respectively. The major theme of one chapter becomes a contributing element to the major theme of the next until, by the end of the third chapter in Stephen's case and the sixth in Bloom's, the situation, the personality, the attitude, and even the thoughts about his destiny of the character have been fully revealed. The two groups of chapters have similar thematic development and other similarities, such as the roles of Malachi Mulligan and Blazes Boylan. Each of the novel's two chief antagonists is shown to be the specific cause of the problems confronting the protagonists in their introductory chapters, and they both begin to function (Boylan through his letter) immediately. In their case, the Homeric analogy is a distinct enrichment; both correspond to Antinous, the chief suitor—Mulligan in

Antinous' relation to Telemachus as mocker and as usurper of his rightful patrimony, Boylan in his suit of Penelope. The novel begins at about eight o'clock on the morning of June 16, 1904, just ten days short of a full year from the burial of Mrs. Mary Dedalus. It begins on the parapet of a "Martello" tower on Dublin Bay, built by the English to frustrate a French expedition in aid of the Irish rebellion of 1798: a monument of Ireland subjected.

1 *the tower*

The first chapter has two principal themes, and "stately, plump Buck Mulligan" is the initiator of both. He introduces the first when the banter with which he begins the novel takes Dublin Bay ("the sea") as its subject:

> —Our mighty mother, Buck Mulligan said.
> He turned abruptly his great searching eyes from the sea to Stephen's face.
> —The aunt thinks you killed your mother, he said. That's why she won't let me have anything to do with you.
> —Someone killed her, Stephen said gloomily.
> —You could have knelt down, damn it, Kinch, when your dying mother asked you, Buck Mulligan said. I'm hyperborean as much as you. But to think of your mother begging you with her last breath to kneel down and pray for her. And you refused. There is something sinister in you. . . . (7)

In response, Stephen "broods" about his mother's illness, death, and visit to him in a dream, "her wasted body within its loose brown graveclothes giving off an odour of wax and rosewood, her breath . . . mute, reproachful, a faint odour of wetted ashes."

Stephen's combination of mourning and self-reproach is interrupted by Mulligan's insistence that he disclose what he has "up your nose against me." When Stephen says that the offense was his remark that Mrs. Dedalus was "beastly dead," Mulligan offers an apology after some preliminary comments on death:

> —And what is death, he asked, your mother's or yours or my own? . . . It's a beastly thing and nothing else. . . . Her cerebral lobes are not functioning. . . . I didn't mean to offend the memory of your mother.
> He had spoken himself into boldness. Stephen, shielding the gaping wounds which the words had left in his heart, said very coldly:
> —I am not thinking of the offence to my mother.
> —Of what, then? Buck Mulligan asked.
> —Of the offence to me, Stephen answered. Buck Mulligan swung around on his heel.
> —O, an impossible person! he exclaimed. (10)

Stephen does not deserve Mulligan's angry response to his statement. In the first place, he is speaking with an assumed bravado, "shielding the gaping wounds which the words had left in his heart," so that he apparently is concerned with the offense to his mother. Secondly, it is not he but Mulligan himself who is "an impossible person." He has called Stephen "poor dogsbody." He holds not that Stephen's body is related to that of a dog, but that Stephen himself is similar to a dog because he is no more than a body. Mulligan is a complete materialist, believes humans to be only highly developed animals. It is his denial of the existence of the soul that he had expressed in "O, it's only Dedalus whose mother is beastly dead," so that Stephen is fully justified in speaking of an offense to himself.

Appeasingly, Mulligan tells Stephen to follow him down for breakfast with their English guest:

> —Don't mope over it all day, he said. I'm inconsequent. Give up the moody brooding.
> His head vanished but the drone of his descending voice boomed out of the stairhead:
> *And no more turn aside and brood*
> *Upon love's bitter mystery*
> *For Fergus rules the brazen cars.* (11)

The lines are from a short lyric by Yeats, printed under the title "Who Goes With Fergus?" and included in the first version of *The Countess Cathleen*. Joyce heard it sung by Florence Farr during the famous controversial premiere of the play in 1899, "set the poem to music and praised it as the best lyric in the world."[2] Mulligan's recitation recalls to Stephen his singing the song to his mother during her last illness, after which "Silent with awe and pity I went to her bedside." Ironically, Mulligan's lyrical advice that Stephen "no more turn aside and brood" further intensifies his brooding. And the word from the song is precise. The chapter shows how Stephen's mind sits on his refusal to obey his mother's last wish that he pray for her and on related thoughts about her: "Memories beset his brooding brain" (11). After Mulligan's exit he thinks again of the dream in which she had come to him and reproached him. Then he thinks of her death-bed and "Her glazing eyes, staring out of death, to shake and bend my soul. On me alone. . . . Her eyes on me to strike me down" (12). He utters a protest ("No, mother. Let me be and let me live"), then joins Mulligan and Haines for breakfast and turns his thought to present problems. The treatment of the first of the chapter's principal themes ends with the introduction of the second: usurpation.

The significance of the theme of Stephen's "brooding" depends upon the fact that the "mother" whose reproach evokes his alternating guilt and protest is more than the dead Mary Dedalus. Mulligan refers to Dublin Bay as "Our mighty mother" (7), and Stephen then associates the Bay and his mother in his thoughts:

> The ring of bay and skyline held a dull green mass of liquid. A bowl of white china had stood beside her deathbed holding the green sluggish bile which she had torn up from her rotting liver by fits of loud groaning vomiting. (7)

The association of Dublin Bay with Stephen's mother seems to relate her to Ireland, motherland. In *The Countess Cathleen*, Cathleen says that Fergus' song was sung to her by the bard to comfort her; and the similarity with the situation in which Stephen sang, and with Stephen's conception of himself, is apparent.

Stephen's mother is also (though more fully in later chapters) associated with the Church. She has always been thoroughly devout, she remains for Stephen the one example of pure love, and she reproaches him, in his brooding, for refusing to pray for her—an offense less to Mary Dedalus than to the God and Church of the Roman Catholics, for he spurns not his mother but the action he is asked to perform. Mary Dedalus represents for her son another Mary, symbol of love and holiness, and the Church so largely devoted to her worship. Stephen is brooding not only about his mother, but also about his "mother country" and his "Mother Church"; for not just one but all three bore him and nurtured him, and he has been an unfaithful son to all three. Stephen's guilty brooding about country and religion may have been catalyzed by his mother's death; it certainly was not prominent in the *Portrait*. But however it came about, the sense of guilt bound up in the word "mother" is complex and is to be with him through much of the day.

A very different feeling about a complementary symbolic parent is also to be with him; and persistent, although slight, hints of it run through the chapter. The first of these is Mulligan's recitation from "Who Goes with Fergus." The nature of Fergus in Yeats' poem is ambiguous. In his other poem about him, "Fergus and the Druid," Yeats identifies the warrior of the Red Branch cycle of Irish legends ("king of the proud Red Branch kings"), Fergus mac Roig, and portrays him as relinquishing his kingdom to become a wizard; Yeats is known to have seen Fergus as a powerful wizard in a séance,[3] apparently combining him in his imagination with one of the gods in the oldest Irish cycle (the Tuatha de Danaan), Fergus leth-derg. However, Fergus mac Roig was said to have risen from the grave to restore one of the ancient epics to Ireland, and to have given up his kingdom either for the mother of his successor or for *poetry*; and another namesake is a poet-prophet of the third (Finn) cycle, Fergus True-Lips.

The ambiguity of "Fergus" is an enrichment in *Ulysses*, of course, but the focus in the present context seems to be on the lord of the heaven and the earth, not of the poetic imagination: Mulligan's three lines counsel Stephen to resign himself to God's will. They also portray the subject of Yeats' poem inaccurately:

Who Goes with Fergus?

Who will go drive with Fergus now,
And pierce the deep wood's woven shade,
And dance upon the level shore?
Young man, lift up your russet brow,
And lift your tender eyelids, maid,
And brood on hopes and fear no more.

And no more turn aside and brood
Upon love's bitter mystery;
For Fergus rules the brazen cars,
And rules the shadows of the wood,
And the white breast of the dim sea
And all dishevelled wandering stars.

The plainly distorted, severe masculine deity of the lines "boomed out" by Mulligan corresponds to the God who took Stephen's mother ("—Someone killed her, Stephen said gloomily"). And although Fergus is not called "father," Mulligan's recitation initiates a "father" motif in the chapter. His announcing to Haines that Stephen has a theory that "he"—the ambiguous pronoun can refer to either Hamlet or Stephen—"himself is the ghost of his own father" (in essence has no father) is the first recurrence of the motif. Haines is explicitly (and obviously) "bemused," for he mentions a theological interpretation of the play as representing "The Son striving to be atoned with the Father." His erudite stupidity serves to associate with the two Hamlets: the Father akin to Fergus, and His Son. Mulligan's response is to sing the "Ballad of Joking Jesus," which asserts the non-paternity of "Joseph the Joiner." Stephen remains silent on the subject, but he thinks of heretical views of Christ, especially those of the Arians and the Monarchians (the school of Sabellius) which are the two principal heresies concerning the relationship of the Father and the Son.

In the words of the *Catholic Encyclopedia:*

> the genuine doctrine of Arius . . . denies that the Son is of one essence, nature, or substance with God; He is not consubstantial . . . with the Father, and therefore not like Him. . . .[4]

The view of the Sabellians was directly opposite, that "the Father and the Son" are "but one Person; . . . God the Father appears on earth as Son";[5] yet Stephen turns impartially from "Arius, warring his life long upon the consubstantiality of the Son with the Father" to "the subtle African heresiarch Sabellius who held that the Father was Himself His own Son" (22). He can do so because the antipodal heresies both deny the Sonship of Christ. Therefore, they deny the corresponding Fatherhood of God. And his own theory about the two Hamlets is the Sabellian religious doctrine of the-Father-His-own-Son in its obverse form—with the stress placed where he wants it.

The difference between Stephen's "parents" is plain and that in his attitudes toward them is equally so. Through most of the book the thought of "father" provides a complement and contrast to his "brooding" about "mother."

Awaiting Stephen at the breakfast table in company with Mulligan is Mulligan's friend, Haines, down from Oxford to see the wild Irish in their natural habitat. The "stranger" is superficial, hypocritical, sententious, prim, and stupid. However, although Stephen does not detect it, he has one virtue which redeems him from condemnation along with Mulligan: he is completely free of malice. Haines' rubbernecking Hibernophilia seems compounded of equal parts of Sassenach guilt and spiritual kinship with those cultured Englishmen who in the late eighteenth century discovered Ossian, the noble Omai of the South Seas, and Ann Yearsley, the poetical milkmaid. Mulligan hopes to exploit him.

Stephen is frightened of him at night, and disapproves of
his presence for nationalistic reasons and because he is, in
Mulligan's words, "dreadful," "ponderous," and "Bursting
with money and indigestion."

The *introit* with which Mulligan the mock priest opens
the novel features a bowl of lather and a razor and mirror
crossed on its rim. The razor and mirror are in the pocket
of Mulligan's dressing-gown. The bowl of lather remains
on the parapet, however, and Stephen, before descending to
join Mulligan and Haines, debates whether or not to take
it down with him:

> He went over to it, held it in his hands awhile, feeling
> its coolness, smelling the clammy slaver of the lather in
> which the brush was stuck. So I carried the boat of in-
> cense then at Clongowes. I am another now and yet the
> same. A servant too. A server of a servant. (13)

Stephen takes the shavingbowl down. At Clongowes Wood
the servant served was the celebrant, the master, the Church.
Now the servant is the jester Mulligan, the master, Haines,
delineating the relationship of the English and those Irish
who "sell much more than she ever had and do a roaring
trade," as Stephen says of a prostitute later in the book.
That Stephen should in turn serve this subtle traitor is
strange, but no less true. Mulligan constantly gives him
orders: "Kinch, wake up. Bread, butter, honey" (13),
"Kinch, get the jug" (15), "Fill us out some more tea,
Kinch" (16). This fact, and Mulligan's humiliating discussion of cast-off clothing he has given and "must give" to the
impoverished Stephen, suggest that a power struggle has
been going on; it is about to reach its conclusion. The
struggle is for rule of the Martello tower, the common home
of the poet and the scientist, like the bay it overlooks a
representative of Ireland. The symbol of control is, quite
properly, the key. Ancient tradition held that the poet rules
Ireland, that he sits on the right hand of the king in council,
and that his wisdom prevails. Correspondingly, Stephen
possesses the key. But today it changes hands. Stephen reflects that the critical point in their unacknowledged struggle has been reached:

He wants that key. It is mine, I paid the rent. . . .
He will ask for it. That was in his eyes. (21)

The poet-prophet has not lost his traditional powers, for
minutes later:

> Stephen turned away.
> —I'm going, Mulligan, he said.
> —Give us that key, Kinch, Buck Mulligan said, to keep
> my chemise flat.
> Stephen handed him the key. (24)

Stephen walks away resolving, "I will not sleep here tonight," determined not to live in his own house (he paid
the rent) subservient to a master who is himself a servant.
Mulligan calls to Stephen from the water of Dublin Bay,
in which he swims so easily, and Stephen waves. He calls
again and Stephen's unexpressed judgment ends the chapter: "Usurper" (24).

That the conflict is truly over Ireland and not just the
lodging of two young men is confirmed during the visit of
the old milkwoman. Stephen sees her as "Old Gummy
Granny," symbol of Ireland, "Silk of the kine and poor old
woman, names given her in olden times," and relates her
to his companions: "A wandering crone, lowly form of an
immortal serving her conqueror and her gay betrayer.
. . ." Haines speaks in Gaelic, and Stephen asks the old
woman if she understands him:

> —Is it French you are talking, sir? the woman said
> to Haines. (16)

So cut off from her traditions, it is no surprise that Ireland
defers to the scientist and ignores her rightful leader:

> —Are you a medical student, sir? the old lady asked.
> —I am, ma'am, Buck Mulligan answered.
> Stephen listened in scornful silence. She bows her old
> head to a voice that speaks to her loudly, her bonesetter,
> her medicineman: me she slights. (16)

Stephen may seem at this point to be making a mountain of a molehill, but Joyce fully supports his symbolization. Earlier in the chapter Mulligan, the scientist, says to Stephen, the poet:

God, Kinch, if you and I could only work together we might do something for the island. Hellenise it. (9)

Even if he is only speaking of the two of them literally, Mulligan acknowledges that they represent opposing forces and that "the island" ("the old woman") is their concern.

Not only in the wooing of the milkwoman but in the larger symbolization to which he relates it, that of usurpation, Stephen is Joyce's spokesman. Three prominent historical figures bore Mulligan's Christian name, and all three seem to be associated with him. The first of these was the Hebrew prophet, author of the Book of Malachi; though not chronologically last, it is last in the Authorized Version of the books of the Old Testament, and followed only by the two books of Maccabees in the Vulgate. (Malachi is said to have prophesied about 460 B.C.) Malachy II reigned as undisputed High King of all Ireland from 980 to 1001 A.D., when he submitted to Brian Boru. Finally, Saint Malachy (*ca.* 1095-1148) was an Irish archbishop, the personal representative in the Irish Church of the Pope, and the chief Irish cleric of his time. The associations join with Mulligan's implicit correspondence to Antinous, the attempted usurper of Telemachus' patrimony: Malachi Mulligan, prophet of the new religion and, to its followers, the Irish people, priest and king, has dispossessed the poet-prophet of Irish tradition. Mulligan's name even recalls the key word in a phrase used by Hamlet when he is describing for Ophelia the significance of the dumb show which portrays regicide and the usurpation of a throne and a wife: "Marry, this is miching mallecho; it ["mallecho"] means mischief" (III, ii, 139).

Mulligan is much more than an abstraction endowed with a fortuitously meaningful name, however; and, as a result, readers do not easily recognize that Joyce sponsors Stephen's denunciation of the mischief-making usurper. Though most critics think that Mulligan's character has some unsavory aspects, and that Stephen's hostility and testiness are therefore partly justified, there is nothing approaching a consensus of opinion about the witty and entertaining Buck.

The attractive elements of Mulligan's character are not easily exaggerated. He is gay, robust, and intelligent. He has saved people from drowning, and even Stephen acknowledges that he is brave. Above all, he has a gifted wit. Joyce said that Mulligan, who actually appears only four times in the whole novel, "should begin to pall on the reader as the day goes on";[6] he does not. Some of his funniest lines (such as the Latin *oratio* with the punning on *"testibus ponderosis atque excelsis erectionibus"*) are in the fourteenth chapter (hospital) in which he makes his final appearance. His wit cannot be charged against him. It is too good.

Nevertheless, when weighed in the balance, "the exuberant Mulligan" (Hugh Kenner) is wanting, and therefore deserving of the symbolic role allotted to him. Combined as it is with his affluent ways and his humiliating discussions and promises of cast-off clothing, his constant draining of Stephen's meager resources is sinister. His taking twopence from Stephen for a pint is in no way reprehensible, and his intention of borrowing a pound of Stephen's small wages must be measured against Stephen's debt to him of nine pounds. Yet it was the impoverished Stephen who paid the year's rent on their lodgings, and Mulligan's plans for a drinking bout at Stephen's expense can only be another element in his effort to dominate Stephen, who would thereby be a month without funds. Mulligan is shown consistently to be a glutton; in the present chapter, among other things, he butters a slice of bread on both sides. And the glutton is a subtle traitor. He endeavors to exploit Haines by acting as a minstrel or jester; he provides Haines with entertainment which he hopes will be repaid with pints and hot buttered scones, is in the fullest sense the willing Irish servant of the English master. Haines owns a silver cigarette case with a green stone set like an island in the center of it. It is Mulligan's ilk that, as Stephen sees it, "allowed a handful of foreigners to subject them," and betrayed "the Emerald Isle" to the Saxon.

Mulligan is selfish, cynical, gluttonous, traitorous ("her gay betrayer"), and a devastatingly sincere materialist. Toward Stephen, he is disloyal and finally treacherous. The ultimate vindication of Stephen's attitude toward him in the present chapter is that the betrayer and usurper *does* try to sneak away from Stephen and lock him out of the tower later on. But the chapter itself provides sufficient evidence that, despite his attractive qualities, Mulligan is as Stephen sees him. In the first book of the *Odyssey* (in the words of the translation probably most familiar to Joyce), Antinous says to Telemachus, "Never may Cronion make thee King in seagirt Ithaca, which thing is of inheritance thy right." [7] The action involving the old milkwoman and that concerning the key to the tower illustrate the new situation in Ireland, and the reason why the last paragraph is the one word, "Usurper." Ultimately, this second theme unites with the theme of Stephen's brooding: while that presents his consciousness of his wrong to his "mother," this concerns his consciousness of her wrong (in one of her aspects) to him.

2 *the school*

The second chapter is less than thirteen pages long and the shortest in the novel. (The third [strand-Stephen] is only one page longer; almost every other chapter is longer than both of them combined.) The chapter is dominated by two themes, which are extensions of the principal themes of the opening chapter. Both themes are introduced during the three-page passage with which the chapter begins, the depiction of Stephen's class at its history and poetry lessons. The more prominent one is a question of history; the other is the subject of the poetry to which Stephen and the class turn exactly midway in the passage.

At that point, the history lesson has not been satisfactorily completed. The pupils are ignorant and uninterested, and Stephen himself has to consult the text for the facts he is testing them on. Nevertheless, the meaning of history preoccupies the server of a servant for the opening page and a half—until the lesson simply runs down, the pupils ask Stephen to tell them a "ghoststory," and he responds by directing them to their poetry lesson, "Lycidas." The lines recited (actually, read furtively) by a pupil:

> —*Weep no more, woeful shepherd, weep no more*
> *For Lycidas, your sorrow, is not dead,*
> *Sunk though he be beneath the watery floor* (26)

disclose the new theme by asserting the more comforting of its two opposing elements—that ghosts do exist. However, the lines are no more effective in allaying the brooding of the "woeful shepherd" than the more austere trio of lines offered by Mulligan. Whereas that recitation made him think of his singing of Yeats' song to his mother when she lay dying, this prompts him to wonder if indeed his mother "is not [beastly] dead" but a living spirit—if she has a soul. He hears the lines, finds in Aristotle's *Metaphysics*, characteristically, a conclusion to his "interior monologue" on history, and turns to reassuring phrases from *About the Soul* ("The soul is in a manner all that is: the soul is the form of forms," 27). Then he offers the class a ghost story of his own, the riddle of the fox, which is apparently changed in two significant ways from one traditional [8] in Ireland: the traditional riddle has a different introductory couplet, and the answer involves the fox's mother, not his grandmother. Stephen's alterations, whether intentional or not, indicate that the riddle is no banter, and his "shout of nervous laughter" confirms this. P. W. Joyce, the Irish antiquarian (no relation), speaks of "the delightful inconsequence of riddle and answer";[9] but for Stephen they are consequential, in both senses of the word. The relationship of riddle and answer is complicated, almost a riddle itself, but too illuminating to be passed by.

The fox which expects "his grandmother," "this poor soul," to go to heaven is plainly human, and he would not be burying her covertly had he not killed her; on the next page, the same "fox" is described as having "red reek of rapine in his fur" and "merciless bright eyes." Stephen has represented himself as the fox; he may have killed his mother by his "merciless" behavior to her. In the first chapter he was faced with this proposition by Mulligan. Now he is facing himself with it. When all the other pupils have left to play hockey, and he is helping the quiet, timid, and dull Cyril Sargent with his lesson, he thinks:

> Yet someone had loved [Sargent], borne him in her arms and in her heart. . . . She had loved his weak watery blood drained from her own. Was that then real? The only true thing in life? His mother's prostrate body the fiery Columbanus in holy zeal bestrode. She was no more: . . . an odour of rosewood and wetted ashes. . . . A poor soul gone to heaven: and on a heath beneath winking stars a fox, red reek of rapine in his fur, with merciless bright eyes scraped in the earth, listened, scraped up the earth, listened, scraped and scraped. (28-29)

Cranly had said in the final conversation in the *Portrait*, "—Whatever else is unsure in this stinking dunghill of a world a mother's love is not," and Stephen now, after the experience of his mother's death, wonders if Cranly was perhaps not right all along. Thus he associates himself with Saint Columbanus, who abandoned his mother for an abstract ideal,[10] and with the merciless fox. The "odour of rosewood and wetted ashes" identifies Mary Dedalus explicitly.

However, although his mother has gone to heaven, he, the gore-begrimed fox, is scraping in the earth. His thoughts in the next chapter, while he watches the gypsies' dog with its "rag of wolf's tongue redpanting," confirm that the fox (a member of the canine family) is not burying but digging up:

> His hindpaws then scattered sand: then his forepaws dabbled and delved. Something he buried there, his grandmother. He rooted in the sand, dabbling, delving and stopped to listen to the air, scraped up the sand again with a fury of his claws. . . . vulturing the dead. (47)

Why should Stephen, who has "buried" his mother, be digging her up? And for what does he listen?

In the first chapter, thinking of the dream-visit of his
mother's corpse, Stephen recalled "her breath bent over
him with mute secret words" (12). In the fifteenth chapter
(nighttown), when he imagines that his mother's corpse
is upbraiding him, he asks of it:

> *(Eagerly.)* Tell me the word mother, if you know now.
> The word known to all men. (566)

The murdering fox listens for what he so badly wants his
"grandmother" to tell him. His "scraping" is not co-
ordinate with this but contrary to it, just as it is contrary
to his "burying" her in the riddle; the alternating scraping
and listening symbolize the opposed elements of Stephen's
troubled thought.

Stephen's riddle and "Lycidas" are *ghost* stories; in the
riddle he accuses himself of having killed his mother, but
he also confidently places her in heaven. However, the
previous chapter revealed his distress at the prospect that
she is "beastly dead." The opposite of GOD is DOG, and
Stephen does not know to which his mother is akin. It is
for this reason that the riddle is succeeded in his thoughts
by an image of its fox scraping and listening: the fox-dog
scrapes up the ground in order to see if he will exhume all
the remains of his "grandmother"-victim; he "stopped to
listen to the air," for "bells," the evidence that the "grandmother" is not buried in the earth below him but a living
soul in the heaven above. What Stephen wishes her to tell
him is as yet unclear, but his brooding ("scraping") would
be partly relieved if the mother he accuses himself of having
killed ("buried") should speak to him from heaven—if the
riddle and answer should truly go together. Meanwhile he
scrapes and listens—doubts and hopes that the burial was
only temporary, his mother is not in the ground but a
ghost, a "soul," gone "to heaven."

Stephen's changing the "mother" of the riddle to "grandmother" is a revelation of the intensity of his feeling of
guilt. And the introductory couplet he offers,

> *Riddle me, riddle me, randy ro.*
> *My father gave me seeds to sow*

in place of the original innocuous one relates to his (in this case strictly literal) mother, his other parent. As in the first chapter, Stephen does not feel toward his "father" as he does toward his mother. He has not solved the riddle; God has not revealed to him if people have souls, if He has been merciful and granted man the possibility of salvation. And he strongly suspects that He has not been so.

At the beginning of the chapter Stephen is teaching history, and "history" is the subject of all but the brief interlude comprising the lines from "Lycidas," the riddle, and Cyril Sargent, which has just been discussed. In the *Portrait* Stephen declared his refusal to pay in his "own person and life" for the faults of his ancestors, to pay a claim made on historical grounds. But the preceding chapter reveals that, although he finds it impossible to remain in Ireland, an unacknowledged server of a servant, in his brooding he has associated his mother country with his mother. In *Ulysses* Stephen Dedalus is no longer able to ignore complications and contradictions. During the present chapter, he reconsiders his long-standing decision to leave his homeland— reappraises the significance of history, the past, for the present.

His very first thought in the chapter is Blake's dismissal of history as "Fabled by the daughters of memory" (25); but he cannot deny to himself that "it was in some way if not as memory fabled it," if only because the non-existence of history would be equivalent to the end of the world:

> I hear the ruin of all space, shattered glass and toppling masonry, and time one livid final flame. What's left us then? (25)

Stephen's acceptance of the fact of history has an almost immediate effect, for within a few lines he thinks of supplying a witticism to "Haines's chapbook" that night. This dramatic change of attitude toward Haines, in turn, prompts him to reappraise the historical relationship of his people with the English:

> A jester at the court of his master, indulged and disesteemed, winning a clement master's praise. Why had

they chosen all that part? Not wholly for the smooth caress. For them too history was a tale like any other too often heard, their land a pawnshop. (25)

In the place of his former unalloyed contempt, Stephen now feels some sympathy for the majority of his ancestors and countrymen, believes that they serve the English master at least partly out of despair of being free. They do not respond to the history of their captive nation and its defeated heroes, to the past of the present situation, with fruitless rebellion, like his boyhood friend Davin and the Nationalists; nevertheless, they do not find it necessary to leave their homeland. They hear the "tale" of oppression submissively instead of defiantly and accept a situation they cannot help despite their dislike of it. By offering his witticism to Haines he would be joining the band of "jesters."

Having decided that history is significant and that one ought to submit to rather than defy what it has imposed, Stephen appeases his conscience by concluding that whatever has happened, although it did not have to happen, nevertheless has, and is, therefore, as though inevitable— the one unavoidable reality:

Had Pyrrhus not fallen by a beldam's hand in Argos or Julius Caesar not been knifed to death. They are not to be thought away. Time has branded them and fettered they are lodged in the room of the infinite possibilities they have ousted. (26)

At this point, the middle of the three-page classroom scene, the pupils ask for a ghost story, and the first theme is temporarily displaced by the second. Stephen has accepted the rationalization of those self-styled realists who submit to circumstances they should either defy or escape: the result of his meditation on history is the shrug of the unhappy collaborator. The phrase taken from *Metaphysics* X, ix, with which he leaves History for The Soul, reiterates the rationalization of the jester. Nothing is to be done, for history "must be a movement then, an actuality of the possible as possible." Joyce mocks this decision to submit to a subject Ireland by having Stephen recall that when he read Aristotle's phrase in a Paris library, "By his elbow a delicate Siamese conned a handbook of strategy" (26).

When the treatment of the chapter's second theme ends with the pupil Sargent's departure from Stephen for the hockey field, the school's headmaster, Garrett Deasy, is walking toward Stephen. Mr. Deasy is a living example of the "despairing," "fated" servant of the English Stephen has just entertained the idea of becoming.

However he is not despairing, and he serves eagerly. The three most prominent features of his office are a picture of Edward VII as Prince of Wales, a series of photographs of (English noblemen's) race horses, and a tray of Stuart coins. The furnishings characterize the man. He admires everything English almost to the point of worship, he is analogous to Nestor ("the tamer of horses"), the aged Achaean king who gave Telemachus wise advice about protecting his patrimony, and his advice to Stephen is in terms of the Stuart coins—an exhortation to avarice after the example of the English. The Homeric analogy is ironic, of course: Mr. Deasy is the headmaster of a shoddy boys' school, and his wisdom consists of worshipping the English and money, quoting Iago as "Shakespeare," and justifying rank anti-Semitism as an awareness of Divine justice; even his sensible appeal for Koch's treatment of hoof and mouth disease is expressed with laughable triteness. But the irony is double, for Stephen's Nestor does unknowingly guide him.

More important than the parodic identification of him with Nestor is the presentation of Mr. Deasy as the complete Irishman:

> —I have rebel blood in me too, Mr Deasy said. On the spindle side. But I am descended from Sir John Blackwood who voted for the union. We are all Irish, all kings' sons.
> —Alas, Stephen said.
> —*Per vias rectas,* Mr Deasy said firmly, was his motto. (32)

Stephen's "alas" is as much caused by Mr. Deasy's identification of himself as ultimate descendant of the heroic Irish kings as it is by the weight of the historical responsibility they both have as kings' sons. And Mr. Deasy's firm pronouncement of the motto of his Ulster ancestor who voted for union with England (in the corrupt plebiscite of 1800 that produced the Act of Union) is a statement of his own upright ethic. He will restate it in a few pages, at the climax of his defense of anti-Semitism.

It is that aspect of the mentor's wisdom which guides Stephen. Thus, when he accuses "the jew merchants" of destroying "old England," it is with "eyes open wide in vision," and while he is standing in "a broad sunbeam" (34). Stephen objects, and:

> —They sinned against the light, Mr Deasy said gravely. And you can see the darkness in their eyes. And that is why they are wanderers on the earth to this day. (34-35)

The key words are "and that is why"; Mr. Deasy not only affirms the proposition that Stephen has just tentatively accepted, that history has power over the individual, the past over the present, but considers this condition a manifestation of divine justice; as in his servitude to the English, the old and experienced complete Irishman does not merely accept a historical situation that has caused a people suffering but glorifies it. And he is so eager a servant that he fails to see the obvious analogy between the disinherited Jews and his own oppressed nation.

Stephen perhaps does see it; at any rate, he refuses to regard the victimizing of a whole nation as the manifestation of justice, divine or otherwise. He asks "Who has not?" sinned against the light; and when Mr. Deasy responds by becoming literally slack-jawed, he defines the attitude he realizes he must take to the history he has so recently accepted. The passage is rich in meaning. At Stephen's "Who has not?", Mr. Deasy's "underjaw fell sideways open uncertainly"; Stephen thinks, "Is this old wisdom? He waits to hear from me," and elucidates his dissent:

> —History, Stephen said, is a nightmare from which I am trying to awake.
> From the playfield the boys raised a shout. A whirring whistle: goal. What if that nightmare gave you a back kick?
> —The ways of the Creator are not our ways, Mr Deasy said. All history moves toward one great goal, the manifestation of God. (35)

Stephen cannot deny the power of history, cannot even deny that he is almost totally vulnerable to it, but he can and does insist that it is a "nightmare." Correspondingly, in response to Mr. Deasy's statement of his comfortably pious view of history, the view implicit in his remarks about the Jews, Stephen identifies the "manifestation" toward which "all history moves" by punning on "goal": he gestures toward the soccer field, on which a goal is being announced and cheered, and says "That is God," "A shout in the street" (35). He agrees that God ordains history, but protests against "the ways of the Creator." For he is not merely insulting God by identifying Him as he does, he is accusing Him. He has already likened the soccer game to a bloody battle (33), and therefore to the battles and their "corpsestrewn plain[s]" with which he had identified "history" on the first page of the chapter. God is responsible not merely for quotidian reality, but for all the nightmare.

Mr. Deasy completes his justification of the suffering of the Jews by recounting the "errors" of other suffering groups, the Trojans and the Irish, and insisting that they did not commit "the one sin" against Jesus, and by restating in English his inherited moral principle, "I will fight for the right till the end." Stephen can only conclude "here what will you learn more?" and impatiently rustle Mr. Deasy's letter. They have agreed that he will not be at the school for long. Our last sight of "old wisdom" is of his back. Having delivered a final insight about the Jews, he turns and walks away, laughing almost hysterically:

On his wise shoulders through the checkerwork of leaves the sun flung spangles, dancing coins. (37)

The encounter with Mr. Deasy decides Stephen against simple submission to the nightmare, which he had been entertaining at the beginning of the chapter; he will *try to* "escape." He accepts his historical identity—he finally (36) decides to help Mr. Deasy in his campaign on behalf of Irish husbandry; furthermore, he is aware that God can cause him to suffer a "back kick." But he cannot emulate Mr. Deasy. That vain, petty, avaricious, and uncharitable man not only accepts history but glorifies it, and, so, eagerly embraces the historical role allotted him as an Irishman: servant and admirer of English pomp and power. In Book III of the *Odyssey*, Nestor not only gives Telemachus advice on his patrimony but inspires him to continue his journey and provides the means for his doing so.

Although his guilty "brooding" is no less intense in this second chapter than in the first, again Stephen's emotional attitude is balanced by a rational one. In the first chapter it was his recognition that the modern scientist had usurped his rightful place as the poet in his homeland. In the present chapter it is a realization of the true grounds of his long-standing opinion that he cannot submit to life in Ireland.

In both chapters, Stephen combines with the indictments of his environment, which are familiar from the *Portrait*, but dramatically developed and integral in *Ulysses*, a new insecurity and guilt. He is no longer arrogant and self-righteous, but a suffering young man. The third chapter is devoted to a vivid presentation of his suffering.

3 *the strand (stephen)*

This chapter, which concludes the initial representation of Stephen Dedalus, is almost exclusively the "interior monologue" of a highly erudite young man. There is very little exposition, and only one line of dialogue ("—Tatters! Out of that, you mongrel," 47). The action is, next to that of the last chapter, the sparest in the novel. Stephen walks along Sandymount Strand. Two women cross the strand to the water and walk out of sight. Stephen sits on a rock by the water's edge. A dog runs toward him from the direction taken by the women. Two gypsies, a man and a woman, owners of the dog, approach, wade into the water, and dip their bags of recently gathered cockles. The male gypsy commands "Tatters" to leave a dog's corpse he has found, the dog "scrapes" the ground and "listens," and dog and gypsies depart. Stephen composes and writes down a quatrain, reclines on the rock, sits up again, wipes a finger with which he has picked his nose on the rock, and turns to see if he is observed. Behind him a ship with sails furled is moving by.

Stephen thinks about many and apparently widely diverse things in this chapter, including abstract metaphysics, phylogeny, his maternal uncle, an exiled patriot of his acquaintance, ancient Dublin and its Viking attackers, his soul. By a nimble power of association that is itself part of Joyce's characterization of him, one thing leads to another in the course of the chapter until all that is vital to Stephen Dedalus is touched upon. His preoccupations are those we have been led to expect: his mother; her death; his guilt; his one-time cocky vanity; the nature of divine Fatherhood; the nature and power of history; the usurpation of his place by the scientist-jester; the existence or non-existence of the soul; and language, the material of the artist he has so completely failed to become.

The "Protean" character of the chapter is generally said to lie chiefly in the changes rung on language. It is more closely related to the fact that through its changing forms Stephen's thought, like Proteus, retains its single essence. Joyce is not drawing an idle parallel with the *Odyssey*, and he is not presenting a contrived and meretricious exposition of his character's state of mind. Stephen has done a very common thing—stopped at the water's edge on a deserted beach, to think. He is beset by anxiety, guilt, self-contempt, and even practical worries, for he can no longer abide his companions or his work, and he no longer has a place to sleep. He will not stay in Ireland but cannot leave, will not teach but cannot write, will not submit to circumstances (history, God) but cannot deny their hold. He has reached the end of the road set out on when he smugly welcomed life, and is taking stock, asking himself where he can go from a dead end. The Homeric parallel serves to make the point that this inquiry is the essential nature beneath the changing subjects of Stephen's thought, and therefore the ultimate subject of the chapter.

As Menelaus explained to Telemachus, Proteus, the old man of the sea, napped on the shore every day at noon. If, at that time, a person desiring information about the future

succeeded in holding the demi-god fast despite his metamorphoses, he was obliged to grant the prophecy. Stephen's
thought contains no mention of Proteus, but he does identify
the time as "the faunal noon" (50); and when he recites
"Won't you come to Sandymount,/ Madeline the mare?"
on the first page, he is unknowingly invoking Mananaan
MacLir (not only are the names similar in sound and
rhythm, but *mare* and *lir* are Latin and Gaelic for "sea"),
the sea-diety, who was one of the two chief Irish Celtic gods,
and who had Proteus's metamorphic power. Thus, on the
next page he thinks that "The whitemaned seahorses . . .
the steeds of Mananaan," are approaching.

Joyce associates the two sea-deities in order to disclose
what essentially is happening in the chapter. But the fact
that they are sea-deities is also important; and he stresses
the sea by direct means such as the attention Stephen gives
to the action of the waves, and by indirect means such as
having phrases from *King Lear* occur to Stephen, *"lear"*
being a variant of *"lir."* Stephen has always avoided water,
the source of life as Mulligan observed at the beginning of
the novel. Like its Proteus and Mananaan, the sea, life,
conceals its nature and withholds its truth under an ever-
changing surface. In facing the sea in this chapter—confronting reality, coming to grips with his condition and
persisting through all the shifts of his thought—Stephen is
attempting to discover what Menelaus had sought from
Proteus, knowledge of how he could continue on his way.
Stephen concludes his endeavor in despair. Yet he is not
as fully equipped to judge what he sees and thinks as
Joyce enables the reader to be.

Quite characteristically, Stephen tries to determine his
condition by a controlled formal procedure. And quite
characteristically, his thoughts are almost wholly direct or
indirect expressions of his various preoccupations—the
central facts of that condition. He begins well enough, with
a quasi-Aristotelian determination of first principles. Following the line of Aristotle's discussion of sense perception
in *About the Soul* (II, vii, viii), he decides first that sight
reveals an undeniable mode of reality (the "ineluctable
modality of the visible," 38), one mode despite all the
specific forms it assumes: space ("the *nebeneinander*");
and next that hearing reveals another such mode ("the

ineluctable modality of the audible") : time ("the *nachein-ander*). He then deduces experimentally (having continued walking with his eyes closed) that reality exists independently of his senses—his experience of its Protean modes ("There all the time without you").

The formal inquiry gets no further than this promising beginning before he sees the two women walking onto the beach and converts them into midwives—initiates the long train of revealing observations, memories, allusions, speculations, and fancies that is the body of the chapter. The most isolated phrase and the most transitory association makes its contribution, yet the substance and meaning of the whole can be derived from certain principal elements in their sequence.

Having made midwives of the two women who are "Like me . . . coming down to our mighty mother" (38), Stephen thinks about the line of generation back to The Beginning, and about himself as one of the children "made not begotten"—as only matter. His inversion of the description of Jesus in the Nicene Creed ("begotten, not made") leads him to speculation on the Fatherhood of God. "He willed me and now may not will me away or ever. A *lex eterna* stays about Him" (39), he declares, and wonders if he has discovered the reconciliation of the Arian position: that the Father and the Son are consubstantial, as the Church says, because the Father shares the inferior position that the Arians ascribe to the Son, under the real predominance of the *lex eterna*—because the Father is not the absolute Father.

At this point he thinks of "the steeds of Mananaan" (whom he unwittingly invoked before seeing the two women), and asks himself if he will turn off the beach to visit the home of his maternal uncle, who is despised by his father and who is not a much better provider. He imagines the visit, calls the Dedalus and Goulding houses "houses of decay" (40), and recalls how he had romanticized his uncle when a child at Clongowes. His "Come out of them, Stephen. Beauty is not there" is reminiscent of the description of Stephen's dedication to beauty on the same beach at the end of Chapter IV and the sordidness of his actual life at the beginning of Chapter V in the *Portrait*; it serves as a subtle corrective to his earlier joy. He himself

seems to recall the experience on the beach, if not his folly,
for he thinks of the opportunity to study for the priesthood
which he had refused that afternoon. His appraisal of the
life of the "gelded" priesthood becomes mockery of himself
for impiety, lechery, and finally intellectual and physical
vanity:

> You bowed to yourself in the mirror. . . . Hurray for
> the Goddamned idiot! Hray! . . . Books you were going
> to write with letters for titles. Have you read his F?
> O yes, but I prefer Q. . . . (41)

The bitterness of the mockery is dramatic evidence of
Stephen's mood. But something has been accomplished. As
he realizes, he has "passed the way to aunt Sara's"; furthermore, he has been walking near the water's edge and the
steeds of Mananaan in the amorphous wet sand. "He . . .
crossed the firmer sand towards the Pigeonhouse" (42),
and "pigeon" invokes a blaspheming French joke about
the father of Christ and a phrase from the "Ballad of
Joking Jesus." He resumes his mockery of himself with
his "flight" to Paris, "pretending to speak broken English
. . . " (43), and is diverted from this only by the memory
of receiving his father's telegram informing him that his
mother was dying.

Perhaps because he has walked away from the sea, his
thoughts do not dwell on his mother but on Paris. He
remembers his conversations with a fugitive patriot dynamitard, Kevin Egan, who tried to "yoke me" to "our common cause" (44). He thinks of Egan as a "spurned lover"
of Ireland: "They have forgotten Kevin Egan, not he
them" (45).

At this point, "He had come nearer the edge of the sea"
and, "his feet beginning to sink slowly in the quaking
soil," his thoughts return to himself. Like Egan, he has
been spurned by Ireland; but he will not emulate Egan,
will not return to his servitude in the tower: "they [Mulligan
and Haines] wait . . . around a board of abandoned plat-
ters. Who to clear it? He has the key. I will not sleep there
when this night comes." He makes a frightening characterization of the tower-Ireland (Mulligan, its new lord, is a
bird dog because he is both "beastly" and a betrayer): "A

shut door of a silent tower entombing their blind bodies, the panthersahib and his pointer"; and he declares that he can afford to relinquish that patrimony to the beastly usurper:

Take all, keep all. My soul walks with me, form of forms. So in the moon's midwatches I pace the path above the rocks, in sable silvered, hearing Elsinore's tempting flood.

He has a soul, then is all soul and his own father (King Hamlet's ghost) as well.

The word "flood" makes Stephen aware of how close the water is, and he goes back a few steps to sit on the rock on which he remains through the rest of the chapter. From this point his wrestling with the Proteus of his thought becomes more intense, and events combine with thoughts to develop the climax and resolution of the chapter. Immediately he is confronted with a refutation of his last comforting assertion: "A bloated carcass of a dog lay lolled on bladderwrack," and a few moments later a live dog is running toward him. Fearful of attack he appraises the situation, but with ironic self-ridicule: "Respect his liberty. You will not be master of others or their slave. I have my stick" (46). He sees the two gypsies in the distance (the dog is "Tatters"), thinks they are the two women he had seen earlier, and decides that they have gotten rid of a misbirth—all there was of a human.

Just after Stephen sees the dog's carcass, the often-quoted line "These heavy sands are language tide and wind have silted here" occurs. It is concerned primarily not with language but with the past—the sands are a kind of historiography. While Tatters runs along the strand, Stephen thinks of the invading Vikings who debarked there, of the people of Dublin butchering a school of beached whales during a famine, of a time when the Liffey froze over; his reference to King Malachi II, "When Malachi wore the collar of gold," is, appropriately, a line from Thomas Moore's "Let Erin Remember the Days of Old." He declares, "Their blood is in me," and imagines himself in one of those earlier times among the other ancient Irish; yet, "I spoke to no-one: none to me."

The dog has been barking and approaching in an irregular fashion. He thinks "Dog of my enemy"; and when he returns to Irish history, his mocking "Paradise of pretenders then and now" is promptly turned upon himself, with Mulligan as his comparison. The next sentence is, "He saved men from drowning and you shake at a cur's yelping." A sharp self-examination follows, during which he admits that he would not be capable of Mulligan's feat, and which ends with an alteration of the pronoun into the feminine; "I could not save her. Waters: bitter death: lost."

Almost immediately after his mother's death returns to Stephen's thought, Tatters discovers the dead dog's carcass. The passages quoted during the discussion of the second chapter—the description of Tatters' "rag of wolf's tongue redpanting" (47), and the account of his alternately scraping up the sand and listening—occur here, along with other direct connections Stephen makes to his fox-riddle thoughts in the schoolroom. The gypsy man utters the one line of dialogue in the chapter, calling his dog away from the carcass, but not before Stephen has reiterated the two alternative propositions of his riddle, so fundamental to his brooding. He says, "Ah, poor dogsbody"; but he immediately alters the phrase so that the despairing exclamation is followed by a reassuring statement: "Here lies poor dogsbody's body"—specifically *only* that corporeal part of him, there being therefore another part which has risen.

As the dog scrapes, Stephen likens him to a pard, and so recalls the dream he was having at about the time Haines, the "panther-sahib," had his nightmare involving a black panther:

> After he woke me up last night same dream or was it? Wait. Open hallway. Street of harlots. . . . I am almosting it. That man led me, spoke. . . . The melon he had he held against my face. . . . In. Come. Red carpet spread. You will see who. (47-48)

The dream is strange, to say the least, and perhaps for this reason it sticks in the reader's mind, but its significance for the story of Stephen Dedalus will not become clear until much later in the novel.

As Stephen is recalling his dream, the gypsies approach. He thinks about their lives, plays with their argot, watches them glance at his "Hamlet hat" as they pass, and thinks, "If I were suddenly naked here as I sit? I am not." He continues to play with language, thinks of the gypsies as eternally journeying "to the west, trekking to evening lands," concentrates on the gypsy woman, and then combines all three matters by composing a crude quatrain about the coming of a personified death to his mother, "mouth to her mouth's kiss." Although he writes it down, the reader does not see it until he next appears, in the seventh (newspaper) chapter; by that time it is far more polished, and the last line has become "Mouth to my mouth" (131). He then thinks about his writing and moves naturally to thinking about his soul: "she" clings to him although "shame-wounded" by his sins, and he does not know where he is taking "her." He begins his self-ridicule again, this time over his attentions to girls, but his bravado breaks down and he makes a moving direct appeal:

> Touch me. Soft eyes. Soft soft soft hand. O, touch me soon, now. What is that word known to all men? I am quiet here alone. Sad too. Touch, touch me. (49)

A sense of isolation has shared prominence with self-blame in Stephen's thought. His inability to tolerate his uncle and cousin; his separation from his living father as well as his dead mother (a break in the umbilical cords that "link back"); the abandonment of Kevin Egan (with whom he therefore identifies himself) by his country; his isolation among the ancient Dubliners ("I spoke to no-one: none to me"); even his observations on language and on the difference, preventing communication, between his idiom and the cant of the gypsies—all ring changes on the theme of isolation, of his loneliness. Having become more and more consciously manifested in his thoughts, it now prompts a naked appeal. Once again the unsuccessful injunction of the first chapter is made: *And turn no more aside and brood* (50). This time it causes him to think about Mulligan. He is defiant still, but his loneliness is intensified:

"He now will leave me. And the blame? As I am. All or not at all."

His sense of loneliness having become as sharp as his self-ridicule, Stephen is in almost abject despair, and this mood persists to the very end of the chapter. He thinks for some time about the "weary," "sighing" weeds in the water, helpless, moved throughout their existence by a sea which for them is literal reality-life: "Day by day: night by night," "To no end gathered: vainly then released." The symbolic personal relevance of the passage becomes clear when he moves to the similar action of the sea (now not "our mighty mother" but "Old Father Ocean") on the drowned man, who is expected to rise soon. He likens the corpse to Lycidas, and so to his mother, but only in passing. What he dwells on is the awful "seachange" the drowned man undergoes; he then makes explicit his thoughts about death's pervasiveness in life, concluding, "Dead breaths I living breathe, tread dead dust, devour a urinous offal from all dead" (51).

Approaching its end, Stephen's line of thought is apparently interrupted, but only apparently, when he notices that the sky is clouding over, and remarks "Allbright he falls, proud lightning of the intellect, *Lucifer, dico, qui nescit occasum.*" He is probably thinking of Isaiah's mocking of the "day-star":

How art thou fallen from heaven, O Lucifer, son of the morning! . . .
For thou hast said in thy heart. . . .
I will ascend above the heights of the clouds; I will be like the most High.
Yet thou shalt be brought down to hell. . . . (Isaiah 14: 12-15)

For having taken stock of his situation, wrestled with his Proteus through its many changes of subject, he looks upon the lowering sky as a judgment or omen and reaches his conclusion, secures an answer. Following his apostrophe to the star of the morning, "who knows no setting," he announces his destination: "Where? To evening lands." For, like Lucifer, he has fallen from proud assurance into hellish misery. He has run the gamut from the arrogance of the morning star to the resignation of "evening will find itself in me, without me," from the "Welcome, O life!" at the end of the *Portrait* to the acceptance of a journey "to the west, trekking to evening lands." The answer he derives from his Protean inquiry is nothing more promising than a life that is like death, until the release of death itself.

It is when his despair has reached this climactic and conclusive point that Stephen, who has been picking his nose, searches in vain for his handkerchief and, prompted by the thought that he may have been observed, turns and sees the schooner "Rosevean." A brief description of the "threemaster" ends the chapter.

But although it is the theme of Stephen's meditation, despair is not the theme of the chapter. Rather, the chapter has been moving toward a specific statement about Stephen's despair, a foreshadowing of his destiny that corresponds to the pronouncements sought from Proteus. Not only in folklore, but in medieval science, the nose was considered the passage to, and an expurgative of, the brain. In a sense Stephen has been "picking at" his mind during the chapter— his nose-picking is a counterpart to his brooding meditation. Throughout the *Portrait* he misread omens, and the suggestion is that he has done so again with the lowering sky, and that in view of the conclusion he has reached, the sum of his thoughts is equal to the "dry snot" he picks from his nose. The last lines of the chapter make the point:

> He laid the dry snot picked from his nostril on a ledge of rock, carefully. For the rest let look who will.
> Behind. Perhaps there is someone.
> He turned his face over a shoulder, rere regardant. Moving through the air high spars of a threemaster, her sails brailed up on the crosstrees, homing, upstream, silently moving, a silent ship. (51)

Stephen wonders if his nose-picking is observed, turns, and sees only the ship. Earlier, he had looked behind him for the same reason: "Who's behind me? Out quickly, quickly!" (46), and despite his lonely appeal had been generally

concerned about being exposed, revealed to an observer:
"If I were suddenly naked here as I sit? I am not." (48);
"Who watches me here?" (49).

Not only is Stephen's "I am not" mistaken, but the one
who "watches" him has the "soft eyes" and "soft soft soft
hand" he appealed for; to Him, he is "naked." The
"threemaster" with the silhouetted masts and "crosstrees"
is a specific symbol of the crucifixion. The correct term for
the spar supporting a sail is "yard" (when this was pointed
out by his friend Frank Budgen, Joyce called "crosstrees"
"essential"[11]); the incorrect technical term which so con-
veniently combines two synonyms for the cross is actually
identical with the neologism Stephen uses in the ninth
chapter (library), when he speaks of Christ as "starved
on crosstree." Stephen's plea has been heard. Although he
thinks his façade is intact, he has been seen naked; and
although he feels totally alone, the reader is pointedly
advised that he is not, and furthermore that he may not
be lost to love or to salvation.

In view of Joyce's lifelong apostasy from the Catholic
church (he refused to permit the office of a priest at his
deathbed, or even at his burial), the Protean prophecy of
Stephen's future which he provides the reader—the suggestion of divine grace—seems strange. Nevertheless, the
religious burden of the chapter cannot be avoided. When
Menelaus tells Telemachus of his successful encounter with
Proteus, in Book IV of the *Odyssey,* he says that he learned
from Proteus that Odysseus was alive—that Telemachus'
quest is not a vain one. This has an obvious, but secular,
relevance for Stephen's situation at the end of the third
chapter of *Ulysses.* However, Menelaus' chief business with
Proteus, his reason for wrestling him, is more significant.
Menelaus was totally becalmed on an island whose shore
was the site of Proteus' noontime naps. He tells Telemachus
that when he had defeated Proteus, he put his question to
him, and it is very similar to Stephen's question of Bloomsday morning:

" 'I am holden long time in this isle, neither can I find
any issue therefrom, and my heart faileth within me.
Howbeit do thou tell . . . which of the immortals it is

that bindeth me here . . . and . . . how I may go over
the teeming deep.'
    "Even so I spake, and he straightway answered me
saying: 'Nay, surely thou shouldst have done goodly
sacrifice to Zeus and the other gods ere thine embarking.
. . . For it is not thy fate to see thy friends . . . till
thou hast . . . offered holy hecatombs to the deathless
gods who keep the whole heaven. So shall the gods grant
thee the path which thou desirest.' "[12]

Important as his destination was to him, Menelaus had set
out for it with too much self-assurance and too little reverence. When he wrestled with Proteus, he was trapped and
despairing. The pronouncement of Proteus was that he had
to worship "the gods." Menelaus did so, he tells Telemachus,
"and the deathless gods gave me a fair wind."[13] Stephen
may be as fortunate as Menelaus; he is more reluctant to
worship his God, and he misunderstands the Protean pronouncement; but his God watches over him with soft eyes.

in search of stephen

The reader brings two facts about Stephen Dedalus to
Ulysses: there is an undeniable connection of some sort
between him and the young Joyce; and his life from early
childhood up to a point less than fourteen months before
June 16, 1904, was the subject of a previous novel by the
author. The first of these facts is one aspect of the complex
relationship between Joyce's fiction and actuality, discussed
in Chapter Five under the heading "Joyce's Dublin and
Dublin's Joyce." The second puts *Ulysses* in the position of
being a sequel with respect to Stephen—makes the depiction
of him in the *Portrait* part of what is given in *Ulysses*.
    But by the end of the third chapter of *Ulysses*, it has be-
come quite clear that neither of the two familiar—and directly opposed—critical views about Joyce's portrait of that

younger Stephen can be reconciled with the Stephen of Bloomsday morning. If the young man of the *Portrait* is damned,[14] or if on the other hand he has fulfilled, begun the process of fulfilling, or prepared himself to fulfil his artist's destiny,[15] then Joyce has capriciously created two essentially different Stephen Dedaluses in his two novels.

The problem is not with the older Stephen's state of mind in his three introductory chapters, of course; the change from his former proud assurance is fully motivated. It is with Joyce's presentation of him as neither damned nor an artist. And because not the character of the young man handed on to *Ulysses,* but his creator's earlier disposition of him—the essential meaning or ultimate point of the *Portrait*—is at issue, that earlier novel will have to be considered as a whole. As I understand it, Joyce's treatment of Stephen in the *Portrait* is not only completely consistent with but prepares for his appearance in *Ulysses.* My debt to advocates of both of the two prevailing points of view about the *Portrait* is extensive, but my answer is not a compromise between them, for they are irreconcilable. It is an attempt to consider the book anew.

The first significant point to be made about it is that it is psychological in a very precise sense, whatever may be true about the influence or confluence during its composition of "the new Viennese school," as Stephen calls the Freudians in the ninth (library) chapter of *Ulysses.* Specifically, the whole first part of *A Portrait of the Artist as a Young Man* is almost literally the early history of a "psyche," and the remainder of the book is determined by what has been formed. Questionable as this conception of the *Portrait* may seem, Joyce leads us to it in the very beginning. The two-page "overture" in which the structure of Chapter I and the major themes of the book can be discovered, as Hugh Kenner has pointed out,[16] is explicitly the account of a very young child's responses to his environment; and from Simon Dedalus' tale of baby tuckoo to Dante's threat, it presents the book's themes precisely in terms of environmental influence on Stephen.

The first part of the *Portrait* is not its first chapter. Like those of *Ulysses,* the five chapters are shaped more to perform narrative functions than to subdivide the action, while the book's form reflects the three phases of its subject: Stephen's childhood, his adolescence (the clinical term is the most appropriate), and his ultimate stance as a young man. The first part ends in Chapter II, when the pandying incident of Chapter I is concluded; the second extends from that point, with its abrupt two-year transition to the Whitsuntide play, until Stephen sees the wading girl at the end of Chapter IV; the third is congruent with Chapter V, which takes place after a transition of four years, at the very end of his university career. The first part ends when Stephen learns that he will be able to go to Belvedere College (a secondary school), the second when he learns that he will be able to go to the university, the third when he learns that he will be able to go to Paris. Although this pattern distinguishes perfectly normal stages in human growth (as well as formal education), and ignores the chapter divisions, it not only exists but is important; for the three stages in Stephen's younger life are complication, unraveling, and conclusion of its story.

The idea of psychogenesis, the virtual molding of human character by specific childhood experiences and early environment, is a truism today, and its use for the motivation of literary characters almost a cliché. But despite that embarrassing fact, the first part of the *Portrait* presents something different from the normal tension between experience and character found even in the remainder of the *Portrait*. I speak of it as the early history of a psyche because Joyce's portrayal of Stephen Dedalus' childhood (his "formative years" in that originally psychoanalytic term) seems to be primarily a record of the development of Stephen's way of perceiving and dealing with, respectively and explicitly, the external world and his own feelings—the development of precisely that to which the "new psychology" gave the name "ego":

> As the child grows older, that part of the id which comes in contact with the environment through the senses learns to know the inexorable reality of the outer world and becomes modified into what Freud calls the ego.[17]

The ego tests and evaluates reality. It determines the

kind of adaptation the individual makes to internal and
external pressures; . . . its way of handling the pressures requiring adaptation determines the personality of
the individual.[18]

Although he does not use the term in the book and probably was ignorant of the psychoanalytic concept, Joyce
seems to have intuitively understood, as Freud said of artists
with respect to the unconscious, what psychologists named
and studied—and to have considered it of vital importance.
The recently published prose piece, "A Portrait of the
Artist," [19] clearly the first form of the work that became
Stephen Hero and ultimately the *Portrait,* begins:

> The features of infancy are not commonly reproduced
> in the adolescent portrait for, so capricious are we, that
> we cannot or will not conceive the past in any other
> than its iron memorial aspect. Yet the past assuredly
> implies a fluid succession of presents, the development
> of an entity of which our actual present is a phase only.
> Our world, again, recognizes its acquaintance chiefly by
> the characters of beard and inches and is, for the most
> part, estranged from those of its members who seek
> through some art, by some process of the mind as yet
> untabulated, to liberate from the personalized lumps of
> matter that which is their individuating rhythm, the first
> or formal relation of their parts.

This piece was written in the winter of 1903-4, when
Joyce was only twenty-one, and at about the time the process
of the mind was being tabulated at Vienna. Despite the
decade of literary activity before his completion of the
Portrait, Joyce did not relinquish his belief that "the first
or formal relation" of a subject's "parts" is linked to his
"development," and that this "individuating rhythm" is
vital to an "adolescent portrait." The *Portrait* depicts the
development of Stephen's ego and the persistence of that
"entity" or way of being throughout his adolescence and
into young manhood. (It even persists, in fact, on Bloomsday morning.)

The development of Stephen's ego, his way, in his own

words, of "battling against the squalor of his life and against the riot of his mind" (p. 91),* begins before the advent of either squalor or riot. In Chapter I, his circumstances are still comfortable and his mind innocent; yet, from the story of baby tuckoo, he is (in a phrase from *Finnegans Wake*) "jung and easily freudened."

The chapter is an excellent example of Joyce's exploitation of structural elements. It has four sections, which are separated by asterisks. (Those between the second and third sections are missing in American editions although a space for them is provided.)

The four sections are two sets of alternating episodes of home and school, which are significantly different from each other. The first pair of episodes of home and school, the "overture" and the first scene at Clongowes, are almost completely subjective in point of view. Except for some snatches of dialogue, almost nothing interrupts the record of Stephen's perceptions, feelings, memories, and attitudes. The scene at Clongowes begins with his memory of his parents as they deposited him with Father Conmee and left. He is young, weak, lonely, and bullied, and his illness makes his misery extreme. He anticipates in his feverish reverie and dream the end of the term, the triumphal trip from school, his home, and his first Christmas dinner.

The actual Christmas dinner follows, and is the first occasion in the *Portrait* on which the facts, as Stephen later thinks (p. 87), "give the lie rudely to his phantasies." The distinction between the two pairs of episodes of Chapter I is precisely that of "phantasy" and fact: the subjective record of a child's idealized assumptions about his world (home and school) is negated by an objective depiction of that world itself, reality juxtaposed against idealization stylistically as well as substantially, in the same formal unit. Moving as it is, the dinner episode is not in the book

* For the remainder of this chapter, Arabic numerals in parentheses accompanied by "p." or "pp." indicate pages in the Compass Books edition of the *Portrait* (New York, 1958), unless otherwise specified. Quotations from the text of the novel have been revised to eliminate errata specified by Joyce and listed in Peter Spielburg, "James Joyce's Errata for American Editors of *A Portrait of the Artist*," in *Joyce's "Portrait": Criticisms and Critiques*, ed. Thomas E. Connolly (New York, 1962), pp. 318–28.

to represent Ireland's predicament at the time, or the destruction of her "uncrowned king," but to show the subject confronted with these facts, Stephen's fervent anticipation of the feast of love before the hearth of home rudely disappointed and disillusioned. The irony with which Joyce invests the Christmas colors is part of Stephen's formative experience. He has learned that Church and country are not harmonious, that there can be no green rose after all. As on one or two other significant occasions in the first part of the novel, Stephen's reaction to his experience is not given. But it can readily be inferred; his confusion (p. 36), Dante's "O, he'll remember all this," and the echo of her prediction by Mr. Casey, spokesman for the other extreme, are all to the point.

The last episode in the chapter, which carries forward the confuting of the protected child's assumptions about the world, seems on its surface to be very different. The boys speak in the yard of revolting against the school's "unjust and cruel and unfair" discipline, but Stephen alone has the courage to do so. When his trust in the authority placed over him by home and society is seemingly vindicated and his admiring schoolfellows lift the shy and unpopular child aloft, the similarity with the note of fulfilment at the end of the book is apparent.

But deep ironic undercuttings show the reader the episode's place in the pattern of the chapter. Stephen is very soon "alone"; the cricket bats that had played in the background when the boys were discussing the punishment (pandy bat) of their schoolmates return; furthermore, the skull on Father Conmee's desk, beside which he takes Stephen's hand across the desk, and his attempt to excuse Father Dolan's action on sophistical grounds suggest that the triumph of justice has not been absolute.

Stephen undergoes the disillusionment in Chapter II, at the end of the first part of the book. His reaction to Simon's unwitting revelation that the justice of Father Conmee was absolute cant and that Simon himself is unable to recognize the moral issue ("O, a jesuit for your life, for diplomacy!") is not shown. But the dramatization in Chapter I of his intrepid appeal to Father Conmee and of the feelings that preceded and followed it is one index of what the reader may infer about the general nature and the intensity of that reaction; and another is the fact that the imitation of Father Conmee's laugh with which Simon Dedalus ends his anecdote is followed directly by the end of the section (the asterisks are missing in American editions, although a space for them is provided) and by a forward jump of two years. The first part of the book is defined not so much by the transition in time to the midst of Stephen's high-school days as by the suggestion that the discovery he makes about Father Conmee completes the pandying affair and so fulfils the pattern of the child's disillusioning experience of home, society, and Church, set up so symmetrically in Chapter I.

The depiction of Stephen's formative years is completed at that point. But before the point is reached, his experience broadens to include squalor and riot. Chapter II begins the summer after his year at Clongowes, and almost immediately he is weaving his fantasies about Dantes' betrothed in *The Count of Monte Cristo*. The association he makes between Mercedes and the Virgin Mary is more overt than that involving his first *inamorata*, the Protestant neighbor, Eileen, yet he seeks Mercedes constantly in real rose gardens. The principal subject of Chapter II is this struggle against the "riot" of his sexual impulses, but "the squalor of his life" is also articulated. His idealized view of the cows at summer pasture is the first fantasy rudely given the lie in the chapter—autumn comes, and "the first sight of the filthy cowyard" sickens him so he can not even "look at the milk they yielded." The note of squalor is promptly reinforced as he becomes aware of the effects of his family's declining fortunes. The sudden loss of his material security complements the loss of his emotional security, dramatized in the Christmas dinner scene; the author makes the point explicitly:

> those changes in what he had deemed unchangeable were so many slight shocks to his boyish conception of the world. (p. 64)

Whereupon, "He returned to Mercedes and, as he brooded upon her image, a strange unrest crept into his blood" (p. 64). The author tells in the next three pages (pp. 64-67)

of Stephen's isolate wanderings and reveries about travel
to exotic places, his "restless heart," his feeling of difference from other children and almost total withdrawal from
their society, his incapacity for either amusement or pleasure, his endeavor "to meet in the real world the unsubstantial image which his soul so constantly beheld," his
belief that with that meeting "he would be transfigured."

These new developments in Stephen's character are
strange neither to experience nor to literature, although
they are extreme in intensity. However, the author takes
care to link his behavior to the carefully laid-out set of
"shocks" Stephen has undergone; and when he has described
that behavior, he identifies Stephen's antagonists explicitly:

> He was angry with himself for being young and the prey
> of restless foolish impulses, angry also with the change
> of fortune which was reshaping the world about him into
> a vision of squalor and insincerity. (p. 67)

To this point what I have designated the first part of the
Portrait not only presents a history of the child Stephen's
experiences of the world about him and his own impulses
but does so explicitly and in those very terms of world
and self. Still, all human experiences must be of one or
the other, and Freud gave the name "ego" to an active
quality of mind which we develop *as a way of perceiving
and dealing with* external reality and our feelings. Before
Simon's anecdote (pp. 71-73), only two more incidents
occur—Stephen's first meeting with E.C. (pp. 68-70), and
his attempt to compose a poem about the meeting (pp.
70-71). But he has come to recognize the antagonists
troubling him. In that meeting and its consequence he
shows the way he has developed for dealing with them.

E.C., whom Stephen makes another avatar of the Virgin
and the answer to his longing (her eyes speak "to him from
beneath their cowl," and "he had heard their tale before,"
p. 69), is indeed beckoning to him as they stand on the
tram steps. He recognizes that "I could hold her and kiss
her," and has been shown to want nothing in the world
more. "But he did neither," the author says, and turns to
Stephen's poetic effort of the following day. The attempt
to render the vivid incident is futile until:

by dint of brooding on the incident, he thought himself into confidence. During this process all those elements which he deemed common and insignificant fell out
of the scene. There remained no trace of the tram itself
nor of the trammen nor of the horses: nor did he and
she appear vividly. The verses told only of the night and
the balmy breeze and the maiden lustre of the moon.
Some undefined sorrow was hidden in the hearts of the
protagonists as they stood in silence beneath the leafless
trees and when the moment of farewell had come the kiss,
which had been withheld by one, was given by both.
(pp. 70-71)

By dint of brooding on the incident, he succeeds in removing every element of reality from it, idealizing and blurring
until he is able to bring about the very opposite of what
happened to him. The probable quality of Stephen's poem
is incidental here; what is central is his development of a
pattern for dealing with the world and himself. His dis-
appointments, disillusionments, shocks, the "two years' spell
of reverie," the worst possible thing for him (which is to
end directly, when his father secures his admission to
Belvedere during the revelatory meeting with Father Conmee)—all have resulted not in a revision of his discredited
ideals concerning his own feelings and the world about him
but in his denial of reality for the sake of those ideals and
consequent inability to act in reality to achieve them. If
his ambiguous words at the end of the book, "I go to
encounter for the millionth time the reality of experience,"
assert that he himself had encountered it the other times,
the boast is not only one of the most grandiloquent in English literature but one of the most hollow as well.

That the Stephen of the *Portrait* is among those heroes
of fiction who tend to deny reality has been pointed out
before,[20] but the relationship of this tendency to his character as a whole and the careful and (as I have shown) systematic presentation of its genesis have not; and these additional elements of Joyce's portrayal qualify the tendency
itself significantly. The view of the book as "The picture
of a soul that is being damned for time and eternity,"[21]
as the portrait of "a matured, self-conscious, dedicated,
fallen being," [22] derives mainly from a judgment upon
Stephen's rejections and self-delusions: they are an attempt

to achieve "metaphysical self-sufficiency" because of "spiritual pride." Yet the supposed moral tragedy of this "anti-Christ" is actually presented as the result, in large part, of a child's encounters with a treacherous world and with the "strange unrest" of his own inchoate adolescence. Although his way of dealing with life is his own and not determined, Stephen is explicitly denied some degree of responsibility. Joyce's *Bildungsroman* is not about a tragic Luciferian but about a boy who is ludicrous, pathetic, and full of admirable potentialities.

This is confirmed by the culmination of Stephen's search for his ideal woman, in which he supposedly "falls" into "sin" for the first time. Joyce treats it more severely than he does the ultimately touching incident on the tram that foreshadows it. When he first conceives the woman at the beginning of Chapter II, Stephen imagines that upon their meeting "weakness and timidity and inexperience would fall from him." Unable to see that he has found his ideal in E.C. and failed it, he continues his search throughout the chapter until his meeting with the prostitute at the end, which is couched in terms that elaborately parody the imagined meeting:

> . . . a premonition which led him on told him that this image would, without any overt act of his, encounter him. They would meet quietly as if they had known each other and had made their tryst, perhaps at one of the gates or in some more secret place. They would be alone . . . and in that moment of supreme tenderness he would be transfigured. He would fade into something impalpable under her eyes . . . . Weakness and timidity and inexperience would fall from him in that magic moment. (p. 65)

> He wandered up and down the dark slimy streets
>
> .   .   .   .
>
> A young woman dressed in a long pink gown laid her hand on his arm. . . .
>   —Good night Willie dear!
>   Her room was warm
>
> .   .   .   .
>
> He wanted to be held firmly. . . . In her arms he felt that he had suddenly become strong and fearless and sure of himself. . . .

> . . . . he read the meaning of her movements in her
> frank uplifted eyes. . . . He closed his eyes, surrendering
> himself to her. . . . (pp. 99-101)

The accusation of lechery may or may not be implicit;
but although Stephen himself and the critics who see him
as "being damned for time and eternity" hold his first
mortal sin at face value ("from the evil seed of lust all the
other deadly sins had sprung forth," p. 106), sin is not the
author's chief concern. The "disembodied grin" of Joyce's
ubiquitous irony is mocking and disapproving, but it is
human rather than ghoulish. Adolescent boys frequently
both glorify objects of infatuation and engage in sexual
adventure rather than have a balanced relationship with
any one girl; Stephen's idealism is an extreme case. The
depiction of him seeking his ideal, finding her real equivalent, but failing himself, and continuing to seek until ultimately he is subjected to an elaborate parody of his dream,
might be so sadistic as to be intolerable were it to signify
not merely folly but self-damnation. Stephen's problem is
that he refuses to face the fact of his own growing masculinity; his ego, the way of being he has developed, tries to
deny his senses rather than discipline them, to climb away
from all sense and to pure spirit, union with "Mercedes."
His attitude is not simply Christian but Platonic: he conceives an ideal relationship with an ideal mate that will
come about under ideal circumstances in an ideal way.
What Joyce presents in his double satire is a boy Platonist
who persists in etherealizing his sexual feelings until he is
made helpless by them and "transfigured" into bestiality—
and the search of Chapter II reaches its comic fulfilment.

The fact of Stephen's faults is not synonymous with their
gravity. Unless the *Portrait* also provides a Roman Catholic standard for taking their measure, critical discussion of
"his persistent sin" or his "denial of metaphysical fact, that
is Divine fact," and consignment of his soul to eternal fire
infers such a standard in spite of the very different one which
the book does provide. Joyce's treatment of Stephen's experiences with sex exemplifies its true tone, which is less the
damnation of a corrupted vision than the chastisement of
youthful folly; and the book shows the development of that

folly from "the features of infancy" on and thereby tempers the chastisement. The references it contains to Stephen's Icarus-like "falling" have been unfortunate in one sense, for they have been too readily taken out of their pagan context. He is no satanic hero who systematically, because of "spiritual pride and autonomy," falls; he is a young man who repeatedly, because of a twisted way of being, flops.

Precisely because he flops, Stephen also cannot be the developing artist who by the end of the book has fulfilled, has begun the process of fulfilling, or has prepared himself to fulfil, his destiny. There is no doubt of his bravery, integrity, and dedication to the values of art. His appeal to Father Conmee in Chapter I, his resistance to the bullying of his schoolfellows in Chapter II, his entering a room he fully and literally believes to contain fiends waiting to take him to hell in Chapter III, his deliberations after the invitation to join the Jesuits in Chapter IV, and, in Chapter V, both the contrast between his aspiration and the shabby, materialistic self-seeking of his schoolfellows, and his firm willingness to risk eternal damnation—all show that unlike "Sunny Jim" Joyce as Stephen Dedalus may have been in some ways, he shared those three considerable virtues of his creator. Nevertheless, the view that "the whole book points toward the selection of a calling by the hero" [23] replaces a harsh and alien religious judgment of Stephen with a neglect of the judgment which Joyce actually makes. It is not of his immortal soul, his failure is no fall through corruption. But beneath the protestations, proclamations, and maturations that mark his progress through and beyond adolescence, the postulant artist persists in the way of being he has fully developed by the time Simon's anecdote about Father Conmee completes his rude removal to the world outside tuckoo's nursery; and for this reason he is found wanting. Whether a lapwing, as he calls himself in *Ulysses*, or a thoroughgoing dodo, he is not the Dedalion.

The second part of the *Portrait* ends when Stephen goes down to the beach, sees the wading girl—"the likeness of a strange and beautiful seabird"—and affirms his personal destiny and vocation. The girl seems to provide him with the key to all the problems depicted throughout that part of the book, to exemplify a wedding of his sexual (Chapter

II), religious (Chapter III), and artistic (Chapter IV) aspirations: he will worship the beauty of the created world, and his work will be "to recreate life out of life!", in his own fervid phrase. Just as the first part of the novel can be said to take the child Stephen from his father's fanciful nursery tale to his wordly anecdote, the second can be said to extend from the fictional Mercedes to the girl in the water—Stephen's discovery of Dumas' character at the beginning of Chapter II is his unpromising intro-duction to sex, religion, and literature, and his encounter with the bird-girl at the end of Chapter IV convinces him that his problems are resolved. Some readers have agreed with Stephen (divorcing him from his condition in *Ulysses)* and called Chapter V anticlimactic and an artistic error. But the progress of the second part of the novel to that fervid denouement indicates that Stephen has deluded them and himself both, as he seems to realize when he (signifi-cantly) returns to the beach in the third chapter of *Ulysses.*

First of all, Joyce creates in Chapter II an advertisement of the force and importance of Stephen's problem—a vir-tually unbroken series of examples of the denial of reality by deception and self-deception. On the first page one reads that the bankrupt parasite Uncle Charles (who acts like a prosperous burgher with the tradesman), made to leave the house when smoking, calls "the reeking outhouse" "his arbour"; on the second the weakling boy is "trained" as a runner by the derelict athletic coach; thereafter, Stephen's daydreaming about Mercedes, his pastoral idyll, the women's admiration of "the beautiful Mabel Hunter," Stephen's idealization of E.C., the writing of the poem, Father Conmee's justice, the play production in general and in detail ("—Is this a beautiful young lady? . . . Upon my word, I believe it's little Bertie Tallon . . . "), Simon's attempted return to the Cork of his youth, and the exotic delicacies, theater parties, and pink paint of Stephen's last desperate effort "to build a breakwater of order and elegance" with his essay prize money before surrendering to his frustration in nighttown—all have that quality in common. Its ubiquity in Stephen's world actually serves to temper one's judgment of him as well as to make his developing problem unavoidably apparent.

Furthermore, the chapter meaningfully charts Stephen's descent of the Platonic scale to the stews. In the two years between his first experience of E.C. and the night of the Whitsuntide play, the two years passed over in the book, he has not seen her. He has spent that day thinking about her. Furthermore, he is aware that "poetry" will no longer do him any good:

> The growth and knowledge of two years of boyhood stood between then and now, forbidding such an outlet (p. 77)

even though the basis of her hold on him is unchanged:

> He tried to recall her appearance but could not. He could remember only that she had worn a shawl about her head like a cowl and that her dark eyes had invited and unnerved him. (p. 82)

The night of the play something unique in the novel occurs, a contradiction of the tendencies in Stephen that Joyce shows to be deplorable:

> He saw her serious alluring eyes watching him. . . . Another nature seemed to have been lent him. . . . For one rare moment he seemed to be clothed in the real apparel of boyhood. . . . (p. 85)

During his religious reversion in Chapter III, Stephen chastises himself for replacing "boyish love," "chivalry," and "poetry" with "brute-like lust." But a moral distinction between pious chivalry and bestiality is irrelevant: they are alike in significance, are the alternative symptoms of his real fault. In Stephen's explicitly transforming experience of E.C.'s eyes, Joyce both makes this point and presents the corrective for Stephen's fault; and his placement of the episode in the chapter creates the meaningful chart.

Saying that Joyce works almost diagrammatically here may seem to denigrate him, but the serious witty game he made of his art results in, and supports, greater whimsies. Both of the extremities between which Stephen moves during the chapter in dealing with his sexual feelings are inadequate to the real nature of such feelings. However, midway on his descent from the ideal to the bestial, from the eyes of Mercedes to the obscene ("frank uplifted") eyes of the prostitute, he experiences an alternative to the two baneful extremes which is simply the mean between them: he sees E.C.'s eyes, both longed for and inviting, doing violence to neither spirit nor sense. And his ability to deal with his experience transforms him.

Unfortunately, not for long. And it should be noted that once more circumstance is the villain. When he rushes out of the theater after the play, not only willing to act but full of purpose (p. 95), E.C. is gone. In the next incident, the trip to Cork, his reaction to the carved word "Foetus" reveals that he has begun to have "monstrous reveries." The final step in his gradual descent follows his unsuccessful "breakwater of order and elegance": he makes E.C. a succubus. At this point he resumes his search, but not in neighborhoods with rose gardens.

When Stephen confesses his carnal sins at the end of Chapter III, the priest tells him to turn to the Virgin; but the place of E.C.'s eyes in Chapter II, as point of balance between complementary extremes and as cure of the troubles of which the extremes are the symptoms, suggests both that the priest's advice is singularly poor and that Stephen cannot satisfactorily turn to the prostitute either. The beginning of Chapter III is primarily an extended exposition of Stephen's new sensuality, but it reveals that his commitment to all the deadly sins—"his soul lusted after its own destruction"—is as deluded as are his former and future aspirations to pure spirituality; for at the same time, "The glories of Mary held his soul captive." Furthermore, his inability to reconcile spirit and sense has badly perverted both:

> If ever his soul, reentering her dwelling shyly after the frenzy of his body's lust had spent itself, was turned towards her . . . it was when her names were murmured

softly by lips whereon there still lingered foul and shameful words, the savour itself of a lewd kiss. (p. 105)

The religious reversion that fills the remainder of Chapter III is also explicitly undercut, not only by the crudeness of Father Arnall's theology and Stephen's simpleminded responses of fear followed by smugness, but also by precisely the device used in connection with his ideal woman in Chapter II: parody. The chapter begins with Stephen's anticipation of eating a greasy stew and ends with precisely the same sensual anticipation, although its object ("White pudding and eggs and sausages and cups of tea") is decorous enough to support his self-delusion. Joyce reiterates the point blasphemously, by concluding the chapter at that place in the Communion service at which Stephen is about to accept the host: "The ciborium had come to him."

Chapter II begins with Stephen's attempt to exist on a purely spiritual plane and records his progressive descent to the purely sensual. Chapter III begins with Stephen's attempt to exist on a purely sensual plane and records his progressive ascent to the purely sprirtual. Chapter III ends with the Communion, Chapter II with the prostitute, but both kinds of fulfilment are undercut. And the two chapters are clearly complementary, depicting in concert Stephen's being flung from pillar to post by his inability to reconcile his impulses with his idealizations. The descent through Chapter II and ascent through Chapter III is a kind of geometrical trope, whose very symmetry suggests the futility of Stephen's actions and the worthlessness of both his denial that his genitals are part of him (p. 161) and his reversion to the opposite extreme of the Platonic scale. By the end of Chapter III, he has resolved nothing.

Joyce has made his depiction of Stephen's troubled adolescence a simplistic criticism of that scale itself, a refutation of Plato's view of reality and human experience through that of Aristotle. The true dichotomy he offers is that between the whole range of Stephen's frenetic conduct, on the one hand, and, on the other, his brief and luckless coping with E.C.'s real eyes—with the tension between spirit and sense of normal human experience. The form of Chapter II, with Mercedes at one end, the prostitute at the other, and Stephen's unique and salutary experience of E.C.'s eyes between, suggests the paradigm.

The two chapters representing Stephen's personal suffering are followed by Chapter IV, whose principal subject is his quest for vocation ending in the revelatory sight of the wading girl. But, just as the implicit comment on Stephen's delusion about Father Conmee at the end of Chapter I is made explicit at the beginning of Chapter II, and the implicit comment on his escape into sensuality at the end of Chapter II is made explicit by his visits to the shrine of the Virgin, so the beginning of Chapter IV explicitly mocks his reversion from sensuality, which has already been implicitly refuted in the white pudding and Communion. His piety is methodical and crass ("he seemed to feel his soul . . . pressing . . . his purchase . . . in heaven," p. 148); he still feels indifference for others; above all, after a while his devotions lose their meaning—until he discovers a "world of fervent love and virginal responses" in an old prayer book in which "the imagery of the canticles was interwoven with the communicant's prayers":

> An audible voice seemed to caress the soul . . . bidding her arise as for espousal . . . look forth, a spouse, from Amana and from the mountains of the leopards; and the soul seemed to answer with the same inaudible voice, surrendering herself: *Inter ubera mea commorabitur.* (p. 152)

The bulk of the allusions are to the fourth chapter of Song of Songs, which contains the famous physical description of the mistress and the "Thou hast ravished my heart, my sister, my spouse" passage. The pun on *"ubera"* in the Latin of the soul's response makes the sexual cast of the passage unmistakable. Stephen is still engaged in his characteristic folly, and his "I have amended my life, have I not?", with which the episode almost immediately ends, is Joyce's characteristic mockery of it.

The next episode in the chapter presents the interview between Stephen and the director of the school, and the perceptive and enobling grounds on which he rejects the

invitation to prepare for the Jesuit order. The third and
final episode depicts his discovery of vocation. It begins
with his learning that he is to enter the university and
feeling that he has therefore "passed beyond" the authority
and pressures of his society. He wonders about "the end
he had been born to serve," reflects upon the "dappled
seaborne clouds," composes his phrase, and decides that
he is interested in language and that, like the clouds, he
is to "wander." He comes on his swimming classmates,
whose schoolboy Greek causes him to consider his name.
He has a vision of "a winged form flying above the waves
and slowly climbing the air," "a hawklike man flying sunward," and decides that along with the clouds this vision
is significant of his destiny:

> What were they now but cerements shaken from the
> body of death—the fear . . . the incertitude . . . the
> shame that had abased him within and without. . . .
>   His soul had arisen from the grave of boyhood, spurn-
> ing her graveclothes. Yes! Yes! Yes! He could create
> . . . as the great artificer whose name he bore. . . .
> (pp. 169-70)

He sets out, freed from distraught adolescence, full of assurance and joy, and sees the bird-girl, who like the girls
before her looks in his eyes. The chapter ends in his rhapsodic affirmation of life in nature and of his destiny as its
celebrant.

Unfortunately, his sense of vocation is no more meaningful for him than was either of the complementary motive
forces, spiritual aspiration and sensual indulgence, that
preceded it; and he is as wrongly praised for finding himself and his vocation as he is charged with losing his
immortal soul. Joyce denied the value of Stephen's vocational commitment in the very process of revealing it.
Stephen's two omens are ironic—that is to say, he misreads
them (characteristically) to suit his wish: the clouds are
travelling westward, have gone from the continent to Ireland; the artist of his vision is "flying sunward," "climbing
the air," acting not like the fabulous artificer but like his
foolish son, as the text promptly confirms:

An ecstasy of flight made radiant his eyes and wild his
breath and tremulous and wild and radiant his wind-
swept limbs.
—One! Two! . . . Look out!—
—O, Cripes, I'm drownded!— (p. 169)

Stephen must fail to realize the artist's calling because
he will repeat, is inclined by his whole way of being to
repeat, the fault of his first poem to E.C. Throughout the
book, water has the symbolic meaning that it has in
Ulysses: it represents life or reality. Thus, Stephen always
refuses to swim and is reluctant to wash (as in *Ulysses*).
In Chapter I, water dropping into a bowl is linked with
pandying, the life of a priest is likened in Chapter IV to
turf-colored water, and in Chapter II the association is
made the vehicle for a statement of Stephen's condition in
terms familiar to this discussion:

He had tried to build a breakwater of order and elegance
against the sordid tides of life without him and to dam
up . . . the powerful recurrence of the tide within him.
Useless. From without as from within the water had
flowed over his barriers: their tides began once more
to jostle fiercely above the crumbled mole. (p. 98)

Joyce said in his student essay "James Clarence Mangan,"
"so long as this place in nature is given us, it is right that
art should do no violence to that gift." The creative process corresponds to the flight of Dedalus because in both
cases success depends upon remaining close to the water;
and Stephen's misconception of that process dooms him
to failure. The point is made in the chapter before the
advent of omens and bird-girl, when Stephen thinks with
amusement of his father's gardener, "the man with the hat,"
and

of how the man with the hat worked, considering in turn
the four points of the sky and then regretfully plunging
his spade in the earth. (p. 162)

The lesson for the artist is lost on him. Being the way he
is, he naturally inclines to "soar" "sunward" himself rather
than turn over the earth and create "out of the . . . earth

a . . . soaring . . . being." Despite his rhapsodizing about
mortal beauty, the young Stephen has provided the reader
with a prognosis of failure in his artistic aspiration that
is consistent with his unchanged character. The long-
limbed bird-girl who seems to him an augury of his emergence from boyhood, of the end of the trials begun with
his encounter with Mercedes, and who seems the embodiment of his successful reconciliation of spirit and sense
through vocation is depicted very clearly as a water bird.

The last part (and chapter) of the book has for its subject the young man who is the product and veteran of
Stephen's experiences of childhood and adolescence. Far
from being superfluous, it is required by what has gone
before. It presents the result of the development in childhood and the living out in adolescence of Stephen's way
of being. What the young man who emerges is, determines
what the *Portrait* is about in the most elementary sense.
Some critics feel that Joyce withholds the answer to the
elementary question, and so does not truly end the book at
all. But it does end, for Joyce truly does portray and
judge Stephen. He does not indicate Stephen's destiny in
the full sense of the grandiloquent word; but such an indication is not called for—the portrait is of the artist specifically as a young man. The method at the end of the
novel is consistent and familiar. The five chapters, both
discrete and sequential, a pentaptych much like a Hogarth
progress, are linked by corresponding revelations about
Stephen's major delusions, each made implicitly at the
end of a chapter when the delusion reaches its climax, and
then explicitly at the beginning of the next. Because of
this method, the *Portrait* does end, and yet *Ulysses* is its
sequel with respect to Stephen: when he appears at the
beginning of *Ulysses* he is precisely what the end of the
Portrait showed him, by ironic suggestion, to be.

Stephen saw in the bird-girl the beauty of the created
world, which would be the matter of his art. But when
the page is turned and the time suddenly becomes the end
of that university career the anticipation of which a few
pages before had led to his rhapsodic affirmation, the explicit revelation of that climactic delusion of his adolescence is made:

Chapter V

He drained his third cup of watery tea to the dregs
and set to chewing the crusts of fried bread that were
scattered near him. . . . The yellow dripping had been
scooped out like a boghole and the pool under it brought
back to his memory the dark turfcoloured water of . . .
Clongowes. The box of pawn tickets at his elbow had
just been rifled and he took up idly one after another
in his greasy fingers. . . . (p. 174)

Fundamentally Stephen is unchanged; despite the true
nature of the world out of which he must make his art,
he is still dedicated to the bird-girl he had seen years
before and still assumes that he need only "fly" to the
continent to fulfil himself. He has changed enough super-
ficially to confirm his belief that "his soul had arisen from
the grave of boyhood"—he is confident, even smug, in
his consciousness of potentiality, is gregarious, sententious,
assertive, and resolute. It is precisely because these characteristics are superficial that they are so fully overwhelmed
by his troubles in *Ulysses*. The fundamental fact is focussed
on again and again in the chapter. Despite the multitude
of boys' names that contrasts so completely with the preceding chapters, he is still isolate. In a consistent pattern,
he taunts his mother for her tenderness toward him, walks
to school alone, spurns the flower girl ("a type of her
race and of his own"), fails to communicate with the dean
of studies ("I meant a different kind of lamp, sir," "No,
no—said Stephen smiling—I mean . . . "), rejects McCann
the internationalist and Davin the nationalist, and really
has no meaningful relation with either Lynch or Cranly,
although they compete for him. (He is little more than
a prestigeful curiosity to Lynch; he does all the talking
in their intellectual "discussions," so that his blushing
"We are right" is pathetic. He unconsciously associates
Cranly with John the Baptist and confides his most intimate
feelings to him, yet Cranly is as kind to "the captain," the
symbolic dwarf in the National Library, as he is to Stephen;
Temple, the "flaming floundering fool" who is "a believer
in the power of mind," is a comic version of Stephen himself, and Cranly's intolerance of Temple is a meaningful
index.)

Stephen's essential isolation joins with the box of pawn tickets, "speckled with louse marks," to confirm that his triumphant joy at the end of Chapter IV was unjustified and he is still unable to cope with his own feelings or the world about him. The remainder of the chapter simply takes this fact and ironically juxtaposes it against his final stance as artist and individual; Joyce's tone and method both are precisely what they are in the anticipatory triumph at the end of Chapter IV.

Joyce shows Stephen as artist in the composing of his villanelle. The process is recorded from beginning to end, and the passage beautifully combines the images and ideas of the aesthetic discourse with Lynch. Shelley's "fading coal," the phrase from Galvani, the Aquinian phases of artistic apprehension, the process of creation by stages— all are related in the making of a poem which, when made, exemplifies the defects of an aesthetic that nowhere admits value to the object itself, that is not Thomistic but, like Stephen's morality, Platonic, separating experience and idea. Stephen awakes with a "morning inspiration." The subject and agent, E.C. and his own soul (the ideal in two aspects), are combined into one "she." With this ideal he associates females symbolic of Ireland, such as the flower girl. He sees himself as "a priest of the eternal imagination, transmuting the daily bread of experience into the radiant body of everlasting life" (p. 221). And Joyce invests the incident with its final bit of significance by having him think that he "had written verses for her again after ten years" and recall the ride on the tram that inspired his last previous composition of a whole poem.

He is still a failure as an artist, and for the same reason. The poem is consummated when his soul, one aspect of "the temptress of his villanelle," is aroused sufficiently, with the whole incident suggesting Stephen's familiar confusion of the sexual, the religious, and the artistic; and the villanelle is a vague piece full of figurative possibilities without a literal base—Joyce's own poetry of the period pushed beyond image to vapor. There is no transubstantiation of experience into everlasting life, only sweet sound and an echo, appropriately, of Shelley's apostrophe to the "weary" celestial wanderer, quoted in Chapter II. Joyce shows him going wrong during the process. "Shrinking from that life" of the world around him, he nurtures his inspiration, "imaging a roseway from where he lay upwards to heaven." His reversing the direction of the primrose path may not be morally significant, but it is poetically so. As he did when a child, he has taken the easy way out, left the earth and climbed sunward. One can measure the extent to which he has failed his aspirations against Joyce's own well-known literary accomplishments at his age, and against the fact that the protagonist of *Stephen Hero* is said on page 211 of that book to have composed "some ardent verses which he entitled a 'Vilanelle of the Temptress'" and on page 226 tells his brother Maurice that he has burned his whole volume of poems because "they were romantic," lacked precisely the virtue of "bend[ing] upon these present things" which Joyce's essay on Mangan cites in arguing the superiority of the "classical" attitude over the "romantic."

Stephen watches the birds in flight from the steps of the library, thinking of Thoth and Dedalus and advising himself that he is watching the birds for an "augury," immediately after his composition of the villanelle. He construes (p. 225) that the birds are indeed an augury of flight and creation, in the tradition of Dedalus and "Thoth, the god of writers." But Thoth has the head of an ibis, which is a water bird; and Stephen concludes that "he was to go away" and create just when "they came back with shrill cries. . . . " He has once again caused himself to misread the omens; like the clouds and the vision of Dedalus, the birds and the vision of Thoth signify for him as man and as artist the very opposite of flight from the Irish earth, either toward the continent or toward the heavens. From this point to the end of the book, Joyce persistently invalidates Stephen's expectations and assumptions. After interpreting the omens, Stephen seeks out Cranly for the "Easter duty" conversation, and declares with as much bravery as bravado his willingness to risk eternal damnation. However, as Cranly points out, he believes in the validity of the sacraments, his "mind is supersaturated with the religion in which you say you disbelieve," so that a flight from

Ireland would be futile with respect to the "net" of religion. Another pall is cast on his prospective departure by the circumstances in which he finally decides that he will make it. Cranly sings "Rosie O'Grady," Stephen adds Rosie O'Grady to the symbols of Ireland embodied in E.C., thinks that E.C. prefers Cranly to himself, and concludes:

> Away then: it is time to go. A voice spoke softly to Stephen's lonely heart, bidding him go. . . . Yes, he would go. He could not strive against another. (p. 245)

Although his escape is at least occasioned by apparent dismissal, he proceeds to make his self-deluding proclamation about the things he will not serve and the "arms" he will use for his "defense." Cranly mocks his stance ("Is it you? You poor poet, you!"), and the action gives way to the excerpts from his journal.

These confirm Cranly's judgment. By the end of the book, Stephen has associated E.C. with his ideal woman, with the Church, with Ireland, and even with his own soul. (E.C. is completely absent from *Ulysses* for the good reason that all her symbolic functions are taken over by Stephen's dead mother.) His decision to make his melodramatic "flight" is prompted by the belief that E.C. has rejected him (it seems never to have occurred to him that Mercedes married Monte Cristo's enemy, although it must have occurred to Joyce that she fared badly as a result). And despite all his previous concern about omens and his triumphant pronouncements during the course of the journal passage, E.C. comes up eight times in the six and a half pages—she is his only constantly recurring subject, and Joyce may well have used the device of the journal primarily to show Stephen's preoccupation with her; she keeps appearing until, just before the end, he reveals that he met her and expresses a willingness to throw up calling, flight, freedom, and all if only E.C. (with her whole freight of meaning) will have him:

> Yes, I liked her today. . . . Then, in that case, all the rest, all that I thought I thought and all that I felt I felt, all the rest before now, in fact. . . . (p. 253)

He recognizes however that his courtship is futile, and turns to the exultant apostrophe to life and boast about his millionth encounter with the reality of experience with which the book ends half a page later. The passage is one with his poem about the tram-car tryst at the end of the first part of the book, and his paean to the created beauty of the bird-girl at the end of the second. Joyce shows him to be fundamentally unchanged in Chapter V, and his aspirations to continue to be futile: both his poetic practice in the chapter and his inability to relinquish or even put out of mind that which he protests he would escape testify to the fact.

The ending is complete and without ambiguity. After all the ironic revelations of the chapter, Stephen is caused to make his exultant boast and to invoke Dedalus. However, just as he is more like Monte Cristo than like Christ, both in his own nature and in his relations with his bride, he is more like Icarus than like Dedalus. And the weight of the irony generated when this already familiar point is not only made again, through Stephen's references to "the wings of their . . . youth" and to Dedalus as "father," but is also amplified by the whole context of false analogy—Dedalus had only to separate himself physically from what he wished to escape while Stephen's island prison is also within him; Dedalus had been able to fly close to the water; Dedalus had been returning to his home from exile—brings to a decisive end the portrayal of an attractive and impressive young man who is neither damned nor fulfilled, but self-deluding and ineffectual.

Just as the tone of Joyce's portrait of Stephen Dedalus is complicated but not ambiguous, so is its basic argument. Stephen's expectations at the end with regard to himself and his future are vain, and his suffering and sense of futility when he reappears a year and seven weeks later are expected, the explicit representation of that former vanity. But Stephen's failing has been fully articulated in the *Portrait* and its correction is plain. He must come to apprehend and to accept reality, submit to the laws of his existence, in terms both of the condition of the created world and the limitations of human nature. Joyce is not suggesting that he spend his life in a milieu whose hypocrisy and squalor helped to develop that failing but, as the omens reiterated, his going "forth" in his condition was mistaken, for to do so was only to avoid more successfully the reality he would sooner or later have to, and by his mother's death was forced to, confront.

Therefore, not only has the failure of Stephen's consummate aspiration in the *Portrait* been inevitable, it has been necessary for his rescue from complete spiritual breakdown. And not only is the Stephen of the *Portrait* not irreconcilable with the Stephen of *Ulysses*, but *Ulysses* is Stephen's only chance.

1. Hugh Kenner, "The Portrait in Perspective," in Givens, pp. 132–74, 164.

2. *James Joyce*, p. 69.

3. See Virginia Moore, *The Unicorn* (New York, 1954), p. 69.

4. *Catholic Encyclopedia* (New York, 1907), I, 708.

5. *Ibid.* (New York, 1911), X, 449.

6. See Budgen, p. 116.

7. S. H. Butcher and A. Lang, *The Odyssey of Homer Done into English Prose* (4th ed.; London, 1883), p. 13. The familiar old Butcher and Lang translation was the standard one throughout Joyce's lifetime.

8. For a discussion of its origins, see Joseph Prescott, "Notes on Joyce's *Ulysses*," *Modern Language Quarterly*, XIII (1952), 149–62.

9. *Ibid.*, p. 149.

10. Saint Columbanus (d. 615) was, according to Butler's *Lives of the Saints* (London, 1938), "the greatest of the Irish missionary monks on the continent of Europe" (XI, 276). "He left his mother, grievously against her will" to follow the monastic calling (*ibid.*). A work with the same title (Edinburgh, 1914) by the Reverend S. Baring-Gould is more explicit about the incident alluded to in *Ulysses*: "His mother attempted to deter him, prostrating herself on the threshold of the door; he stepped over her, and left . . ." (XIV, 489–90).

11. See Budgen, p. 56.

12. Butcher and Lang, pp. 62–63.

13. *Ibid.*, p. 66.

14. See, e.g., Kenner, "The *Portrait* in Perspective," and Caroline Gordon, "Some Readings and Misreadings," *Sewanee Review*, LXI (1953), 388–93.

15. See, e.g., Eugene M. Waith, "The Calling of Stephen Dedalus," *College English*, XVIII (1957), 256–61, and the chapters named for the *Portrait* in Dorothy Van Ghent, *The English Novel, Form and Function* (New York, 1953), and in *Joyce*.

16. Kenner, "The *Portrait* in Perspective," pp. 136–41.

17. A. A. Brill, Introduction to *The Basic Writings of Sigmund Freud* (New York, 1938), p. 12.

18. Irene M. Josselyn, *The Happy Child* (New York, 1955), "The Growth of the Ego," p. 170.

19. Edited, with an Introduction, by Richard M. Kain and Robert E. Scholes, *Yale Review*, XLIX (1960), 355–69.

20. "The *Portrait* is throughout a tragedy of ideals without matter; the tragic conflict is always between the dream and life . . . ," Kenner, "The *Portrait* in Perspective," p. 172.

21. Gordon, p. 389.

22. Kenner, "The *Portrait* in Perspective," p. 142.

23. *Joyce*, pp. 120–21. Mr. Waith states that Joyce "never fails . . . to indicate what is unlikeable, weak, or foolish" in Stephen, but focusses on the extent to which he is made right-minded or even admirable, and his striving toward fulfilment as a man and an artist is supported.

chapter two

4 *the kitchen*

The fourth chapter of *Ulysses* is the first of the group of three chapters devoted to introducing Leopold Bloom. Not only are the two trios of chapters structurally parallel, but the first, second, and third chapters of each, respectively, have similar thematic patterns. For example, the present chapter and Stephen's first chapter are chronologically simultaneous, and embody parallel rather than continuous actions—the respective situations "at home" of Stephen and Bloom. But the correspondence goes further. Like Stephen, Bloom is a servant; and like the poet, the husband has been dispossessed.

The chapter begins with the unique, dramatic fact of Bloom's servitude:

> he moved about the kitchen softly, righting her breakfast things on the humpy tray.
>
> . . . .
>
> Another slice of bread and butter: three, four: right. She didn't like her plate full. Right. (55)

And that he is not merely granting his wife a unique privilege is made quite clear during its course:

> —Poldy!
> —What?
> —Scald the teapot (62)

Everything on it? Bread and butter, four, sugar, spoon, her cream. Yes.

.   .   .   .

—What a time you were, she said. (63)

As in the first chapter, a key figures in this chapter, and a similar significance must be attached to it. On his way to the porkbutcher's, Bloom realizes that his latchkey is "In the trousers I left off" (56), but decides not to "disturb" Molly and hopes that his house will not be entered while his wife is in bed if the door remains unlocked (57). In symbolic terms: he would have to *disturb* Molly in order to secure the proprietary key; the fault is his because he has "left off" the "trousers" with which it belongs; the consequence on the morning of the novel is that he must feebly hope that his unlocked house, with his wife in bed, will not be entered.

A number of other facts are revealed in the chapter: Bloom is a newspaper-advertising salesman; his wife is a concert soprano; the day is Thursday, June 16; the midwife who had delivered the Blooms' son eleven years before "knew from the first poor little Rudy wouldn't live"; the surviving child, Millicent, who was fifteen the previous day, works away from home; the morning's mail includes a letter to Bloom and a postcard to Molly from Milly, and a letter to Molly from the manager of her impending concert "tour," Hugh ("Blazes") Boylan (actually, only one concert is scheduled, for June 25 in Belfast). From its first words the chapter also provides, through Bloom's "interior monologue," an introduction to his singular values, intelligence, and sensibility.

When he reads in Milly's letter of the attentions of a young student, Alec Bannon, Bloom feels the inevitable consternation of the father of a pretty, adolescent girl; but he promptly resigns himself:

A soft qualm regret, flowed down his backbone, increasing. Will happen, yes. Prevent. Useless: can't move. Girl's sweet tight lips. Will happen too. He felt the flowing qualm spread over him. Useless to move now. Lips kissed, kissing kissed. Full gluey woman's lips. (67)

And the transition with "Will happen too" from "Girl's sweet light lips" to "woman's lips" is wholly understandable. Milly is a younger and slimmer version of her mother, "Molly" with the difference of the vowels: "Marionette we called her" (440). Similarly, Bannon is of the order of Boylan. Thoughts of Milly and Bannon inevitably associate with thoughts of Molly and Boylan, who present a much more pressing problem.

Molly's secretiveness about Boylan's letter would have aroused Bloom's suspicions if that were necessary. But the "Bold hand" of the address is sufficient. Bloom remembers too well how Molly's first sight of Boylan at "the bazaar dance" had affected her (69), and knows Boylan's reputation. His fear is confirmed when Molly tells him that Boylan is bringing her the program of her concert and that she is to sing "Love's Old Sweet Song" and "La ci darem" from *Don Giovanni*. He does not dwell on the first selection's obvious irony, but thinks instead:

> *Voglio e non vorrei.* Wonder if she pronounces that right: *voglio.* (63)

The line sung by Zerlina is "Vorrei e non vorrei." Bloom unconsciously substitutes the indicative "I will" for the conditional because he knows the attitude his wife (who is to sing the part of the peasant girl equivocating about succumbing to Don Giovanni because of a desire to be faithful to her betrothed, Masetto) will take toward the blandishments of her own Don. He corrects himself when he repeats the line in the sixth chapter (92), so his error is not the result of ignorance; yet in every instance after that he persists in the substitution.

It is significant that, although Bloom is made to serve Molly and is betrayed by her, he has no resentment for his wife. His attitude is in direct contrast to that of Stephen in the corresponding situation. He is a willing servant, is repeatedly concerned throughout the novel with pleasing Molly. Thus, before going for his kidney in the present chapter:

> She might like something tasty. Thin bread and butter
> she likes in the morning. Still perhaps: once in a way (56)

and en route:

> Boland's breadvan delivering with trays our daily but
> she prefers yesterday's. . . . (57)

The chapter makes it apparent that he loves her, even dotes on her. For example, he recalls remarks of hers he had scribbled on his cuff—remarks that the unprejudiced reader finds very ordinary—and his thoughts about writing a "sketch" include sharing the author's credit with her (69).

Bloom almost abjectly serves Molly, and with solicitude rather than resentment. If she appears to be analogous to Calypso, the Homeric correspondence is a significant contrast, for Odysseus resented strongly his years of subjection in the cave of the nymph. Loving her, he is upset about her imminent adultery, would like to win her back; the title of the "prize titbit" he reads in the outhouse, "Matcham's Masterstroke," and its opening words, "Matcham often thinks of the masterstroke by which he won the laughing witch who now," recur in his thought throughout the day. Yet even here he shows no resentment. Can his doting on her be sufficient reason for his failure to resent either servitude or betrayal? To complicate matters, there is a suggestion that solicitude is his response not only to Molly's exploitation of him but, subconsciously, to her betrayal of him as well—that he has a propensity for bawdry. After the neighbors' servant girl has disappeared outside the pork-butcher's:

> The sting of disregard glowed to weak pleasure within his
> breast. For another: a constable off duty cuddled her in
> Eccles Lane. (59)

When his "weak pleasure" at being spurned for another is coupled to his enthusiasm for his servitude, one is led to suspect Bloom of masochism. The chapter introduces a character who is frustrated father and husband, on the one hand,

and enthusiastic servant and perhaps even co-operative cuckold, on the other.

5 *the post office*

The action of this chapter takes place in and around the
branch post office on Westland Row to which Bloom goes
for the letter sent to "Henry Flower, Esq." by a probably
equally pseudonymous "Martha Clifford." He secures the
letter at the Westland Row Postal Annex, but as he leaves
he meets M'Coy, an acquaintance, who inquires about Molly's
forthcoming concert tour, tells how he learned about Paddy
Dignam's death, and asks Bloom to have his name placed on
the list of mourners at the funeral. He escapes from M'Coy,
turns the north corner (onto Brunswick, now Pearse, Street),
and around the block (onto Cumberland Street), to the deserted rear of the Westland railroad station, where with continued caution (ludicrous throughout the chapter, while
Molly's caution with Boylan's letter was understandable) he
reads the letter. He tears the envelope into tiny bits under
the elevated tracks of the railroad, enters the back door of
All Hallow's Church (which, like the railroad station and
the postal annex, fronts on Westland Row), and witnesses
part of a communion service. He leaves the church by its
front door, thus describing roughly a full circle, and goes to
an apothecary shop on Lincoln Place, which is the junction
of the block-long Westland Row and the street just south of
it (Leinster Street), where he orders a skin lotion for Molly.
He decides to have a bath before the funeral and buys a cake
of lemon-scented soap. But again as he reaches the street
he has an unpleasant encounter. He meets a racing tout,
Bantam Lyons, seeking the betting odds on the day's principal race, the Ascot Gold Cup; he offers Lyons his newspaper:

—I was just going to throw it away, Mr. Bloom said.
Bantam Lyons raised his eyes suddenly and leered
weakly.
—What's that? his sharp voice said.
—I say you can keep it, Mr. Bloom answered. I was
going to throw it away that moment.
Bantam Lyons doubted an instant, leering; then thrust
the outspread sheets back on Mr. Bloom's arm.
—I'll risk it, he said. Here, thanks.
He sped off towards Conway's corner. (84)

The chapter ends with Bloom walking "round the corner"
to the "mosque of the baths," imagining himself extended in
his bath.

As this detailed account of Bloom's itinerary suggests, the
designation of the chapter's locale might properly be "Westland Row"—were it not for the central role of Martha
Clifford's letter. The prodigious enterprise Bloom makes of
getting and reading the letter, and his subsequent thoughts
about it and the woman who wrote it, span the chapter.
Furthermore, the "flower" motif running through the chapter, a major element of the Homeric correspondence, is
associated directly with the letter.

The chapter corresponds, of course, to the episode of the
lotus-eaters in the *Odyssey*. Both the pseudonymous Angli-
cized and the original forms of Bloom's name are "flower,"
and so is the last word in the chapter. Familiar phrases using
the word or the names of flowers occur throughout, and the
chapter contains an extensive catalogue of types of flowers.
The effect of Homer's lotus on those who ate it is invoked by
the repetition of such phrases as "flowers of idleness" and by
reference to many types of chemical and institutional narcotics. The details of this correspondence have been fully
delineated;[1] what remains to be considered is its possible
function.

After Bloom secures Martha's letter:

He strolled out of the postoffice and turned to the right.
Talk: as if that would mend matters. His hand went into
his pocket and a forefinger felt its way under the flap of
the envelope, ripping it open in jerks. Women will pay a
lot of heed, I don't think. His fingers drew forth the
letter and crumpled the envelope in his pocket. (72)

At the same time that he is consummating one stage of his epistolary romance, he is thinking of the impending adultery of his wife. Deciding that he cannot deter Molly from her affair, he draws Martha's letter from its envelope. This paragraph, so near the beginning of the chapter, makes unavoidable the conclusion that Bloom associates his own behavior with Molly's. Directly he meets M'Coy; and while he is fingering the letter in his pocket, trying to determine what is pinned to it, he tells M'Coy of Molly's concert tour. M'Coy's "—That so? . . . Who's getting it up?" (74) makes him think of Molly lying in bed, of the "Torn strip of envelope" from Boylan's letter under her pillow, and of a snatch of the significant "Love's Old Sweet Song." He avoids answering and starts to leave. From this point, so near the beginning of the chapter, to its end, Bloom does not think once about the impending rendezvous of Molly and Boylan.

Taken together, the Homeric correspondence, the central place of Martha Clifford's letter in the action, Bloom's association of the letter and his activities related to it with Molly's impending adultery, and Bloom's subsequent avoidance of any thoughts about the adultery reveal the subject and theme of the chapter. The lotus-eaters had eaten of the flower of oblivion and had, as a consequence, become passive, content, forgetful of their responsibilities and of their homes and families. A yellow flower is pinned to Martha's letter. The letter represents the lotus; and Bloom's retrieving, reading, and thinking about it, the chief matter of the chapter, represents his particular kind of lotus-eating. The Homeric correspondence is Joyce's device for indicating the nature and significance of what Bloom is doing: he is using the letter to help him forget his home and the acute problem it presents, to help him forget his responsibility to try to solve that problem.

Martha's letter is not by itself the whole delineation of Bloom's lotus-eating. It is rather the principal and unifying element in a pattern that runs through the chapter. Bloom thinks of gelded horses, "Might be happy all the same that way" (76); of cab drivers, "no will of their own" (76); and of *castrati* in church choirs, "Suppose they wouldn't feel anything after. Kind of a placid. No worry. Fall into flesh don't they? . . . Eunuch. One way out of it" (81). With

comic impatience he awaits a sight of the ankles of a woman
about to mount a carriage, and he thinks of a number of
other inaccessible women. He walks about almost in circles
and idles away the time. Again and again it is he who is
relaxed, "lolling," floating, in his mental images of *dolce
far niente*. All these thoughts and images are expressions of
his desire to escape from his marital problem, which is
clearly shown to be his responsibility as a man, into passivity.
Thus, despite Martha's importunities he avoids meeting her:
"Thank you: not having any" (77). And when her name
reminds him of a picture of Christ preaching to the two
sisters, Martha and Mary of Bethany, in their home, he
associates himself and his Martha with the persons in the
mixed but celibate group:

> Nice kind of evening feeling. No more wandering
> about. Just loll there: quiet dusk: let everything rip.
> Forget. Tell about places you have been, strange customs.
> The other one, jar on her head, was getting the supper.
> . . . She listens with big dark soft eyes. Tell her: more
> and more: all. Then a sigh: silence. Long long long rest.
> (78)

"The other one" is, of course, Martha, who complained to
Jesus that her sister only sat and listened to Him while she
worked. Jesus praised Mary for doing so. Bloom would
just as soon have his Martha busy herself, for the woman
who in his fancy "listens with big dark soft eyes" is his
Mary-Marion—it is to Molly that Bloom wishes to tell all,
and with her to rest. He exchanges titillating letters with the
likes of Martha because Molly, from all appearances, would
have none of that sort of thing.

Almost all Bloom's thoughts in the chapter, then, whether
about flowers, narcotics, floating, castration, religion (the
lulling comfort of faith, the passivity of the Buddha),
women, or Martha Clifford, reflect a single theme: his endeavor to forget his marital problem and the responsibility
to try to solve it. Directly paralleling Stephen in the second
of the three chapters presenting him (school), Bloom here
in his second chapter attempts to avoid the consequences of
his situation. In contrast to Stephen, he succeeds so well

that as he is about to read the letter he is metamorphosed
from the poor betrothed of the peasant girl into the bold
and seductive Don:

> *Là ci darem la mano*
> *La la lala la la.* (76)

For a different Zerlina now occupies his thoughts.

The end of the chapter is the consummate statement of this
theme of escape and dereliction of responsibility, and the
consummate exploitation of the Homeric correspondence
as well. When he decides upon taking a bath, Bloom de-
tects a "curious longing," apparently the result of Martha's
letter, and resolves to masturbate in the bath, "Combine
business and pleasure" (83). Although he ultimately does
not do so ("Damned glad I didn't do it in the bath this
morning over her silly I will punish you letter," 362), the
anticipation is presented, for it is a fitting consummation
to his shabby epistolary affair. It is also a fitting climax
to the chapter, to his whole attempt to evade his responsibility—escape his problem—as Molly's husband; the reader
can have no delusions about the significance of what the
eager servant, possibly eager cuckold, and reluctant mate,
is doing. And the final paragraph of the chapter explores
its implications, and so completes the chapter thematically
and structurally:

> He foresaw his pale body reclined in it at full, naked, in
> a womb of warmth. . . . He saw his trunk and limbs
> riprippled over and sustained . . . and saw the dark
> tangled curls of his bush floating, floating . . . around
> the limp father of thousands, a languid floating flower.
> (85)

What Bloom's mind "saw" is a symbol of the consequence
of his attempt to escape into passivity and forgetfulness. To
renege on his duty as Molly's husband is to renege on his
function as a man; it is to make "limp," to make "a languid
floating flower"—a lotus, the very emblem of that reneging
—what should be the emblem of the husband and father.

6 *the cemetery*

The sixth chapter begins, as Joyce might have said, epi-phanically:

> MARTIN CUNNINGHAM, FIRST, POKED HIS SILKHATTED HEAD
> INTO the creaking carriage and, entering deftly, seated
> himself. Mr Power stepped in after him, curving his
> height with care.
> —Come on, Simon.
> —After you, Mr Bloom said.
> Mr Dedalus covered himself quickly and got in, saying:
> —Yes, yes.
> —Are we all here now? Martin Cunningham asked.
> Come along, Bloom.
> Mr Bloom entered and sat in the vacant place. (86)

Bloom's relationship to his group, to those he thinks of as social equals and as friends (the closest thing to a community in a modern city), is fully characterized. After they are "all here," Bloom is invited to occupy the vacant place. His "after you" to Simon Dedalus is quixotic politeness, because Dedalus has already been specifically prompted to enter the carriage next. The "we all" distinguished from the occupant of a "vacant" place focusses the relationship sharply.

There is nothing in the chapter to contradict this picture of Bloom in company. Until one specific occurrence, he is not addressed spontaneously by any of his companions, and their conversation rather ignores than pointedly excludes him ("O draw him out, Martin, Mr Power said eagerly. Wait till you hear him, Simon, on Ben Dollard's singing of *The Croppy Boy*," 89). When he offers an observation there is some response, but the give-and-take of the conversation of the three others is absent.

The specific occurrence which changes their behavior follows by seconds Bloom's thought, "He's coming in the

afternoon" (91). The text mentions only "the white disc
of a straw hat," but the phrase is a metonymic figure, and
subsequent more elaborate descriptions of Boylan seem
almost superfluous. Bloom's thoughts show that he has
already given up his attempt of the last chapter to ignore
his problem; but the appearance of Boylan, and the eager-
ness with which his companions seize the opportunity, show
how foolish the "lotus-eating" was. Boylan passes, Bloom
assiduously examines his fingernails, and Power suddenly
becomes interested in Molly's concert tour. He even specifically asks Bloom "—Are you going yourself?"

The cuckold-baiting has no more than begun when it is
interrupted by Cunningham's sight of the Shylock-like
moneylender, Reuben J. Dodd. After Power and Dedalus
have expressed their small affection for Dodd, Cunningham
says "—We have all been there," then looks at Bloom and
amends his statement: "—Well, nearly all of us" (93).
Bloom's reaction to this first hint of Jew-baiting is appeasement: he tries to tell the anecdote "about Reuben J. and the
son." The scheme to escape the baiting by joining the baiters
does not succeed, however. Dedalus keeps interrupting him
until "Martin Cunningham thwarted his speech rudely," and
the story is taken bodily from him by Cunningham. When
Cunningham has finished, he is still trying: "—Isn't it
awfully good? Mr Bloom said eagerly," but Dedalus replies
"drily," and Power laughs.

There is no suggestion that Bloom's companions are
vicious. As they do M'Coy and Kernan, they consider him a
second-class friend, mildly contemptible, and so deserving of
their condescension and casual malice. He is not despised,
however, or hated. When Power begins to condemn suicide,
Cunningham does his best to change the subject and to
qualify the condemnation. And Power himself, when he
later learns of Bloom's father's suicide, is genuinely sorry.

It is important to keep in mind that these four men know
each other fairly well, are social compeers, and are associated
in this chapter under ordinary circumstances. That is to say,
there is no reason to feel that the coolness of the others
toward Bloom, the baiting of him, or his subsequent attempt
at appeasement is other than completely normal.

Once the group has left the carriage, the focus of the
narrative shifts to Bloom's thoughts as he follows the corpse
of Dignam and sees it interred. However, at the very end
of the chapter the focus shifts again. John Henry Menton,
the solicitor, is the most distinguished mourner in the
company. Bloom had beaten him in a game of bowls seventeen years before, in the presence of Molly, then unmarried,
and another girl, and knows that Menton dislikes him for
it. Nevertheless, he tells Menton of the dent in his hat and
is soundly rebuffed for his kindness.

Menton is representative of the best in Ireland. Catholic,
distinguished, kind enough to attend the funeral of a former
employee cashiered for drunkenness and to contribute hand-
somely to his family's support, he is also one of Dublin's
(i.e., Ireland's) important public officials. He is comparable
with the dead Parnell, for whom Bloom had done a similar
service, and been thanked graciously in the midst of a riot;
Bloom himself later mentions the analogy and the historical
significance of their differing behavior (634 and 639).

As it began with an epiphany of Bloom's normal relation
to his "friends," the chapter ends with an epiphany of that
which Bloom's second-class status represents—the unjust
rejection of him by Catholic Ireland, of which he supposes
himself a part.

The action of the chapter, which involves its other principal characters and depicts Bloom's relations with them, is
less prominent than the thoughts Bloom himself has throughout. Almost at the very beginning, he sees Stephen walking
(toward Sandymount strand) and points him out to his
father. The elder Dedalus guesses that he is going "Down
with his aunt Sally" (87), derides Stephen's uncle, and then
strongly denounces Mulligan. Bloom thinks:

Noisy selfwilled man. Full of his son. He is right.
Something to hand on. If little Rudy had lived. See him
grow up. Hear his voice in the house. Walking beside
Molly in an Eton suit. My son. Me in his eyes. (87-88)

This second thought of Rudy in the novel, prompted at least indirectly by his sight of Stephen, reveals that Bloom is actually strongly affected by the loss of his infant son. In keeping with the revelation, Bloom begins to show his unusual concern with families and maternity in the present chapter. He thinks about Dignam's wife and family (100) and extensively about the wife and family of Mr. O'Connell, the cemetery caretaker (106-7). He will comment in the eighth chapter on the large families of Theodore Purefoy, Dedalus, and Queen Victoria.

The relevance of Bloom's concern about children to his own condition is hinted at in the passage quoted above. The expressions "Something to hand on" and "Me in his eyes" are echoes of the concept evolved by Stephen in the third chapter—actually being evolved at about the same time—of the umbilical chain of ancestry (39), which reflects Stephen's sense of isolation and loneliness. Vital to Bloom, this concept is more fully presented later in the chapter, when the hearse with a child's coffin passes the carriage with the four men. Bloom thinks of the child as Rudy in his "white-lined deal box," then thinks "Rattle his bones. Over the stones. Only a pauper. Nobody owns" (95). The others begin to discuss the dead child, and Power brings up suicides. Bloom thinks about the cruelty of society toward suicides, about Martin Cunningham, whose attempt to divert Power's conversation he appreciates, and then, in a separate paragraph, about the inquest after his father's suicide, and about his father's corpse. This separate paragraph is preceded by "Rattle his bones," and is followed by "No more pain. Wake no more. Nobody owns." The phrases were applied a few lines earlier to the child he had identified with his son, but now it is his father who lies dead ("Rattle his bones"), and he himself who is the son, he whom "Nobody owns." Again Bloom has thought in terms of a chain of ancestry, of a continuous relationship of father and son who is in turn father. And following this development of the concept he has come to see that he is in isolation, cut off before and behind. He owns nobody and nobody owns him, for he has neither father nor son, neither root nor branch.

The reason for his having failed to have a son after Rudy's death is not revealed in the chapter, although he does say

"If it's healthy it's from the mother. If not the man. Better luck next time" (94). That he is cut off from his heritage is abundantly clear, however. He reveals (89) that his legacy from his father was the latter's dog Athos (a-theos— "dog" is the opposite of "god"). Later in the novel (477), he will reel off the first four letters of the Hebrew alphabet plus a dozen words denoting Jewish holidays, ceremonial objects, and religious and popular expressions—the sum of his Judaism. In his first chapter he had reveries about traveling to the East (57), and the "Agendath Netaim" advertisement focussed his attention on Palestine; but he was too aware there that he had just bought a pork kidney, which had been wrapped in one of the circulars by a pork-butcher who may be a Jew, and he even quashed his enthusiasm for the project, whose headquarters are located on "Bleibtreustrasse" in Berlin, with a reappraisal of the "land of promise," a devastating conception of sterility and decay (61). He habitually associates the East with some earlier happy condition (the reason why it was so prominent in his "lotus-eating" reveries); but he recognized in the early morning that, in terms of his ethnic origin, his roots, any return is impossible. He is the son of neither man nor tradition.

It is perhaps apparent that the present chapter has not two principal themes, but one: both the action at the beginning and the very end and the interior monologue that occupies most of the chapter are concerned with Bloom's isolation. It is a compound isolation, both contiguous and continuous. He is cut off from those around him and he is cut off from his family line.

Which kind of isolation is more significant for Bloom is almost revealed in the fact that he is a Jew. For not only is he therefore automatically set apart from those about him, he is also under certain obligations. The code of Jewish law (*Shulhan Aruch*) declares that a man must "fulfil the precept of propagation" by begetting a son and a daughter capable of having children. Bloom is far from being a devout Jew, and yet his distress over the death of Rudy is linked in the present chapter to that over the death of his father, with the ultimate source of distress, his sense that he is isolated in what should be a chain of descent; and it is not such a chain because of his failure to fulfil the precept of propagation. Joyce has been quoted as saying that Jews "are better husbands than we are, better fathers, and better sons." [2] He has made Bloom a Jew at least partly because as a Jew his main character is motivated to become a good husband, father, and son.

The central business of the chapter—the funeral; all the conversation about dying, murder, and suicide; and Bloom's increasingly morbid thoughts about these subjects and about age, animal slaughter, corpses, burial alive, the activity of graveyard rats, and his own graveplot—conforms to, and supplies the background for, the chapter's basic theme. Furthermore, Bloom's isolation is extending to Milly and, because of Boylan, to Molly. In the chapter he decides that Milly is Molly "watered down" (88), and that to pay her a surprise visit would be unwise: "Catch them once with their pants down. Never forgive you after" (99). With regard to Molly herself, he thinks: "Could I go to see *Leah* tonight, I wonder. I said I" (90-91); and he associates Molly with the widow Dignam, "She would marry another. Him? No," and himself with the deceased: "alone under the ground: and lie no more in her warm bed" (101). His isolation portends a fruitless, lonely existence, a death in life that will end in death.

As with the two previous chapters, this third chapter in the group that presents Bloom has a thematic similarity to the third chapter in the group that presents Stephen. In both chapters the character is concerned with his situation and what it signifies for his future. In both, isolation and mockery (Stephen of himself) cause the same despairing conclusion. The use of Homeric correspondence is also parallel; in both cases the analogue in the *Odyssey* is, appropriately, a quest for information—from Proteus and Tiresias respectively.

The analogy between this chapter and the descent to Hades episode (Book XI) of the *Odyssey* is an inexact one, for that involves a prophecy of success. Still, before his rebuff from Menton, as he is leaving the cemetery at the end of the chapter, Bloom does decide to leave his morbid thoughts with it: "Enough of this place. . . . They are not going to get me this innings. Warm beds: warm full-blooded life" (113). Whether his decision signifies a resumption of escapism or something more in keeping with the episode in the *Odyssey* remains to be seen.

mr. leopold paula bloom

There may be a sense in which Bloom is the Everyman ("Bloom or mankind," "Bloom, or Everyman") which so many critics see—the sense in which all powerfully individual literary figures become archetypes upon reflection. But this is not a primary sense, and F. Scott Fitzgerald's stricture, "Begin with an individual and you will end with a type. Begin with a type and you will end with nothing," may be applied to the reader as well as to the writer.

Certain aspects of Bloom's character tend to reinforce the Everyman conception. When the description of him emerges, detail by detail, Bloom is seen to be not so much undistinguished in history and appearance as *indistinguishable*. The only child of an Irish Protestant mother and a Hungarian Jewish father who was converted to his wife's religion after his arrival in Ireland, Bloom was born a Jew, was baptized in his mother's church, and then converted because of his marriage (much as did his father), to his bride's religion. He became unfaithful to both the adopted faiths as he had been to the inherited one, and so his religious history roughly parallels that of Western civilization itself. Unlike the thin young man with the deacon's hat and the ash stick, he attracts no public notice. He is of average height (5 feet 9½ inches) and weight (162 pounds) for his time, and has an olive complexion and a prominent nose and eyes. He has a mustache, is moderately handsome, and wears a derby. And, reinforcing his indistinguishable qualities, his attitudes bear the stamp of the world in which he lives. He is the citizen who follows his leaders along the path of materialist atheism, science, and debased culture.

However, a closer look shows the superficial nature of Bloom's "Everyman" characteristics. For example, the interlocutor in the next-to-last chapter of the novel says euphemistically: "his tendency was towards applied, rather than towards pure, science" (667); in plainer terms, he is principally a gadgeteer whose understanding of science is so limited that he cannot comprehend Archimedes' law (71), and whose interest is the collection of legends, simple facts, and mechanical devices of popular scientism. But Bloom's scientism is unlike that of the average man—is marked by a singular intensity and sincerity. He experiments often during the course of the day in a pure exercise of *intellectus*. At one point, speculating on synesthesia of touch and sight, he tries to feel the color of his arm, but decides that the hairs ruin the experiment. He considers the problem of creating a valid experimental situation, and concludes that his belly would be the most favorable area of research. Immediately, although walking in the street, he separates his clothing and proceeds with the experiment (179).

In the quality of his culture, too, Bloom is only apparently typical. He had read in Shakespeare for "moral guidance" (661). He cites as his musical favorites: in "the severe classical school"— Mendelssohn; in "light opera"—*Martha* and *Don Giovanni* (!) (645). He thinks often of the "modern art of advertisement" (667), conceiving advertisements and devices for displaying them and judging with a critical eye all those he sees. But that "literary" criticism itself shows his bourgeois cultural conceptions to be a disguise for purer stuff. Examples of his witty wordplay abound in his opening chapters (of a watering cart, in the fourth chapter: "Watering cart. To provoke the rain. On earth as it is in heaven," 60). In the eighth chapter he thinks of an advertisement he saw in the morning paper: "What is home without / Plumtree's potted meat? / Incomplete. / With it an abode of bliss"; and remarks "What a stupid ad!" (169). Joyce is being ironic, for both literally (659) and figuratively Bloom has Plumtree's potted meat at home. But in addition he is showing Bloom to be perceptive; Bloom's response is not primarily to the quality of the verse, nor even to the claim that the jar of Plumtree's in his pantry has made his home "an abode of bliss," but to the placement of the advertisement under the obituary notices.

Joyce shows Bloom favor in other ways. His politics—pacifist, internationalist, mildly socialist—are the same as Joyce's, he is the age Joyce would have been had he finished *Ulysses* when he expected to (thirty-eight), and Joyce even enriches his inner monologue with a figure of his own:

> Chamber music. Could make a kind of pun on that. It is a kind of music I often thought when she. Acoustics that is. Tinkling. (278)

Bloom's inner language—unlike that he speaks to others—is occasionally gifted, and his wit reveals itself constantly. His good sense has fewer opportunities to reveal itself, but it is persistent. One example of it is his rejection of the "Agendath Netaim" pseudo-Zionism of the Italianate Moses whose name contains yet another cognate to Bloom's own (Moses Montefiore). Another example is his ultimate response to the ballad of the "Croppy Boy," who reveals his complicity in an uprising to a British "yeoman captain," thinking the soldier a confessor. Ben Dollard's moving rendition of the song is mentioned in the funeral car. When he sings it in the eleventh chapter (Ormond), Bloom emotes along with the other auditors, but then has a second thought: "Breathe a prayer, drop a tear. All the same he must have been a bit of a natural not to see it was a yeoman cap" (285).

Bloom is capable of disgusting acts, and has many petty faults; for example, he frustrates M'Coy's attempt to permanently borrow a valise in the fifth chapter (post office), yet he had planned to beg a train pass of M'Coy, and is constantly planning, preparing, or trying to get something for nothing from an acquaintance. But he has intelligence, wit, perceptiveness, compassion ("They used to drive a stake of wood through [a suicide's] heart in the grave. As if it weren't broken already," 95), good sense, and an appreciation of the value of life and love (the pork kidney, example of the organic meats he "relishes," is both associated with Molly and an index of his sanguine humor). He is a unique spirit disguised even from himself within a common, an indistinguishable, externality. It is as though he were a living example of the tension between natural endowment and environmental influence. To the extent that a culture and a set of attitudes and values can impose themselves on a man, modern bourgeois industrial civilization has molded Bloom. But his claim upon our interest and sympathy comes from his showing again and again an innate superiority to the Everyman his environment would have him be.

1. Most fully in Gilbert, pp. 153–58.
2. Frank Budgen, "James Joyce," in Givens, pp. 19–26, 23.

chapter three

The first and fourth chapters of *Ulysses* introduce their respective protagonists as they are on the morning of June 16, 1904—in serious trouble. Significantly, Stephen resents his loss and broods about his guilt, while Bloom's thoughts avoid direct acknowledgment of either loss or responsibility. The very similar conditions of the two obviously antedate the novel; but the novel begins at an appropriate point, the point of developing crisis: the first thing Bloomsday morning, an outright act of usurpation is initiated against each protagonist and makes his situation acute.

The second and fifth chapters are corresponding elaborations of the first and fourth chapters. They present Stephen's brooding and Bloom's escapism in their most intensive form; and they portray the characters' first attempts to cope with their troubles. Characteristically, while Stephen acknowledges his powerlessness before cosmic circumstances but defies them and their creator, Bloom sordidly accommodates himself to his domestic situation by means of paper philandering and projected masturbation.

The third and sixth chapters show the protagonists (simultaneously) evolving despairing prognostications. And the two characters finally come together for the first time in the novel when the presentation of both has been completed.

7 *the newspaper office*

The seventh chapter actually makes much less of the meeting of Bloom and Stephen than of the circumstances in which it occurs. Bloom is mildly interested in Stephen and observant enough to notice that he has much better "boots" (identified earlier as "a buck's castoffs") than when he had seen him last; Stephen ignores Bloom completely. The major subject of the chapter is the political character of the Irish nation.

Although Joyce directs the chapter to this end, it is an integral part of the developing action of the novel. He makes his political tract an expression of Stephen's viewpoint, with which he then deftly identifies himself. Stephen is at the newspaper office to deliver one copy of the letter given him by Mr. Deasy in the second chapter to one of the two editors he knows "slightly"; Bloom is there to prepare the layout for "Keyes' ad," something he had decided at the cemetery (106) to do immediately after the funeral. The chapter presents the poem Stephen wrote on the beach during the third chapter (that is, a few minutes before); and two things mentioned by Bloom's companions during the sixth—the trial of Samuel Childs for the murder of his brother (98), and a sentimental and pretentious panegyric to Ireland delivered the night before by "Dan Dawson" and printed in the morning's paper (90) —are prominent and important in it.

In addition to the nationalistic speech in the newspaper and a courtroom speech made by the well-known Irish barrister Seymour Bushe in defense of the fratricide Childs, the chapter gives a prominent place to a famous speech by John F. Taylor, barrister and orator, which advocated the revival of Gaelic.[1] (Taylor, who became the first Chief Justice of Ireland, was the spokesman for the successful propagandistic group in the National Literary Society when Yeats attempted in 1892 to make poetical values ascendant over doctrinal ones.) These three orations combine with a large number of other elements in the chapter to establish its "Aeolian" nature. As Aeolus does to Odysseus, the newspaper editor sends Bloom away with good humor, but dismisses him angrily when he returns. The chapter dwells on newspaper personnel, plant, format, production, and distribution. And countless details such as a reference to Dawson as "the inflated windbag" (bag of winds) reinforce the analogy to the court of the god of the winds in the *Odyssey*.

However, the fact of that analogy—or of the incorporation of actual speeches by contemporary Irishmen, or the parodies of newspaper headlines which punctuate the chapter—is itself not its justification. This is also true of Stephen's "Parable of the Plums"; it cannot be dismissed as "intentionally cryptic" or "suggestive," because its title makes clear that it calls for interpretation, and because it eventually becomes the central matter of the chapter.

All these typically Ulyssean elements of the seventh chapter of *Ulysses* are (also typically) functional; James Joyce makes them the medium of his statement about the political character of the Irish people. The principal locale of the chapter is the outer office of Myles Crawford, the editor of the *Evening Telegraph*, which shares a building behind Dublin's General Post Office with the *Freeman's Journal*. Other parts of the newspaper building are involved, and at the beginning and end of the chapter the locale is Nelson's Pillar, which is around the corner, in front of the post office, and is a replica of the pillar in Trafalgar Square. Newspaper building and monument are bound together thematically. From the latter, lines of track radiate to Dublin suburbs and outlying towns; the chapter begins with a description of the trams moving out along those lines, and the very first words (in the boldface "headline" type, so that they seem to form a title) are "IN THE HEART OF THE HIBERNIAN METROPOLIS." The pillar, a servant's replica of a monument in the capital of the master nation, marking the central battleground, Joyce knew when he was writing *Ulysses*, of the abortive Easter 1916 rebellion, combines with the radiating tram lines before it to symbolize the heart of that "metropolis" which is in turn the heart of Ireland. And the association of pillar and tramlines with the building from which two important newspapers are published indicates the heart which is symbolized. Journalism and oratory are the two media of social communication, the vehicles of expression for the molders of public opinion. The winds of Aeolus directed the ship of Odysseus. The modern Aeolian winds direct the ship of state. The gathering in Myles Crawford's office during the major part of the chapter is composed entirely of "Aeolists," guides of society, with the exception of Stephen: Professor MacHugh is a teacher; J. J. O'Molloy is a trial lawyer; O'Madden Burke, Crawford, and Lenehan are editors.

Stephen is aware of the position of the public rhetorician, and feels that it has been usurped from society's rightful guide, the poet. After Professor MacHugh recites the nationalistic oration of John F. Taylor, he thinks, in phrases reminiscent of his observation in the first chapter about the old milkwoman's deference toward Mulligan: "Love and laud him: me no more" (142). And the orator shares the position of leadership with the journalist—both play the Hibernian harp in Aeolian fashion. The advertisement with which Bloom is occupied throughout the chapter identifies Catholic Celtic Ireland as the "house of keys." Crossed keys are the emblem of the parliament of the Isle of Man (Bloom sees the advertisement accomplishing "innuendo of home rule") and part of the emblem of the Vatican. And the key of public rule which is denied to Stephen (Bloom himself neglects to take the key of domestic —home—rule when he leaves the house in the morning) is granted to Editor Crawford, whose concern for and use of his office and desk keys is mentioned twice (129 and 142).

During the chapter, the guides of society express themselves on a variety of subjects, including Bloom and Stephen. The attitude toward Bloom is not different from that of his companions during the ride to the cemetery; his Jewishness (123), appearance (128), and wife (133) are touched on. The attitude toward Stephen is in sharp contrast to this. At one point, Crawford tells Stephen that he wants him to "write something for me," "Something with a bite in it. . . . Put us all into it, damn its soul" (133-34), and attempts to encourage him with an anecdote about the journalistic gifts of Ignatius Gallaher (the reporter on a visit home from London in Joyce's story "A Little Cloud"). During his account:

> The professor came to the inner door.
> —Bloom is at the telephone, he said.
> —Tell him to go to hell, the editor said promptly.
> X is Burke's public house, see? (135)

Crawford's respect for Stephen's intellectual ability is as fully shared by the others as is his contempt for Bloom. When the young man first enters the office, he is greeted solicitously (130-31). Before rendering his excerpt from Seymour Bushe's defense of Childs, J. J. O'Molloy directs his descriptive remarks to Stephen, and when he has finished:

> —Fine! Myles Crawford said at once.
> —The divine afflatus, Mr O'Madden Burke said.
> —You like it? J. J. O'Molloy asked Stephen. (138)

Even Lenehan recites for Stephen's private appreciation a limerick he has composed (132). In fact, judging from the intellectuals and other Dubliners he meets, here and in the National Library, Stephen is much more highly regarded than he tells himself.

If the group represents Ireland's spokesmen and guides, their attitudes toward Stephen and Bloom are no surprise. Of much greater interest is the picture of the group themselves. Their conversation is composed of nostalgia, nationalism, learned wise-cracking, buffoonery, and oratory. More important, all of them are idle, one (Lenehan) is a shameless sponger, and another (O'Molloy) has come to borrow money. Finally, the group soon retires to a public house. Joyce's portrait of the Aeolian guides of Ireland is like his implicit portrait of the ordinary Irish citizen wherever that citizen appears—impoverished, idle, sentimental, nationalistic, and, above all, alcoholic—a portrait of futility.

This portrait is one principal element of the subject of the chapter—the political character of the Irish nation. The symbolic complex of newspaper office and pillar and tramline is another. Actually, there is very little in the chapter that is not directly related to the subject. The professor makes speeches about Roman and British materialism and about Hebrew, Greek, and Irish spirituality; and he recites John F. Taylor's "vision" of an admonition to Moses by an Egyptian priest to forsake his own primitive religion and language for the culture of Egypt (a fanciful reconstruction of the speech actually delivered). O'Molloy's quotation from Seymour Bushe concerns the Moses of Michelangelo and the distinction between Roman (British) law and Mosaic law and so is associated with Taylor's speech. Dan Dawson's turgid rhetoric, read mockingly from the morning paper at the beginning of the chapter by Ned Lambert, bears the title "Our Lovely Land" and appears under the headline "ERIN, GREEN GEM OF THE SILVERY SEA."

Even the treatment of Stephen and Bloom is largely in terms of the general motif. Not only is the public view of them rendered by the guides of and spokesmen for their fellow-citizens, but each is himself preoccupied throughout the chapter with a characteristic manifestation of his citizen-ship: Bloom, practitioner of the art of advertising, is endeavoring to complete arrangements for the advertisement with "innuendo of home rule"; Stephen, inchoate bard, composes and narrates an allegory about his country which has long been an enigma to readers and is ultimately the central matter of the chapter.

In a short essay primarily about the speech and its author, Horace Reynolds calls the "vision" of John F. Taylor "one of Ireland's great speeches." He points out that it was extemporaneous, and was prompted by a formal address "against the practicality of reviving the Irish language." Yeats "gives two versions of it in his autobiographies" and Joyce "also reports this speech in the newspaper chapter," he says, and concludes, "Both advocates [i.e., Yeats and Joyce] convince us that this was a great oratorical moment." [2]

Whether or not Joyce may be called an "advocate" of Taylor's speech is open to question. But there is little doubt that he recognized both its quality as oratory and its social and political significance; his version of it is apparently the only thing in *Ulysses* he ever consented to record, and it has a central place in this tract about the Irish nation.

After having heard the "vision" of the Egyptian priest's admonition and Moses' rejection of it, the emotional and rhetorically elevated appeal of an idealistic nationalist for faith in the Irish nation, the group "adjourns" to Mooney's public house. The professor and Stephen are walking together when Stephen says "I have a vision too." Later, when he tells the title of his story, "I call it *A Pisgah Sight of Palestine or the Parable of the Plums,*" the professor recognizes that Stephen is contradicting not merely Taylor's point of view but the very terms in which it is couched:

> —I see, he said again with new pleasure. Moses and the promised land. We gave him that idea, he added to J. J. O'Molloy. (148)

What Stephen thinks of Taylor's (and his own companions') romantic conception of the Irish nation as a new Hebrew people with a great destiny of their own is apparent. His "vision" is an allegorical presentation of his own antithetical view of their nation and its destiny. The two old women who are the subject of the story are both "Old Gummy Granny" *(Sean Van Vocht,* "the old woman"), like the milkwoman of the first chapter, symbolic of Ireland. The statue of the imperial warrior, Nelson, symbolizes their conqueror, England. After eating, the old women go to the edge of the pillar and look down—not only on the "heart" of Ireland but on her other "master," as Stephen calls the Church in the first chapter:

> They see the roofs and argue about where the different churches are: Rathmines' blue dome, Adam and Eve's, saint Laurence O'Toole's. But it makes them giddy to look so they pull up their skirts. . .

THOSE SLIGHTLY RAMBUNCTIOUS FEMALES

> —Easy all, Myles Crawford said, no poetic license. We're in the archdiocese here.
> —And settle down on their striped petticoats, peering up at the statue of the onehandled adulterer.

—Onehandled adulterer; the professor cried. I like that.
I see the idea. I see what you mean.

DAMES DONATE DUBLINS CITS
SPEEDPILLS VELOCITOUS
AEROLITHS, BELIEF

—It gives them a crick in their necks, Stephen said,
and they are too tired to look up or down or to speak.
They put the bag of plums between them and eat the
plums out of it, one after another, wiping off with their
handkerchiefs the plumjuice that dribbles out of their
mouths and spitting the plumstones slowly out between
the railings.
He gave a sudden loud young laugh as a close. (146)

The Irish nation, old woman that she is, can neither truly
communicate with herself (speak) nor look (down) at her
Church-ridden and -dominated self realistically, nor pay
homage to (look up to) her sinful but potent temporal
conqueror. Instead, she enjoys life (eats plums) as best
she can, "donating" "belief" to herself: the nation's leaders (like Taylor and those who are listening to Stephen)
spouting nationalist sentiments to "Dublin's cit[izen]s"
which are not only as worthless as plumstones but as incidental. Myles Crawford had enjoined Stephen to produce
"Something with a bite in it," and to "Put us all into it,
damn its soul." He has had his wish.

Stephen calls his little story a vision, and he gives it a
title that functions in two ways as a refutation of Taylor.
First, as the professor remarks ("I see . . . Moses and the
promised land"), it indicates a contradictory conception
of the "promised land" of which Taylor was speaking.
Where the orator sought to elevate Ireland by using ancient
Israel as a metaphor, Stephen denigrates it by the specific
association of the old women with Moses, Nelson's Pillar
with the mountain range from one peak of which Moses
viewed the Promised Land, and Dublin below them with
that land; he follows the implications of the metaphor and
demonstrates its vanity.

The title shows the story to be a satiric attack not only
on the validity of Taylor's basic metaphor but also on the
whole approach to Ireland's problem by the Nationalist

movement. It is the same as that of a work by Bishop Fuller printed in 1650. Fuller's *A Pisgah Sight of Palestine* is a long (six hundred and fifty folio pages) account of the tribes of Israel and of Old Testament geography and civilization, which is thoroughly factual and realistic in nature. Stephen's short oral "Pisgah Sight" is a corresponding treatment of Taylor's "Palestine" appropriately couched, in direct contrast to the impassioned rhetoric of Taylor's "vision," in a hypernaturalistic idiom:

> —They buy one and fourpenceworth of brawn and four slices of panloaf at the north city dining rooms in Marlborough street from Miss Kate Collins, proprietress. . . . (143)

What he implies by his reference to Fuller and by his naturalism is that his own "vision" is true and Taylor's hopelessly romantic and inaccurate.

When Stephen has concluded his "parable," Professor MacHugh, consistently the perceptive one in the group, expresses an acute understanding not only of the young man's viewpoint but also of his mental state. He likens him to Antisthenes, enemy of Plato and of idealizing, and founder of the Cynic school:

> —You remind me of Antisthenes, the professor said, a disciple of Gorgias, the sophist. It is said of him that none could tell if he were bitterer against others or against himself. (147)

Nevertheless, he has not refuted Stephen's perception of Ireland. For following his remark, under the headline "HELLO THERE, CENTRAL!", which points to the symbolic meaning of the radiating tramlines:

> At various points along the eight lines tramcars with motionless trolleys stood in their tracks, bound for or from Rathmines, Rathfarnham, Blackrock, Kingstown and Dalkey, Sandymount Green, Ringsend and Sandymount Tower, Donnybrook, Palmerston Park and Upper Rathmines, all still, becalmed in short circuit. (147)

Stephen has been telling his companions his opinion of them and their aspirations. The author describes them in the chapter in terms that suggest a similar opinion. Now Joyce explicitly endorses Stephen's "vision" and thus rejects Taylor's. The relationship between heart and members is "in short circuit." The leadership and impelling force that enable a nation to realize its ambitions are dead. There is nothing but the spitting out of plumstones. In one of the series of letters concerning *Dubliners* sent to Grant Richards the British publisher in 1906, Joyce had said, "I chose Dublin for the scene because that city seemed to me the centre of paralysis."

The chapter ends very shortly. The "headline" device is plainly not just a stylistic correspondence to the principal locale of the chapter but an oblique method of exposition, a representation (as are real headlines) of the burden of what follows and frequently the source of illumination of otherwise cryptic details. The final example of this functional narrative device is perhaps the most expressive. Stephen has told his companions the title of his story. The professor, comprehending, stops to look at the statue of Nelson "through the meshes of his wry smile." A "headline" and two remarks that follow conclude the chapter:

DIMINISHED DIGITS PROVE TOO TITIL-
LATING FOR FRISKY FRUMPS. ANNE
WIMBLES, FLO WANGLES—YET
CAN YOU BLAME THEM?

—Onehandled adulterer, he said grimly. That tickles me I must say.
—Tickled the old ones too, Myles Crawford said, if the God Almighty's truth was known. (148)

With Nelson the "onehandled adulterer" representing his nation, which maintains a corresponding illicit relationship with Ireland, the unconscious irony of Crawford's statement and the relevance of the question posed in the "headline" are clear. Joyce is speaking of the seduced servant and her master, of the fact that, as Stephen has repeatedly said in both the *Portrait* and *Ulysses*, the Irish people "sell much more than [the old prostitute in the cabmen's shelter] ever had and do a roaring trade" (617). And he is posing in his own voice the question of blame posed by Stephen in the opening pages of the second chapter: "Why had they chosen all that part? Not wholly for the smooth caress. For them too history was a tale like any other too often heard, their land a pawnshop" (26).

The seventh chapter brings Bloom and Stephen together for the first time (although they do not meet) and in other ways advances their story; but the major subject is the political character of the Irish nation, and the theme is self-deception, paralysis, futility. Stephen is the author's spokesman for the most part, and he clearly presents James Joyce's view of the state of the Irish nation. And ultimately the "newspaper chapter" is, as is a newspaper in a more petty and transitory way, a report to the nation about itself.

about "episodes" and correspondences

In his essay on Joyce in *Axel's Castle*, Edmund Wilson says:

> It is now apparent, however, that "Ulysses" suffers from an excess of design rather than from a lack of it. Joyce has drawn up an outline of his novel, of which he has allowed certain of his commentators to avail themselves, but which he has not allowed them to publish in its entirety (though it is to be presumed that the book on *Ulysses* which Mr. Stuart Gilbert has announced will contain all the information in it). . . .[3]

The first actual critical study of *Ulysses* was part of a lecture delivered while the novel was still in proof. Valery Larbaud, the French writer and critic, gave it to help introduce Joyce and his work to literary Paris.[4] Larbaud called *Ulysses* "a book which has a key," and went on to say:

> Where then is the key? It is, I venture to say, in the door, or rather on the cover. It is the title: *Ulysses*.[5]

Having identified its most overt element, he gave a paradigm of the whole "design" depreciated by Mr. Wilson:

> Upon [the general arrangement of *Ulysses*, in three sections to correspond with the *Odyssey*], Joyce traces a particular design in each of his panels or episodes. In this way, each episode deals with a particular art or science, contains a particular symbol, represents a special organ of the human body, has its particular colour (as in the catholic liturgy), has its proper technique, and takes place at a particular hour of the day. But this is not all: in each of the panels, thus divided, the author inscribes more particular symbols and relations.
>
> To make this clear, let us take an example, Episode V [sic] of the adventures. Its title is Aeolus. It takes place in the offices of a newspaper. The hour is noon. The relative organ of the body: the lungs. The art of which it treats: rhetoric. Its colour: red. Its symbolic figure: the editor-in-chief. Its technique: the enthymeme. Its relations: a person who corresponds to the Aeolus of Homer; incest compared with journalism; the floating isle of Aeolus to the press. . . .[6]

Gilbert's well-known book, *James Joyce's Ulysses*, in fact appeared before *Axel's Castle*. Using Larbaud as a model (as Gilbert himself suggests),[7] it thoroughly delineates Joyce's schema and even reproduces his "outline." [8]

Ezra Pound, whose literary taste and judgment during this period were as unerring as Mr. Wilson's, shared Mr. Wilson's attitude toward the sets of correspondences. Although he raised money for Joyce, praised *Ulysses*, and touted it far and wide, Mr. Pound called the Homeric correspondences "mere mechanics,"[9] and so could hardly have looked more kindly on the other patterns.

Of course, Joyce put into *Ulysses* itself a characterization of it as "this chaffering, allincluding most farraginous

chronicle," and my Introduction suggests that the novel is
not flawed because he endeavors to give it an encyclopedic
quality (and perhaps to assert his belief in the ultimate
order of the real and verbal worlds) by planting in each
chapter inconspicuous patterns of "colour," "organ," "art,"
"symbol," and "tehnic." Furthermore, the Homeric correspondences (and similar literary and historical allusions)
invoke comparisons—of Bloom with Odysseus and Stephen
with Hamlet, for example—that are not only mock-heroic
but mocking-the-heroic, that cut both ways,[10] and these are
part of both characterization and theme.

But these considerations do not answer the question raised
by Edmund Wilson, whether or not *Ulysses* "suffers from
an excess of design." And it is not answered by the un-
earthing of more deeply buried details of one pattern of
correspondence or another, by the disclosure that Joyce's
favorite childhood book was the *Odyssey*, by the assertion
that "Naturally, Joyce has traced for himself, and not for
the reader, this minutely detailed scheme," [11] or by the
explanation that "Joyce's high spirits made him see many
parallels of this kind." [12] A recent critic asks of "Joyce's
analogical method": "Can he be excused from what seems
an inveterate habit of idiosyncratic and irresponsible association?" [13]

Those who have elucidated the sets of correspondences
have supposed that they have the vital function of unifying
each of the individual chapters. However, most of the
"design" crumbles under examination. To say that each
chapter has its "particular hour of the day" is to say little
more than that things happen in sequence; indeed, when
they happen simultaneously, as in the first and fourth,
second and fifth, and third and sixth chapters, the chapters
are obliged to share the same "hour of the day." The
"technics" are either facetious—for example, "Narrative
(young)" and "Narrative (mature)" for the first and third
chapters, or simply descriptive—for example, "Hallucination" for the fifteenth (nighttown). The set of colors and
that of human organs, neither of which is carried through
all eighteen chapters according to Joyce's "outline," are
unobjectionable precisely because they are so inconspicuous that they had to be pointed out by the author. As a

result, they can have no structural force in a rich and complex book which, above all, is about neither the human body nor the spectrum. The only set of "episode" by "episode" correspondences that is not patently forced and artificial as a structuring device is the Homeric. And the almost universal use of the word "episode" to refer to the eighteen chapters of *Ulysses* is not only revealing of the general critical attitude toward the chapters but ironic; for beginning with Larbaud's lecture itself (Joyce's own loose use of the word may have been the actual precedent), students of Homeric and other ostensibly unifying sets of correspondence carried "episode" over from its legitimate use in referring to incidents occurring in various books of the *Odyssey*.

The discussion of the first seven chapters has tried to show that they are not episodic but organic wholes. On the other hand, they are not independent. Like the tiles in a mosaic, they have a subordinate integrity; they are seven discrete units of one book. And subject and theme, rather than an arbitrarily planted pattern of references, are the vehicle of their integrity. This is true of all eighteen chapters.

It is precisely because the Homeric correspondences involve subject and theme that they are vital to the novel and not "artistic caprice." *Ulysses* does not celebrate the *Odyssey*, or even simply invoke it for ironic reflection on either work or both. As the Introduction said of all the special elements of the novel that call attention to themselves, *Ulysses* brings up the *Odyssey* in order to use it. The fact that it brings it up in such detail is merely an index of the use it makes of it.

Only in two chapters up to now has a Homeric (or any other) allusion or analogy been the basic unifying element: the third and the fifth. In the third chapter Stephen corresponds to Menelaus, who wrestled Proteus, not to Telemachus. In the fifth Bloom is the lotus-eater, although Odysseus was not one of those who ate the lotus. In the chapter just discussed, the chapter chosen by Larbaud to illustrate Joyce's "design," Bloom corresponds to Odysseus, but only in order that Myles Crawford may be identified with Aeolus. Bloom is then largely ignored, and Crawford's companions are associated with his Homeric identification; not Ulysses but "Aeolism," as he enables himself to develop and define it, is Joyce's reason for invoking the *Odyssey*. In two of the next three chapters, the ninth (library) and the tenth (city), Bloom plays a part and yet it is Stephen who is made to correspond to Odysseus. And the *Odyssey* does not even have a "wandering rocks episode" to which the tenth chapter can be an analogue.

Of course, if Joyce had been creating the kind of book suggested by his "outline," he would, in the case of the *Odyssey*, for example, have worked in all the important incidents, have preserved the order they have in the poem, and so on. And perhaps he would have ruined his novel. All the actually invoked allusions and analogues (of which, significantly, only the Homeric were mentioned in the elaborate "outline") have purpose; all the chapters have formal integrity (often through the ingenious use of allusion or analogue) and not contrived "design." During a dinner party in Paris, Simone Téry, a French critic, asked Joyce why he "followed the pattern of the Odyssey" in *Ulysses*. His answer was:

Everyone has his own way of working.[14]

1. The trial of Childs occurred in October, 1899. Taylor's speech was made at the Law Students' Debating Society on October 24, 1901. For Joyce's connection with both, see *James Joyce*, pp. 94–95 and nn. 47 and 49.

2. Horace Reynolds, "Speaking of Books," *New York Times Book Review*, August 15, 1954, p. 2.

3. Wilson, p. 211.

4. See Introduction, note 19, *supra*.

5. Larbaud, p. 97.

6. *Ibid.*, pp. 101–2.

7. See Gilbert, p. 40.

8. *Ibid.*, p. 41.

9. Quoted from *Joyce*, p. 306.

10. See Von Abele, *passim*.

11. Larbaud, p. 102.

12. *James Joyce*, p. 370.

13. Richard M. Kain, in *Joyce*, p. 306.

14. Quoted in *The James Joyce Yearbook*, ed. Maria Jolas (Paris, 1949), pp. 189–90.

chapter four

8 *davy byrne's*

From its first words, a catalogue of kinds of candy, to its
last, this chapter of *Ulysses* invokes the episode in Book X
of the *Odyssey* in which most of the Achaeans are slaughtered by the cannibalistic Laestrygonians. Myriad references to food, eating, digestion, and the slaughter of meat
animals complement more precise analogues, such as the
echo of Homer's climactic description of the Laestrygonians
decimating the harbor-bound Achaean fleet, "And like folk
spearing fishes [bearing] home their hideous meal," [1] in
Bloom's thoughts about a community kitchen: "Want a
soup pot as big as the Phoenix Park. Harpooning flitches
and hindquarters out of it" (168).

Insistent as the Homeric correspondence is, Bloom is
not in danger of being eaten, and does not himself eat a
great deal. When the last words of the chapter draw it
more subtly, however, the altered terms of the correspondence indicate its real purpose. The adventure of Odysseus
with the Laestrygonians ends as follows:

> Quickly then I called to my company and bade them
> dash in with the oars, that we might clean escape this
> evil plight. And . . . to my delight my barque flew forth
> to the high seas away from the beetling rocks. . . .[2]

At the end of the chapter, Bloom is rushing to the museum entrance in order to escape the notice of Boylan:

> The flutter of his breath came forth in short sighs. Quick. Cold statues: quiet there. Safe in a minute.
> No, didn't see me. After two. Just at the gate.
>
> .   .   .   .
>
> Afternoon she said.
>
> .   .   .   .
>
> Hurry. Walk quietly. Moment more. My heart.
> His hand looking for the . . . soap lotion have to call. . . . Ah, soap there! Yes. Gate.
> Safe! (180-81)

Although there is no mention of food, the parallel is plain. Furthermore, Bloom's Laestrygonian attacker is Boylan, and linked thoughts of Molly's lotion and the soap which he associates with the East, her place of origin, interrupt those of escape and the "cold statues" with which he will be "safe"; he even notices that it is "After two" o'clock and recalls "Afternoon she said." The episode concludes two patterns that run through the chapter, and it combines them. One is the Homeric correspondence; the other is a pattern of references to Molly, Bloom's former happiness with her, and her increasingly imminent rendezvous with Boylan.

For example, Boylan and the time of day occur again and again in Bloom's thoughts. Soon after the chapter begins, while thinking of advertisement media, he remembers the posters of a "quack doctor for the clap," and:

> If he . . .
> O!
> Eh?
> No . . . No.
> No, no. I don't believe it. He wouldn't surely?
> No, no.
> Mr Bloom moved forward raising his troubled eyes.
> Think no more about that. After one. (151-52)

He dismisses the possibility that Boylan has a venereal disease, but his "after one" is the first indication in the chapter that he cannot dismiss the situation itself. A dozen pages later, when he has decided to have lunch, it imposes itself unrelentingly. He reviews more fully than he had done in the fourth chapter (kitchen) the circumstances of Molly's meeting with Boylan twelve days before, and concludes: "Stop. Stop. If it was it was. Must" (165). He then enters the Burton restaurant, whose repulsive nature and gluttonous patrons provide the most blatant Laestry-gonian parallel, and promptly decides to leave it. Before he does so, however, "He gazed round the stooled and tabled eaters" until "His eyes said," "—Not here. Don't see him" (167). His searching for Boylan in a place he intends to leave is unusual enough; but, as he would know in a normal frame of mind, there is absolutely no possibility that the affluent and natty rake would patronize a restaurant like the Burton. When he finally does secure his lunch at Davy Byrne's public house, he must face conversation about Boylan from Nosey Flynn, which in turn prompts him to observe: "Time going on. Hands moving. Two. Not yet" (170). He then plans for his dinner: "Just a bite or two. Then about six o'clock I can. Six, six. Time will be gone then" (172), and recalls his earlier sight of Boylan, during the funeral (91). Leaving the public house, he hums a snatch from the ubiquitous *Don Giovanni,* part of the pas-sage in which the Commendatore is preparing his revenge (177). Although he mistranslates it slightly, he understands its context; and the pathos of his wish fulfilment over-shadows the irony of his identification with the Commenda-tore. He thinks of another chance sight of Boylan (178) and then, as a climax to the pattern, is confronted by Boy-lan in the flesh outside the National Library and Museum— the end of the chapter culminates both the correspondence to the episode of the Laestrygonians in the *Odyssey* and Bloom's distress over Molly and over her rendezvous with Boylan.

Boylan and his impending visit to Molly plague Bloom most after he decides to eat lunch because the references in the chapter to food, eating, and the rest are the vehicle for an analogy between the predatory ferocity of the ancient Laestrygonians and that of Bloom's anxieties. Precisely as do the "Laestrygonian" diners in the Burton, the impending

rendezvous takes away his appetite; he will eat at six, for
"Time will be gone then." The Homeric correspondence is
thus a symbolic statement of the major action of the chapter, which is Bloom's constant suffering because of remind-
ers of his situation, both in his thoughts and in events.

Because the major action is what it is, Bloom's conversation with Nosey Flynn is significantly similar to an
earlier conversation with M'Coy (74). Flynn asks after
Molly and asks if she is doing any singing. He mentions
the "tour" to Belfast, and Flynn says:

—No. O, that's the style. Who's getting it up? (170)

The Belfast concert had also come up in the conversation
with M'Coy in the fifth chapter (post office):

—That so? M'Coy said. Glad to hear that, old man.
Who's getting it up? (74)

Bloom had explained "It's a kind of tour, don't you see.
. . . Part shares and part profits," and M'Coy, satisfied,
had prepared to take his leave. Now, after a little delay,
punctuated by the concluding verses of an ironically relevant bawdy limerick (*"His five hundred wives / Had the
time of their lives / It grew bigger and bigger and bigger"*),
he responds to Flynn:

—Getting it up? he said. Well, it's like a company
idea, you see. Part shares and part profits.
—Ay, now I remember, Nosey Flynn said, putting his
hand in his pocket to scratch his groin. Who is this was
telling me? Isn't Blazes Boylan mixed up in it?
A warm shock of air heat of mustard haunched on Mr
Bloom's heart. (170)

The recurrence of the same phrase, as the form of the
critical question, serves to accentuate the fact that in this
chapter Bloom ceases to find it possible to avoid thinking
about his situation, something he was able to manage for
long stretches in previous chapters; both the phallic motif

of his limerick and Flynn's scratching make the sexual pun in the phrase unmistakable. All occasions do inform against him. He is beset by "Laestrygonians." (Flynn goes on to discuss Boylan's virtues, concluding, "O, by God, Blazes is a hairy chap.")

The sixth chapter (cemetery) disclosed that Bloom's situation involves much more than the imminent prospect of his wife's taking a lover; that is only an immediate manifestation of it. His son is dead, and his wife is becoming progressively more estranged. No less distressing than his thoughts about Molly's affair with Boylan are those about his own relationship with her. Again and again in the chapter Bloom thinks about Molly and their former happiness together, and these thoughts gnaw at him fiercely:

> Milly was a kiddy then. Molly had that elephant-grey dress. . . . She didn't like it because I sprained my ankle first day she wore. . . . Fitted her like a glove, shoulder and hips. Just beginning to plump it out well. . . . People looking after her.
> Happy. Happier then. Snug little room. . . . Milly's tubbing water. . . . Funny she looked soaped all over. Shapely too. Now photography. (153)
> Windy night that was I went to fetch her. . . . Remember her laughing at the wind, her blizzard collar up. . . . Remember when we got home raking up the fire. . . . Could see her in the bedroom from the hearth unclamping the busk of her stays. White.
> Swish and soft flop her stays made on the bed. Always warm from her. Always liked to let herself out. Sitting there after till nearly two, taking out her hairpins. Milly tucked up in beddyhouse. Happy. Happy. (154)

And, as the nadir of his misery, he remembers rhapsodically the consummation of their love on the Hill of Howth, and then makes a relevant comparison:

> Stuck on the pane two flies buzzed, stuck.
> Glowing wine on his palate lingered swallowed. . . . Touched his sense moistened remembered. Hidden under wild ferns on Howth. Below us bay sleeping sky. No sound. The sky. . . . Pillowed on my coat she had her hair, earwigs in the heather scrub my hand under her nape, you'll toss me all. O wonder! Coolsoft with oint-

ments her hand touched me, caressed: her eyes upon me
did not turn away. Ravished over her I lay, full lips full
open, kissed her mouth. Yum. Softly she gave me in my
mouth the seedcake warm and chewed. Mawkish pulp her
mouth had mumbled sweet and sour with spittle. Joy: I
ate it: joy. Young life, her lips that gave me pouting.
Soft, warm sticky gumjelly lips. Flowers her eyes were,
take me, willing eyes. Pebbles fell. She lay still. A goat.
No-one. High on Ben Howth rhododendrons a nanny-
goat walking surefooted, dropping currants. Screened
under ferns she laughed warmfolded. Wildly I lay on her,
kissed her; eyes, her lips, her stretched neck, beating,
woman's breasts full in her blouse of nun's veiling, fat
nipples upright. Hot I tongued her. She kissed me. I
was kissed. All yielding she tossed my hair. Kissed, she
kissed me.
  Me. And me now.
  Stuck, the flies buzzed. (173-74)

This passage and the poetic device Joyce employs in it
call for some comment. He is not using the refrain to associate as in verse but to set off a passage of prose from what
precedes and follows it. The refrain is a frame, an adaptation of that other resource of poetry, typographical arrangement. Its most apparent effect is emphasis, which is war-
ranted; not only is Bloom's revery important in the present
chapter, but the incident on Howth is also the subject of
Molly's final thoughts in the book. A second effect is the
drawing together of that which is framed—the line "Me.
And me now" is yoked to the revery. As a result, the state
of mind Bloom's despondent comparison represents is
dramatized and the comparison validated. The frame itself
is no arbitrary image, no casual smuttiness. The copulating
flies associate directly with the prospective lovers on Bloom's
mind, are a comment on their relationship and their attitude
toward it. The frame is both a meaningful contrast with
the spirit of Bloom's revery and an ironic reflection of one
aspect of his situation "now."
  The gnawing thoughts that are the major action of this
chapter, thoughts of Boylan, of the forthcoming rendezvous,
of the difference between the past and the present, and of
Molly's desirableness, are all distilled in Bloom's "Me. And
me now," in the four words with which he acknowledges

to himself that he has lost his happiness, his wife, and his self-respect—all of which, for him, are won or lost together.

Bloom's situation "now," on the day of the novel, which he drearily regards in this chapter, is fully clarified in the chapter as well. The fourth chapter, which introduced him, revealed that he serves Molly, and not with resentment despite her shrewish exploitation of him but dotingly, so that he is very troubled over the impending adultery. At the same time he regards it as inevitable, and even possibly derives the "weak pleasure" of a bawd from the affair. The next chapter depicted his various devices for escaping the problems of his relationship with his wife, all of them tawdry, and none likely to be very successful. In the sixth chapter, he considered briefly the significance of the increasing deterioration of that relationship. He is isolated from his social peers and, through the deaths of his father and his son, isolated from his family line. Estrangement from Molly will deprive him of his last meaningful contact with other human beings and any chance of restoring his familial ties through a son.

Bloom's concern about families and its obvious connection to his own lack of a son came up in the sixth chapter. But it is most prominent in the present one. He thinks not only of families but of women in terms of maternity. Beginning with the first page he reflects on: Mrs. Purefoy's arduous labor (156); the large families of Dedalus (149), Mrs. Breen (154), Mrs. Purefoy (158), and Queen Victoria (159); the old midwife Mrs. Thornton (159); the attitude toward motherhood of a "gay divorcee" (158); Queen Victoria's aptitude for reproduction (159); and the "Funny sight two of them together, their bellies out. Molly and Mrs Moisel. Mothers' meeting" (159).

The reason why Bloom is as interested in the conception and bearing of children as in children themselves is suggested in one of his "Laestrygonian" comparisons of his present state with the past:

I was happier then. . . . Twenty-eight I was. She was twenty-three when we left Lombard street west something

> changed. Could never like it again after Rudy. Can't
> bring back time. Like holding water in your hand. Would
> you go back to then? Just beginning then. (165)

Bloom and Molly have not had normal sexual relations since
the birth and death of Rudy (for "a period of 10 years, 5
months and 18 days," the seventeenth chapter declares just
before Molly's soliloquy). Furthermore, his reflection makes
clear that the infant's death caused the disruption in those
relations and that his situation "now," which in the present chapter is so dramatically clear to him, had its "beginning" in that disruption. Thus his thoughts about Rudy on
the ride to the cemetery:

> Our. Little. Beggar. Baby. Meant nothing. Mistake of
> nature. If it's healthy it's from the mother. If not the
> man. Better luck next time. (94)

are not for consolation but for mockery. There had been
no next time and there apparently will be no next time.

Bloom's interest in large families naturally reflects his
grief at the loss of his son. It also reflects his belief that
he will never have any more children himself. And the
interest in procreation and maternity which accompanies
it reflects the belief that he will fail to have a son not
because Molly will bear one and that one too will die but
because he will, as he has done since Rudy's death, prevent
her from bearing one. The extent of his interest in procreation and maternity is an index of his frustration in
presuming that he will provide neither.

Molly vigorously protests against Bloom's sexual perversions during her soliloquy. She does not understand,
and the author does not declare, the reason for them. But
it can be inferred from the declared source of Bloom's
inhibition—Rudy's death. Bloom himself knows only that
he "could never like it again after Rudy." However, he also
believes that Rudy's death is his fault ("If it's healthy it's
from the mother. If not the man"). Without being aware
of it, he fears beginning again a cycle of conception and
eagerly-awaited birth that will end in death.[3]

BLOOM's failure to seek a son with her estranges him from
Molly; estrangement from Molly denies him a son. This
dilemma, which began to plague him ten and a half years
before the day of the novel and threatens to continue doing
so until he is destroyed, is the key to Leopold Bloom's apparently contradictory actions and attitudes.

For example, preceding chapters show him combining an
inclination toward promiscuous skirt-chasing with ardent
love for Molly. In the present chapter his repeated "Laestrygonian" thoughts about Molly's physical desirableness and
about his former happiness with her are punctuated by a
lengthy, almost frantic, sexual revery, which is associated
with "eating" motifs:

> Perfume of embraces all him assailed. With hungered flesh
> obscurely, he mutely craved to adore.
> Duke street. Here we are. Must eat. The Burton. Feel
> better then.
> He turned Combridge's corner, still pursued. Jingling
> hoofthuds. Perfumed bodies, warm, full. All kissed,
> yielded: in deep summer fields, tangled pressed grass, in
> trickling hallways of tenements, along sofas, creaking
> beds.
> —Jack love!
> —Darling!
> —Kiss me, Reggy!
> —My boy!
> —Love!
> His heart astir he pushed in the door of the Burton
> restaurant. (166)

The link between the two gnawing concerns of sexual
hunger and longing for Molly is the same thing as the
cause of his decision to visit the "naked goddesses" in the
museum—who "don't care what man looks" (174)—immediately after his climactic expression of love and sexual
frustration, his memory of the incident on Howth. It is the
estrangement from Molly which he found himself obliged to
initiate upon the death of Rudy.

By the day of the novel its effect on her has become
eager acceptance of a lover who is rich, handsome, lusty,
and gay. For himself it has resulted in suffering. His
frantic search through his pockets while he rushes to the

museum entrance at the end of the present chapter is
prompted by shame. As in the sixth chapter, where he
inspected his fingernails while his companions greeted Boylan, he is ashamed to face his cuckolder. But its object
suggests that his search is also an attempt to find Molly
secure. He locates the soap, finds it still in his possession,
just as he reaches the gate, and the last word of the chapter
("Safe!") refers not only to himself but, in his frenzied
wishes, to his wife as well. Yet, despite love for Molly,
distress over her affair with Boylan, and sexual frustration,
he does nothing to stop the affair. He considers it inevitable: it is the result of his neglect of her. The reason
why he is so uncomplaining is the same. He not only
cannot, or even will not, stop it, he believes that he has no
right to stop it.

Other attitudes and actions also fall into place. Bloom's
first chapter showed him serving Molly with alacrity and
also inclining to bawdry. In the present chapter a character tells of seeing him buying "her cream" (Bloom's
words) for Molly's breakfast tray (174). And after trans-
lating the snatch from *Don Giovanni* in which the Commendatore lays the ground for his revenge, Bloom calculates his prospective income for the near future and thinks:

> Could buy one of those silk petticoats for Molly, colour
> of her new garters.
> Today. Today. Not think. (177)

The passage reflects his love for Molly, desire for her, and
solicitous service of her; but above all, it shows the punctuation of distress over his wife's imminent adultery by the
thought of buying attractive underwear for the adulteress.

Bloom almost wants Molly to take a lover, so guilty is he
about having betrayed his responsibility to her as a husband. His sense of guilt makes him unable to attempt to
prevent her from having an affair, causes him to feel
unworthy of the role of husband and master in the household, and prompts him to a solicitude which extends from
gratifying Molly's every whim, to serving her ignominiously,
to helping her adorn herself for her lover. All the apparent
incongruities in his character—skirt-chasing and sexual

frustration, despite his love for Molly; failure to attempt to stop her adultery and even manifestations of encouragement of it, despite his distress; thoughtfulness and willing service, despite Molly's oppressive manner—are natural developments of a situation that arose out of the death of the infant Rudy ten and a half years before the day of the novel. Having perverted his relationship with Molly because he blamed himself for their feeble child, he has caused a situation for which he deserves blame; and having accepted that blame, he has developed into the degraded sufferer finally revealed in this chapter.

Gnawed at by his anxieties and memories, and revealing the complex mainspring of his behavior, Bloom in this chapter becomes fully sympathetic perhaps for the first time. The chapter is principally an exposition of the manner and extent of Leopold Bloom's suffering, and the nature and source of its causes.

Almost everything that is not part of this exposition is part of a complementary portrayal in the chapter of the major elements of Bloom's character—his politics, his verbal wit, his concern with advertising and "science," and his kindness. His politics is given the most prominent treatment. He has thoughts on Ireland, public kitchens, mass demonstrations, conspiracy, infant subsidy, the British secret police, landowning. As the previous chapter clearly establishes the politics of Stephen, and of Joyce, this one does so for Bloom; it shows him in full agreement with them about Ireland and the Nationalist movement. Thus he says of the chess-playing John Howard Parnell, "His brother used men as pawns" (162). The remark expresses his reverence for "Ireland's uncrowned king" and disdain of contemporary politicians, and is one of many examples of his ability to use language:

> Sad booser's eyes. Bitten off more than he can chew. . . .
> That last pagan king of Ireland Cormac in the school-
> poem choked himself. . . . Saint Patrick converted him
> to Christianity. Couldn't swallow it all however. (167)

One significant example of the portrayal of his concern with advertising is that the disturbing thought that Boylan might have a venereal disease grows out of a "meditation" on the subject. In the first four pages of the chapter alone he thinks about newspaper advertisements, floating advertisements, billboard advertisements, and sandwichboard advertisements. Manifestations of his scientism are not as prominent; but, during the course of the chapter, he thinks of gravity, parallax, solar eclipse, and the work of a noted astronomer, and conducts two "experiments" in sensory experience.

To complete the portrait, the chapter provides many instances of Bloom's mercy. Aside from recurring concern for the plight of Mrs. Purefoy and pity for Mrs. Breen, which are related to his interest in families and maternity, there are such uncomplicated pure examples of his kindness as the incident at the very beginning of the chapter in which he buys two Banbury cakes from a peddler for "those poor birds" and feeds the gulls on the Liffey (151), and the last incident in the chapter before the sighting of Boylan, in which he meets and assists the blind "stripling," taking care to avoid making the boy self-conscious (178).

The two examples of kindness neatly straddle the chapter, and for good reason. Bloom's mercy is one aspect of a significant pattern of association begun in this chapter. It is as vital a part of the story of *Ulysses* as the nature and cause of Bloom's abject condition, and it is the final significant element in the portrait of him. The two prominent incidents in the chapter that have not yet been considered concern this element of his character. They are his receipt of a handbill announcing the forthcoming appearance in Dublin of the American evangelist, John Alexander Dowie (1847-1907), as the chapter opens, and the discussion in Davy Byrne's of horseracing and that day's Gold Cup race at Ascot.

The discussion involves only Nosey Flynn and Byrne, at first. Bloom wonders if he should tell Flynn that Lenehan's choice (overheard in the newspaper office) is Sceptre, recalls that Flynn knows already, and remains silent. A short while later, three other horserace addicts enter. Paddy Leonard informs Flynn and Tom Rochford that Bantam

Lyons "has some bloody horse up his sleeve for the Gold cup." Lyons refuses to reveal the name of the horse and Leonard exasperatedly asks him who gave him the tip:

> Mr Bloom on his way out raised three fingers in greeting.
> —So long, Nosey Flynn said.
> The others turned.
> —That's the man now that gave it to me, Bantam Lyons whispered.
> —Prrwht! Paddy Leonard said with scorn. (176)

Bloom clearly has no special information; and he has met Lyons only once before during the day. At the end of the fifth chapter (post office), Lyons borrowed his newspaper to look at the list of Ascot entries. He suggested that Lyons keep the paper, explaining "I was just going to throw it away." The statement excited Lyons; and when he repeated it, Lyons excitedly said, "I'll risk it," and ran off.

The revelation by Lyons in this chapter that Bloom provided his tip for the Gold Cup at Ascot is linked to the incident at the very beginning of the chapter in which Bloom is given the evangelist handbill; for that is referred to as "a throwaway," and the little-used term is insisted on always in preference to "handbill" or "leaflet." Furthermore, the "throwaway" is identified with Bloom, source of the "throw it away" tip. He very shortly throws it away: he thinks momentarily of throwing himself into the Liffey, of committing suicide, sees gulls wheeling over the water, and then drops the "throwaway," crumpled, from the bridge instead (151). And when he first takes the handbill, the identification is suggested by an almost strained device:

> Bloo . . . Me? No.
> Blood of the Lamb. (149)

The reason for the identification is that Bloom is thereby associated at the beginning of the chapter with the two subjects of the handbill, which speaks not only of Christ but of the coming of Dowie, who, in 1901, had announced

to the world that he was "Elijah the Restorer" reincarnate.
The association of Bloom and Elijah is developed promptly.
He reads that "Elijah is coming," reaches the bridge over
the Liffey, and contemplates suicide—a direct parallel to
Elijah's asking God for death in the wilderness near Beer-
sheba. He throws in the crumpled handbill, then thinks of
"those poor birds," and feeds the gulls wheeling over the
river—an inverse parallel to the miraculous feeding of Elijah by ravens in the desert. He actually calls the Banbury
cakes "manna" (151), and later in the novel he will associate the gulls with the handbill's "Elijah" ("Penny the
gulls. Elijah is com," 275). Finally, of course, he has acted
in a prophetic capacity, granted a revelation, although
unwittingly, of the outcome of the Ascot Gold Cup race.

While the association of Bloom and Elijah is suggested in
the first action of the chapter, that of Bloom and Christ is
initiated in the very first paragraphs, in which the handbill
incident occurs. The chapter opens with an excellent example of Joyce's verbal play in *Ulysses.* A combination of
Bloom's experiences and interior monologue, the first paragraphs actually form a catalogue of the chapter's subjects.
The passage warrants quotation in full:

PINEAPPLE ROCK, LEMON PLATT, BUTTER SCOTCH. A
SUGARSTICKY girl shovelling scoopfuls of creams for a
christian brother. Some school treat. Bad for their tum-
mies. Lozenge and comfit manufacturer to His Majesty
the King. God. Save. Our. Sitting on his throne, suck-
ing red jujubes white.

A sombre Y.M.C.A. young man, watchful among the
warm sweet fumes of Graham Lemon's, placed a throwaway in a hand of Mr Bloom.

Heart to heart talks.

Bloo . . . Me? No.

Blood of the Lamb.

His slow feet walked him riverward, reading. Are
you saved? All are washed in the blood of the lamb.
God wants blood victim. Birth, hymen, martyr, war,
foundation of a building, sacrifice, kidney, burntoffering,
druid's altars. Elijah is coming. Dr. John Alexander
Dowie, restorer of the church in Zion, is coming.

Is coming! Is coming!! Is coming!!!

All heartily welcome.

Paying game. Torry and Alexander last year. Polygamy. His wife will put the stopper on that. Where was that ad some Birmingham firm the luminous crucifix? Our Saviour. Wake up in the dead of night and see him on the wall, hanging. Pepper's ghost idea. Iron nails ran in.

Phosphorous it must be done with. If you leave a bit of codfish for instance. I could see the bluey silver over it. Night I went down to the pantry in the kitchen. Don't like all the smells in it waiting to rush out. What was it she wanted? The Malaga raisins. Thinking of Spain. Before Rudy was born. The phosphorescence, that bluey greeny. Very good for the brain. (149)

As does the "Bloo . . . Me?" reference, the linking of Christ to the bit of codfish through the luminous crucifix effects an association of Christ with Bloom. Not only is the fish associated with Bloom as part of a personal memory, but later in the chapter, when Bloom remembers his boyhood nickname, it turns out to be the name of a fish that is symbolic of Christ: "Mackerel they called me" (160). Furthermore, Christians of the Roman era used the fish as an emblem of Christ, and the chapter is as full of the names of fish: salmon, sardine, herring, lobster, oysters, sturgeon, sole, as it is of examples of Bloom's mercy.

Manifestly, the same words that initiate the "throwaway" matter—literally, symbolically in the association of Bloom with Christ and Elijah which is effected through the handbill, and figuratively in the punning reference to the horserace tip—also initiate the parallel with Homer's Laestrygonians through reference to a slaughtered lamb and through Bloom's thoughts about a "blood victim." The passage as a whole also provides examples of Bloom's concern with science, advertising, and politics, his verbal wit, and his considerateness. Finally, in Bloom's memory of an incident involving Malaga raisins for Molly and leftover codfish that explicitly occurred before Rudy's birth, it suggests the connection between the Laestrygonians correspondence and the true principal subject of the chapter, which that correspondence illuminates.

In fact, while it announces the chapter's subjects, the opening passage asserts by its form that all of those subjects are related. The first paragraph, with its candy and eating imagery, is linked to the second, which introduces the "throwaway" matter, through the repetition of "lemon" in the name of the candy shop. Bloom's reading and thinking about the handbill from there to the beginning of the fourth paragraph links the Laestrygonian motif to the references to Christ and Elijah, and to the association of himself with Christ. The luminous crucifix in the fourth paragraph links with the phosphorescent codfish in the fifth, and so asserts that the whole complex of "throw-away"-Christ-Laestrygonian matter is related to Bloom's memory of Molly before the birth of Rudy.

The relating of horserace tip and handbill, the associating of Bloom with Christ and Elijah, and the linking of these new elements in the novel with the principal subject of the chapter, the nature and condition of Leopold Bloom, are all done unobtrusively; but they are done and must be acknowledged, although the reason why they are done is not apparent. As the next chapter, the ninth, does for Stephen, this chapter completes the presentation of Bloom. The rest of *Ulysses* develops what is presented here.

style in ulysses

. . . The novel may now be starting upon a fresh life, after the tremendous career it has had already. The discovery of the degree to which it may be enhanced dramatically—this may be a point of departure from which it will set out with vigor renewed; perhaps it has done so by this time. Anyhow it is clear that an immense variety of possible modulations, mixtures, harmonies of method, yet untried, are open to it if it chooses to avail itself. . . . [4]

When Percy Lubbock's *The Craft of Fiction* appeared in 1921 with this speculation, part of *Ulysses* had already been printed, and the whole novel was less than a year from publication. Lubbock's book, which Allen Tate has compared to Aristotle's *Poetics*, is primarily a discourse on the exploitation of point of view for the enhancement of dramatic representation in fiction. It uses the later novels of Henry James as examples of a fully autonomous narrative art: "The Ambassadors, then, is a story which is seen from one man's point of view, and yet a story in which that point of view is itself a matter for the reader to confront and to watch constructively."[5]

Whether or not James showed subsequent writers "that the craft of fiction has larger resources than might have been suspected," as Lubbock believes, James and Joseph Conrad were the first of a line of British and American novelists whose work is almost characterized by its eschewing of the omniscient narrator for one or another indigenous "eye" whose "point of view is itself a matter for the reader to confront and to watch." The technique is at least as old as Petronius' *Satyricon*, of course. However, Lubbock's prophecy of "an immense variety of possible modulations, mixtures, harmonies of method" following James' consummate development of it has been borne out in the twentieth century.

Joyce's use of the technique can be seen even in *Dubliners*. The child of "Araby," Mr. Duffy of "A Painful Case," Maria of "Clay," Lenehan as he appears in "Two Gallants," for example, all lend the author their diction and their eyes, either consistently or intermittently. The method of the *Portrait* is precisely that of presenting Stephen's point of view as "a matter for the reader to . . . watch." Furthermore, Stephen's discourse on art in Chapter V of the *Portrait*, although characteristically lacking a sense of the importance of reality, asserts the value of the dramatic quality in a literary work. When Stephen says "art necessarily divides itself into three forms progressing from one to the next," he is describing stages in the process of artistic creation, levels of accomplishment, and not literary genres. That is why he then poses the question, *"Is the bust of Sir Philip Crampton lyrical, epical or dramatic?"*

The lyrical form of a literary work, he says, is "a rhythmi-
cal cry." The next higher form such a work can take, the
epical "form progresses till the centre of emotional gravity
is equidistant from the artist himself and from others."
The dramatic form "is reached" if and when an artist has
succeeded in the highest aim of art: if his personality,
which has responded, then expressed itself, "refines itself
out of [the] existence [of the work]"; in the almost identical words of T.S. Eliot's essay "Tradition and the Individual Talent": "Poetry . . . is not the expression of
personality, but an escape from personality." And the
image with which Stephen concludes his assertion, which
many readers have taken to be a self-projection of the arrogant, indifferent (nihilistic) Joyce,

> The artist, like the God of the creation, remains within
> or behind or beyond or above his handiwork, invisible,
> refined out of existence, indifferent, paring his finger-
> nails[6]

is really a final expression of the characteristically modern
concern for the autonomy of the work of literature, of
which both the Jamesian method in fiction and depersonal-
ization in poetry are manifestations: the successful artist
can pare his fingernails, or do whatever else he wishes, for
"The mystery of esthetic . . . creation is accomplished"
—the work is dramatic, has its own life.

Joyce's three volumes of fiction reveal his increasing
concentration on refining the author out of the work's
existence. Used intermittently in *Dubliners*, the method of
the later Henry James is used fully in the *Portrait*. In about
the first half of *Ulysses*, Joyce took the first step beyond
that "point of departure"—a heavy reliance on the literary
device (today a convention) of representing consciousness
or thought in words, as though it were verbal, in order
to achieve a fiction that is almost wholly the speeches,
perceptions, and thoughts of characters. The most common
term for the device, "interior monologue," is from the
French *monologue intérieur*, which is more aptly rendered
"inner monologue." This portion of the novel, the first
eleven chapters (through Ormond) and some of the thir-

teenth (strand-Bloom), has an omniscient narrator and the only style, properly speaking, in *Ulysses*. It is akin to the style of the *Portrait* but richer and more difficult, with abrupt transition from one element to another of its characteristic combination of dialogue, the representation of characters' thoughts, and occasional exposition by the author-narrator; in keeping with Joyce's general strategy, even the exposition is sometimes from the point of view of the character (wholly subjective), so that all of the narrator but his voice has been refined out. Throughout the remainder of the novel, Joyce created a series of "modulations, mixtures, harmonies of method," chapter after chapter, that dazzle and perplex the reader who confronts them for the first time. Each of these special varieties of narrative ("styles" would be an inadequate word even if the method were not the avoidance of an identifiable personal style) has its functional purpose, but all are also calculated to eliminate the eye and voice of the omniscient narrator completely; and in the last seven chapters, with the exception of the mentioned portion of the thirteenth, not one word can be identified as his.

Various as they are, the literary devices or methods used in *Ulysses* are almost all of only three fundamental kinds. "Inner" monologue is the most important. It is introduced gradually, but by the third chapter Joyce represents Stephen's thoughts on the beach almost uninterrupted by either dialogue or exposition; the corresponding treatment of Bloom, which occurs in the eighth chapter, just discussed, is only a little less pure; and in every other chapter between the third and the end of the ninth (the end of the first of the novel's two formal parts), inner monologue dominates and all but determines the style. After the tenth and eleventh chapters and part of the thirteenth, it is not employed again until the last. There Molly's consciousness has its turn; and Joyce provides an example of the ultimate form of the method, in which absolutely nothing interrupts the character's thought, and which is most meaningfully called "stream-of-consciousness." Next in importance after inner monologue is parody. It is the basis of the anti-styles of the twelfth (Kiernan's), fourteenth (hospital), and sixteen (shelter) chapters, and of most of the thirteenth (strand-Bloom) ; it is prominent in the seventh (newspaper) chapter; and in the eleventh (Ormond), operatic conventions are parodied so extensively that even while maintaining the characteristic style of those preceding it, the chapter effectively begins the succession of changing narrative manners which marks the second part of the novel. Lastly, there is the quasi-dramatic format of the fifteenth (nighttown) chapter, which is almost one-fourth of the whole novel.

Thus, all the tricks and kinds of writing that characterize the various chapters of *Ulysses* (with the sole exception of the seventeenth, which is both parody and burlesque) derive from three literary devices. The novel is not stylistically bizarre; and considered in historical context, it is even less so. It is in the tradition that followed the "dramatic" fiction of James and Conrad, and that includes Virginia Woolf, John Dos Passos, and William Faulkner, among many others—the tradition, foreseen by Lubbock, which brought to fiction the explosive developments in form undergone by all the arts in the first part of the century and now pretty much assimilated. It stands out in that tradition because the "variety" of "modulations, mixtures, harmonies of method" in it is so very "immense."

Furthermore, all three of Joyce's basic devices have precedents, and to some extent their sources, in earlier literature. Again Nero's courtier Petronius can be mentioned, for the *Satyricon* relies heavily on the parody of genres; and parodies of style go even further back to Aristophanes. The parody newspaper headlines in the seventh chapter were anticipated in the student publication at University College, *St. Stephen's*, in at least one humorous piece the young Joyce must have seen, for it is partly about him. Furthermore, *St. Stephen's* had occasion to mention "Mr. Joyce" (also "the mystic Joacax," "dreaming Jimmy," "the dreaming one of Nola," and "the mad hatter") frequently, so it probably was read by him; and while it printed serious articles, including one by Joyce himself, it was not above parodies of newspaper and cheap-novel styles, puns, portmanteau words, and other tricks.[7]

Two sources or inspirations for the narrative manner of the fifteenth (nighttown) chapter which have been suggested by critics are the Walpurgisnacht scene in Goethe's *Faust* and Flaubert's *La Tentation de Saint-Antoine*.[8] Another one, which is strikingly similar to it, is Strindberg's *Ein Traumspiel (The Dream Play)*.[9] Blake's "The Island in the Moon" and the "Forecastle-Midnight" scene (Chapter XL) of *Moby-Dick* could be added to these (and undoubtedly other things as well). All are at least precedents, and Joyce probably knew all but the chapter from *Moby-Dick*.

The term *monologue intérieur* was used as long ago as 1845, in *Vingt ans après* by Dumas *père*, the sequel to *Les Trois Mousquetaires*. However, its present meaning was given it by Joyce's French friend and publicist, Valery Larbaud, in his preface to the 1924 reprint of *Les Lauriers sont coupés*, by Edouard Dujardin, a novel Joyce had read as a young man. It is a confessional novel whose protagonist-narrator discloses what is on his mind in the present tense, and is interrupted only by occasional dialogue. Upon the publication of *Ulysses* and afterward, Joyce insisted that he had taken inner monologue from Dujardin's book, and both the reprinting of 1924 and a resurgence of reputation for the old French writer were at least partly brought about by Joyce's active promotion. Nevertheless, Joyce's avowed indebtedness to Dujardin was openly challenged; while Larbaud and William Carlos Williams wrote inner-monologue novels on the examples of Dujardin and Joyce, Dorothy Richardson and Virginia Woolf lit upon the technique themselves; finally, once again a number of anticipations which may also have been inspirations have been suggested by critics,[10] and whole books have been written about the origins and development of inner monologue (usually calling it "stream-of-consciousness"). Even if Joyce's chief narrative device and the primary stylistic element in *Ulysses* did not have a more illustrious source, if he did take it from Dujardin, it had considerable precedent.

Discussing Dujardin and Joyce's relations with him in his biography of Joyce, Richard Ellmann declares summarily, "The method of the *monologue intérieur* was of consequence only because Joyce saw what could be done with it."[11] Ultimately, the truth about the origins of the stylistic and narrative elements of *Ulysses* which give such an impression of novelty, variety, and bizarreness is less important than what Joyce does with each. One function that all of them have is the removal of the author, the creation of a dramatic fiction. But this end does not require such a multiplicity of means; indeed, that multiplicity actually draws attention to the author who is so shy of being his own narrator. The essential reason for all of the different stylistic techniques and narrative devices is the same as the reason for every other special element in *Ulysses*—each helps to tell the story. Just as the parody headlines in the seventh chapter elucidate theme and symbol, so are the parodies in the later chapters vehicles of meaning. Generally, they have definite models. The eleventh chapter is not just an exercise in musical effects but a parody of a specific opera; the twelfth does not parody in its narrator just the speech of the lower-class quarter of Dublin called The Coombe but a specific chronicle; the thirteenth does not just parody "dollar-novel," "dime-novel," or "penny novelette" style but a specific sentimental book. And every parody has a definite narrative purpose. The format of the nighttown chapter makes possible the dramatic presentation of a concrete action, the fantasies of Stephen, those of Bloom, and the very vital interrelations of the three elements. Inner monologue, an effective method of psychological portraiture, and often limited to that in fiction, is tailor-made for a novel whose essential action occurs inside its chief characters' heads, as in fact that of *Ulysses* does.

That convention of representing thought as a sequence of words on the page and thereby making it action, like dialogue, is also tailor-made for a writer intent on fully exploiting every resource at hand. The sequence of words must suggest the quality of thought in its style by such things as compressed syntax and elliptical phrasing; and it must suggest the processes of thought in its form, fundamentally through association of words and ideas. Almost alone among writers who have used inner monologue, Joyce turned this necessity into an opportunity for packing his text with meaning.[12] He creates, through the style and form of passages of inner monologue, articulated constructs whose elements relate to one another like those in a lyric poem; the passage at the beginning of the eighth chapter, linking different subjects of Bloom's thought and thereby asserting that the apparently diverse matters these subjects represent are really related, and the passage in the body of the chapter in which Bloom's revery of the idyll on Howth and his abrupt concluding observation are framed and set apart are only two such constructs. Furthermore, he takes advantage of the fact that the mind invokes matters that concern it when given the slightest pretext, and he invests the inner monologue everywhere it occurs with a freight of references to objects, concepts, memories, phrases, in such a way that the context of each is invoked and exploited. Paralleling the pattern of correspondences, allusions, and parodies in *Ulysses* is a wholly internal network of references, a web of intrinsic associations that permeates the novel. Its nature and the uses to which Joyce put it are such that the inner monologue is not simply written but built up. Joyce's correspondence abounds with notes and postcards to his typists asking them to add words and phrases at certain points; when reading proof for the novel, he "insisted on five sets, and made innumerable changes, almost always additions, in the text, complicating the interior monologue with more and more interconnecting details";[13] memoirs by friends mention frantic trips to the printers at Dijon to make changes in press; and studies of the manuscripts and galleys of *Ulysses* confirm that there was a constant thickening of the web of associations, primarily in the inner monologue of Bloom.[14] Irish critics have likened this quality of the novel to the graphic style of "The Book of Kells," Ireland's famous illuminated manuscript of the Gospels, dated at about the seventh century. The delicate lacework ornamentation of that and similar manuscripts, a purely Irish art, is almost unbelievably elaborate; and yet nothing is random, the designs are symmetrical, a web, not a chaos.

A reasonably good example of the fruits of Joyce's elaborative process would suggest its close dependence on the qualities of inner monologue, its functionality, its validity in the naturalistic world of the novel, and the gusto with which he wove his thick texture. In the fourth chapter

Bloom and Molly are introduced, and the central fact of
the novel, that he is about to be cuckolded, is disclosed.
Boylan and Molly are to rehearse, that afternoon, "*La ci
darem*" from *Don Giovanni* and "Love's Old Sweet Song."
Both are perfectly ordinary choices for a popular chanteuse
at the turn of the century, so they are appropriate in
naturalistic terms. The obvious irony that Molly is to rehearse "Love's Old Sweet Song" with Boylan invests the
song with a significance for the reader that he soon learns
is shared by Bloom. Ten pages later, in the next chapter,
M'Coy asks, "Who's getting it up?"; and before giving
his evasive answer, Bloom thinks that Molly is lying in bed
telling her fortune with cards, and concludes:

> Dark lady and fair man. . . . Torn strips of envelope.
> *Love's*
> *Old*
> *Song*
> *Comes lo-ve's old* (74)

In the eleventh chapter (Ormond), Bloom sees Boylan set
out for his rendezvous with Molly and imagines his progress. When he calculates that Boylan has arrived at the
Bloom residence, the title of the song works its way into
his inner monologue (269-70). Before the end of the
thirteenth chapter, the cuckolding of Bloom has occurred,
and in that chapter the associative value with which the
song has been endowed by the previous references is exploited. Details in the action correspond to phrases in
the song; however, now it not only represents the consummation of Boylan's tryst with Molly but Bloom's sense of
the significance of that tryst. Echoing the first "verse" of the
song in her sentimental idiom, Gerty MacDowell thinks,
"Perhaps it was an old flame he was in mourning for from
the days beyond recall" (358). Which is precisely the
case. Knowing what has happened during the afternoon,
Bloom considers his happiness as husband and father to
be "dear dead days beyond recall."

Having fully exploited a rather bad popular song, Joyce
might have let it drop, but a prose style of elaboration
provides room for a bit of bawdy humor. After one of

the whores in Nighttown badgers Stephen to sing the song, that one detail in the novel makes its final appearance. In the seventeenth chapter Bloom is examining the re-arranged furnishings in his parlor. On the music rest of the piano is "Love's Old Sweet Song." The author lists the directions presumably followed by the pianist, Boylan, in concluding his part of the rendition of the song. The score is:

> open at the last page with the final indications *ad libitum, forte*, pedal, *animato*, sustained, pedal, *ritirando*, close. (691)

Of course, even here the stitch in the design is functional.

Furthermore, Molly's other selection is also important. "*La ci darem*," one of the most famous love duets in all operatic literature, if not the most famous, is one of the most important elements in the novel.[15] But perhaps the last point to be made about Joyce's stylistic art in *Ulysses* is that his representation of the directions at the end of "Love's Old Sweet Song" actually follows the standard score of the song precisely, except for the necessary transposition of "*animato*" and the hold ("sustained") mark.

1. Butcher and Lang, pp. 156–57.

2. *Ibid.*, p. 157.

3. Damon says, p. 34, "Since his son's death, [Bloom] has not had normal relations with his wife; his inner self perhaps refuses to risk more such tragedies. . . ."

4. Percy Lubbock, *The Craft of Fiction* (New York, 1957), p. 173.

5. *Ibid.*, p. 170.

6. The passage is on pp. 250–52. See also Chapter Five, n. 26.

7. See Patricia Hutchins, *James Joyce's Dublin* (London, 1950), pp. 51–52, 60–61, 63–67, and especially pp. 69–70. Most of this material is reprinted in Miss Hutchins' *James Joyce's World* (London, 1957).

8. See, e.g., Gilbert, pp. 312–15 (esp. n. 1, p. 313), 331.

9. See, e.g., Tindall, p. 46.

10. In an extended discussion, Harry Levin shows the similarity of inner monologue to passages he quotes from Fanny Burney's diary, Cooper's *The Spy*, *The Pickwick Papers*, and *Moby-Dick*, and men-

tions that Gide found similarities in Dostoevsky's *The House of the Dead* (Levin, pp. 90–93). Richard M. Kain mentions Tolstoy's first (unfinished) story, "The Story of a Yesterday," as having "an interesting anticipation" of it (Kain, pp. 18–19).

11. *James Joyce*, p. 534 n.

12. For a general discussion of form in the inner monologue of *Ulysses*, see Goldberg, pp. 242–53.

13. *James Joyce*, p. 527.

14. For example, R. F. Roberts says, in "Bibliographical Notes on James Joyce's 'Ulysses,'" *Colophon* (New Series), I, 4, 565–79, 569: "The first three episodes remain almost without alteration, but the succeeding ones all bear marks of revision and addition—especially in the enlargement of Mr. Bloom's *monologue intérieur*."

15. For a discussion of the allusions to *Don Giovanni* in the novel, see Vernon Hall, Jr., "Joyce's Use of Da Ponte and Mozart's *Don Giovanni*," *PMLA*, LXVI (1951), 78–84.

chapter five

9 *the library*

The ninth chapter has been called "the subtlest and hardest
to epitomize of all of the eighteen episodes of *Ulysses*";[1]
it is also one of the most important. The chapter has three
major elements. The most prominent by far is Stephen's
involved forensic speech; it has prompted a great deal of
critical discussion of the relationship of Shakespeare to
Ulysses, but is primarily a narrative device. Then, Bloom
appears twice, the second time to cross Stephen's path;
but clearly Stephen is the "Ulysses" of the chapter, and
what Bloom is seems less clear. Finally, according to
Joyce's schema, the chapter is analogous to the adventure
in Book XII of the *Odyssey* of the monster on the rock
(Scylla) and the consuming whirlpool (Charybdis); but
setting aside its possible function, prodigious searching
for the very details of the correspondence has had small
results.

The scene of the chapter is the National Library in
Dublin. The action is dominated by Stephen's exposition
of his theory about the place of Shakespeare the man in
Hamlet and the other works, and by the comments of
Stephen's auditors. Before the speech has really gotten
under way, the most distinguished of them, George Russell
—the poet A.E., who was one of the leaders of the national

literary revival in Ireland—leaves. Stephen has come to
the library from drinking with the "Aeolists" in order to
give A.E. the second copy of Mr. Deasy's letter for the
Irish Homestead, of which he is an editor. But Stephen
stays on. When he has delivered his first climactic paragraph, Mulligan enters; and there is what Stephen thinks
of as an *"entr'acte"* of clowning by the new arrival. Although Mulligan has received Stephen's telegraphed message that he would not meet Mulligan and Haines at "The
Ship," as they had agreed in the morning, and buy drinks
for them, Stephen leaves the library with Mulligan when he
has completed his exposition. As they reach the entrance,
Bloom walks between and past them.

The nature and function of the Homeric parallel are
more easily determined than either the nature and function
of Stephen's speech about Shakespeare or Bloom's role in
the chapter.

The chapter is begun characteristically by "the Quaker
librarian," Thomas W. Lyster, director of the National
Library in 1904, presented as a platitudinous moderator,
ridiculously dogged in his courteous service and pacifying
zeal:

> URBANE, TO COMFORT THEM, THE QUAKER LIBRARIAN
> PURRED:
> —And we have, have we not, those priceless pages of
> *Wilhelm Meister*? A great poet on a great brother poet.
> A hesitating soul taking arms against a sea of troubles,
> torn by conflicting doubts, as one sees in real life. (182)

Stephen has been talking about *Hamlet*. Mr. (W.K.) Magee,
the Irish writer and editor known as "John Eglinton,"
mentions tauntingly a plan Stephen had for rewriting
Paradise Lost with the help of six "medicals" from a Blake-
ian, anti-Jahwistic viewpoint—as *The Sorrows of Satan*—
and says, "I feel you would need one more for *Hamlet*.
Seven is dear to the mystic mind. The shining seven W.B.
calls them" (182). Having twitted Stephen and cited
Yeats, he "sought the face, bearded amid darkgreener
shadow, an ollav, holyeyed" of A. E.; Stephen thinks:

He holds my follies hostage. . . . Gap-toothed Kathleen, her four beautiful green fields, the stranger in her
house. And one more to hail him: *ave, rabbi.* . . .
My soul's youth I gave him. . . .
Mulligan has my telegram. (182-83)

Stephen, too, had once been a disciple of the theosophist
high priest. Now he thinks of him (in terms of Yeats' play
The Countess Cathleen) as the emissary of the devil after
the soul of (wanton) Ireland. And he associates the A.E.
he rejected with the now-rejected Mulligan. The nature
of their relationship to Stephen, and to each other, is defined by the Homeric correspondence.

With respect to the simple creation of that correspondence, it is difficult to understand how Joyce's explicit identification of A.E. with Charybdis has been overlooked.
A.E. sits in the background, in shadow. When he attacks
(with justice) Stephen's biographical approach to Shakespeare's work and turns for agreement to the fifth member
of the group, Richard I. Best, like Eglinton an assistant
of Lyster's (in 1924 he became a successor), Stephen
thinks of the effect A.E. has on Ireland's young intellectuals
in terms of a passage from the poet's play *Deirdre*:

Flow over them with your waves and with your waters,
  Mananaan,
Mananaan MacLir (187)

—as the sea-god, engulfing them in his swirling water.
Finally, when the Hermetic high priest discloses that he
may be unable to attend a literary soirée at (George)
Moore's house that night because "We have our meeting,"
Stephen again thinks of his religious activity, this time in
terms that establish beyond a doubt the connection between
A.E. and the whirlpool in the *Odyssey*:

Yogibogeybox in Dawson chambers. *Isis Unveiled.* . . .
The faithful hermetists await the light, ripe for chelaship,
ringroundabout him. . . . Filled with his god he thrones,
Buddha under plantain. Gulfer of souls, engulfer. He-

souls, shesouls, shoals of souls. Engulfed with wailing
creecries, whirled, whirling, they bewail. (189)

In direct opposition to A.E. as he is pictured here is the
flippant blaspheming high priest of science (materialism),
who in the first chapter suggested that he and Stephen
"work together" to "Hellenise" Ireland, and whom Stephen,
so self-consciously the poet, identified as the "usurper,"
the old milk-woman's "medicineman: me she slights" (16).
Mulligan's second appearance in *Ulysses* reveals no change
in Stephen's attitude. A.E. has left, and Stephen has just
made a cryptic identification of Shakespeare with King
Hamlet and his canon with the prince:

> —Amen! responded from the doorway.
> Hast thou found me, O mine enemy?
> *Entr'acte.* (195)

Although A.E. and Mulligan are both Stephen's enemies,
they are not enemies of a similar kind. Mulligan's witty
but terribly sincere materialism was amply disclosed in the
first chapter, and the ethereal solipsism of A.E.'s religion
is treated in this; but there is another respect in which
they are opposed: the attitude of each toward the Irish
literary revival. A.E. is one of its leaders. Most of Mulligan's speeches in the chapter are concerned with ridiculing
one or another of its aspects. On page 195 he finally succeeds in identifying Shakespeare ("The chap that writes
like Synge"). To this criticism of the group's hyperbolic
self-praise he adds a parody of their "folk idiom" (197)
and a mocking use of Gaelic (203). He has a short
exchange with Stephen:

> —The tramper Synge is looking for you, he said, to
> murder you. He heard you pissed on his halldoor. . . .
> —Me! Stephen exclaimed. That was your contribution
> to literature. (197)

Leaving the library with Stephen, he mocks the Abbey
Theatre (213) and, on the same page, Lady Gregory's
"drivel" and Yeats' extravagant praise of it.

As the antipode to the "engulfer," Mulligan is analogous to Scylla, the monster on the rock, and the first fruit of the Homeric analogue is immediately apparent. In describing Scylla and Charybdis to Odysseus, Circe says:

> Never mayest thou be there when she [Charybdis] sucks the water, for none might save thee then from any bane, not even the Earth-shaker! But take heed and swiftly drawing nigh to Scylla's rock drive the ship past, since of a truth it is far better to mourn six of thy company in the ship, then all in the selfsame hour.[2]

The reason for Stephen's past association with Mulligan the monster (philosopher of "beastliness") and Mulligan's fellow medical students is that their materialism and mockery protected him from the literary parochialism and religious extravagance of the sole artistic group in Ireland at the time. In consorting with the devil he has been paying a price, but he has escaped the deep sea.

For a long time the Homeric correspondence has been seen as representing an opposition of Plato and Aristotle; in fact it represents, in Mulligan the monster on the rock of materialism and A.E. the whirlpool of mysticism, the two extremes of the Platonic scale in human conduct: the denial of spirit and the denial of matter. Nevertheless, Plato and Aristotle are opposed in the chapter, and meaningfully so.

The one time the clear-witted Eglinton loses his temper in the whole chapter is when Stephen says that Aristotle "would find Hamlet's musings about the afterlife of his princely soul . . . as shallow as Plato's" (184). Eglinton ignores the slight to the most famous soliloquy in all Shakespeare:

> —Upon my word it makes my blood boil to hear anyone compare Aristotle with Plato.
> —Which of the two, Stephen asked, would have banished me from his commonwealth? (184)

The retort is ironic, for Eglinton's group both consciously identifies itself with Plato and has excluded Stephen, as Plato would exclude the free poet from his ideal society.

Stephen just as consciously sees himself as Aristotelian. Following his retort, he tells himself, "Unsheathe your dagger definitions. Horseness is the whatness of allhorse." He mocks their theosophy: "Streams of tendency and eons they worship." (The word "eons" is also a pun on the original form of Russell's pen-name: Æon.) A few pages further on, he meditates on the existence of his soul in terms of Aristotle's *About the Soul* (187). And later in the chapter he conducts privately what he calls "Aristotle's experiment" (190).

This loose identification of Stephen's point of view and that of A.E.'s group as Aristotelian and Platonic respectively is part of the chapter's portrayal of Stephen-Odysseus as trying to navigate a safe course between the two extremes of that group's "whirlpool" and the "beastliness" of Mulligan and his "medicals." It brings into the general symbolic situation represented in the Homeric correspondence, the question which Stephen debates with himself again and again throughout the book; indeed, the existence of the soul, which Mulligan categorically denies and A.E. categorically assumes, is for Stephen on Bloomsday the fundamental point of opposition between the two.

In this chapter Stephen's debate with himself is disguised by comic punning. It is "Aristotelian," an exercise in reliance on experience and reason in order to steer a mean course between opposite excesses. He remembers that he owes A.E. a pound. Reluctant to pay it, he is not sorry to think:

> Wait. Five months. Molecules all change. I am other I now. Other I got pound.

To the materialistic assumption he opposes, not the Platonic one, but Aristotle's concept:

> But I, entelechy, form of forms, am I by memory because under everchanging forms.

This he tests by recalling snatches of experience from youth and childhood:

I that sinned and prayed and fasted.
A child Conmee saved from pandies.

Then, by means of what must be called punctuational symbolism, he poses the two alternatives:

I, I and I. I.

Because of the fact of memory, pointed out by Aristotle, he comes (temporarily) to the *rational* conclusion that the soul exists, that man is more than mere changing molecules, for his next and final thought, also in capital letters, is a catalogue of the vowels:

A.E.I.O.U. (187)

By invoking Odysseus' experience of Scylla and Charybdis, the ninth chapter represents in *Ulysses* the same two extremes of attitude between which Stephen had alternated so violently and with such futility as a boy in the *Portrait*. His debate about the soul will go on, but just as he has grown painfully beyond his self-delusions, he has grown wisely beyond his alternating commitments to the bestial and the ethereal in the world; and those antitheses are shown to have caught, together, so many of his contemporaries. His problems are much more serious now than they were in his younger days, but the contrast Joyce insists on in this respect, from both his former self and the young Dublin intellectuals around him, does him credit.

The representation of the social and intellectual situation Stephen is in, and his "Aristotelian" sagacity in dealing with it, are almost obscured in the chapter by his talk on Shakespeare. This has not progressed far when Mulligan enters the librarian's office and by completing the Homeric analogue defines Stephen's relationship to his auditors. Stephen is speaking to men hostile, not only to his argument, but to himself. And he is, if possible, more hostile to them.

After Mulligan has clowned for four pages, Bloom's search for the Keyes advertisement he must copy brings him to the office door, prompting a sample of Mulligan's uncomplicated anti-Semitism and the remark to Stephen, "He knows you. He knows your old fellow." With this, the "*entr'acte*" comes to an end, for Stephen's effort has had some effect at least.

> —We want to hear more, John Eglinton decided with Mr Best's approval. We begin to be interested in Mrs S. (198)

And his theory of Shakespeare's place in his works is an ingenious one. However, it is not a set piece, but another element in the action of the novel, and for this reason its complex argument must be examined carefully.

Stephen opposes the view, common to his audience and apparently popular at the time, that Hamlet is a self-portrait of Shakespeare. The chapter begins during one of the many interruptions he is to endure; when he resumes (and the reader is introduced to) his argument, it is in a paragraph which begins with the question, "What is a ghost?" and ends with the question, "Who is king Hamlet?" The paragraph explicitly answers the first question: a ghost is "One who has faded into impalpability through death, through absence. . . ." And it implies the answer to the second: the dead King Hamlet is Shakespeare.

Describing the premiere of *Hamlet*, with Shakespeare playing the king and Richard Burbage the prince, Stephen expands his argument:

> —Is it possible that that player Shakespeare, a ghost by absence, and in the vesture of buried Denmark, a ghost by death, speaking his own words to his own son's name (had Hamnet Shakespeare lived he would have been prince Hamlet's twin) . . . did not draw . . . the logical conclusion of those premises: you are the dispossessed son: I am the murdered father: your mother is the guilty queen, Ann Shakespeare, born Hathaway? (186-87)

Stephen's argument that Shakespeare charged his wife with adultery in the situation in *Hamlet* arouses A.E.'s protest that he is "prying," and Eglinton's more substantial observation that Shakespeare's marriage was merely a youthful, ultimately unimportant, mistake. But the charge of adultery is only part of Stephen's point. Not only had Shakespeare been ultimately betrayed by his wife, but he was seduced and overborne by her, an older woman, to begin with. In direct answer to Eglinton, Stephen argues that she must have been beautiful, and says:

> He chose badly? He was chosen, it seems to me. If others have their will Ann hath a way. By cock, she was to blame. She put the comether on him, sweet and twenty-six. (189)

This brief passage is a good example of the way in which Stephen has saturated his exposition with references to Shakespeare's works,[3] factual and apocryphal material relating to Shakespeare and Elizabethan England, and the English idiom of the time. The pun on Ann Hathaway's name is also a parody of the first verse of sonnet 135: "Whoever hath her wish, thou hast thy will." The next sentence is a line from one of Ophelia's mad songs *(Hamlet, IV, v)*, with the sex of the pronoun changed. Stephen's whole assertion relies heavily on the evidence of Ann Hathaway's age provided by her tombstone, and on parish records of their marriage and the baptism of their first child five months later.

After an interruption caused by the departure of A.E., Eglinton warns Stephen that "if you want to shake my belief that Shakespeare is Hamlet you have a stern task before you" (192), and Stephen says that the other plays present the same situation—the "unquiet father," the betrayed husband. Against the retort that the late plays "breathe another spirit," "the spirit of reconciliation," he has a brilliant rhetorical defense:

> —There can be no reconcilation, Stephen said, if there has not been a sundering. (192)

He goes on to say "look to see when and how the shadow lifts," and to talk of the lovely daughters of the protagonists (all analogous to King Hamlet in age and rank) of *Pericles,*

The Winter's Tale, and *The Tempest.* In the late plays Shakespeare did become reconciled, he says, but to his grandchild, who was at the same time a replica of the still-faithful wife he had loved when young and "His own image" (193).

At this point the librarian breaks in with some relevant bibliography. His chief subject is Frank Harris, who published a series of articles in 1898 (and a book in 1909) devoted to biographical reconstruction from Shakespeare's writings. (Joyce is being unkind to Lyster, for Harris' work is very shabby in most respects.) Harris, Lyster says, "draws for us an unhappy relation with the dark lady of the sonnets." The Quaker peacemaker is trying to compromise the issue between Stephen and the others by suggesting that Shakespeare did write of a betrayer, who, however, was not his dear wife but the court lady, Mary Fitton, whom Harris and others had identified as "the dark lady." Harris had written:

> What binds the two series [the sonnets to "W. H." and those to "the dark lady"] together is the story told in both . . . that Shakespeare first sent his friend [William Herbert, Earl of Pembroke] to the lady, most probably to plead his cause, and that she wooed his friend and gave herself to him.[4]

But all Lyster does is provide grist for Stephen's mill:

> —That may be too, Stephen said. . . . Why does he send to one who is a *buonaroba,* a bay where all men ride, a maid of honour with a scandalous girlhood, a lordling to woo for him? . . . Why? Belief in himself has been untimely killed. (194)

Developing this new aspect of his argument, Stephen speaks of the "goad" (a sort of psychological emasculation—"the tusk of the boar of *Venus and Adonis* has wounded him there where love lies ableeding") that resulted from Ann's seduction and subsequent betrayal of Shakespeare and that caused his passion for the dark lady, regarding which passion "A like fate awaits him and the two rages commingle in a whirlpool" (194),

The next paragraph follows logically this consummate depiction of Shakespeare's intense suffering and its causes (which is so reminiscent of the preceding chapter). Saying that "The poisoning and the beast with two backs that urged it king Hamlet's ghost could not know of were he not endowed with knowledge by his creator" (194), Stephen discusses Shakespeare the creator figuratively, with his creature King Hamlet as the vehicle, and comes to the conclusion that Shakespeare had devoted all his work to erasing that suffering ("the creation he has piled up to hide him from himself"), but had failed and had returned to Stratford to die, "an old dog licking an old sore." The works remain "because loss is his gain" (earlier, Stephen had said regarding Shakespeare's marriage, "A man of genius makes no mistakes. His errors are volitional and are the portals of discovery"); but as for their creator, "he passes on towards eternity . . . untaught by the wisdom he has written. . . . He is a ghost, a shadow now . . . a voice heard only in the heart of him who is the substance of his shadow, the son consubstantial with the father" (194)—in the "heart" of the works, the Shakespeare canon, child of the poet's oppressed spirit.

The "—Amen!" with which Mulligan announces his presence occurs at this point. Presumably he has refrained from interrupting Stephen's eloquent termination of one phase of his argument. When Eglinton admits that Stephen's attempt to "shake [his] belief that Shakespeare is Hamlet" has at least disturbed it by asking Stephen to fill out the details of his thesis, the *"Entr'acte"* caused by the new arrival ends, and Stephen moves toward completing his description of the conditions motivating Shakespeare's works.

Backtracking slightly, he discusses Shakespeare's "rich" life and "scortatory love," asks rhetorically what "poor Penelope in Stratford" was doing "those twenty years," and probes the second betrayal of the poet, brought up by the librarian: "the court wanton spurned him for . . . his dearmylove" (199). Eglinton pointedly refuses to recognize the allegation of homosexuality, probably intended in part for his and Best's discomfiture; but it is an aside, and is relinquished without a struggle, for Stephen is more concerned with an important new element in his thesis:

But she, the giglot wanton ["the court wanton"] did not break a bedvow. Two deeds are rank in that ghost's mind: a broken vow and the dullbrained yokel on whom her favour has declined, deceased husband's brother. (200)

At this point Stephen identifies Ann's lover in terms of the situation in *Hamlet* in order to provide another reason for Shakespeare's hatred of her. He charges that the burden of proof is with those who would deny that King Hamlet's denunciation of his widow is addressed to Ann. He offers as his chief support Shakespeare's will.

When Eglinton objects, Stephen describes Shakespeare's "sense of property" and opportunism. Following the paragraph, he tells himself, "I think you're getting on very nicely," and indeed his rhetoric is beautiful and seductive. Ironically however, at this point Eglinton challenges the powers of the speaker. Probably because of Stephen's likening of Shakespeare to Shylock, he "dares" Stephen:

—Prove that he was a jew. . . . (202)

With the aid of Aquinas on incest ("Saint Thomas . . . likens it . . . to an avarice of the emotions"), a paraphrase of the commandment against covetousness, and a subtle *non sequitur*, he meets the challenge. And Eglinton takes refuge in a categorical refusal to entertain his theory, expressing agreement with A.E.'s criticism of it as "prying": "I feel that Russell is right. What do we care for his wife and father" (204).

Eglinton's casual reference to Shakespeare's father has a dramatic effect on Stephen. First he thinks of Eglinton as denying his father—envisages the elder Magee, "a rugged rough rugheaded kern," visiting his son. Then he thinks of his own father on his return from Paris to his mother's death bed. When he speaks, it is to dismiss Shakespeare's father absolutely. It is Shakespeare who is King Hamlet the father:

If you hold that he, a greying man with two marriageable daughters . . . is the beardless undergraduate from

Wittenberg then you must hold that his seventy year old
mother is the lustful queen. No. The corpse of John
Shakespeare does not walk the night. . . . He rests, dis-
armed of fatherhood, having devised that mystical state
upon his son. (204)

And he does not stop there, but launches into a discussion
of fatherhood that has slight relevance if any to his observations on Shakespeare. He repeats an idea he had in the
schoolroom, "*Amor matris,* subjective and objective geni-
tive, may be the only true thing in life." And he balances
against this, assertions that "Paternity may be a legal
fiction," that the annals of sexual crime "stained with all
other incests and bestialities" hardly record a breach of
the "sundering" of father and son, that "The son unborn
mars beauty: born he brings pain, divides affection, increases care" (205).

At length, he relates his digression to Shakespeare—gives
his final demonstration of the identity of Shakespeare and
King Hamlet's ghost, probably the proof "by algebra" that
Mulligan spoke of in the first chapter when he told Haines
of Stephen's theory. However, he utilizes in it the Sabellian
heresy concerning the relationship of the Father and the
Son, which he had found so attractive in that chapter:

—Sabellius . . . subtlest heresiarch . . . held that the
Father was Himself His Own Son. The bulldog of Aquin
. . . refutes him. Well: if the father who has not a son be
not a father can the son who has not a father be a son?
(205)

Stephen asks how, if Aquinas is right and fatherhood cannot exist without the existence of a (discrete) son, sonhood
can exist without a (living) father. And John Shakespeare
was dead at the time of the composition of *Hamlet.* On the
other hand, if Aquinas is wrong and Sabellius right, then
Shakespeare can be father and son both, whether John
Shakespeare be alive or not.

With this Stephen has finished discussing the identity of
Shakespeare and King Hamlet and the treatment of the
poet by his wife. When he speaks next, it is to explore the

path only pointed out when he resumed his discourse following the *"Entr'acte,"* with the reference he made to "the
dullbrained yokel on whom [Gertrude-Ann's] favour has
declined, deceased husband's brother":

> —As for his family, Stephen said, his mother's name
> lives in the forest of Arden. . . . Hamlet, the black
> prince, is Hamnet Shakespeare. . . . But there is another
> member of his family who is recorded.
> —The plot thickens, John Eglinton said. (206)

Eglinton has perceived the introduction to the new phase of
Stephen's argument.   Stephen's identification of Ann's
lovers as Shakespeare's brothers Richard and Edmund
("The playhouse sausage filled Gilbert's soul. He is nowhere"), this final flagrant wrenching of Shakespeare's biography, is possible only because of what has gone before.
The assertion of Ann's adultery and that of Shakespeare's
identification of himself with the ghost have been carefully
presented. Stephen is now asserting that the analogy with
his own situation which Shakespeare created in *Hamlet*
extends to Claudius. And not until Stephen has accommo-
dated Claudius does he seem able to conclude what he has
to say about Shakespeare. It is almost as though the first
part of the speech was a prelude to this new development.
Anticipating the significance Stephen is to place on the
names "Richard" and "Edmund," Eglinton questions the
importance of characters' names and then calls Stephen's
name "strange enough." The casual remark causes Stephen
to castigate himself for the failure of his "flight" to Paris.
He calls himself "Icarus" and "lapwing," the bird whose
erratic flight is so contrasted to that of the "Fabulous artificer, the hawklike man" his name suggests and which for
the Elizabethans was the type of precociousness. (In *Hamlet,* Horatio calls Osric the fop a lapwing when Osric runs
off prematurely.) Stephen remains silent until:

> John Eglinton touched the foil.
> —Come, he said. Let us hear what you have to say of
> Richard and Edmund. You kept them for the last, didn't
> you? (208)

Again, he does not deny Eglinton's charge. He spends a few lines developing the relationship of the poet's brothers' names to the characters in the plays, and then presents the climax of the speech, his theory of the universal theme in Shakespeare:

> . . . the theme of the false or the usurping or the adulterous brother or all three in one is to Shakespeare what the poor is not, always with him. The note of banishment, banishment from the heart, banishment from home, sounds uninterruptedly from *The Two Gentlemen of Verona* onward till Prospero breaks his staff . . . and drowns his book. . . . But it was the original sin that darkened [Shakespeare's] understanding, weakened his will and left in him a strong inclination to evil. . . . an original sin and, like original sin, committed by another in whose sin he too has sinned. . . . It is in infinite variety everywhere in the world he has created, in *Much Ado about Nothing*, in *Measure for Measure*, and in all the other plays which I have not read.
> He laughed to free his mind from his mind's bondage. (209)

On the very next page Stephen ends his speech. For a few lines he talks of Shakespeare's self-torture, and then he presents his final paragraph, a well-turned conclusion the burden of which repeats the idea expressed briefly just before Mulligan announced his presence: that in all his works with all their various characters, Shakespeare was trying to hide from, but constantly coming upon, himself. Whomever we meet, we are always meeting ourselves:

> Maeterlinck says: *If Socrates leaves his house today he will find the sage seated on his doorsteps. If Judas go forth tonight it is to Judas his steps will tend.* (210)

Because God *("dio boia,* hangman god") is in all of us.

The oration completed, Mulligan is the first to speak. He shouts "Eureka!" over an idea he has had for a bawdy play *("Everyman His Own Wife or A Honeymoon in the Hand")*. It is a mockery not only of the cuckoldry and fatherhood of Shakespeare, but of: the wifeless Eglinton

and Best, young devotee of Wilde, both of whom Stephen,
Mulligan, and Joyce himself regard as homosexuals
(Stephen and Mulligan also so regard Shakespeare; Mulligan, Lyster and Bloom; and Stephen—according to his
monologue on the beach in the morning [50]—Mulligan);
of a point Stephen was trying to make about himself and
fatherhood; and even, ironically, of the expedient Bloom is
to resort to later because of his estrangement from his wife.
The attitudes of Eglinton and of Stephen are also
characteristic:

> —You are a delusion. . . . You have brought us all
> this way to show us a French triangle. Do you believe
> your own theory?
> —No, Stephen said promptly. (211)

But although the theory is less than valid, which Stephen
promptly admits, it has shown them more than a "French
triangle," which none of them perceives.

Stephen's rejection of his own elaborate and at times
impassioned speech is no summary decision. He has been
insincere throughout: at the high point just preceding Mulligan's interruption, he thought, "They list. And in the
porches of their ears I pour" (194); when congratulating
himself that he was "getting on nicely," he told himself
to "mix up a mixture" and, punning on "mix," recited the
paradigm of the Latin for "urinate" (202); when speaking
of Shakespeare's return from visits to Ann by the light of
the star that appeared at his birth, he remarked, "Don't
tell them he was nine years old when it was quenched"
(207). He has a good reason for his sophistry—he wants
to impress his "foes" with his intellectual and artistic ability. Perhaps he wants also to embarrass them, to have the
satisfaction of seeing them unable to rebut what they are
told is untrue. An hour or two earlier, hearing John F.
Taylor's speech in Myles Crawford's office, he had thought,
"Noble words coming. Look out. Could you try your hand
at it yourself?" (140). He had then created his "parable."

Actually, that was the second, and this is the third, attempt Stephen has made to create since morning. On the beach he had written the quatrain about death the vampire which is reproduced in final form in the seventh (newspaper) chapter. The change of the last line from "Mouth to her mouth's kiss" (48) to "Mouth to my mouth" (131) is significant of his state of mind; but it and other revisions also reveal that he had done little more than unconsciously plagiarize the last quatrain of "My Grief on the Sea," one of the translated Irish poems in Douglas Hyde's *Love Songs of Connacht* (1894). His "Parable" had perplexed all the "Aeolists" except Professor MacHugh. In the present chapter he characterizes Shakespeare's plays as nakedly lyrical, the purgative device of a poet troubled by "a French triangle," and his tour de force is punctured by Eglinton, who obliges him to admit his sophistry. Joyce has presented Stephen as failing as an artist, much like his younger self in the *Portrait* but for different reasons.

This fact about Stephen is significant here because of the motivations behind his Shakespeare talk. Some have been mentioned. The immediate practical one is his desire to interest Eglinton in his theory for *Dana,* the periodical Eglinton helps to edit (211). But none of these can explain his excitement or his constant self-prodding ("Folly. Persist," 183; "Come, mess," 206; "On," 209; etc.). An additional motive is suggested in the digression on the nature of fatherhood. His conclusion:

> Paternity may be a legal fiction. Who is the father of any son that any son should love him or he any son? (205)

was followed by a question put to himself and answered almost viciously:

> What the hell are you driving at?
> I know. Shut up. Blast you! I have reasons.

Apparently, Stephen was "driving at" something extraneous to Shakespeare. This something had manifested itself

in earlier parts of his speech, had in fact been with him
early in the morning. Before his first abortive attempt to
create, on the beach, he had been invited to do so twice,
once in each of the preceding chapters. In response to the
children's request for a ghost story in the second chapter
he had recited a traditional riddle that had perplexed them
as much as his "parable" had the men in the seventh chapter. When in the first chapter Haines had asked, "What is
your idea of *Hamlet?*", he had declined "listlessly" to
tell it.

However, Mulligan had been more amenable:

> It's quite simple. He proves by algebra that Hamlet's
> grandson is Shakespeare's grandfather and that he him-
> self is the ghost of his own father.
> —What? Haines said, beginning to point at Stephen.
> He himself? (19)

Mulligan's account is facetious, of course, but only to an
extent. For he then:

> . . . bending in loose laughter, said to Stephen's ear:
> —O, shade of Kinch the elder! Japhet in search of a
> father. (19)

Having heard Stephen's theory (perhaps as often as Stephen
has heard his analogous "Ballad of Joking Jesus"), and
being nothing if not shrewd, Mulligan knows that it presents Stephen's attitude toward the nature of fatherhood as
well as his attitude toward the nature of Shakespeare.
Mulligan even gives equal weight to the fatherhood theme.
And he interprets correctly (in order to mock) the point
Stephen is driven to make through his treatment of Shakespeare. What Stephen does in this chapter is to finally
deliver himself of the thesis solicited in the first chapter
and the ghost story solicited in the second ("—He will have
it that *Hamlet* is a ghoststory, John Eglinton said. . . ."
185). He asserts both points Mulligan has delineated regarding Shakespeare—that the poet is King Hamlet's ghost
and that he is his own father; and ultimately he asserts as
well the point embodied in Mulligan's ambiguous "he him-

self," the point he is "driving at," driven to make, in his compulsive digression on fatherhood—that he, Stephen Dedalus, is his own father, shade of Kinch the elder as well as Kinch, father and son in one body.

Stephen's presentation of his view has not been too successful. In the first chapter, in contrast to Stephen's diffidence, Mulligan not only stated the nub of the issue but presented his analogous "Ballad of Joking Jesus." In the present chapter, Mulligan has his sketch of a play, again a mocking version of Stephen's thesis. The others in the room will have none of that thesis; and instead of joining them to hear it, Haines has gone to a bookseller's—to buy the book containing the original of Stephen's quatrain, *The Love Songs of Connacht* (184). But convincing others of his thesis with regard to Shakespeare is far less important a motive than convincing himself of relevant aspects of it with regard to himself.

In the first chapter, Stephen's thoughts impartially entertained both the opposing heresies which deny the Sonship of Christ and the Fatherhood of God: that of "Arius, warring his life long upon the consubstantiality of the Son with the Father" and that of "the subtle African heresiarch Sabellius who held that the Father was Himself His own Son. Words Mulligan had spoken a moment since in mockery to the stranger" (22). His reference to Mulligan's richly ambiguous "he himself" of three pages before makes clear the connection between Stephen's theory about Shakespeare and the Sabellian doctrine which he finds so attractive; appropriately, the other two times that doctrine figures in the novel occur during Stephen's discourse on Shakespeare. When Mulligan makes known his presence in Lyster's office, Stephen uses the phrases "brood of mockers," and mentions "Photius" and "pseudomalachi" (195). The passage is an echo of "Photius and the brood of mockers of whom Mulligan was one" (22), the beginning of the catalogue of heretics that culminated in the references to Arius and Sabellius quoted above. Then Stephen converts the Apostles' Creed (or perhaps it is the Nicene Creed, which was formulated explicitly to oppose the Arians) into an expression of the Sabellian identification of Father and Son:

> He Who Himself begot . . . and Himself sent Himself,
> Agenbuyer, between Himself and others . . . Who let
> Him bury, stood up, harrowed hell, fared into heaven
> and there these nineteen hundred years sitteth on the
> right hand of his Own Self. . . . (195)

His caricature of his own thesis about fatherhood is a transistory weakening. When the doctrine comes up for the last time, in a passage already quoted, Stephen's "algebra" asserts that whether *either* Aquinas *or* Sabellius be right, Shakespeare by analogy had no father, and so:

> he was not the father of his own son merely but, being no
> more a son, he was and felt himself the father of all his
> race. . . . (205)

That is, he was the divinely-inspired poet, the bard revered in Irish tradition.

The first words to follow Stephen's climactic statement of Shakespeare's unique condition are spoken by Mulligan:

> —Himself his own father, Sonmulligan told himself.
> (205)

The apparent reference is to the apparent subject, Shakespeare; but plainly Stephen has been talking about himself as well, and Mulligan's words, which echo the ambiguous remark he made to Haines in the morning, point this out. Stephen had thought about himself in similar terms while on the beach. When he saw himself as King Hamlet's ghost (45), he was not only asserting that he was a spirit, possessed a soul, but was identifying himself, the troubled Prince Hamlet, as his own father. Furthermore, his conception of Shakespeare's consummate "fatherhood" as the great artist of his people reflects an assumption about himself. Eglinton's remark at the beginning of the chapter (183) comparing "Our young Irish bards" unfavorably to "Saxon Shakespeare" has ironic relevance, for Stephen audaciously identifies himself with the great poet in his mind. For example, he wonders when he too will be "overborne"

(189) and, after discussing the W configuration in the Cassiopeia constellation, asks where his own celestial configuration is (207).

If it is true that Stephen has been discussing himself as well as Shakespeare, it is equally true that he has been addressing himself as well as the others; indeed, there is no indication that any one of them except Mulligan is even aware of the personal dimension of his speech. There is also no indication that he has convinced himself. In the heat of his most radical denial of fatherhood, when he asks himself, "What the hell are you driving at?" (205), he must prod himself on, *"Amplius. Adhuc. Iterum. Postea,"* and then ask "Are you condemned to do this?" This follows by only half a page his thought of his father's kindness to him on his return from Paris:

> I touched his hand. The voice, new warmth speaking.
> . . . The eyes that wish me well. But do not know me.
> —A father, Stephen said, battling against hopelessness, is a necessary evil. (204)

The subsequent paragraphs are his battle against the hopelessness of denying one's sonship, his attempt to prove (it must be to himself) that paternity is a legal fiction, and therefore that it is possible to be, as he says of Shakespeare, "being no more a son . . . the father of all his race." The significance of this attempt becomes more clear in the light of the two other preoccupations he reveals in his speech.

Almost as prominent as his preoccupation with the matter of fatherhood is Stephen's sense of his relationship to his auditors, the relationship represented in terms of the Homeric correspondence. Clearly the basis of Stephen's safety from the "engulfment" of most of his contemporaries is what he has called "banishment," and he is acutely aware throughout the chapter that he is being spurned by those who should recognize his abilities and admit him to their "commonwealth."

The situation is not a simple one. Stephen was shown respect by the "Aeolists," and he is shown respect by the representatives of Dublin's dominant intellectual group. All except A.E. hear him out and contend with him; and A.E.'s early departure is part of the Homeric pattern, along with Mulligan's subsequent arrival and final departure in his company. He has no right to expect that Eglinton will buy from him an article based on a far-fetched thesis he himself does not accept, especially when he is "the only contributor to *Dana* who asks for pieces of silver" (211). Apparently he has written nothing which deserves inclusion in the "sheaf of our younger poets' verses" (190) that A.E. is said to be preparing (the historically important *New Songs,* a selection from the work of eight young Irish poets which A.E. edited, appeared in 1904). It can even be argued that Stephen rejects the mystical-nationalistic "whirlpool" so thoroughly that he has no right to expect to be accepted by those who are committed to it. Specifically, of its representatives in the room, he regards A.E. as the god or evil genius of the whirlpool that once threatened to engulf him, and looks on Lyster as a fool and on Best as a fool and a fop; he respects only Eglinton—whom he even flatters (204).

Nevertheless, the rudeness with which they discuss in his presence, not only A.E.'s anthology, but the literary soirée that evening, to which both members of the revival group and mockers of it like Mulligan (in fact, even the "stranger" Haines) are invited—figuratively at least, to which every literary person in Dublin except Stephen is invited—is not justified. We learn in this chapter (196) that while Mulligan and Haines were waiting in The Ship to buy drinks with Stephen's small (and last) teacher's pay, he was spending it on drinks for the guides of "Dublin's Cits," who showed him acceptance and respect even before he invited them to Mooney's tavern, although they refrained from criticizing his bewildering "parable" after he had done so.

The latter fact is as significant of Stephen's attitude as of theirs, for he did not tell the parable until after he had extended the invitation (142-43). In the present chapter when the foolish librarian, embarrassed by the rudeness of the others, detaches himself from the cluster around A.E. at the door and, "blushing," compliments Stephen on what he has been saying, Stephen is grateful (190-91). Before he does so, Stephen, sitting in isolation, regards the cluster and thinks, "See this. Remember," and, "Cordelia. *Cordoglio.* Lir's loneliest daughter" (190).

The Italian for "sorrow" associates phonetically and thematically with the reference to Cordelia, the wronged, rejected, unappreciated, and banished daughter of the king. "Lir's loneliest daughter" is a phrase from Thomas Moore's "The Song of Fionnuala." Fionnuala is the daughter of Lir, the first Tuatha de Danaan sea deity. Mananaan is her foster brother. Mananaan's mother casts Fionnuala out (turns her into a swan). "Lir" is a pun involving the Celtic deity, the parent of Cordelia, and the Gaelic *lear* or *lir,* "the sea" (actually, they are all related). The relevance of the situation of the unappreciated British king's daughter to Stephen's situation is apparent; the relevance of that of Fionnuala is similar, for another child is preferred over her, too—Mananaan, whom Stephen associated at the beginning of the chapter with A.E. The general allusion to the sea invokes the association of mother, sea, Ireland-family-Church made in the first chapter and recalls Stephen's despairing thoughts near the end of the third, while he sat before the sea:

> I am lonely here. . . . I am quiet here alone. Sad too. (49)

Stephen's disturbance about the very isolation for which he had striven is fresh in his mind when he is delivering his speech on "Shakespeare," and the extent of disturbance is manifested in the speech. Just before concluding it with his statement about the one universal theme in Shakespeare's work, he thinks:

> I am tired of my voice, the voice of Esau. (209)

The voice of the exile, denied his birthright, then goes on to say:

> The note of banishment, banishment from the heart, banishment from home, sounds uninterruptedly from *The Two Gentlemen of Verona* onward till Prospero breaks his staff, buries it certain fathoms in the earth and drowns his book. . . . It is everywhere in the world he has created. . . . (209)

If his preoccupation with the nature of paternity has dominated much of Stephen's "ghoststory," its own essential
burden is an expression of this other preoccupation. And
after stating the universal theme in Shakespeare:

> He laughed to free his mind from his mind's bondage.
> (209)

A third preoccupation to which Stephen's mind is in
bondage is that major subject of the first chapter, his
"brooding" about his mother. To complete the picture of
Stephen's condition given in this chapter, the author has
planted manifestations of his brooding in the Shakespeare
speech and in thoughts connected with it.

The first thought of his mother's death comes to him
when he is discussing Ann's prominence in Shakespeare's
life:

> . . . She bore his children and she laid pennies on his
> eyes to keep his eyelids closed when he lay on his
> deathbed.
> Mother's deathbed. . . . Who brought me into this
> world lies there, bronzelidded, under few cheap flowers.
> *Liliata rutilantium.*
> I wept alone. (188)

More interesting than his remembrance of his grief, which
he has never had explicitly before in the novel, is the unconscious association of his mother with the wronged
Shakespeare (the linking of "his deathbed" and "Mother's
deathbed," the pennies on Shakespeare's eyelids and his
mother's "bronzelidded" eyes). Once made, the association
functions infrequently—for example in Stephen's use of
the phrase, taken from Iago's speech to Brabantio in the
opening scene of *Othello*, "the beast with two backs," in
connection with Gertrude and Claudius; it concerns not
adultery but a child's disloyalty. At any rate, with this
brooding present (though he nowhere indicates awareness
of it), his repeated insistence on Shakespeare's sense of
guilt may, like almost everything else Stephen says, be
considered as in part reflexive, and "His unremitting intellect is the hornmad Iago ceaselessly willing that the moor

in him shall suffer" (210) be considered an intimation that
Stephen's own unremitting intellect will not cease from
causing the moor in him (that part of him capable of
love) to suffer.

The first major part of this chapter dealt with Stephen's
relationship to his social and intellectual peers, which the
ninth chapter of *Ulysses* represents primarily by invoking
the Scylla and Charybdis episode of the *Odyssey;* Stephen's
Shakespeare talk was reviewed in the next part; and its
revelation of Stephen's preoccupations has just been discussed. Stephen is injured by his isolation and lack of
recognition. At the same time, he strives to convince himself that he has no father, is self-contained—and therefore
is profoundly isolated. And as in the first chapter, his feelings about fatherhood exist side by side with brooding
about his disobedience to his mother on her death bed.

It was pointed out in that chapter that the word "mother"
has symbolic as well as literal meaning; and the suggestion
was made there that the same is true of "father." As Simon
Dedalus is presented, he is not sufficient reason for Stephen
to question the principle of fatherhood by means of heresies
concerning the relationship of Christ and God, or of theories
concerning the relationship of Shakespeare and the two
Hamlets. The complementary terms "mother" and "father"
are metaphors. And they are metaphors, not for contrasting
things, but for contrasting attitudes toward the same thing.

In his conversation with Cranly at the end of the *Portrait,*
the dedicated poet, a year and a few months younger than
on Bloomsday, discussed his refusal to obey his mother's
wish that he do his Easter Duty, announced that he would
"fly" from Ireland, and then made some bold declarations,
the first of which was: "I will not serve that in which I
no longer believe, whether it call itself my home, my fatherland or my church" (p. 247). That which formed Stephen,
from which he derived, but in which he tried and still
tries to no longer believe—whose claim (and mark) on him
he so vigorously attempts to deny, "whether it call itself
. . . home . . . fatherland or . . . church"—he thinks of
in paternal terms, as the manifestations of his "father." But

as she is treated in *Ulysses*, Stephen's mother represents his family ("home"); identified with Dublin Bay, she represents Ireland; supremely devout, she represents the Church. And growing out of this, on a different level, she represents God's love.

Just as Stephen's guilt is not caused merely by disloyalty to the late wife of Simon Dedalus, his attempt to deny the paternal relationship is not aimed merely at the genial Simon himself. Furthermore, the correspondence between the two terms is complete. While "mother" represents God as love, "father" represents God as authority; and Stephen's "I will not serve . . ." is in part a *Non serviam!* which is rooted more in the indignation of a Blake or an Ivan Karamazov than in the pride of a Lucifer, and is directed at a Deity (*"dio boia,* hangman god") whom Stephen accused in the second chapter of responsibility for the "nightmare" of war and suffering that is history—a God he acknowledges but cannot worship. He denies not the existence but the claim. Thus, we learn at the beginning of the present chapter, he would rewrite *Paradise Lost* as *The Sorrows of Satan*. He asserts (and later he will actually use Blake's term) that the Father of us all is really "Nobodaddy," not even the Father of the Son—that "A *lex eterna* stays about Him" (39). In associating himself with Shakespeare, he assumes the semi-deification ("After God Shakespeare has created most," 210), as well as the freedom from external paternity, of "the father of all his race."

That Stephen's attempt to deny his "father" is a conscious "battling against hopelessness" has been pointed out. It is ultimately an attempt to deny his descent from God, and the final sentence of his Shakespeare talk is his statement of defeat:

> The playwright who wrote the folio of this world . . . the lord of things as they are whom the most Roman of catholics call *dio boia,* hangman god, is doubtless all in all in all of us. . . . (210)

Stephen must acknowledge that he is the child of God just as he must acknowledge that he is the child of his family, church, and country. He *can* not deny any aspect of the "father" he *will* not serve. And his continual "brooding" has been caused by feelings of guilt toward and love for these very same loyalties—focussed in terms of his mother. The respective parents represent his conflicting attitudes toward family, country, faith, all of which are manifestations of God himself.

With the clarification of Stephen's contradictory attitudes, the question implicit throughout *Ulysses* is also clarified: what is he doing in Dublin, in circumstances of poverty and hostility, circumstances in which he cannot work, when he should logically "fly" again to Paris (in his speech he had drawn the analogy: Stratford is to London as Dublin is to Paris)—that is, go to a place beyond the "nets" set to ensnare him? Why, in terms of the chapter under discussion, does he make his speech about Shakespeare at all? This, of course, is the basic problem that confronts Stephen, and it is directly analogous to Bloom's basic problem. Flight in order to be able to create his work is to the artist Stephen what conjugal reunion in order to be able to recreate himself is to the man Bloom.

Stephen is too intelligent and too self-conscious not to understand his problem, and he confronts himself with it explicitly in the present chapter. At that interruption in his speech when he castigates himself for being a "lapwing," he goes on to say:

Speech, speech. But act. Act speech.
They mock to try you. Act. (208)

Ironically (doubly so because Lyster is unable to perceive it when it is revealed), the speech of the librarian which begins the chapter, in which he paraphrases from Goethe's *Wilhelm Meister*, is stating Stephen's condition before Stephen has revealed it:

A hesitating soul taking arms against a sea of troubles, torn by conflicting doubts, as one sees in real life. (182)

Stephen is no delicate vase like Goethe's Hamlet, but he too is beleaguered by his sea of troubles. He has stayed

out of the reach of the whirlpool, has been able to endure
the monster on the rock. But he must go past them, as
Odysseus did—must, as he tells himself and as Hamlet
also tells himself, "act." It is in this respect that the two
bodies of allusive reference in the chapter unite with the
literal narrative; straddled by enemies, required to act
(sail past them, fly by them), Stephen combines the situations of both Odysseus and Hamlet in his own. How does
he fare? Like Hamlet (and in contrast to Odysseus!), he
reads *"au livre de lui-même,"* talks instead of acting in
the face of his problem.

The three declarations which a younger and more brash
Stephen made to Cranly at the end of the *Portrait* clearly
have not been lived up to. He has not successfully cut
himself away from "home," "fatherland," and "church";
he has not exiled himself and has distinctly not remained
silent; and he fears exactly what he thought he did not
fear ("I do not fear to be alone or to be spurned for
another or to leave whatever I have [i.e., whatever he would
be reluctant] to leave"). He does not leave Dublin because
of fear of loneliness, because of distress over rejection,
because of guilt about disloyalty to everything he thinks
of as his mother, because of the inability to convince himself that these same things have no claim on him. And he
talks in a vain attempt "to free his mind from his mind's
bondage." Thus the three themes of his speech: banishment from his home, independence of his "father," guilt
regarding his "mother" (Shakespeare's cuckoldry, auto-
paternity, and sinning). The paean of "Welcome, O life!
I go to encounter for the millionth time . . . " at the very
end of the *Portrait* is the last part of a diary entry the
rest of which reads:

> April 26. Mother is putting my new secondhand clothes
> in order. She prays now, she says, that I may learn
> in my own life and away from home and friends what
> the heart is and what it feels. Amen. So be it. (p. 253)

His mother's prayer and his supporting invocation have
been answered.

As the chapter moves to a close, Stephen and Mulligan are leaving together, Stephen submitting to the company of his enemy with silent rancor:

Life is many days. This will end (212)

Jest on (213)

Offend me still. Speak on. (215)

Mulligan has invited Stephen to accompany him with a characteristically knowing remark:

Come, Kinch. Come, wandering Aengus of the birds. (212)

Angus was the son of the Dagda, supreme god among the Tuatha de Danaan. The birds of inspiration were said to fly about his head. However, there is a "Mad Sweeney of the birds" in Irish legend. Furthermore, the most familiar element in the Angus mythology is his long search for his ideal mate, who appeared to him in a dream: she was a changeling, and became a swan before his eyes; whereupon he changed into a swan and flew away with her and her retinue of white birds. The phrase "wandering Aengus" and the fact that Stephen has not been able to become a bird and fly away as the prince of the Sidhe had done indicate that Mulligan is mocking Stephen for wishing to be like the hero of the myth but actually being like Yeats' version of him in the poem "The Song of Wandering Aengus," in which Angus spends his whole life wandering in a fruitless search for the girl (who is not a bird but a silver trout).

Standing on the steps of the library, Stephen elucidates Mulligan's remark: "Here I watched the birds for augury. Aengus of the birds." His reference is to the situation in the *Portrait* that precedes the talk with Cranly, in which he stood on those steps watching birds and misread out of their coming and going an augury of "flight." On this day, however, there are "No birds," only two plumes of smoke; and so he tells himself "Cease to strive," and the chapter comes to a quiet close with a passage from the conclusion of *Cymbeline* which alludes to the smoke of homage to the gods. As the preceding chapter does for Leopold Bloom, this chapter reveals the manner and extent of Stephen Dedalus' suffering, and the nature and source of its causes. And as is true with respect to Bloom, the rest of *Ulysses* develops what is presented here.

The conclusion of Stephen's ordeal in the library is much more complex (and positive) than he himself seems to realize—in part because of the appearance on the scene of Mister Bloom. Stephen suffers the attacks of the monster on the rock, still unable to "act," to escape past him. His "Cease to strive," however, is fatalistic rather than submissive: he again looks for birds to repeat the situation that first inspired him to depart, and he awaits that (birds or whatever) which will liberate him: "That lies in space which I in time must come to, ineluctably" (214).

His attitude is not necessarily foolish. As he is leaving the library, Bloom causes him to step away from Mulligan— passes between them; and it is then that he is impelled to think:

> Part. The moment is now. Where then? . . . Why? That lies in space which I in time must come to, ineluctably. (214)

In the sixth chapter Bloom had seen Stephen from the funeral car; in the seventh he had interrupted the progress of Stephen and the "Aeolists" to Mooney's in order to speak to Myles Crawford; in the present chapter he appeared at the door of the librarian's office and was spoken of and linked to Stephen (and to Stephen's father) by Mulligan: "He knows you. He knows your old fellow" (198). Having come closer and closer to it, Stephen now has his first encounter with Bloom. And, although he decides to wait for the fated "ineluctable" circumstance, this encounter initiates an important revelation about that circumstance. As Bloom is passing between him and Mulli-

gan, Stephen makes his fatalistic statement; when Bloom
has done so, he recalls that he had "watched" the birds
"for augury" on those steps, and he thinks of the dream
which he had first recalled in the morning, while on the
beach:

> They go, they come. Last night I flew. Easily flew. Men
> wondered. Street of harlots after. A creamfruit melon
> he held to me. In. You will see. (215)

In his earlier recollection, Stephen had asked:

> After he [Haines] woke me up last night same dream
> or was it? (47)

Apparently the dream of the Levantine man ("Haroun al
Raschid" in the third chapter, "he" in this one) which
followed Stephen's awakening during the preceding night
was the remainder of a dream in the first part of which
Stephen actually "flew"; and this dream of deliverance
was interrupted by Haines' nightmare involving a panther.
Bloom is likened to a panther here: "A dark back went
before them. Step of a pard . . . " (215). In the third
chapter Stephen associated the panther with the "beastly"
canines, the dog and the fox; but the panther is also a
traditional symbol for Christ. Mulligan's remarks, again
amazingly knowing, associate with and clarify Stephen's
dream. Though he thinks Bloom's interest homosexual
("He is Greeker than the Greeks"), he speaks the truth:

> Did you see his eye? He looked upon you to lust after
> you. . . . O, Kinch, thou art in peril. Get thee a breech-
> pad. (215)

The last word ironically reveals the way in which Bloom
will really "lust after" Stephen. A child is generally
"breeched" by his father. Stephen fails to recognize the
augury he so wishes for or its verification by the mock-
prophet, even though his "Hast thou found me, O mine
enemy?" on Mulligan's arrival at Lyster's office associated

Mulligan with Elijah;[5] he thinks "Offend me still. Speak on." To the reader, however, who knows a great deal about both principal characters at this point in the novel, the chapter has in one sense been moving toward this encounter; and to the reader the episode on the library steps suggests that the deliverance which Stephen fatalistically awaits, his redeeming "flight," will somehow be related to Bloom's "leading" him and extending an invitation to him.

Although Stephen has gone to great pains in this chapter to associate himself with fathers, Joyce has built up a quite different pattern. For the paradigm at the heart of the chapter—of exiled husband, lost wife, troubled son, and hated usurper or usurpers, exemplified by Odysseus, Penelope, Telemachus, and the suitors in the case of the *Odyssey*, by King Hamlet, Gertrude, Hamlet, and Claudius in the case of *Hamlet*, by Shakespeare, Ann, Hamnet, and Shakespeare's brothers in the case of Stephen's theory—is also manifestly exemplified by Bloom, Molly, Stephen, and Boylan. Stephen's similarity to Hamlet has been discussed. His theory helps Joyce invoke his own association of Bloom and Shakespeare. (Both were overborne by their wives; both were then cuckolded; each lost his only son when a child; Bloom has a daughter, Shakespeare two daughters; and so on.) And Bloom is all the other fathers as well. He has been Odysseus, and Mulligan calls him "Greek"; being Shakespeare, he is King Hamlet; and being Shakespeare, he is the one greater Creator and Father, who like Bloom and Shakespeare "would be bawd and cuckold" if "the economy of heaven" permitted it (210).

Of course, the parallel cannot be pushed too far. Although Bloom knows Stephen's father, will desire to breech Stephen, and is the true analogue to all the fathers with whom Stephen has been trying to associate himself, Stephen is not Bloom's son; also, Stephen is faithful to his mother and not, like the prince of Denmark, to the ghost of his father. Nevertheless, this pattern of analogy links up with and confirms the meaning of the things that occur on the steps of the National Library: Stephen's encounter with Bloom, Mulligan's "augury," and Stephen's remembered dream. Bloom is to "lust after" Stephen in the future, effect a quasi-paternal relationship with him, and thereby somehow provide the means of his deliverance. It is Bloom's action that Stephen fatalistically awaits.

The little episode at the library entrance over, Stephen's role in the subsequent action of the novel—and much of Bloom's—defined, their potential meaning to each other represented, the characters follow each other "down [the steps], out by the gateway," "*exeunt*," and the first part of *Ulysses* comes to an end.

joyce's dublin and dublin's joyce

Following Joyce's death the British Broadcasting Corporation solicited the participation of Dr. Richard I. Best, of Dublin, senior professor in the School of Celtic Studies of the Dublin Institute of Advanced Studies and retired director of the National Library, in a program it was preparing about the writer. Purportedly, Best said, "What makes you think *I* have any connection with this man Joyce";[6] the B.B.C. representatives responded, "But you can't deny your connection. After all, you're a character in *Ulysses*"; and Best said indignantly, "I am not a character in fiction. I am a living being."[7] *James Joyce's Dublin*[8] is the title of a book that considers Joyce's work as a record of the Dublin of his experience; *Dublin's Joyce*[9] is the title of a book that considers his experience of Dublin as a motive of his work. Between them they represent the gamut of possibilities regarding a difficult but important question: What is the relationship between James Joyce's art and the precise historicity out of which that art is so largely made? That question must be considered in this study because *Ulysses* is the most extreme example of his method (if method it is, for the word begs the question).

Ulysses is not merely a *roman à clef*, but a work of seemingly compulsive historical preciseness. The public events of June 16, 1904, that enter into it are all documented in the Dublin newspapers of that day,[10] and the public figures mentioned are apparently real persons. Furthermore, almost all the scores of minor characters are named for, or modeled on, or composites of, actual Dubliners; Richard Ellmann points out that even the dog Garryowen, companion of Bloom's antagonist in the twelfth chapter (Kiernan's), "was not made up of stray barks and bites, but belonged to the father of Joyce's Aunt Josephine Murray, whom Gerty MacDowell accurately identifies (346) as 'Grandpapa Giltrap.' "[11] Joyce freely admitted what he had done,[12] and on at least one occasion admitted it to one of his subjects: an extant letter to Mr. Alfred Bergan, his father's closest friend, states, "You are in this book by name with so [?] many others of Pappie's friends."[13] Even the English barber's letter of application for a job of hanging, which Bergan displays in the twelfth chapter and which is so central there, is based on a true experience of Bergan's which Joyce remembered from his boyhood.[14]

These and similar facts about *Ulysses* seem to signify no more than an extreme case of a writer's exploiting his experience. And Joyce implied a practical purpose in his use of real materials when he told one colleague[15] "that many of the characters in *Ulysses* had been friends of his father whom he had a good chance of studying closely and whose conversation he noted." However, the extent of the novel's historicity is too great to be explained on practical grounds.

In the second chapter (school), Stephen compiles a list of his debts which includes among his creditors not only "Russell" and "Mulligan" but "McCann" of the *Portrait*, and such real people who never appear and are never mentioned in any of Joyce's works, either *in propria persona* or under pseudonyms, as (C. P.) "Curran" and "Mrs McKernan." That list is largely if not wholly one of Joyce's own debts on June 16, 1904,[16] to A. E., Oliver St. John Gogarty, Francis Skeffington (the models for Mulligan and McCann), and others. Stephen says that he owes the unidentified "Mrs McKernan," "five weeks' board"; and Stanislaus Joyce's diary records that for a few days in June, 1904, his brother slept elsewhere than in his rented room at the house of a family named McKernan—until he found sufficient money to make a token payment on his rent in arrears.[17]

A memoir by one of Joyce's closest friends provides more extensive evidence of this compulsive historical preciseness. John Francis Byrne's *Silent Years*[18] not only confirms a fact that has long been recognized, that he is the model for Cranly in the *Portrait*, but also discloses the sources of elements in *Ulysses*, in which novel Cranly does not appear. The pedantic narrator of the seventeenth chapter describes every action of Bloom and Stephen on their way to Bloom's house. When they arrive, Bloom discovers that he has forgotten his key and gains entrance by climbing down to the kitchen, which is on the basement level. Byrne's memoir reveals that 7 Eccles Street was his address in Dublin at the time of the novel. It recounts precisely how he and Joyce walked the streets of Dublin and then gained entrance to his house, and concludes:

> Joyce narrates in minute detail our arrival at the hall door of number 7 Eccles Street; my belated discovery that I had forgotten my key; my dropping over the railing to enter by the area door, and my reappearance as I opened the hall door.[19]

"Joyce" also narrates the precise location of the weighing scale, only mentioned by Byrne, which was used by the pairs of men in life and fiction. And while Byrne's description of his house shows that it is reproduced accurately in *Ulysses*, the novel presents a detail of it overlooked by him. When Bloom goes from his kitchen to his front door to admit Stephen, the pedantic narrator of the chapter says that "The glimmer of his candle was discernible through the semitransparent semicircular glass fanlight over the halldoor" (653). According to *James Joyce's Dublin*, one of the sons of Joyce's aunt Mrs. William Murray "Used to be sent out to verify whether a certain fanlight was in colored glass or plain!"[20] Finally, there is one element in Joyce's compulsive verisimilitude which Byrne could not have been aware of, for it concerned precisely the difference between himself, the historical source, and Bloom, the fictional product, in the episode in question. In a letter to his aunt, Joyce first thanked her for information provided and then asked:

> Is it possible for an ordinary person to climb over the railings of number 7 Eccles Street either from the path or the steps, lower himself from the lower part of the railings till his feet are within two feet or three of the ground and drop unhurt [?] I saw it done myself but by a man of rather athletic build.[21]

A passage from Joyce's student essay on James Clarence Mangan, quoted in the discussion of the *Portrait* at the end of Chapter One, asserts that "so long as this place in nature is given us, it is right that art should do no violence to that gift." And the suggestion that that is a statement of principle is borne out by the more interesting of two accounts Oliver Gogarty gives of his second meeting with Joyce. He tells of having come upon a young man in the National Library who was intently applying compasses to a map. Recognizing Joyce, whom he'd met "some months before," he greeted him; Joyce's response was, "From Ushant to Scilly is more than thirty-five leagues." Whereupon, Gogarty noticed that the map was one of the English Channel, and Joyce sang the first "verse" of a sea chanty, "Then," Gogarty relates:

> with his voice filling and his finger beating time and, as it were, admonishing me, he continued
>
> We'll rant and we'll roar like true British sailors;
> We'll rant and we'll roar across the salt seas,
> Until we strike soundings in the Channel of England;
> From Ushant to Scilly is thirty-five leagues.
> It's forty.[22]

Joyce's admonition was subsequently made explicit, for Gogarty quotes him elsewhere as saying, "Don't exaggerate.

Tell the truth." And Joyce's terse observation on the sea chanty was literary criticism. He was saying that the poem is defective because it distorts incontrovertible fact.

Joyce spoke of having read every line of four writers all of whom are distinguished by their faithfulness to reality (although they did not always write in the realistic mode): Defoe, Flaubert, Ben Jonson, and Ibsen.[23] It would be simple to say that he early adopted as a primary guiding principle of his art the greatest possible verisimilitude; that he began with *Stephen Hero* or the stories of *Dubliners* to realize in practice this classical (Aristotelian) principle of holding "the mirror up to nature"; and that in *Ulysses* he achieved its full realization. But artistic principle does not quite explain his concern that a particular Dublin areaway be negotiable by a perfectly normal, but not young and athletic, man; it does not explain the "numerous truncated references" in the novel to real "material which [Joyce] does not intend to explain," mentioned and given the name "blurred margin" by Richard Ellmann;[24] and it seems hardly relevant to Stephen's list of debts and creditors.

That list suggests one motive for Joyce's practice other than the objective belief that the artist should "tell the truth": the creation of autobiography. A third motive is suggested by the high value placed on the created world in the statement quoted from the essay on Mangan: reverence for that creation, for reality. Both of these possibilities demand careful examination.

The inspiration for some of the most absurd speculations about autobiographical statement in Joyce's fiction is the distinction Stephen makes, during his discourse on art in Chapter V of the *Portrait*, between the lyric, the epic, and the dramatic forms of art (pp. 214-15). It was only a decade ago that the critics who variously fitted Joyce's canon (in some cases including works written after the *Portrait*) into Stephen's categories were taken to task. An essay entitled "Joyce's Categories"[25] pointed out what was mentioned near the beginning of the discussion of "Style in *Ulysses*"—that Stephen's statement "Art necessarily divides itself into three forms progressing from one to the next" is concerned not with genres but, as the word "progressing" suggests, with high art and the process that creates it. A work of art begins in subjective expression, "a lyrical cry or cadence." Even a small talent can develop this to the mediate form Stephen calls "epical." But high art is achieved when a work is made itself, an autonomous whole thing; in his words, "The dramatic form is [then] reached."

The essay quite rightly reproves critics, not only for their misreading, but also for predisposing themselves to it by too readily identifying Stephen and his creator—by assuming autobiographical purpose on Joyce's part.[26] Ironically, however, recently published evidence about the young Joyce reveals that this sophisticated refutation of the popular treatment of the passage as the vehicle of such purpose is not sophisticated enough. "A Portrait of the Artist," the autobiographical essay quoted from in the discussion of the *Portrait* above (and rejected for *Dana* by editor John Eglinton, who did in fact accept some of Joyce's poems), although painfully egotistical in both style and substance, is plainly the first "form" of the work that became *Stephen Hero* and then the *Portrait*. In other words, Stephen's delineation of three forms of art refers to Joyce's canon after all; for Joyce's work of art about the young Dubliner who aspires to be an artist "progressed" through the form of a lyrical declamation and that of a naturalistic memoir before, as the result of a decade of maturation and work, *A Portrait of the Artist as a Young Man* was finally "reached."

The place of autobiography in *Ulysses* cannot really be discussed adequately until precisely what happens in the novel has been established. But although it is difficult to accept the extreme proposition that "nothing has been admitted into the book which is not in some way personal and attached,"[27] the example of Stephen's discourse on the forms of art in Joyce's earlier novel makes plain the extent to which his creative power might have enabled him to secrete autobiographical statement in functional elements of his later one.

One of the most bizarre facts about Joyce's mature years is his expressed desire that a radically different writer, James Stephens, take over *Finnegans Wake* if he should give it up or die before finishing it. And the reasons for his choice are more bizarre still: he carried photographs of the portraits by Patrick Tuohy of his father, himself, and Stephens; Stephens' name combined his first name and that of "my hero in [the *Portrait*]"; Stephens was born in Dublin, and on the day that he himself was born.[28] Joyce's subsequent feeling of identification with the Irish tenor John Sullivan was based on less dramatic coincidences, but was almost as strong.[29] In both cases he was expressing an attitude that is surprisingly foolish for a man of such intellectual power, unless he was applying rigorously the orthodox belief that a divine intelligence governs the world. If that were so, then coincidence was for him not accident but conjunction. His full commitment to this belief would explain his well-known superstitiousness, and his constant pointing out of coincidences to friends.[30] And his commitment would explain such seeming coyness as the picture Padraic Colum reports having seen in his Paris apartment of the city of Cork, framed in cork.

What these facts of Joyce's life suggest, then, is that correspondences of various kinds (even in language—puns and portmanteau words) are so prominent in his later work for more than functional literary reasons, that his art expressed his conviction about the nature of reality: it is ordered, things are meaningfully related. Even if one limits speculation to *Ulysses*, whether or not this is truly the case is a question best deferred until the book itself has been discussed; but the possibility provides the third feasible motive for Joyce's extreme historical preciseness: adherence to an artistic principle of verisimilitude; the creation of autobiography; a belief that the world, reality, is sacred.

Even if the motives for it are difficult to fix, Joyce's compulsive historicity is a simple enough proposition to assimilate as a fact. Unfortunately, compulsive as it is, it is not a consistent fact. Joyce violates history; furthermore, he sometimes violates it gratuitously. The English barber whose letter of application to Alfred Bergan for a job of hanging was mentioned above is given the name of a man against whom Joyce had a grievance.[31] There are other examples of this sort of caprice; and while many people represented in the novel are given their own names, some, without apparent reason, are not. However, the capricious violations of history in the novel are not exten-sive. And most violations of it are absolutely functional.

Of course, by definition a work cannot be both fiction and history; and there was no real Leopold Bloom even in the sense that there was a real Stephen Dedalus. Yet in what sense was there a real Stephen Dedalus? For Joyce deviated from particular historical facts in the case of Stephen, and in many other respects; and he did so for functional reasons.

Where he made up his story of Bloomsday out of whole cloth, there is no definable relationship between Joyce's Dublin and Dublin's Joyce. Where he recorded history faithfully, even compulsively, as his story, the relationship is plain, although his motives are difficult to fix. Where he incorporated history with capricious distortion no consider-ation is possible.[32] But where Joyce made up his story out of history, transmuted fact purposefully in the creation of fiction, there will be found the greatest and most valuable part of whatever answer exists to the question so important for *Ulysses* which was posed at the beginning of this dis-cussion: "What is the relationship between James Joyce's art and the precise historicity out of which that art is so largely made?"

One such transmutation of fact is neither unusual nor very significant. Like many other novelists, Joyce com-bined in his important characters qualities of different people he knew. Bloom's similarities to Joyce himself were pointed out in the discussion of "Mr. Leopold Paula Bloom" in Chapter Two. The indignation J. F. Byrne expresses in *Silent Years* over Joyce's apparent use of him as a model for the middle-aged Jewish cuckold as well as the model for Stephen's young crony is largely wasted; but the extent to which Joyce exploited a nocturnal walk with Byrne and visit to his house was suggested above, and some similarities between Bloom and Byrne, as he appears in his auto-biography, do exist. Joyce went beyond himself and Byrne; for example, his father worked as an advertising solicitor for the *Freeman's Journal*,[33] and had a son who died in infancy, and whose death affected him greatly,[34] before the author, his oldest surviving child, was born.

Although this kind of transmutation of history is conventional, it is worth noting because Joyce has in fact imposed on his unconventional, extreme historicity precisely the same, and a similar humble, transmutation in most of the important elements in the novel. This can best be shown by a consideration of that aspect of historical reality to the use of which he was most plainly committed—himself when young. He gave Bloom certain of his own youthful as well as later characteristics and attitudes; in fact, Mr. Deasy's efforts on behalf of Irish cattle were his own, and even the shabby old bigot of the twelfth chapter (Kiernan's), "the citizen," echoes some statements he made in political articles; but his commitment is really embodied, of course, in the most prominent character in his fiction.

The two examples of Joyce's use of fact in connection with Stephen Dedalus that will be discussed are two central elements of *Ulysses*: Stephen's refusal to pray for his dying mother, and his character.

Regarding the first of these, Stanislaus Joyce wrote in his short "memoir":

> Here I am pleased to demolish a legend. I have read in certain articles on Joyce that his dying mother begged her son to kneel and pray for her, and that Joyce refused. The episode happened otherwise. The order, a peremptory one, came from an uncle and went unheeded. His mother, by that time, was no longer conscious.[35]

However, he went on to point out that Joyce felt guilty about his religious differences with his mother; and Byrne's account of a conversation with Joyce about a contention between mother and son in which "The point at issue . . . was her wish that he would make his Easter duty, and his refusal to do so,"[36] reveals a good reason for Joyce's guilt.

In the conversation between Stephen and Cranly near the end of the *Portrait*, which is plainly based on this real event, Cranly asks Stephen about his mother's age and Stephen replies that she is "not old." At the end of the novel, on April 27, 1903, Stephen "flew" to Paris. Only a few weeks later, the reader learns in *Ulysses*, he had been

recalled to Dublin by his father's telegram, his mother had
asked him to pray for her, he had refused, and she had
died. *Ulysses* discloses that she was already buried two
months after his "flight": "interment . . . 26 June 1903"
(680).

Joyce reached Paris on December 3, 1902, and remained
until the morning after the night of April 10, 1903 (Good
Friday), when his father's telegram had arrived.[37] His
own stay, therefore, not only was much longer than Stephen's
five or six weeks but ended before Stephen's began. This
is significant because the question of Joyce's own Easter
duty arose not before his "flight" to Paris, but after he
was summoned back; although his mother lingered on for
a few months, he had been called to her deathbed, and
Byrne describes his decision as a "refusal to comply with
what he knew was practically her dying wish."[38]

By altering the chronology of actual historical events
when incorporating them in his fiction, Joyce eliminated
from the issue of the Easter duty presented in the last
chapter of the *Portrait* any question about Stephen's
mother's health. His young man's antagonism toward religion and filial disobedience were what he wanted to present
there, and a dying mother would have complicated the
issue and would even have blunted the conclusion of the
novel, for she would not have fitted with Stephen's vain-
glorious "flight."

James Joyce did not refuse his dying mother's request
for prayer in behalf of her soul, he refused an uncle's
command after she had lost consciousness. However, as
Byrne points out, he did something equivalent when he
refused to make his Easter duty.

Because of his artistic purpose in the *Portrait,* Joyce
completely suppressed the vital fact of his mother's condition when he adapted his and Byrne's discussion of the
Easter duty matter to that novel. And for the same reason,
he employed in *Ulysses* the effect upon him of that vital
fact, his feeling of guilt, by transferring to his character's
mother an action of his own uncle.

Joyce's transmutation of reality in his characterization
of Stephen was the product of a similar flexibility, and was
dedicated to the same purpose. There can be no doubt of

the fact of a relationship between Stephen and his creator. In their homes, their schools, the significant incidents in their lives, in virtually all external circumstances, Joyce depicted his own young life. As a young child, he had been "baby tuckoo,"[39] and he had been told (by Mr. Vance, the father of the real Eileen, not by Dante Conway, the real Dante) that if he did not apologize, "the eagles will come and pull out his eyes," and had chanted "Pull out his eyes, / Apologise";[40] and the connections are no less close in Stephen's subsequent experiences.

However, although this is true about the external circumstances of the lives of creator and creature, although Joyce himself expressed feelings about the Church, Irish nationalism, the artist, and other things, which were essentially identical with Stephen's, and although Joyce at the time of *Ulysses* was the rowdy companion of medical students, dressed himself as Stephen does in the novel, carried an "ashplant," and signed private letters and his first three published *Dubliners* stories "Stephen Daedalus," the relationship between history and fiction is by no means a direct one. It is true that the critics of the recent past, who discredited the simple identification of Joyce and Stephen which had been so common for so long by showing that Joyce had perspective on his character, dealt with the identification of Stephen and the older author who wrote the *Portrait* and *Ulysses*, not with that of Stephen and the Joyce who had been Stephen's contemporary. Yet that young man was no more simply Stephen Dedalus than was the mature Joyce Stephen Dedalus grown older.

Certain discrepancies of fact between the portrayal of Stephen and Joyce's own life may seem at first glance trivial; for example, Stanislaus Joyce's book about his own and the author's early years, *My Brother's Keeper*, says of the schoolboy Joyce's career at Clongowes:

> Even in sport he distinguished himself. When . . . he left Congowes, we had at home a sideboard full of cups and a "silver" (electroplate) teapot and coffee pot that he had won in the school hurdles and walking events.[41]

But a moment's consideration makes it plain that young Stephen Dedalus could not have been the "boy amongst

boys"[42] described here—that the seemingly trivial discrep-
ancy of fact is the manifestation of a fundamental discrep-
ancy of character, and that that is why it exists. A similar
suppression:

> My brother was very fond of swimming, too. He was
> a splashy swimmer but fast. Over a short distance he
> could beat his burly friend Gogarty . . . [43]

has a complicating element. Not only would Joyce's own
love of swimming have been incongruously athletic, but
he invests the attitude toward water of his "unwashed bard"
with symbolic meaning.

As might be expected, Joyce's physical robustness did
not exist in isolation. His brother speaks of him as one

> who in boyhood and youth was of such a cheerful and
> amiable disposition that in the family circle he was given
> the nickname . . . of "Sunny Jim."[44]

Of the fully-grown young man, he says:

> If the Dedalus of *Ulysses* were intended to be a self-
> portrait, it would be a very unflattering one. In tempera-
> ment he was as unlike that figure, mourning under the
> incubus of remorse, as he could well be. He had a lively
> sense of humour and a ready laugh.[45]

And he says that Yeats told Joyce, during his stopover in
London on his way to Paris in 1902, "that he had never
met anybody, except William Morris, in whom he felt the
joy of life to be so keen."[46]

The significance of this difference in temperament is
great. Unlike the young Stephen, Joyce took his family's
increasingly straitened circumstances in stride. Padraic
Colum retells an account Joyce gave him of one of the
family's many moves forced by no longer patient landlords:

> Joyce's own part in this particular removal was the
> carrying of two family portraits, one under each arm;
> I can imagine his humming an Italian air as the family
> deployed in the moonlight.[47]

Colum's image of Joyce echoes significantly a description Stanislaus Joyce gives of their father on such occasions, walking behind the moving van, "lilting to himself one of his songs"; Stanislaus goes on to say:

> In all these movings he used to make a great to do about the family pictures. . . . Later at Trieste and in Paris my brother, too, following him in this, set great store upon them.[48]

Joyce "followed" his father not only in that but in many things. Like John Joyce, the writer was a spendthrift, a heavy drinker, a low-life; like him, he had gaiety, wit, and a love of song; above all, like him, he had a robust joy in living and sense of humor about life. So it is not surprising that Joyce's attitude toward his father was very different from the embittered hostility and contempt Stephen Dedalus felt for Simon Dedalus. For example, like Stephen Dedalus, Joyce accompanied his father when he went to sell his property in Cork. Stanislaus Joyce writes:

> My brother accompanied my father on a few rare trips out of Dublin, and seemed to enjoy travelling with him. At least he went willingly. . . . In *A Portrait of the Artist*, the visit [to Cork] . . . awakens in Stephen a raw sense of unrest and spiritual discomfort, but my brother's letters home at the time were written in a tone of amusement even when he described going from one bar to another.[49]

Joyce simply did not have Stephen's feelings "even" about bar-hopping—or about his father. And Joyce's solicitous affection for his father (which was reciprocated, and which never changed) extended to his whole family.[50]

The differences between Stephen and Joyce that have been discussed are not intellectual but temperamental. Joyce's writings and pronouncements when a young man prove that he shared Stephen's attitudes; they, and the testimony of others, also prove that he was a lot more discreet than Stephen in the expression of those attitudes. And that latter fact is another manifestation of the essential difference: no matter how paranoid and difficult he became in later life, the young writer was athletic and gay, witty and bibulous, affectionate, loyal, tolerant of faults, and reluctant to offend and hurt[51]—once again, he had like his father a robust joy in living and a sense of humor about life. If he became troubled, like his creature Stephen and unlike his presumably unreflective and morally insensitive father, his inner distress was incongruous with his temperament (and apparently successfully masked by it), not an appropriate complement to it.[52]

Stephen Dedalus is estranged from his peers and from his family and nakedly antagonistic to his father. His manner is so sober as to be almost melancholy. He lacks physical robustness and spiritual warmth. It is because of these qualities as well as because of certain impressive principles and values which his creator did share that Stephen is an uncompromising—and soberly intolerant—iconoclast, an *avant-garde* prig.

He is, in fact, a familiar type, the melancholy, young, rebellious artist that the Romantic aesthetic tradition gave to literature and society. And that fact signifies that there are many possible sources for the alternative Joyce provided to the portion of history (his own temperament) which he suppressed in creating Stephen. Certain specific literary models have been suggested by one critic, principally the poet Michael Kramer, hero of Gerhard Hauptmann's play, and James Clarence Mangan (1803-1849), whom Joyce once called "the most significant poet of the modern Celtic world," as Mangan revealed himself in his "Fragment of an Unpublished Autobiography."[53]

Joyce's familiarity with and interest in *Michael Kramer* are proven by the fact that he translated it in 1901, the year after it was written, when he was nineteen.[54] And in addition to the example of a dedicated artist embodied in the hero, Kramer's son Arnold provided him with an example of a melancholy, romantic, and gifted youth who rebels against his father and is destroyed by a combination of his own willfulness and bourgeois society.[55]

The playwright whom Joyce considered Hauptmann's mentor and who was for a while his own idol, Henrik Ibsen, provided models that are more significant, both because Joyce was more greatly influenced by Ibsen's work in other

respects and because of that playwright's apparent attitude
toward those characters.

Ibsen's attitude was not very different from that expressed
in *Michael Kramer* at first. An early (1862) play, a
drawing-room comedy called *Love's Comedy*, has as its
fully sympathetic protagonist a young poet named Falk,
who proclaims among other things:

> The poet, yes; for poets all men are
> Who see through all their labors
>
> .   .   .   .
>
> The Ideal's lone beacon splendour flame afar.
> Yes, upward is my flight; the winged steed
> Is saddled; I am strong for noble deed

and:

> I go to scale the Future's possibilities.[56]

Four years later, in the romantic play *Brand*, the idealistic
clergyman of that name who is the hero is treated by his
creator equivocally rather than with complete sympathy,
as Hugh Kenner points out. Mr. Kenner goes on to say:

> In the five chapters of *A Portrait of the Artist as a
> Young Man* Joyce rewrote the five acts of *Brand*. . . .
> It is from Brand . . . that many of the most humor-
> lessly arrogant gestures of Stephen Dedalus are derived:
> his behavior at his mother's death-bed, his rejection of
> the Christianity of the clergy, his romantic positives.
> . . .[57]

Ibsen's attitude toward romantic idealism seems to have
fully hardened by the latter plays, in which Joyce was most
interested. Solness the architect in *The Master Builder* and
Rubeck the sculptor in *When We Dead Awaken* are both
idealists striving to fulfil themselves only to end in disaster.
All critics do not agree either that that was Ibsen's view
of the idealist-heroes he created toward the end of his
career, or that it is the correct view of them. But Joyce had

read the classic statement of it, George Bernard Shaw's *The Quintessence of Ibsenism*, when a student; and in his youthful (1900) essay in the distinguished *Fortnightly Review*, "Ibsen's New Drama" (which is primarily about *When We Dead Awaken*), he criticizes both Rubeck and the other artist, Solness, for being idealists so bent on self-fulfilment and so dedicated to their art as to alienate themselves from life and suffer destruction.[58] The similarity to his ultimate conception of Stephen Dedalus is plain.

Like his interest in Hauptmann and Ibsen, Joyce's interest in Mangan is easily documented. His essay "James Clarence Mangan," already quoted from above and in the discussion of the *Portrait*, was published in the University College newspaper just before he graduated in the spring of 1902; and five years later, he delivered in Italian a lecture in Trieste which was an expanded version of the earlier piece, but in which, significantly, he was more critical of Mangan's art and "dissociate[d] his own personality from Mangan's fainting rhythms." [59]

In that lecture, which he composed about half a year before beginning work on the *Portrait*,[60] Joyce spoke of Mangan as "a stranger in his native land, a rare and bizarre figure in the streets, where he is seen going sadly and alone," said of the face revealed by Mangan's death mask, "it is impossible to discover anything but melancholy and great weariness," and after describing "a childhood passed in the midst of domestic cruelties, misfortunes, and misery," declared:

He had always been a child of quiet and unresponsive nature, secretly given to the study of various languages, retiring, silent, preoccupied with religious matters, without friends or acquaintances.[61]

What Joyce had to say about Mangan's childhood indicates that he had read the "Fragment of an Unpublished Autobiography," which he mentioned and quoted indirectly.[62] In that piece Mangan describes a childhood whose external circumstances are very like Stephen's (and Joyce's own): a Jesuit education, in which he distinguished himself, and, at home, rapidly declining circumstances because of his

father's profligacy. Furthermore, Mangan expresses an unequivocal attitude toward his father:

> It was his boast . . . that "we [the children] would run
> into a mouse-hole" to shun him. While my mother lived,
> he made her miserable. . . . If anyone can imagine such
> an idea as a human boa-constrictor, without his alimentive
> properties, he will be able to form some notion of the
> character of my father.

And when he describes himself as a child:

> For me, I sought refuge in books and solitude. . . . I
> loved to indulge in solitary rhapsodies. . . . I . . . felt
> . . . that between me and those who approached me, no
> species of sympathy could exist: and I shrank from com-
> munion with them . . .[63]

not only the substance, but the very style of his portrayal is
familiar.

Plainly, Joyce did not lack literary models for Stephen
Dedalus; and Mangan, at least, provided a detailed model
for Stephen's temperament. Yet, it is very likely that, as
he did Stephen's intellectual attitudes and the external events
of Stephen's life, Joyce actually got Stephen's temperament,
too, from history—only not from his own.

After noting the similarity between his father's and his
brother's attitudes toward the family pictures in the passage
from his book quoted above, Stanislaus Joyce says: "In my
opinion they were furniture-pictures, glazed and wooden
portraits that looked as if the sitters had been seized with
a catalepsy of respectability while being portrayed." [64] The
family called the writer "Sunny Jim" because of what his
brother described as "his cheerful and amiable disposition";
they called Stanislaus Joyce himself "Brother John," "to
hint some imagined staidness in my character."[65] And there
is abundant evidence that the "staidness" is not imagined.
At the age of eighteen he wrote in his diary that he "never
followed" his brother "in drinking . . . in whoring, in
speaking broadly, in being frank without reserve with
others. . . ." [66] He was, he says, the "model" for the sober,

melancholy, moralistic, alienated intellectual (who translated *Michael Kramer*), Mr. Duffy, of the *Dubliners* story
"A Painful Case." [67] He was far more affected than the
writer seems to have been by the family's privation and
their father's responsibility for it.[68] And he himself inadvertently suggests the identity I am trying to establish here
when he writes, after describing a drunken antic of John
Joyce's that embarrassed him while he was walking with
friends:

> I wish I could see now, or could have seen then, the
> funny side of such happenings, as my brother did. And
> yet in *A Portrait of the Artist* he writes that "any allu-
> sion to his father by a boy or a master put Stephen Deda-
> lus's calm to rout and the smile waned on his face." It did
> not seem so, but, of course, Stephen Dedalus is an imag-
> inary, not a real, self-portrait and freely treated.[69]

There is more than Stanislaus Joyce's staidness, dour
attitude toward the family's privations, and hatred of his
father ("I loathe my father"[70]) to confirm that his temperament is the primary source for that of Stephen Dedalus.
Richard Ellmann contrasts the "cool" apostasy of the older
brother with the younger's lifelong hostility toward the
Church, and says that when they were young "James . . .
suggested [Stanislaus] moderate his revolt a little in the
interest of family harmony"; Stanislaus reproduces a conversation about religion between the brothers which the
writer terminated with the comment, "There's a queer, grim,
Dutch touch about your phiz"; and both these reports make
less surprising than it might otherwise be Stanislaus' disclosure that

> I announced that I would refuse to do my Easter duty.
> Jim made a half-hearted attempt to dissuade me from
> my purpose.
>
> .   .   .   .
>
> The painful conflict between my mother and my brother
> originated from my refusal ["in point of time, at least, I
> refused first"]. . . . he told me of a talk he had with
> "Cranly," which was much vaguer and briefer than the
> one in *A Portrait of the Artist*.[71]

When Joyce went to Paris in 1902, he corresponded with both his parents, and solicited and received money and encouragement from both; before going he had arranged not only for Yeats to meet him in London and help him to get work, but for introductions to people in Paris who might be similarly helpful. Stanislaus Joyce says of these efforts what Stephen Dedalus might be expected to say: "I should have liked him to go to Paris without his viaticum of introductions of dubious utility, and I believe he would have succeeded in his adventure if he had not relied on them." [72] And, of course, Stephen makes no such ignoble preparations at the end of the *Portrait*. My point has been perhaps too abundantly documented: Stephen Dedalus has the temperament of Stanislaus Joyce as it is revealed in his autobiography. Maurice, Stephen Daedalus' brother in *Stephen Hero*, was not simply eliminated as a character from the *Portrait* and *Ulysses* for the sake of economy, but assimilated into Stephen Dedalus for a much more important artistic purpose. The young rebel and aesthete who is first self-deluding and then troubled, whose attitudes and circumstances are those of Joyce himself when young (and also to some extent those of his younger brother, although on the evidence of his autobiography Stanislaus Joyce was not troubled in conscience by his own acts)—that young man whom the writer was creating seemed to him more properly staid, dour, arbitrary, intolerant, and hostile than gay, gregarious, athletic, witty bibulous, affectionate, tolerant of faults, and reluctant to offend and hurt: seemed to him more properly like his younger brother than like himself in temperament. And so he took that brother's temperament instead of his own from history. [73]

Joyce's transmutation of history in the cases of Stephen's refusal to pray for his dying mother and Stephen's character is, quite simply, functional. He sometimes incorporated history in *Ulysses* with capricious distortion but not often. He more frequently simply recorded it with compulsive faithfulness, and that fact suggests an attitude toward art, toward himself, and toward the created world. But the most important element in the relationship history has with *Ulysses* is as the novel's functional source: things are in it as they were in life, except where the demands of art require that they be changed,[74] and then life is not discarded but rearranged or recombined whenever possible.

Joyce's transmutation of history, where it is important in the novel, exemplifies the making of fiction as fully as possible out of fact. And like his use of correspondences, it not only is "a way of working" but suggests an attitude toward the created world. Therefore it combines with that and with his faithful recording of history—to suggest that the making of Stephen Dedalus, for example, out of a Hamlet and a Telemachus, a Joyce and a Stanislaus Joyce, is an act of belief as well as an act of art.

1. Gilbert, p. 209.

2. Butcher and Lang, p. 184.

3. For lists of allusions to Shakespeare and his works in *Ulysses,* see: B. J. Morse, "Mr. Joyce and Shakespeare," *Englische Studien,* LXV (1930–1931), 367–81; Arthur Heine, "Shakespeare in James Joyce," *The Shakespeare Association Bulletin,* XXIV (1949), 56–70; and especially, Schutte, Appendix B, which assimilates the two earlier lists. I am indebted in this chapter, in various ways, to Mr. Schutte's erudition.

4. The quotation is from Harris' book, *The Man Shakespeare and His Tragic Life Story* (New York, 1909), p. 203. This is one instance in *Ulysses* in which Joyce may have committed an historical error. Harris' articles were published in fourteen numbers of the British *Saturday Review,* running from March to December of 1898. At the end of the introductory series of March and April, Harris promised three more "essays," one on Shakespeare's women, one on the sonnets that would not be published for half a decade intentionally, be "reserved for publication in book form" (*Saturday Review,* LXXXVI, 400). This was true of the latter two; all the other articles that appeared were about "Shakespeare's Women." Joyce's memory may somehow have confused the articles, which he probably saw when a high-school senior and college freshman, with those two parts of the book that had not been printed previously in the *Saturday Review.* However, it is also possible that he caused Stephen and Lyster to talk in 1904 about a discussion of Shakespeare's sonnets that would not be published for half a decade intentionally, because he considered the anachronism necessary. For a list of functional (and most likely intentional) anachronisms in the novel, see Robert Martin Adams, *Surface and Symbol: The Consistency of James Joyce's "Ulysses"* (New York, 1962), pp. 4–8.

5. See I Kings 21:20.

6. Actually, they had been better friends than either the remark or Joyce's portrayal of Best in the ninth chapter of *Ulysses* suggests. See *James Joyce,* pp. 122, 156, 161, 168, 208, 314.

7. Quotations taken from *James Joyce,* p. 374.

8. Patricia Hutchins, *James Joyce's Dublin* (London, 1950).

9. Hugh Kenner, *Dublin's Joyce* (Bloomington, Ind., 1956).

10. See Kain, p. 55 ff.

11. *James Joyce*, p. 376. This discussion of Joyce's use of historical material is considerably indebted to Mr. Ellmann's authoritative biography.

12. See, e.g., Mary Colum, *Life and the Dream* (New York, 1947), p. 397.

13. The letter, dated May 8, 1932, bears the letterhead of a Zurich hotel. It is in the Margaret McKim Maloney collection at the New York Public Library and is used by permission of the Library and the Society of Authors, London, the literary representative of the Estate of James Joyce.

14. See *James Joyce*, pp. 43–44.

15. Mary Colum, *loc. cit.*

16. See, e.g., *James Joyce*, pp. 157, 168.

17. *James Joyce*, p. 157.

18. J. F. Byrne, *Silent Years: An Autobiography with Memoirs of James Joyce and Our Ireland* (New York, 1953).

19. *Ibid.*, p. 158.

20. Hutchins, p. 91.

21. *Ibid.*, p. 94; *Letters*, p. 175.

22. "The Joyce I Knew," *Saturday Review of Literature*, XXIII (January 25, 1941), 3–4, 15 ff., 3. For the other account, see *Mourning Became Mrs. Spendlove and Other Portraits, Grave and Gay* (New York, 1948), p. 51.

23. See Budgen, p. 181.

24. *James Joyce*, p. 377.

25. Ellsworth Mason, "Joyce's Categories," *Sewanee Review*, LXI (1953), 427–32.

26. It was identification of them that led some critics to attack Joyce for escapism or callousness because Stephen concludes the passage with his image of the artist as "invisible, refined out of existence, indifferent, paring his fingernails" (p. 215). The observation was made in the discussion of "Style in *Ulysses*" that the image is a vehicle for the point that a "dramatic" work of art is autonomous; Joyce artfully has Stephen focus on the artist who has achieved that independence of the work from himself in keeping with his portrayal of Stephen's aesthetic as debased by subjectivity, as Neoplatonist rather than Aristotelian: in Hugh Kenner's phrase, the aesthetic of a mind "centered on *ego* rather than *ens*" (Kenner, "The Portrait in Perspective," p. 154).

27. *James Joyce*, p. 375.

28. *Ibid.*, pp. 604–5.

29. See *ibid.*, pp. 632–34.

30. Some readers may have seen recently a relevant example of the kind of thing that so excited him. A reply to a query in the *New York Times Book Review* of June 11, 1961, concerns "James Lovebirch," the appropriately-named author of the salacious novel *Fair Tyrants*, which Bloom considers buying before he decides on *Sweets of Sin* (232). The italics are mine: "R.M.A. (May 7) asks

for a turn of the century play in which a Mrs. Scarli appears. Such a woman appears in *"Leopoldo,"* one of a collection of *eighteen episodes of marital infidelity* by an obscure artist, *Jack Lovebirch.* These first appeared about *1904."*

The letter is made most remarkable by the name of its writer, "Joyce J. Augustine."

One should not be complacent about Joyce's belief, but investigation has not confirmed the existence of correspondent, "artist," or work.

31. Sir Horace Rumbold, the British Minister to Switzerland in 1918.

32. A related issue worth mentioning here is more properly editorializing than caprice: Joyce's treatment of some things about which he had strong feelings, such as the Church in Ireland. See William T. Noon, S.J., "James Joyce: Unfacts, Fiction, and Facts," *PMLA*, LXXVI (1961), 254–76, for a discussion of "the distance that separates" those things as they appear in his fiction from "the facts out of which the fiction grew."

33. *James Joyce*, p. 39.

34. He is quoted as having said, "My life was buried with him." —*Ibid.*, p. 20.

35. Stanislaus Joyce, "Memoir," p. 491. For a more elaborate account of the incident, and a discussion of Joyce's behavior at the time of his mother's sickness and death, see Stanislaus Joyce, *My Brother's Keeper: James Joyce's Early Years*, ed. Richard Ellmann (New York, 1958), p. 233 ff.

36. Byrne, p. 85.

37. He also returned to his home for a three-week visit at Christmas time. For dates see *James Joyce*, pp. 113, 115–16, 120, 123, 132–33.

38. Byrne, p. 85.

39. Noon, p. 260.

40. See VI in James Joyce, *Epiphanies*, ed. O. A. Silverman (Buffalo, 1956), p. 6. See also, *James Joyce*, p. 25.

41. Stanislaus Joyce, p. 41.

42. *Ibid.*

43. *Ibid.*, pp. 41–42.

44. *Ibid.*, p. 23.

45. *Ibid.*, p. 187.

46. *Ibid.*, p. 195.

47. Mary and Padraic Colum, *Our Friend James Joyce* (New York, 1958), p. 52.

48. Stanislaus Joyce, p. 122.

49. *Ibid.*, p. 60.

50. See, e.g., his brother's account of his consoling their sister Mabel at the time of their mother's death (Stanislaus Joyce, pp. 236–37).

51. See, e.g., Stanislaus Joyce's account of their talks about religion, in which the writer tried to persuade his brother to moderate his position (Stanislaus Joyce, pp. 103–5, 138–39).

52. After enumerating differences between Joyce and Stephen, Maurice Beebe says, "Joyce, it is clear, was a better rounded—alas, better adjusted—person than his fictional surrogate."—Beebe, p. 73.

53. The critic is Marvin Magalaner; see *Joyce*, pp. 27–30. His later suggestion (*Joyce*, p. 63) that Ivan Dmitrich Gromov of Chekhov's short story "Ward No. 6" resembles Stephen is less convincing; Gromov is a similar type, but is a paranoiac. For a more extensive list of possible models, see Beebe, pp. 74–77. Joyce's statement is from an Italian lecture on Mangan (1907), translated and printed in *The Critical Writings of James Joyce*, ed. Ellsworth Mason and Richard Ellmann (London, 1959), pp. 175–86, 179; although he did translations of Gaelic poems, Mangan wrote in English.

54. He was unable to render every passage of the play's Silesian dialect; see *James Joyce*, p. 91.

55. I am indebted for this observation, and for most of what I have to say about the possible influence of Ibsen and of Mangan's autobiographical piece on Joyce's characterization of Stephen, to an unpublished undergraduate honors essay by Robert Stein, "The Backgrounds of Stephen Dedalus" (Clark University, 1961).

56. Quoted from Vivienne Koch Macleod, "The Influence of Ibsen on Joyce," *PMLA*, LX (1945), 879–98, 892–93. For an extensive discussion of Ibsen's influence on Joyce, see that essay and Mrs. Macleod's "The Influence of Ibsen on Joyce: Addendum," *PMLA*, LXII (1947), 573–80.

57. Kenner, *Dublin's Joyce*, p. 81.

58. See "Ibsen's New Drama," in *Critical Writings*, especially pp. 53, 54, 57, 58, 62, 66.

59. Printed in *Critical Writings*, pp. 73–83 and 175–86; the quotation is from the editors' comment, p. 175.

60. See *James Joyce*, pp. 268, 269, 274.

61. *Critical Writings*, pp. 180, 178, 177.

62. *Ibid.*, pp. 76, 180–81. In both essay and lecture Joyce used the "boaconstrictor" figure (in the latter it is changed to "human rattlesnake"), which he presumably could have gotten from no secondary work on Mangan. See Marvin Magalaner, "James Mangan and Joyce's Dedalus Family," *Philological Quarterly*, XXXI (1952), 363–71.

63. James Clarence Mangan, "Fragment of an Unpublished Autobiography," *The Irish Monthly*, X (1882), 675–90, 678, 679.

64. Stanislaus Joyce, pp. 122–23.

65. *Ibid.*, p. 135.

66. *Ibid.*, p. xiii. He may have been nineteen; the entry containing this passage is not one for September, 1903, as stated, according to the editor of the diary (see n. 70 below), but that for August 13, 1904.

67. *Ibid.*, p. 54.

68. *Ibid.*, pp. 50–51, 59.

69. *Ibid.*, p. 48.

70. Diary entry for April 12, 1904. *The Dublin Diary of Stanislaus Joyce*, ed. George Harris Healey (Ithaca, 1962), p. 28. For the

similarity between Stanislaus' and Mangan's views of their fathers, compare the entry for September 26, 1903, especially pp. 16–18, with Mangan's "Fragment."

71. Stanislaus Joyce, pp. xii, 138–39, 103–6.

72. *Ibid.*, p. 199.

73. Maurice Beebe says, "Joyce combined certain aspects of his brother's character with his own and thus gave Stephen the strength of two young Joyces."—Beebe, p. 70. Kevin Sullivan, in *Joyce among the Jesuits* (New York, 1958), comes even closer to this conclusion. He says in a note: "Stanislaus' attitude toward his father [as expressed in *My Brother's Keeper*] closely resembles that of Stephen toward Simon Dedalus, nor is this the only point of resemblance between Joyce's 'hero' and his younger brother. It is possible that Stanislaus rather than James served as model for some of the less attractive traits of the Dedalus" (p. 54, n. 79).

74. This principle would validate the anachronisms of a functional nature in the novel; see n. 4 above.

chapter six

10 *the city*

The introductory paragraph of Stuart Gilbert's analysis of "The Wandering Rocks" says:

> It consists of eighteen short scenes followed by a *coda* describing a viceregal passage through Dublin. . . . In its structure and its *technic* ('labyrinth') the episode may be regarded as a small-scale model of *Ulysses* as a whole. The first . . . ["section"] describes the peregrinations of Father Conmee . . . 'the decentest rector that was ever at Congowes' (vide *A Portrait of the Artist*). Other sections describe the movements of Stephen Dedalus, of Mr Bloom . . . and the wanderings of several minor personages, who reappear in the course of *Ulysses*.[1]

The paragraph neatly presents three critical observations about this chapter that are generally accepted and that not only cannot be reconciled with, but absolutely prevent an understanding of, its true nature.

First of all, it comprises not eighteen episodes and a coda but nineteen episodes, and the only valid dividing of these produces seventeen framed by the first and the last. Consequent upon this fact, it is not "a small-scale model of *Ulysses* as a whole," even though most of the novel's characters appear in it, some for the first time. A model it is, but it represents Dublin, which in the author's terms represents Ireland, not *Ulysses;* "the city" is not only its locale but also its subject, for the chapter is largely an expansion of the statement about Ireland made in the seventh (newspaper) chapter. And finally, the Father Conmee portrayed in its first episode is not very decent.

For reasons that will become apparent, this last point must be established first. The common misconception of it [2] undoubtedly owes something to the knotty relationship between Joyce's created Dublin and historical Dublin's James Joyce. Father John Conmee was kind to Joyce on at least the two occasions on which his fictional namesake is shown being kind to Stephen Dedalus: he sustained the boy's protest at being unjustly pandied by Father James Daly ("Father Dolan") for breaking his glasses; and he secured his admission to Belvedere College without fees. But Joyce's portrayal of Conmee goes well beyond the expression of any putative tenderness he personally felt toward the priest.

The first page alone of the episode—the first page of the chapter—contains a sufficient indictment of any cleric. After Conmee is introduced with ironic pomp as "The superior, the very reverend John Conmee S.J.," the opening paragraph presents his thoughts about the case of young Patrick Dignam II. Martin Cunningham, leading the efforts to aid the Dignam family, has undertaken three major projects, two of which were mentioned in the sixth (cemetery) chapter: a collection of money (101) and an effort to place the Dignam boy at what seems to be a Catholic orphans' school at Artane (100). The third, an attempt to secure the unmortgaged portion of Dignam's life insurance, which has been blocked by an incorrect mortgage procedure, will occupy him (and, far more important, Bloom) in the twelfth chapter. In the present chapter Cunningham is making his collection, and he expresses the belief that young Dignam "will be all right" (242) because he has written to Father Conmee about the boy's plight. The priest's trip to Artane, the basic action of the Conmee episode, is thus the expression of Conmee's co-operation in the Dignam matter. However, in contrast to the simple charity of the

lawyer, "the superior, the very reverend John Conmee S.J."
thinks, in the opening paragraph of the chapter:

> Five to three. Just nice time to walk to Artane. What
> was that boy's name? Dignam, yes. *Vere Dignum et jus-*
> *tum est.* Brother Swan was the person to see. Mr Cun-
> ningham's letter. Yes. Oblige him, if possible. Good
> practical catholic: useful at mission time. (216)

Joyce's indictment of Conmee takes another form in the
second paragraph. A one-legged sailor stops "before the
convent of the sisters of charity" and extends his cap

> for alms towards the very reverend John Conmee S.J.
> Father Conmee blessed him in the sun for his purse held,
> he knew, one silver crown.

This incident invites comparison not only with such characteristic examples of Christian charity as Saint Martin's parting his cloak with a beggar and the more directly relevant
gesture of the founder of Conmee's order, Saint Ignatius
Loyola, who traded his aristocratic finery with a beggar for
the latter's rags, but with incidents in the chapter itself.
Molly, who before this chapter has made anything but a
good impression, responds to the one-legged beggar's appeal (222); and in contrast to Conmee's attitude with
regard to both charity and the Dignams, Bloom not only
is to give freely of his time in the insurance matter and to
become the victim of unjust contumely as a result, but has
contributed five shillings to Cunningham's collection, a sum
generous enough to draw comments from Cunningham's
companions (242-43).

In the third paragraph Conmee's self-righteousness is
revealed:

> He thought, but not for long, of soldiers and sailors,
> whose legs had been shot off by cannonballs, ending their
> days in some pauper ward, and of Cardinal Wolsey's
> words: *If I had served my God as I had served my king*
> *He would not have abandoned me in my old days.*

The paragraph ends when he sees approaching "the wife of Mr David Sheehy M.P."

The full stop between Sheehy's name and his social status is sufficiently eloquent of Conmee's sycophancy. Nevertheless, Sheehy's title and name are repeated lower down on the page in a satiric paraphrase of Conmee's toadying, to drive home the point:

> Father Conmee was very glad to see the wife of Mr David Sheehy M.P. looking so well and he begged to be remembered to Mr David Sheehy M.P.

before Joyce moves on to his vanity. Father Conmee smiles a great deal to Mrs. Sheehy, "And smiled yet again in going. He had cleaned his teeth, he knew, with arecanut paste."

The portrait sketched out on the first page of the episode is elaborated through the remainder of it. For example, the "millions of" non-Christian souls in the world that must perish are "a waste," the priest decides (220); and the deaths of those involved in the "General Slocum" disaster in New York Harbor, announced in the day's papers, are "unfortunate" because they died unshriven, but "Still, an act of perfect contrition" (218). As the episode nears conclusion, he becomes in a revery "Don John Conmee," smiling "at smiling noble faces," marrying "a bride and . . . a bridegroom, noble to noble" (220).

The importance of understanding Joyce's portrayal of Father Conmee becomes clear when the form of the chapter is clear. The individual episodes present no problem. They are, as critics have pointed out, a portrait gallery. They are interconnected through Joyce's recounting the same incidents in different episodes, presenting successive incidents of a sequence in successive episodes, referring to the same objects and characters by the same phrases in different episodes, and by similar devices. The difficulty lies with the formal entity that comprises them, the chapter as a whole. If it were indeed a small-scale model of *Ulysses*, the form of the chapter would be exhibitionism, without real purpose;

but the extra episode (the "tail") nicely invalidates that proposition, and perhaps that is why there are nineteen episodes.

At the end of the preceding chapter, Stephen, seeing "no birds," resigned himself to the attacks of Mulligan, the monster on the rock, told himself to "cease to strive." The concluding lines of the ninth chapter, and of the first part of the novel, are:

Offend me still. Speak on.
Kind air defined the coigns of houses in Kildare street. No birds. Frail from the housetops two plumes of smoke ascended, pluming, and in a flaw of softness softly were blown.
Cease to strive. Peace of the druid priests of Cymbeline, hierophantic: from wide earth an altar.

Laud we the gods
And let our crooked smokes climb to their nostrils
From our bless'd altars. (215)

The two plumes of smoke were the inspiration for Stephen's "crooked smokes" quotation from *Cymbeline*. In turn, he apparently linked to the Shakespearean passage itself the beginning of the speech with which Cymbeline closes the play, his decision to "cease to strive" for freedom; for he said that instead he would accept the "peace of the druid priests of Cymbeline." Disregarding Bloom and the true augury of deliverance, he considered two plumes of smoke to be augurs in place of the birds of "flight" he had hoped for, augurs of his subjection to the peace of Cymbeline's druid priests. And so he determined to "cease to strive" against it.

The nature of the peace to which Stephen resigned himself is defined by Cymbeline in the words that follow directly the passage which closes the ninth chapter. He says (V, v, 481-84):

Publish we this peace
To all our subjects: Set we forward: let
A Roman and a British ensign wave
Friendly together: so through Lud's town march.

Although the Rome referred to by the ancient British king
is different from the Rome which was in Stephen's mind,
he clearly associated his presumed "augurs," the two
plumes of smoke, with the two "ensigns" of Cymbeline's
speech through the medium of the unspecified number of
"crooked smokes" of that speech (presumably Cymbeline
would have many more sacrificial fires for the auspicious
event). The plumes of smoke are therefore symbols of the
two masters of all Irishmen, and omens of the subjection to
those masters which threatens Stephen.

This concluding passage of the preceding chapter is
directly relevant to the present one. The tenth chapter is
fundamentally a depiction of the peace to which Stephen
just resigned himself—the subjection of Ireland to the
Roman church and the British crown. Joyce has fulfilled
Cymbeline's command and has "published" the peace in
question, in the manner Cymbeline prescribes—with a
Roman and a British ensign (in that order) waving friendly
together, sharing between them the rule of the (in this
case, Irish) nation. Correspondingly, the "march" of the
ensign bearers is not through the capital of Britain but
through that of Ireland.

The ensign bearers are, of course, the superior, the very
reverend John Conmee S.J., whose procession opens the
chapter, and the Right Honourable William Humble, earl
of Dudley, G.C.V.O., lord lieutenant general, and general
governor of Ireland, whose procession closes it. The conclusion of Shakespeare's play functions not only as the very
appropriate expression of the conclusion of an endeavor
(Stephen's in the preceding chapter), whose vehicle is
Shakespeare and whose apparent result is the specific
"peace" to which Stephen submits, but also as the basis
of the depiction of that peace in the following chapter.
And it thereby links the first part of the novel with the
"*entr'acte*" which, as Joyce described it, follows the "first
part of *Ulysses*," and is fundamentally outside the action.

Father Conmee is made the representative of the Church
for good reasons. He is unchanged from the gentle rector
of the *Portrait*. He thinks of walking in the evening across
Clongowes field and hearing the boys at play, while the
reader is told, "He was their rector: his reign was mild"

(221). He is genial with some Belvedere boys on the street, and the reader is told, "Father Conmee liked cheerful decorum" (219). Even some of Joyce's satire is of a sympathetic kind—for example, that at the very end of the Conmee episode, when the priest naïvely blesses a young man (Lynch, we learn in the fourteenth [hospital] chapter) and woman who emerge from some bushes and turns to the next section of his breviary, that named for the Hebrew letter "*Sin.*" Perhaps he cannot see what is going on under his nose, but he is less sinister for it.

Nevertheless he is calculating, sycophantic, subtly corrupted in motive and attitude. And it is significant that the superior is unchanged from the rector of the *Portrait* in these ways also. Conmee's sympathetic response to the young Stephen when he protested the prefect's unjust pandying of him at Clongowes and total indifference (the discovery of which so affected the boy) to the moral point at issue reveal a character that is not very different from the one which calculates, years later, that placing a boy in an orphans' school would be worthwhile largely because the "useful" Martin Cunningham asked it.

The worldly Simon Dedalus had not regarded Conmee's conduct in the earlier incident as unique; "O, a jesuit for your life, for diplomacy!", he had said. The nature of Conmee's role in the chapter, his clerical position, his conduct—all rule out the possibility that Joyce is exposing a fraud. He is depicting a representative Jesuit priest, conscientious and diplomatic, with his calculation placed at the service of his Church. It may even be that Conmee's toadying is devoted to the service of his Church. His many faults show him to be a weak vessel, but there is no indication that he is to be considered uniquely so and therefore unqualified to bear the "Roman ensign."

Conmee's representational role is not easily recognized because he is portrayed so intimately. But that portrayal is prescribed by the necessity for presenting (and indicting) the Church in moral-spiritual terms, the only terms that are valid. His refusal to part with his silver crown is completely normal by ordinary standards: it is impractical to give so much money away, and his tram fare was to come out of the coin ("he disliked to traverse on foot the dingy way past Mud Island"). His calculation, physical vanity, and social climbing are also common in our world. Joyce is suggesting not that the priest is vicious but that he has embraced the values of the world, that he has become secular.[3] As represented by Father Conmee, the Church no longer burns heretics. But it schemes and calculates, toadies and exploits, striving to gain or preserve power at the sacrifice of the spiritual value that justifies its existence.

With respect to the Crown, there is no necessity for spiritual examination. Its essence is simply the power of a foreign conqueror. Correspondingly, the bearer of the "ensign" of the Crown is treated in completely external terms, terms of the control of public ceremony, pomp, strength, and sovereignty. And there is no question of the representational nature of the Right Honourable William Humble, Earl of Dudley, G.C.V.O., lord lieutenant general and general governor of Ireland.

The ensigns of Rome and Britain straddle the city, then, imposing their peace on it. The fact of their domination is suggested in the echoes of Conmee's procession and reports of the viceroy's that respectively follow and anticipate throughout the chapter the episodes of the two ensign bearers. The nature of that domination is represented in their contact with their subjects. In Father Conmee's case such contact is always the same, a sterile communion between Church and people, maintained almost as a matter of form. Thus, all Conmee's contacts with persons during the episode after those with the begging sailor, Mrs. Sheehy, and the schoolboys are represented in the same mechanical manner:

> Father Conmee smiled and saluted (217)

> Father Conmee . . . was saluted by Mr William Gallagher. . . . Father Conmee saluted Mr William Gallagher. . . . (218)

> They [two men] saluted him and were saluted. (218)

> A constable on his beat saluted Father Conmee and Father Conmee saluted the constable. (218)

There is much greater variation in the relationship of the Crown and the Irish people, or at least much more expression of individual attitudes, despite the fact that the beginning of the last episode of the chapter includes the statement in journalese that "The viceroy was most cordially greeted on his way through the metropolis" (248). For example, Tom Kernan is enthusiastic, "Mr Dudley White, B.L., M.A." strokes his nose with his forefinger, Simon Dedalus is obsequious and is graced by a return salute, Gertie MacDowell, of the thirteenth chapter, tries in vain to "see what Her Excellency had on," John Wyse Nolan "smiled with unseen coldness," Buck Mulligan "gaily" ("her gay betrayer") and Haines "gravely" look down from their luncheon table, Blazes Boylan boldly examines and admires the ladies, and the enigmatic man in the macintosh, thirteenth mourner at Dignam's funeral, walks with frightening ominousness, "eating dry bread . . . swiftly and unscathed across the viceroy's path." Joyce's final word on the subject of England is "the salute of Almidano Artifoni's sturdy trousers swallowed by a closing door."

In Joyce's view the Irish nation is more aware, or at least more openly resentful, of the oppression of England than of that of the Church, but is equally victimized by both. And Stephen shares Joyce's view, for it is precisely this double victimization that he resigns himself to at the end of the preceding chapter. This is the peace signified by the "two" plumes of smoke from the druid sacrifices, the two "ensigns." Stephen says to Haines, in the first chapter, "—I am the servant of two masters . . . an English and an Italian" and, pressed for elucidation,

> The imperial British state, Stephen answered, his colour rising, and the holy Roman Catholic and apostolic church. (22)

The present chapter is a representation of the condition Stephen describes. It complements the seventh (newspaper) chapter, because while there the Irish people, and especially their leaders, are indicted for failing to throw off the foreign yoke—Nelson's Pillar and Dublin's churches in Stephen's "parable"—and achieve their own destiny, here the nature of that yoke is focussed on, and the two foreign "masters" condemned.

Once a common misconception is set aside, the Homeric correspondence of the chapter can be seen to be a highly compact reiteration of its theme. The ostensible originals of the "Wandering Rocks" in the *Odyssey* are in the Bosphorus. The common view is that the subjects of the nineteen episodes are analogous to the wandering rocks, or alternatively, that this is so of the citizens portrayed in the seventeen enclosed episodes, while Conmee and the viceroy are the two opposite shores of the Bosphorus, the Asiatic (spiritual) and the European (material).

The opposition of a "spiritual" Conmee and the viceroy is clearly invalid. And identification of the Dubliners with the rocks is no more tenable, in view of Circe's description of the "Rocks Wandering" in Book XII of the *Odyssey*. The rocks are destructive forces, not victims. The victims are the ships that go between them. Neither Bosphorus, nor European shore, nor Asiatic is mentioned; only rocks for ships to attempt to sail between and, with the single exception of Jason's "Argo," to fail. The true nature of the parallel is apparent. The two ensigns whose processions straddle the chapter are the destructive rocks (the association of the Church with a rock is especially apt); they are not strictly wandering, but they are always moving, their processions constituting in fact the action of their respective episodes. And the ships (being) destroyed by the rocks are the Dubliners presented in the different episodes —the Irish nation.

The Homeric correspondence carries with it certain implications that are important. Circe tells Odysseus of the wandering rocks and of Scylla and Charybdis simultaneously. She advises him to avoid the rocks, which mean certain destruction, and instead to make his way between the monster and the whirlpool, staying close to the former. In the preceding chapter Stephen attempted the course corresponding to that prescribed for Odysseus and, he thought, failed. His presumption of failure caused his resignation to the peace of Cymbeline's priests, which is resignation to the wandering rocks. The Homeric correspondence reiterates the point made in the second chapter: that Stephen's submission to the servitude which has been decreed for Irishmen by the "nightmare," history, would mean his destruction. In addition, it declares that the twin masters of Stephen's countrymen are indeed destroying them (Joyce's political speeches and articles also associate the Church with England as a foreign oppressor of Ireland). Finally, since Odysseus did *not* submit to the wandering rocks, and the present chapter is, analogously, outside the action of the novel—since, in this case, correspondence is also pointed anti-correspondence—it suggests that ultimately Stephen shall turn his back on the destructive situation that his fellow citizens are in.

The seventeen episodes which constitute the body of the chapter are a composite representation of the citizens of subject Dublin, revealing all the major and many of the minor figures in the novel in characteristic, sometimes even what Joyce might call epiphanic, actions. For example, Mulligan takes Haines into a Dublin Bread Company tearoom (the Englishman is to pay), pointing out to the earnest tourist "—Parnell's brother. There in the corner" (244). He mocks his ostensible closest friend to the extent that Haines is moved to sympathize with Stephen at one point. He gulls Haines with his rhetoric, but only as part of his constant endeavor to entertain him. For "some scones and butter and some cakes" (245) which his "watchful eyes" see the waitress bringing; whereupon "He helped her to unload her tray," "plastered butter" over a scone, and "bit off a soft piece hungrily." In a page and a half of text, Mulligan's hypocrisy and treachery toward Stephen, his prostitution ("A jester . . . winning a clement master's praise"), and his essential gluttony are fully portrayed. Haines is characterized, too; although in his case, little is required other than the statement with which he closes the sequence:

—This is real Irish cream I take it, he said with forbearance. I don't want to be imposed on. (246)

In general, the treatment of Stephen and Bloom, like that of Mulligan, Haines, and the other minor characters, is representational, portraying them rather than contributing to the general action of the novel, as befits an *entr'acte*. The exception to this is the series of snatches from a salacious novel read by Bloom in his episode.

Stephen appears in two episodes. In the first of these, less than a page long, he is talking with Almidano Artifoni, his friend and one-time teacher of Italian. The older man, in a combination of Continental politeness and affectionate solicitude, informs Stephen that he too once regarded the world as *"una bestia,"* and deplores the attitude because Stephen, feeling as he does, only sacrifices himself. He repeatedly begs Stephen to consider earnestly what he has said; somewhat abashed, Stephen promises that he will; and Artifoni gently and gracefully takes his leave. Like Mr. Deasy, who had said simply and directly, "I am happier than you are," Artifoni perceives Stephen's inability to come to terms with life. This episode focusses upon that fact.

The second episode portraying Stephen exploits the focus made a dozen pages before. Melancholy thoughts reminiscent of the third chapter are interrupted when "the hum of dynamos from the powerhouse urged Stephen to be on" (238). He asks the dynamos to "Stop!" without success, exclaims "Throb always without you and the throb always within," and declares that he stands "between two roaring worlds." The throbs—roaring "worlds"—Stephen is speaking of in this intricate passage are the dynamos and his heart ("Your heart you sing of") respectively. The dynamos represent external reality, the created world, "history"—the conditions of Stephen's existence laid down by his "father." His heart, in contrast, represents his internal reality, such things as conscience and love—the seat of his trouble regarding his "mother." The throbbing worlds without and within are precisely the macrocosm and microcosm which Joyce delineated in the early pages of the *Portrait*. Stephen himself is no longer a child being molded by "squalor" and "riot," but a fully self-conscious spirit: "I between" his two throbbing worlds, he says.

He goes on to say, "Shatter them, one and both," only to have a sobering afterthought, one recalling the fears of Artifoni: "But stun myself too in the blow." Yet he persists

in defiance of his "father," repeating the epithets he used
in the librarian's office: "Shatter me you who can. Bawd
and butcher, were the words." Promptly he falters and,
although facetiously, pays tribute to God's power. First he
grants that God can "shatter" him at any moment, that
history can give him a "back kick," in his phrase of the
second chapter; then he admires God's creation; finally he
echoes Hamlet's dissembling when the meddling old man
Polonius imposed himself on him (II, ii):

> I say! Not yet awhile. A look around.
>   Yes, quite true. Very large and wonderful and keeps
> famous time. You say right, sir. A Monday morning,
> 'twas so, indeed. (238)

Having succumbed once again to the "father" of the
"throbbing world" "without" him, Stephen faces the
"mother" of the "throbbing world" "within." Walking on
to a bookstall he discovers, in a volume of popular occult-
ism, a talisman for winning a woman's love. His response
is "For me this." The woman is the only woman who
concerns him in the novel, of course, and when his sister
comes upon him, although she cannot possibly know what
he is reading or why, he thinks immediately, "Shut the book
quick. Don't let see." His sister invokes all his familial
loyalty. And feeling the pathos and futility of Dilly's situation, he is tender, for the first time in the novel. He uses
the figure "She is drowning" to describe her situation and,
as he had in the case of the drowned man in the third
chapter, slips into acute brooding about his mother. In a
questionable device of Joyce's, he repeats variations on the
Middle English expression "agenbite of inwit," [4] and concludes with "Misery! Misery!" Between them, the two
episodes portray Stephen as the reader knows him at this
point in the novel.

Bloom's condition, too, is epitomized in a brief sketch.
After touching on his frustrated paternity, his episode represents the devoted and unrequited lover, frustrated emo-
tionally and sexually, who is also both cuckold and pander.
It is less than two pages long, and it depicts his selection
of a salacious book for Molly. He comes upon one with the
title *Sweets of Sin*:

*—All the dollarbills her husband gave her were spent
in the stores on wondrous gowns and costliest frillies.
For him! For Raoul!*
   Yes. This. Here. Try.
   *—Her mouth glued on his in a luscious voluptuous kiss
while his hands felt for the opulent curves inside her
deshabille.*
   Yes. Take this. The end.
   *—You are late, he spoke hoarsely, eyeing her with a
suspicious glare.*
   *The beautiful woman threw off her sabletrimmed wrap,
displaying her queenly shoulders and heaving embonpoint.
An imperceptible smile played around her perfect lips as
she turned to him calmly.*   (232-33)

The first of the three snatches Bloom reads at random echoes
both Molly's cuckoldry of him and his pandering tendency,
for the husband in *Sweets of Sin* is unconsciously abetting
his wife's affair. The second is a reinforcement of "her"
sexuality. The third is the conclusion of the story of "her"
and a "he" who is presumably the lover. A revery follows
in which Bloom is making fervid love to the "beautiful
woman" of the conclusion, the voluptuous wife; he has
already seen himself as Don Giovanni, but his Zerlina was
Martha Clifford. His transition, from his real situation of
the betrayed and rejected husband to the revery in which
he speaks "hoarsely" to the woman who, although "late,"
ultimately comes to him, reveals every aspect of his condition
with respect to Molly.

The passages from *Sweets of Sin*, which are unusual for
this chapter because they are exploited in the action of the
novel, are used chiefly to invoke various aspects of Bloom's
connubial circumstances. The clichéd phrases, "costliest frillies," "opulent curves," "sabletrimmed wrap," "heaving
embonpoint," or parts of them, crop up; and "For him!
For Raoul!", or either half of it, appears frequently.

The link between this chapter and the preceding one has
been discussed. It is also linked with the following chapter,
whose locale is the Ormond Hotel. Lenehan arranges to
meet Boylan at the Ormond during this chapter. Father
Cowley, Ben Dollard, and Simon Dedalus meet and arrange for their active role in the eleventh chapter. Every
important character in that chapter is brought into this one;

aside from those mentioned, there are Bloom, Richie Goulding, Boylan, the blind piano-tuner, and the Misses Kennedy and Douce. Finally, the observation of the viceregal procession by "bronze by gold" (the two barmaids) from the vantage of the hotel's bar, which occurs twice (242 and 249), is repeated twice in the eleventh chapter: at the beginning of the "overture" (252) and the beginning of the chapter proper (253); and it is followed by the barmaids' discussion of the procession which ends the "*entr'acte.*"

Although it separates the two parts of the novel and thus does not contribute to the development of the narrative to any significant extent, the tenth chapter is an integral element in *Ulysses.* Joyce carried out only the first and third parts of his original intention regarding "an *Entr'Acte* . . . after 9th episode," for it was to be "Short with absolutely no relation to what precedes or follows like a pause in the action of a play."

1. Gilbert, p. 225.

2. Richard M. Kain, consistently perceptive about Joyce's characterization, is almost alone in understanding the treatment of Conmee. See Kain, p. 111.

3. While walking on the North Circular Road, Conmee wonders "that there was not a tramline" (217–18), and so conceives of one of the pet projects of the arch-secular Bloom (57–58), (96), (469), (703).

4. Literally "again-biting of the inner-wit," colloquially "remorse of conscience"; the medieval homiletic book of that name seems to have no relevance.

chapter seven

11 *the ormond hotel*

The page and a half of fragmentary phrases that opens the eleventh chapter and the second part of *Ulysses* has long been a source of contention. It is clearly a discrete composition, for it is set off from what follows and it ends on the conclusive note of "Done. Begin!", with each word placed on a line by itself. Furthermore, there is little question that the composition is an incomprehensible one (the story of the difficulties it experienced in getting past the British censor during the First World War is well known).

The essential fact about it is generally recognized—that it is a verbal imitation of an operatic overture. The subject of the contention has been a question of sound and sense: can snatches of language from a larger context communicate as snatches of music do? In this instance the snatches fail to do so. And it does not justify Joyce's device to attack the musical convention from which it derives or to argue that the "overture" is comprehensible post facto, after the chapter proper has been read and the context of each phrase supplied from it. The "overture" makes no sense and has no unity; its structure is simply the result of the extraction of representative snatches of language throughout the chapter, with some interpolation for verbal effect. It is not even a replica of the chapter. It is simply the verbal equivalent, for the chapter, of an overture to an opera.

Joyce was not too stupid to know that his snatches of
language out of context would generally lack meaning and
that they would fail to produce a coherent combination. The
composition does not have to be comprehensible or coherent,
only purposeful, which it is. The chapter begins with the
imitation of an operatic overture because it is being associated with the romantic opera *Martha*, by Friedrich von
Flotow.[1] The overture to *Martha* is made up of excerpts
from the opera proper; its famous tenor aria "M'appari" is
very prominent in the chapter; one of the barmaids brings
up the central soprano aria, Thomas Moore's "The Last
Rose of Summer"; and Bloom is occupied a good deal of
the time with a letter to his penpal, Martha Clifford. The
prominence in the chapter of vocal music in general and
of references to singers and the heavy concentration (with
varying results) on onomatopoeia and other phonetic word
play in the prose serve primarily to reinforce this specific
association.[2]

Martha appears to be the casting of an English Restoration comedy situation into a romantic and moralistic mold,
with the result that the nastiness remains and the wit is
converted to mawkish sentimentality. Lady Harriet, a British noblewoman ("maid of honor to Queen Anne"), decides
to attend the Richmond Fair disguised as a peasant (Martha)
for diversion from the tedium of court life. Her maid
Nancy and a foppish suitor accompany her. Two young
farmers at the fair, attracted by their beauty, offer to hire
the women, who accept the money proffered and thereby
bind themselves. At the farmers' cottage, Lionel, the
adopted brother of Plunkett, declares his love for Martha
(Lady Harriet), who thereupon fans his fervor by singing
"The Last Rose of Summer." Plunkett and Nancy provide
the comic subplot.

The women escape, and the next time Lionel meets the
noblewoman (coincidentally, he has just sung "M'appari")
she is in her proper dress. She has him arrested for effront-
ery when he courts her, and he sends his ring to Queen
Anne via Plunkett. He is discovered to be a noble waif, son
and heir of the late Earl of Derby. Lady Harriet is now
enthusiastic about him (actually, although unwavering in
her duty to her class and herself, she had suffered touching

regrets), but Lionel has become mentally deranged because of her former cruelty. She goes to his farm and sings "The Last Rose of Summer" without success. Her pleas for forgiveness are also rejected. But with the aid of the now betrothed Plunkett and Nancy, Lady Harriet devises a method of therapy: she converts part of her estate into a replica of Richmond Fair, and Plunkett leads Lionel to a repetition of the original meeting between the four. Lionel is cured and wins his Martha. The finale of the opera is a chorus by the full cast of a song to the tune of "The Last Rose of Summer," but with the words, "Behold, April returns / Around the hilltop with flowers in bloom. . . ."

The quality of the book of the opera is apparent. Some similarity to Bloom's situation in *Ulysses* may also suggest itself. The devotion and suffering of the unrequited lover echo aspects of Bloom's relationship with Molly; and the "return" of his Martha is for Lionel a realization of Bloom's deep desire, expressed in his gnawing memories of his and Molly's former relationship in the eighth chapter (Byrne's), and in his revery over the conclusion of *Sweets of Sin* a few pages back. But these are only approximate correspondences, and much closer and more revealing ones exist.

Every word in the "overture" except the final one is designed to reflect some part of the chapter proper. That "Begin!" is more than the cue for the raising of the curtain on the "opera," the eleventh chapter of *Ulysses*. It also functions in the general action of the novel. The chapters through the ninth are a presentation or exposition of an everyday situation, which ends with the intimation of a future development; with the eleventh chapter that unique development begins.

The discussion of the novel's structure in the Introduction included other indications that the rising action begins with the present chapter. At this point the various narrative devices begin to dominate the respective chapters. More important, Bloom's behavior begins to change. The example of change that was cited there is his decision, at the beginning of the chapter, to follow Boylan.

The circumstances of this decision provide an early indication that the "Martha" who figures so prominently in the chapter is not Martha Clifford but, as has been suggested, Molly. Bearing *Sweets of Sin,* Bloom thinks "To Martha I must write" and visits a stationer's:

> Wise Bloom eyed on the door a poster, a swaying mermaid smoking mid nice waves. Smoke mermaids, coolest whiff of all. Hair streaming: lovelorn. For some man. For Raoul. He eyed and saw afar on Essex bridge a gay hat riding on a jauntingcar. It is. Third time. Coincidence.
> Jingling on supple rubbers it jaunted from the bridge to Ormond quay. Follow. Risk it. Go quick. At four. Near now. Out.
> —Twopence, sir, the shopgirl dared to say. (259) 263

Thus the prudent Bloom, formerly anxious to avoid Boylan (in the funeral car he had intensely studied his fingernails; approaching the National Library he had rushed into the museum), at this third sight of him is so intent on taking some action that he forgets to pay for the letter paper. Throughout the chapter his concern for Molly eclipses any thought of Martha Clifford, and there is little doubt that writing to Martha is, as he says, a "bore." He tries to increase his enthusiasm by telling himself that it is the course prescribed by his alienation from Molly and ignoring the obvious fact of its comparative blandness, that it is "sauce for the gander"; but wife takes precedence over epistolary mistress. He reiterates the guilt-motivated desire, expressed in the eighth chapter (Byrne's), to buy Molly "the violet silk petticoats." This time the pandering motif is delineated by allusion to the "costliest frillies. . . . For Raoul!" of *Sweets of Sin,* in combination with thoughts of Molly's imminent rendezvous:

> . . . At four, she said. Time ever passing. Clockhands turning. On. Where eat? The Clarence, Dolphin. On. For Raoul. Eat. If I net five guineas with those ads. The violet silk petticoats. Not yet. The sweets of sin. (256) 260

He alters the line from "Matcham's Masterstroke," the story he read in the outhouse during the fourth chapter, in a

significant way. The two brief excerpts from the story,
*"Matcham often thinks of the masterstroke by which he
won the laughing witch who now"* and *"Hand in hand,"*
indicate that it would have more than ordinary interest for
Bloom, who wants so much to "win" his own "laughing
witch"; in this chapter he confesses, "Matcham often thinks
[of] the laughing witch" (276). He thinks of Molly's
appearance on different occasions (271, 277, 280). And,
of course, he follows Boylan.

Bloom's pursuit of Boylan is what takes him to the
Ormond. When having his "bite" in Davy Byrne's at two
o'clock, he had decided to dine at six o'clock: "Six, six.
Time will be gone then. She . . ." (172); in the passage
quoted from above, he says, "Eat first. I want. Not yet.
At four, she said." He does not want to eat his dinner with
Molly's rendezvous in prospect. However, when Boylan
enters the bar, Bloom meets Richie Goulding, Stephen's
maternal uncle, outside and decides to dine with him:

> Dining room. Sit tight there. See, not be seen. I think
> I'll join you. (261)

They enter the dining room that adjoins the bar and, pursuing his endeavor to "see, not be seen":

> Aimless he chose with agitated aim, bald Pat attending,
> a table near the door. Be near. At four. Has he forgotten? Perhaps a trick. Not come: whet appetite. I
> couldn't do. (262)

His wishful thinking is soon disappointed, for Boylan
leaves the Ormond; and he sadly estimates Boylan's progress
while the author reports it at intervals in the chapter. He
guesses Boylan's arrival at number 7 Eccles Street precisely
right, for his words are followed by:

> One rapped on a door, one tapped with a knock, did
> he knock Paul de Kock, with a loud proud knocker, with
> a cock carracarracarra cock. Cockcock. (278)

Of course, he was helpless to stop the affair or another
like it, as he recognizes while following the usurper to his
home and wife in his imagination:

Jingle jaunty. Too late. She longed to go. That's why.
Woman. As easy stop the sea. Yes: all is lost. (268)

His last remark, which is inspired by a phrase of a song
("All is lost now") just mentioned to him by Richie
Goulding, indicates a *conscious* realization for the first time
in the book of the extent of Molly's importance to him.
This realization is immediately reinforced: Simon Dedalus,
after insistent prodding by his two companions, Ben Dollard and Father Cowley, begins to sing an English version
of "M'appari." The fragmentary English verses that appear
in the text are a rough approximation of the original Italian.
The lover sings of his happiness "When first I saw that
form endearing," tells of the folly of his hope to win
Martha, and ends with an appeal that she go to him. During
the singing of this song, Bloom, listening in the dining
room, thinks of his loss of Molly to Boylan and his distress
at that loss in two paragraphs that exploit respectively
"Love's Old Sweet Song" and *Sweets of Sin* (269-70). He
then has another revery of lovemaking with Molly (270).

However, as he points out, Dedalus is "Singing wrong
words." Bloom is familiar with the aria. He remarks on the
coincidental identity of the name of the opera from which
it comes and that of the woman to whom he is about to
write; he refers to it as "Lionel's song"; and he seems to
know something about the meaning of its original verses.
Furthermore, Dedalus' free English version is "wrong"
with respect to Bloom as well as with respect to *Martha*.
For "M'appari" is a representation of Bloom's lament for
Molly. It is for this reason that he is referred to as "Henry
Lionel Leopold" and "Lionelleopold," and that the reader
is told, when Dedalus concludes his version of the song:

Lionel Simon, singer, laughed. Father Bob Cowley
played. Mina Kennedy served. Second gentleman paid.
Tom Kernan strutted in; Lydia, admired, admired. But
Bloom sang dumb. (272)

In the original Italian, the song Bloom is singing "dumb"
is especially apt. The first of its five stanzas describes the
lover's meeting with his lady, the second her effect on him,

the third his revery with respect to her, the fourth their
meeting (repetition of the first), and the fifth the reality
of "Lionel-leopold's" situation. Literally translated, the
song reads:

> She appeared to me . . full of love;
> My glance fell on her
> So beautiful . . that my anxious heart
> Flew to her.
>
> That angelic beauty
> Wounded me . . kindled my desire;
> Sculpted in my heart . . by love,
> It could not be blotted out.
>
> The thought . . to be able
> To tremble with her in love
> Can allay . . the torment
> Which troubles me and tortures my heart.
>
> She appeared to me . . full of love;
> My glance fell on her
> So beautiful . . that my anxious heart
> Flew to her.
>
> Martha, Martha, you faded away,
> And my heart went with you;
> You robbed me of peace,
> I shall die of sadness.[3]

And there is no doubt that the "Martha" about whom Bloom
sings silently is Molly. He has never seen Martha Clifford,
so that from the very first line the song is inappropriate to
her. Besides, as the chapter makes clear, his epistolary
affair has practically no hold on his interest. Molly's correspondence to the soprano in the opera is fairly precise,
both having abandoned their devoted lovers; and Bloom's
thoughts explicate the correspondence. Echoing the burden
of the first two stanzas, in which Lionel tells how he fell

in love with Martha the minute he saw her at the Richmond Fair, Bloom thinks while the song is being sung:

> First night when first I saw her at Mat Dillon's in Terenure. Yellow, black lace she wore. Musical chairs. We two the last. Fate. After her. Fate. . . . Down she sat. All ousted looked. Lips laughing. Yellow knees.
> —*Charmed my eye.* . .
> Singing. *Waiting* she sang. I turned her music. . . . Bosom I saw, both full, throat warbling. First I saw. She thanked me. Why did she me? Fate. (271)

Thus, the various devices used to associate the chapter with the opera *Martha* effect a highly functional association. Where Bloom was resigned in the sixth chapter (post office) and troubled in the eighth (Byrne's), he is now fully, consciously, aware of his situation and of its significance. He knows that he must get Molly back or he "shall die of sadness." Although his pursuit of Boylan at the beginning of the chapter suggests it, "M'appari" serves as the principal vehicle for representing this awareness.

Ultimately the important thing about Bloom's awareness is whether or not he acts upon it. In following Boylan he acts, although his action is doomed to futility. He acts in another significant way in the chapter, however, a way that directly illustrates his realization of what the loss of Molly means to him.

In this case the author exploits not *Martha* but the *Odyssey.* The analogue to the present chapter is the episode during which Odysseus arranges under Circe's direction to hear the exquisite song of the two Sirens, and yet to avoid the destruction that met all men who had enjoyed the experience. He has his crew stop their ears, tie him to the mast, and disregard any orders he might give that they change course or untie him.

Details substantiating the correspondence abound, and the strongest link is blatant: there are two barmaids who hum and sing, and flirt with the patrons of the Ormond's bar.

Their flirtation is not invariably casual, however, so that they are more than simply representations of Homeric she-demons. For example, when Boylan enters the bar, Miss Kennedy stops reading, and she and Miss Douce compete for his favor until Miss Douce proves more adept (260). Both are jealous over him, for both wonder about the carnation he got at the florist's (261). Finally Miss Douce, after a bit of prodding from Lenehan, exposes her thigh to him and Boylan, following which "mild she smiled on Boylan" (262). To no avail. Boylan leaves for his assignation with Molly, and Miss Douce can only watch him go "pensive (why did he go so quick when I?)." Her spirits rise when George Lidwell, a solicitor, enters the bar and rapidly becomes interested in her; and Miss Kennedy, in keeping with her more decorous deportment, talks decorously with an unwed gentleman who enters the bar.

Not only are the "sirens" more than idle flirts, but with the possible exception of one incident they have nothing whatever to do with Bloom. Neither one is interested in him. In this chapter, as in many others, the Homeric parallel does not function in the terms in which it is drawn. One true siren luring Bloom away from his family and to destruction is Martha Clifford, of course: his purchase of notepaper for a letter to her and writing of the letter figure prominently in the chapter; but his rejection of this siren occurs without great effort. There are much more attractive sirens—quite appropriately, the singers of the songs he hears through most of the chapter.

Bloom observes of Dedalus, "Wore out his wife: now sings," and of Ben Dollard:

> Ben Dollard's voice barreltone. . . . Croak of vast manless moonless womoonless marsh. . . . Big ships' chandler's business he did once. . . . Now in the Iveagh home. Cubicle number so and so. Number one Bass did that for him.
>
> .   .   .   .
> Ruin them. Wreck their lives. Then build them cubicles to end their days in. Hushaby. Lullaby. Die, dog. Little dog, die. (278-79)

To this the author prefixes a description of Dollard's voice as "The voice of dark age, of unlove, earth's fatigue. . . ."

And Father Cowley, the third of the good comrades, is shown worrying about his imminent eviction while he engages in genteel revelry (277). The sirens luring Bloom are the men singing in the adjoining room. Widower, bachelor, and priest, they are unwived and (Dedalus' relationship with Stephen being what it is) sonless. The responsibilities of a husband and father, in Bloom's case the double problem of reuniting with Molly and begetting a son to continue the familial line, are completely avoided by Dedalus, Dollard, and Cowley. Their siren song is simply the example they embody of aging male camaraderie, without the impingement of wife, family, or home, the example of a kind of life that is an easily achieved escape from his predicament.

Bloom deliberates whether to follow their example during the chapter:

> Gone. They sing. Forgotten. I too. And one day she with. Leave her: get tired. Suffer then. Snivel. Big Spanishy eyes goggling at nothing. (273)

But after this deliberation, he has the thoughts about Dollard quoted above and understands the essential loneliness and lack of meaning of the sirens' lives. Continuing to suffer over the more and more imminent consummation of Molly's affair and to recall with admiration aspects of Molly's beauty and personality, he makes his decision. Dollard is singing the sentimental patriotic ballad identified as one of his specialties earlier in the novel (89-90), "The Croppy Boy." It tells of a young "croppy," a member of the revolutionary group of 1798, most of whose leaders were betrayed before they could begin to fight. Preparing for battle, the croppy confesses harmless sins, only to find that the rectory has been occupied by the British and a "yeoman captain" has disguised himself as the priest; the boy is then executed. Hearing Dollard sing "The Croppy Boy," Bloom thinks:

> All gone. All fallen. At the siege of Ross his father, at Gorey all his brothers fell. To Wexford, we are the boys of Wexford, he would. Last of his name and race.
> I too, last my race. Milly young student. Well, my fault perhaps. No son. Rudy. Too late now. Or if not?

If not? If still?
  He bore no hate.
  Hate. Love. Those are names. Rudy. Soon I am old.
(280)

Having acknowledged Molly's importance to him for the
first time in the novel and having followed Boylan for the
first time, Bloom now for the first time expresses the view
that something may yet be done to change his situation.
And, in consequence, he decides to leave immediately,
before Dollard finishes, clearly rejecting the song of the
sirens:

> Ireland comes now. My country above the king. She
> listens. Who fears to speak of nineteen four? Time to
> be shoving. Looked enough.

The last two words refer to another siren call, by Miss
Douce. No more aware that she is offering a lure to Bloom
than are Dedalus, Dollard, and Cowley, she is partly aware
that he has been looking at her. The lure is that of flirtation and concupiscence, a more tangible substitute for reunion with Molly than Martha Clifford's letters and pressed
flowers. And before Bloom does "shove," Miss Douce, still
partly aware that he is looking but "lost in pity for croppy,"
elaborates the lure by symbolic masturbation of a beer-pull
(281). Associated with the croppy boy (as he goes out,
Dollard sings "Pray for him. . . . He was the croppy boy,"
and the author promptly calls him "croppy bootsboy
Bloom"), Bloom also is made to feel that Miss Douce's
gesture is intended for himself (and for Lidwell). But
although grateful, he is undeterred:

> Get out before the end. Thanks, that was heavenly.
> Where's my hat. Pass by her. (282)

Having rejected the siren-songs of Martha Clifford, the
three men, and Miss Douce, Bloom does not succumb to
the dubious attraction of the old prostitute who approaches
him after he leaves the Ormond. Apparently she is Bridie

Kelly, with whom he had his first sexual experience many years before in Hatch Street. He avoids meeting this reminder of a furtive pre-marital experience by looking in a store window while she passes, and the chapter ends with a medley composed of an approaching tram, Bloom's breaking wind, and the concluding words of the patriotic speech made by Robert Emmett, leader of an ill-planned and abortive revolt in 1803, at his trial, which Bloom apparently reads from a picture of Emmett in the store window. Bloom is associated with the young hero through Emmett's traditional (although anachronistic) association with the croppy boy. Nevertheless, his breaking wind as the prostitute passes is his final comment, not only on all the siren lures which she represents, but on the nationalistic sentimentalism that surrounds the composite Emmett-croppy as well; it is at this point that Bloom thinks of the nameless Wexford martyr, "All the same he must have been a bit of a natural not to see it was a yeoman cap."

In the eleventh chapter Bloom has been presented with, and has rejected, various kinds of inducement for reconciling himself to the loss of Molly and a prospective son. He thereby has avoided destruction. The sirens, like the lotus-eaters, offer escape and contentment, but the sirens destroy those they succeed in tempting. Correspondingly, Bloom could crave the forgetfulness of the lotus in the fifth chapter without harm; but had he succumbed to any of the various siren-songs, his ultimate fate would be that of Martha Clifford, the prostitute, and the three old men: loneliness, barrenness, hopelessness. Even the two overt sirens, the barmaids, share this fate. Miss Douce, constantly attracting men, seems to be able to hold none, and Miss Kennedy at least is clearly destined for spinsterhood.

The chapter begins with Bloom's unique, although futile, act of following Boylan, and it ends with an equally decisive contrast with his earlier attitude and conduct—his decision that it may not be too late to do something, that he bears no hatred toward Molly for the Boylan affair, and that if something is to be done, it must be done "soon." Unlike Odysseus, he has had to resist the call of the sirens himself, but both his understanding of his need for Molly and his resolve have proven sufficiently strong. In the next

chapter, too, he will prove himself superior to the Greek
hero, and again in a Bloomian way.

Bloom begins to think and act differently, in this chapter,
from the Bloom presented throughout the first part of the
novel. When Boylan enters the bar, Lenehan greets him in
a characteristically sycophantic manner. It is perhaps not
with sarcasm, considering that Bloom is at that moment
engaged in his intrepid act of following Boylan, that the
author counters Lenehan's with a tribute of his own:

> Lenehan heard and knew and hailed him:
> —See the conquering hero comes.
> Between the car and window, warily walking, went
> Bloom, unconquered hero (260)

and adds to it the epithet "black wary hecat," a reference
not only to a powerful stalking animal but to a savior as
well.

12 *barney kiernan's*

As he prepares to leave the Ormond, Bloom thinks, "Barney
Kiernan's I promised to meet them." The meeting is with
Martin Cunningham and Jack Power, for a visit to Mrs.
Dignam's to discuss the difficulty over her husband's life
insurance. The present chapter concerns what happens when
Bloom arrives at their meeting-place some minutes before
the widow's other advisers.

An anonymous participant, who discloses a great deal
about himself in the process, tells about the incident in a
first-person narrative, the format of which accommodates
both dialogue and his comments to his silent auditor. However, the author interrupts the narrative proper with passages in differing styles, as though it were not fully ade-

quate to the incident. In fact, there is as much of this disguised omniscient commentary as there is story. Interpolations varying in length from a few lines to four pages occur at more than two dozen separate points, after each of which the narrative resumes as though it had never been interrupted. Thus, *Ulysses* is not simply given into a nameless narrator's hands at this point; rather, his story of an incident that occurred at Barney Kiernan's public house is made part of the twelfth chapter, one device the author employs to advance the novel.

The interpolated commentary is generally satiric, employing either ironic contrast or caricature. For example, after Bloom is baited about Molly's projected concert tour with Boylan, and the narrator comments for the reader, "Blazes doing the tootle on the flute," Molly is eulogized ironically (in both style and substance) as "Pride of Calpe's rocky mount, the ravenhaired daughter of Tweedy. . . . The chaste spouse of Leopold is she . . ." (314). An example of Joyce's caricature is a report of a wedding in a burlesque of a society column. The chauvinistic talk in Kiernan's bar has turned to trees, and John Wyse Nolan warns that Ireland will soon be "as treeless as Portugal," "if something is not done to reafforest the land"; for this devotion to Ireland's arboriculture, Nolan is made the groom of "Miss Fir Conifer of Pine Valley" (321). The account begins with a list of the company (Lady Sylvester Elmshade, Miss Virginia Creeper, Mrs. Maud Mahogany, *et al.*) and a description of the bride's dress, which gives her a strong resemblance to a tree, and it continues in a similar vein for almost a page. The pungent ridicule and robust verbosity of most of the interpolations fully justify the comparison often made to Rabelais.

The principal object of Joyce's satire is the modern Irish citizen; his blind chauvinism and the contrast between his society and the Ireland of the past are the themes. The chapter begins with the beginning of the narrator's story, which immediately suggests the correspondence to the Cyclops episode of the *Odyssey*—

I was just passing the time of day with old Troy of the D.M.P. [Dublin Municipal Police] at the corner of

> Arbour hill there and be damned but a bloody sweep
> came along and he near drove his gear into my eye (287)

—and then leads into Joyce's satiric attack on the degenerate state of modern Ireland. Nothing came of the incident, for before he could upbraid the sweep, the narrator says, he saw Joe Hynes approaching. After he repeats a dialogue in which he told Hynes of his endeavors to collect a bill for an unlicensed Jewish merchant who sold a large order of sugar and tea to a larcenous customer, "an old plumber named Geraghty," the first interpolation in the chapter occurs. It is a pompously legalistic bill of sale for this transaction which provides by its incongruity an eloquent statement about the appearance and reality of commerce and a humorous conclusion to the brief account of Geraghty's chicanery. The narrator's account resumes with Hynes' invitation to him to drink at Kiernan's, and the second interpolation begins.

This interpolation lists for almost two pages the natural wealth and abundant produce of "the land of holy Michan," St. Michan's parish in Dublin, the locale of Kiernan's pub and Geraghty's house. The contrast with the way in which Geraghty provides sustenance for himself in the land of holy Michan is obvious, but the comment on the difference between past and present is also made stylistically:

> A pleasant land it is in sooth . . . where sport the gunnard, the plaice, the roach, the halibut, the gibbed haddock . . . and other denizens of the aqueous kingdom too numerous to be enumerated. In the mild breezes of the west and of the east the lofty trees wave in different directions their first class foliage. . . . (288-89)

As a final note of contrast, there is a description of the "superabundance of milk" and dairy products in the region, followed by: "So we turned into Barney Kiernan's . . ." (290).

The nameless narrator's account reinforces the satire, in part because he indicts himself. Joyce conceived his idiom to be that of the Coombe, "a lower quarter of the city," [4] and he is not markedly different from the many other

Dubliners portrayed in the novel. However he is not necessarily an Irish "Everyman": he can be considered more
"typical" than either Bloom or Bloom's fanatical antagonist
in the chapter, "the citizen"; but there is no apparent concern with any universal qualities he may possess, and a
great deal of concern for the development of very particular
ones.

He has been described as "a simple and bibulous Dubliner." [5] Bibulous he undoubtedly is, but he is far from
simple. He seems to know every bit of gossip that exists.
As Bob Doran, still on the bender mentioned by M'Coy in
the fifth chapter (72), leaves the bar, he is able to describe
not only Doran's forced marriage, the subject of "The
Boarding House" in *Dubliners,* but also the circumstances
of Doran's visit to a brothel, including the pseudonym
Doran used and his behavior there. And he reveals during
the chapter intimate and embarrassing information about
Bloom, Hynes, Boylan, Denis Breen, and the citizen. Furthermore, his verbal wit is often funny enough to rank with
the satiric interpolations, and he has the intelligence
and common sense to recognize the folly of the extreme nationalists. The following passage shows both these
characteristics:

> So then the citizen begins talking about the Irish
> language . . . and Joe chipping in because he stuck
> someone for a quid and Bloom putting in his old goo
> . . . and talking about the Gaelic league and the anti-
> treating league and drink, the curse of Ireland. Anti-
> treating is about the size of it. Gob, he'd let you pour
> all manner of drink down his throat . . . before you'd
> ever see the froth of his pint. And one night I went in
> . . . and there was a fellow with a Ballyhooly blue rib-
> bon badge spiffing out of him in Irish. . . . And then an
> old fellow starts blowing into his bagpipes and all the
> gougers shuffling their feet to the tune the old cow died
> of. And one or two sky pilots having an eye around that
> there was no goings on with the females, hitting below the
> belt. (305-6)

The passage shows as well the narrator's outstanding trait—
the pettiness and malice of his character. As he has already
disclosed, Hynes did not borrow the money to provide the

generosity he is enjoying, but is spending his wages, pro-
cured earlier (on Bloom's advice) from the *Evening Telegraph* cashier (113). And Bloom would no more accept
drinks than proffer them, as—again by his own account—
Bloom has just shown.

In fact, even the citizen, who spends his time in bars
ranting about Ireland and accepting proffered treats, does
not impose more blatantly on the generosity of others than
the narrator does; so he is a rank hypocrite as well. When
Hynes has offered the citizen another drink, he berates the
citizen for parasitism before continuing with Hynes:

> And says Joe:
> —Could you make a hole in another pint?
> —Could a swim duck? says I (307)

whose first invitation prompted: "Decent fellow Joe when
he has it but sure like that he never has it."

When to his malice are added his hypocrisy, his self-
centered parasitic exploitation of others, the fact that he is
a bill collector, and such evidence of his refinement as his
vomiting (329), the narrator emerges as a negative character who is too sensible to be the representative Irishman,
and too malicious and calculating as well. Still, he is part
of the typical Irish group in the bar; and through what he
tells about the group and what he reveals about himself, he
provides a constant reminder of the degeneration of Joyce's
Ireland.

The narrator is properly more perceptive and witty than
the others, in view of his function, but he participates as
fully as they do in the central conflict of the two principals,
"the citizen" and Bloom.

The citizen is no more representative a citizen than is
Bloom, and is not even part of Hynes' and Cunningham's
group. He is, rather, a caricature. He is a former shot-
putter and minor revolutionary, currently a fool and barfly.
When the narrator and Hynes enter the bar, the narrator
says, the citizen is "waiting for what the sky would drop
in the way of drink." The citizen begins a childish exchange:

—Stand and deliver, says he.
—That's all right, citizen, says Joe. Friends here.
—Pass, friends, says he.
Then he rubs his hand in his eye and says he:
—What's your opinion of the times? (290)

and the narrator remarks contemptuously, "Doing the rapparee and Rory of the hill."

On the very next page, the author indicates his essential agreement with the narrator. A long description of an ancient Irish giant, parodying romantic translations of Irish sagas, ridicules the actual "hero" by representing the old man as he sees himself. And again and again his intolerance, chauvinism, and stupidity justify the satire:

What do the yellow johns of Anglia owe us for our ruined trade and our ruined hearths? And the beds of the Barrow and Shannon they won't deepen with millions of acres of marsh and bog to make us all die of consumption. (320-21)

The combination here of his execration of the British and his whining complaint that they fail to take certain public health measures is less intolerant, chauvinistic, and stupid than his behavior toward Bloom.

The relatively simple major action of the chapter, comprising the behavior of the citizen and the consequent behavior of Bloom and the others in the bar, is the business of the narrator; but it is only part of the business of the chapter. Certain instrumental details and certain of the interpolated commentaries combine with the action at specific points to accomplish that larger business which is crucial for the novel. The manner in which these various elements combine is shown in the following brief review.

Almost as soon as Hynes and the narrator arrive at Kiernan's, Bloom is brought up; impressed by Hynes' affluence, the narrator is told that "the prudent member gave me the wheeze," and responds, "—I saw him before I met you . . . with his cod's eye" (292). This exchange is immediately followed by a very brief interpolation in the idiom of the heroic age, announcing the approach of "O'Bloom, the son of Rory" (Rory O'Connor, the last High King of all Ireland). After a few minutes the citizen remarks, "—What's that bloody freemason doing . . . prowling up and down outside?" An impending execution is brought up, and Alf Bergan shows the company some letters from hangmen soliciting the commission for despatching the condemned criminal. But the citizen does not participate in the conversation; when he speaks next, it is to say, "staring out," that Bloom has returned. And on the next page the citizen speaks once more—to invite him into the bar; "—So Bloom slopes in with his cod's eye on the dog" (298). (The citizen is not the dog Garryowen's owner, "grandpapa [J. J.] Giltrap," Joyce's aunt's father in real life.) As Bloom enters, Hynes begins to read aloud one of the hangmen's letters.

The intimations of what awaits Bloom in the bar are not long unfulfilled. The talk moves to capital punishment and, in the words of the narrator, "Bloom comes out with the why and the wherefor and all the codology of the business." The citizen begins a tirade, and Bloom attempts to point out to him that he was justifying capital punishment for criminals and not the execution of national heroes by the British. The narrator relishes the situation and discloses some choice gossip about Bloom before telling how the controversy comes to a head. The citizen, "glaring at Bloom," pronounces the Irish nationalistic slogan, *"Sinn Fein!"*, repeats it adding the intensifying *"amhain"* (only, alone), then blatantly refers to Bloom as a stranger and an enemy. The first of three successively more overt affronts, it concludes the first phrase of Bloom's ordeal in Kiernan's. And it initiates the longest interpolated passage in the chapter, a description of "a genuinely instructive treat"—the execution of an Irish patriot by the British, "H. Rumbold, Master Barber," the author of the letter read aloud, officiating.

As he had done in the sixth chapter (cemetery) in the face of less aggressive anti-Semitism, Bloom attempts to override the rebuff. He joins Hynes and the citizen, who seems to be too devoted to Ireland as a whole to know any man in the bar *(except him)* by name, in their nationalist patter. When he mentions "the wife's admirers" (Mrs. Dignam's advisers), his slip is noticed, but the issue is not broached immediately; instead, the citizen's former athletic prowess and Irish sport are dwelt on, and once more he vexes the company, by pointing out the harm in overexertion. His reward follows: Bergan tells of Boylan's clever management of the boxer Myler Keogh. Unlike Nosey Flynn, who brought up Boylan's *coup* in the eighth chapter (170-71), the present company is fully aware of the connection between Bloom and Boylan, and he is unable to divert the conversation either at this point or subsequently.

When the citizen contributes to the cuckold-baiting, he is both more intent and more aggressive: "Pity about [Mrs. Breen], says the citizen. Or any other woman marries a half and half"; and the narrator observes, "Begob I saw there was trouble coming." But the trouble is not imminent. Discussion of Denis Breen's attempts to arrange a libel suit leads the group, now augmented, back to anti-Semitism. A Jew who has swindled prospective emigrants, a Jew who is among his victims, and Reuben J. Dodd, the Jewish money-lender, are discussed. The account of the ruling against Dodd by the recorder (chief magistrate) of the court is followed by an interpolation, in the archaic idiom of most of the commentaries, depicting the judgment of the Green Street Court—metamorphosed into ancient clansmen—against a "malefactor." This is followed in turn by:

Those are nice things, says the citizen, coming over to Ireland filling the country with bugs. (318)

And as the narrator observes, "Bloom lets on he heard nothing." Again he has been directly rebuffed, and again he attempts to reconcile himself.

The third phase of Bloom's ordeal begins with the citizen still spewing his bigotry. The others have deftly turned again to the cuckoldry theme, but the citizen's nationalist zeal cannot be swayed. While Lenehan announces to the others that Throwaway has won the Ascot gold cup "at twenty to one. A rank outsider," and that Boylan bet and lost two pounds on the favorite, Sceptre, "for himself and a

lady friend," he rants at J. J. O'Molloy and Bloom. He
brings up the caning of sailors in the British navy, Bloom
suggests that "discipline" and the use of "force" are "the
same everywhere," and as in the discussion of capital punishment he fails to comprehend Bloom's simple point. There
is general talk of Ireland's plight; other nations are condemned, Hynes orders still another round of drinks (for
everyone but Bloom, who always demurs and, at one point,
denounces "the curse of Ireland"), and Bloom protests
"Perpetuating national hatred among nations." John Wyse
Nolan asks Bloom if he knows "what a nation means?" and
"—What is your nation," and:

> —Ireland, says Bloom. I was born here, Ireland.
> The citizen said nothing only cleared the spit out of his
> gullet and, gob, he spat a Red bank oyster out of him
> right in the corner. (325)

Bloom does not accept this third affront. Ostensibly
speaking of the enslavement of Jews in Morocco, he protests
the persecution of his "race," "This very moment. This
very instant." Then:

> he collapses all of a sudden, twisting around all the oppo-
> site, as limp as a wet rag.
> —But it's no use, says he. Force, hatred, history, all
> that. That's not life for men and women, insult and
> hatred. And everybody knows that it's the very opposite
> of that that is really life.
> —What? says Alf.
> —Love, says Bloom. I mean the opposite of hatred.
> (327)

And he leaves the bar to look for Cunningham at the
courthouse, and to enable Lenehan to suggest that he has
really gone to collect his winnings on the race.

Although from the beginning of the chapter the citizen
has been hostile to Bloom, the author causes Lenehan
to instigate both the greatest injustice done to Bloom by
the group and the citizen's climactic act of violence. Led to

it by his anti-Semitic bias, Lenehan nevertheless has some reason for his presumption. As he explains, he had met Bantam Lyons (at "Lynam's" betting parlor during the tenth chapter, 229-30), when Lyons was about to bet on Throwaway (as a result of Bloom's chance remark about his newspaper during the fifth chapter, 84), and had "put him off it." And just as Lyons had told his companions in Davy Byrne's during the eighth chapter (176), he had told Lenehan in Lynam's that Bloom "gave" him the tip.

The prejudice of the others in the bar is sufficient to support their acceptance, not only of Bloom's supposed bet and deceitful pretext for leaving to collect on it, but of the large amount Lenehan suggests he won as well. The incident is essentially a trial of Bloom—an indictment is brought and, after discussion, a judgment arrived at. A half-hearted defense is made by Nolan, who says that Bloom advised the leaders of Sinn Fein regarding conspiratorial strategy. Cunningham arrives with Jack Power and the Protestant politician named Crofton and confirms Nolan's statement. But it makes no difference. (Ironically, considering Bloom's reason for being at Kiernan's when Cunningham asks about him, Lenehan says he is out "defrauding widows and orphans.") Although when Bloom returns, Cunningham hurriedly ushers Power, Crofton, and him into the carriage that is to take them to Mrs. Dignam's, the indignant citizen follows them outside and shouts anti-Semitic insults. After bystanders join in, Bloom responds by naming great Jews of history who are all, in fact, also non-Jews, just as he is. It is his inclusion of Christ in his list that causes the citizen to return to the bar, secure the large empty biscuit tin, and hurl it as the carriage departs. The end of the chapter is a parody of the ascension of Elijah to heaven in a "chariot of fire" (II Kings 2:11), in Biblical language that becomes briefly colloquial.

The incident at Kiernan's has three essential principals: Bloom, the citizen, and the group of men, of whom the narrator is one, who share a fundamental attitude toward the antagonists—amused tolerance of the citizen, and amused intolerance of Bloom.

Little can be said to extenuate the culpability of the citizen. He sets himself up as Bloom's antagonist the first time Bloom walks past Kiernan's. He is treated with a relentless irony, not only in the interpolated commentaries, but in the account itself. For example, when he protests the Irish origin of British civilization, it is in the most uncivilized way possible. The citizen is, as has been said, a caricature; he is the ultimate development of *the citizens,* the others in the bar—a monster.

Thus, their basic characteristics are bibulousness, not yet reduced to full-time attendance at bars; impecuniousness, not yet reduced to disguised begging; bigotry and malice, not yet reduced to violence; chauvinism, not yet reduced to blind and humorless fanaticism; and inactivity respecting their national problem, not yet reduced to seeking a scapegoat. The portrait is an elaboration of the one sketched in the seventh (newspaper) chapter. In fact, four of the characters appear in the earlier chapter as well: Lenehan, Lambert, O'Molloy, and Hynes. Like the others, the narrator is amused at the citizen's attack on Bloom and upset about his final violence; considers Bloom an outsider; enjoys the high-spirited fun of baiting the Jew and cuckold; and immediately accepts the judgment of Lenehan, which is convincing only because Bloom is a Jew. The only important respect in which he appears to differ from the others is in his hypocritical attitude toward the national question; and since the private attitudes of the others are not known, the reader is left to question to what extent he actually does differ from the representative citizens.

Bloom, the citizen's scapegoat and the butt of the others, is innocent. He is in no sense pro-British; in fact, he may well have done more for the national cause in his youth than any of the others. His reasonable statements about capital punishment and military discipline are twisted by a brutal fanatic. And the amused baiting of the others is no more defensible morally than the similar incident in the funeral carriage. It is clear from that earlier incident that Cunningham, who here attempts to rescue Bloom from the citizen, is nevertheless prejudiced enough to engage in

Jew-baiting when the occasion allows. Even O'Molloy, who
is more insistent than Bloom on giving the British their
due, is anti-Semitic. Only Nolan is a partial exception. Of
course, Bloom is not entirely blameless. His sententious-
ness and his precise appraisal of the various chauvinistic
statements make him something of a bore. However, as the
narrator reveals, his broad (and shallow) knowledge impresses the others; what annoys them is his violating the
code by which they provide themselves with social conversation. While they make the national question a vehicle for
sentimentality, vanity, and vituperation, he takes the political and moral welfare of Ireland seriously. He points out
the debilitating effect of the nation's alcoholism on its aspirations, the injustice of condemning the English for what the
Irish themselves would do if they had a navy, the evil of
persecution and its evil result, hatred among nations; and
supporting these specific points, he asserts that force, insult,
hatred, the contemporary manifestations of historical circumstances, are "not life for men and women." He is
preaching "Love. . . . I mean the opposite of hatred."
And his sudden exit may reflect as much disgust with those
with whom he has been so frank as embarrassment at
his frankness.

Bloom expresses himself poorly and is foolish in trying
to talk seriously to his companions in the first place, but
his thinking and his sentiments are right, and theirs are
wrong. To their blind and empty chauvinism, malice, and
bombast, he opposes common sense, kindness, and sincerity.

Furthermore, Bloom is not simply an innocent victim in
the chapter. As he himself thinks later on, when no longer
able to endure the citizen's vilification, he "departed from
his customary habit to give him (metaphorically) one in
the gizzard" (641). He has acted heroically, "stood up to
injustice" as Nolan has advised him, and he regards his
conduct as the explanation of the citizen's final violence:

> People could put up with being bitten by a wolf but
> what properly riled them was a bite from a sheep. (642)

The similarity between this incident and that in the funeral
carriage establishes beyond any doubt the significance of

Bloom's fortitude: in both cases Bloom's companions are the semi-poor, semi-professional "citizens" in whose circle he nominally belongs; in both, they bait him for amusement; both times the subjects are the same, his Jewishness and his cuckoldry; in both, Cunningham, Power, and a carriage figure prominently; in both, the anti-Semitism is related to the moneylender, Reuben J. Dodd; finally, although he baits Bloom in the sixth chapter, Cunningham acts in both chapters (in the sixth when Power condemns suicides) to extricate Bloom from an ugly situation.

Of course, Bloom's conduct in the present chapter also appears to bear out the parallel for a while. But he does finally upset it, and the significance of this upset is insisted on by the fact that the parallel exists—precisely as his following Boylan to the Ormond in the preceding chapter is made significant by its contrast to his previous behavior toward Boylan. There he was called the "unconquered Hero"; the eulogy with which he is introduced in the present chapter:

O'Bloom, the son of Rory. . . . Impervious to fear is Rory's son: he of the prudent soul (292)

has its similar element of truth.

Finally, just as was his confrontation of his "sirens," Bloom's fortitude when threatened by his "Cyclops" is more creditable than that of his Homeric analogue. For Odysseus, out of vain bravado, causes the Cyclops to hurl the mountaintop and the even greater second missile that nearly wreck his fleet, while Bloom, a timid and prudent man, causes the analogous action by defying bullying and injustice.

In the present chapter Bloom is the victim of ignorance, bigotry, and hypocrisy; and he continues to be significantly different from his former self. But its burden is not so simple as this. Three interpolated passages contribute to it a completely new dimension of meaning: the execution of the

Irish patriot, which comes at the point of the citizen's first major attack on Bloom; the preparation for the trial of the "malefactor," which is sandwiched between the first Jew-baiting of the group and the citizen's second attack; and the final paragraph.

Although the first of these commentaries seems to derive from the citizen's eulogy of Irish national martyrs, whose murder by the British he considers Bloom to be defending, it does not support the citizen in any way. In the first place the Irish spectators enjoy the execution; the passage, actually in part because of its robust humor, is perhaps the bitterest of the novel's indictments of the Irish people for betraying their patriots. Thus it is a parody of a newspaper report—a reflection of the public viewpoint. In the second place the "genuinely instructive treat" is that because the patriot is not only betrayed and abandoned (his "bride-elect" accepts the suit of an Oxonian Englishman before his eyes), but a scapegoat as well. Thus, aside from a "quartering knife" and "various finely tempered disembowelling appliances," the appointments of the scaffold include "two commodious milkjugs destined to receive the most precious blood of the most precious victim."

The review of the action pointed out that Hynes reads aloud the letter of "H. Rumbold," the English barber-hangman, just as Bloom enters the bar; the "worldrenowned headsman" officiating at the execution of the unnamed patriot has the same name. The coincidence of Bloom's entrance and the reading of the real Rumbold's letter; the irony of the citizen's indignant description of Rumbold as "a barbarous bloody barbarian," a description of himself; the placement of the interpolation directly after the citizen's initial attack on Bloom; and the fact that it represents the Irish people as enjoying themselves at the expense of the "victim"—all these elements conjoin with the general situation in Kiernan's to associate Bloom with the martyr-scapegoat, the citizen with "Rumbold" the executioner, and the others in the bar with "that monster audience."

The circumstances of the interpolated execution closely resemble those of Robert Emmett's martyrdom: Emmett was hanged and decapitated; he was to be married to a beautiful girl, and their love figured prominently in the incident; he was an Irish patriot being subjected to a British military execution; he had been betrayed (by his defense counsel). As Bloom prepared to leave the Ormond Hotel in the preceding chapter, he was associated with the "croppy boy" of the patriotic ballad, who is popularly associated with Emmett; and at the very end of the chapter, he was associated with Emmett as well. The martyr is never named and, in conformity with the "betrayal" motif, is much less prominently treated than the spectators, the executioner, and the British army officer in charge. He is called "the hero martyr," "the hero," and the girl's "hero-boy." The terminology suggests not only the croppy and Emmett, but the "unconquered hero," "impervious to fear," as the author has taken to calling Bloom. The croppy boy–Emmett-Bloom complex reiterates that the interpolation is about the victimization of Bloom, with the citizen the agent of victimization and the others in the bar the participating bystanders.

The appellation "hero" is appropriate to Bloom because of the changes in his conduct noticeable since the beginning of the preceding chapter. There is also evidence to support that of "martyr," so insisted on in the Emmett and croppy associations and in the interpolation just discussed. Although he is not killed, Bloom does suffer, unjustly, for the sake of others—he is in Kiernan's on a charitable mission. And he conducts himself throughout in the manner already described: he attempts to turn aside blind chauvinism and xenophobia by appeals to reason and justice. Above all, he preaches "Love. . . . I mean the opposite of hatred." His concern about the suffering of animals (309) and that of Mrs. Breen (315) are instances in the present chapter of the mercy that is one of his prominent traits. And his reward for that mercy is to be despised and rejected by the very men to whom he is attempting to teach his simple doctrine.

The analogy I am drawing between Bloom's situation and that of Christ is intentional. In this twelfth chapter the association of Bloom and Christ made in the eighth chapter (Byrne's), touched on briefly at the end of the ninth chapter, the end of the first part of the novel ("step of a pard"), and in the beginning of the eleventh, the beginning of the second part ("black wary hecat"), is developed. The distinction between the citizen and the group in the bar has been pointed out. The attitude toward Bloom of the ridiculous old crank is in itself irrelevant; he acts as a stimulant to the others, but they are the true citizens, Bloom's fellow men, and only their attitude and their actions are significant. Whether they know it or not, when they turn their thumbs down they make a judgment that is far from casual.

The fact and the nature of its importance constitute the subject of the second interpolation of the three being discussed, that depicting preparations for the trial of the nameless "malefactor," which occurs between the humorous account of a reprimand given by the chief magistrate, Sir Frederick Falkiner, to Reuben J. Dodd, and the citizen's comment on the account, "—Those are nice things . . . coming over here to Ireland filling the country with bugs," his second overt attack on Bloom. The Dodd matter was a civil, not a criminal, case, and Dodd was the plaintiff, not the defendant, so he is apparently not the "malefactor" of the commentary. The reference may be, nominally, to the Jewish swindler mentioned just before Dodd in the Jew-baiting colloquy; but again, Bloom is the actual subject.

Kiernan's public house, adjacent to the Green Street Court (its whiskey cellars actually extended beneath the courthouse), was associated with that court by Dubliners before the transfer of most legal business to the Four Courts caused the bar's decline and eventual closing about twenty years ago. It was even called "the court of appeal" because of all the legal business conducted in it.[6] Joyce's placing of the action in a bar well-known for its association with the court, like the constant talk of trials, court judgments, and executions that appropriately goes on there during the chapter, is functional.

The judge of the interpolated passage is the actual chief magistrate of Dublin, and the court of the passage is his court ("to the solemn court of Green street there came sir Frederick the Falconer"). The interpolation is linked directly to Bloom as well as to Kiernan's. The date of the forthcoming trial is given as "the sixteenth day of the month of the oxeyed goddess [Juno]," and the time "about the hour of five o'clock." Furthermore, the jury is described as:

> the high sinhedrim of the twelve tribes of Iar, for every tribe one man, of the tribe of Patrick and of the tribe of Hugh and of the tribe of Owen . . . there being in all twelve good men and true. (317)

The all-Irish "sinhedrim" of the commentary is an overt representation of the all-Irish group in the bar, which is also preparing to pass judgment on a man guilty of no specific crime, and which also numbers twelve jurors: O'Molloy, Nolan, Lambert, Bergan, Lenehan, Hynes, Cunningham, Crofton, Power, the narrator, the citizen, and Garryowen; Doran leaves the premises early in the chapter, and Terry Ryan, the bartender, remains outside the company; Garryowen, "of the tribe of Owen" (he has the name of a patriotic song, and at least the real Garryowen was an Irish setter), makes repeatedly clear his judgment of Bloom and is represented in one of the interpolated commentaries as parahuman ("synanthropic") and a poet.

The associations between Kiernan's and the Green Street Court, the correspondence of date, time, and "juries," the parallel between the situation of the unnamed "malefactor" and that of Bloom, and the historical fact that Emmett was tried at the Green Street Court make unavoidable the conclusion that the "malefactor" about to be tried represents Bloom. The significance of this fact is crystallized in the word "sinhedrim," under ordinary circumstances an incongruously Hebraic term to apply to a microcosm of the Irish nation. It is a pointed association of the men about to judge and condemn Bloom with the high court of ancient Judaea that condemned Christ. The correspondence extends even to the fact that Bloom is wearing mourning attire, required of a prisoner appearing before the ancient Sanhedrin. The men in the bar are a modern Sanhedrin, representatives of Christian Ireland, swearing fidelity to "him who died on rood" and condemning one who is trying to bring them light, much as the ancient judges proclaimed their faith in the Covenant of the Lord and condemned the one who tried to bring them the light of that covenant.

The association of Bloom and Christ which is the essential burden of this interpolation is suggested throughout the chapter, linked to Bloom in the mock execution, ~~refers~~ presented as a martyr, and mention is made of the "most precious blood" of the hero-martyr-scapegoat. All the talk of hanging and of lynched and legally hanged men during the chapter, linked to Bloom in the mock execution, refers to the modern counterpart of what was, in the time of Christ, the standard method of execution. In speaking later of his altercation with the citizen, Bloom calls himself "a sheep." The narrator repeatedly calls him "cod's eye," making both a reference to the fish symbolism by which Bloom was associated with Christ in the eighth chapter and a pun. While Bergan is talking about the man he saw earlier and thought was the dead Dignam, Bloom happens to look in the door of the bar; and:

—Good Christ! says he. I could have sworn it was him. (297)

Bloom's preaching prompts the citizen to ask, "—Are you talking about the new Jerusalem?" and to say contemptuously, "—A new apostle to the gentiles. . . . Universal love." Later the citizen makes the announcement:

—That's the new Messiah for Ireland! (331)

The association is definitely established, however, at the climax of the action. In the *Odyssey*, the Cyclops hurls the second and greater of two rocks at the hero when Odysseus proclaims his identity. Bloom stands in the carriage and names great Jews, the citizen challenges his including Christ, and he is more explicit:

Christ was a jew like me. (336)

The citizen's reaction is to secure the biscuit tin, and through the unconscious irony of his speech as well as by his Cyclopean action to complete the identification of the hero:

—By Jesus . . . I'll brain that bloody jewman for using the holy name. By Jesus, I'll crucify him so I will.

The distressed narrator can only say "I'll be in for the last gospel" when the tin is hurled, but the author interpolates an account, in a parody of scientific reporting, of an earthquake that corresponds to the earthquake at the crucifixion, and a "perturbation of cyclonic character."

The association of Bloom with Joshua of Nazareth, itinerant rabbi and prophet, the unrecognized Messiah, is not an anagogical revelation of their identity. Bloom is not crucified—not even in the citizen's terms, since the biscuit tin misses him. The citizen is not the spokesman of the "Sanhedrin" anyway—its spokesman is the narrator; but both his personal sentiments and his account of the incident reveal that Bloom was, like Christ, despised and rejected. The non-Catholic in the bar makes the judgment of Christian Ireland complete: "—We don't want him says Crofter [Crofton] the Orangeman or presbyterian."

The representatives of the Irish nation are shown to be beyond salvation. They have "sinned against the light," not by proxy like the modern Jews so accused by Mr. Deasy, but by their own acts. Blasphemy comes up obliquely in the chapter: the drunken Doran reviles Christ; the citizen invokes "the curse of a goodfornothing God"; and patriotic sentiment prompts Ned Lambert to speak obscenely of a Bible inscribed by Queen Victoria. More significant than the blasphemy is the author's comment on the conclusion of the brief "trial" of Bloom in his absence. Cunningham attempts to end the discussion by soliciting a blessing for those who are present, Bloom's judges:

—Well, says Martin, rapping for his glass. God bless all here is my prayer. (332)

The citizen says "Amen," Hynes says "And I'm sure he will," and O'Molloy expresses his agreement. But between Hynes' statement and O'Molloy's is interpolated a two-page burlesque of a procession of saints and clerics to Kiernan's to bless the company. With its strong stress on both Irish and Catholic motifs, the interpolation clearly represents a divine blessing as the men in the bar conceive it. The group of "saints and sages" approaches Kiernan's performing messianic miracles involving loaves and fishes, evil spirits, and the dead, halt, and blind. The ceremony does not conclude until the celebrant, "the reverend Father O'Flynn attended by Malachi and Patrick,"

> prayed that God might bless that house as he had blessed the house of Abraham and Isaac and Jacob and make the angels of His light to inhabit therein. (334)

And, of course, the angel (messenger) of "His light," who is of the blessed "house of Abraham and Isaac and Jacob," has been turned away by "that house." Ironically, the rejected bearer of God's light re-enters the "house" simultaneously with the expression of pious wishes for God's blessing by the company and the author's ironic representation of the form they conceive the blessing to take. But he multiplies no fishes, and he is neither named Father O'Flynn nor followed by a procession chanting "the introit in *Epiphania Domini.*"

The two important interpolations discussed at length above, the execution of the martyr and the trial of the malefactor, relate to Bloom's quasi-trial and quasi-crucifixion in Kiernan's. The last of the three, the chapter's final paragraph, is the sole vehicle of Bloom's quasi-resurrection. Not only a resurrection on analogy with Christ, but an assumption as well; associating Bloom with the Old Testament figure who was thus graced by God, it closely parodies the relevant passage in II Kings. Elijah has triumphed over the priests of Baal. Accompanied by his successor Elisha, he divides the water of the Jordan and passes over:

> And it came to pass, as they still went on, and talked, that, behold, there appeared a chariot of fire, and horses of fire, and parted them both asunder; and Elijah went up by a whirlwind into heaven.

The conclusion of Joyce's parody, "And they beheld Him ben Bloom Elijah [Elijah begotten of Bloom] . . . ascend

. . . at an angle of forty-five degrees . . . like a shot off a shovel," cannot be considered a mockery of all that precedes it. Forty-five degrees is a steep angle, and the meaning of the final colloquial simile reinforces the assumption idea. By combining the idiom of Bloom's Dublin with that of the Bible, Joyce is avoiding a sobriety that would be crudely sentimental and asserting that what is represented in the passage is happening in 1904, on Little Green Street, Dublin. It is this Elijah-like assumption that is the reason for the "cyclonic" counterpart to the earthquake in the interpolation that followed the hurling of the tin. Finally, there can be no doubt that the reference to Elijah is to be seriously applied to Bloom, for Bloom was associated with Elijah previously.

In the opening lines of the eighth chapter Bloom was given the handbill announcing the coming of the evangelist Dowie who, in 1901, had proclaimed that he was "Elijah the Restorer," and Bloom promptly mistook a reference in it to Christ for his own name. He then thought and acted in such a way as to associate himself with the prophet who had wished for death and been fed by birds. Thus, although the three interpolations discussed associate Bloom with Christ and Elijah, both associations were first made early in the novel and, as in the present chapter, they were made together. In addition, Bloom's quasi-apotheosis is firmly grounded in the action of the chapter. The "trial" and "crucifixion" of him are not two elements in an incident between a Jewish advertising salesman and a group of petty men sparked by a bigot which have been arbitarily inflated by the author; the rejection by the men of the figure placed beside Christ and Elijah results, as directly as does their rebuff to the familiar Bloom who is an inconsequential salesman, from their misunderstanding arising out of Bloom's unconscious tip about the horse Throwaway. Like Dowie, Bloom announced the prophet (and Messiah) by a "throwaway," his newspaper; his "I was about to throw it away" in the fifth chapter (post office) was a prophecy in traditionally cryptic form, yet not too cryptic to be comprehended by Bantam Lyons. Furthermore, the action that grows out of the unconscious tip about a racehorse was almost blatantly linked, at the beginning of the eighth chapter, to the association of Bloom with Christ and Elijah,

by the consistent use of the uncommon word "throwaway"
to refer to the handbill that was so instrumental in making
that association. Finally, that action, just ended by the
biscuit tin, began with a "prophecy" and has ended with
a "crucifixion." The previously-established interdependence
of Throwaway tip and Messiah "throwaway" is the foundation for the relationship the author draws in the present
chapter between the action (linked to the first) and the
interpolations (linked to the second), between the insignificant victim of a misunderstanding and the rejected counterpart of both Elijah and Christ.

   With respect to Elijah as with respect to Christ, the
proper word is "counterpart": Bloom is not identified *as*
each (or either) figure but *with* him. The author has not
portrayed a character through half a novel only to declare
that he is really, unknowingly, the avatar of the traditional
Messiahs of both Christians and Jews. Nevertheless, he
is systematically identified with both Messiahs. And that
Elijah as well as Christ is deified as the Messiah is indicated
by the use throughout the concluding passage of capitalized
pronouns to refer to Bloom-Elijah ("the chariot wherein
He stood," "they beheld Him in the chariot").

   Joyce has taken no liberties in calling Elijah as well
as Christ Messiah. The Hebrew word means "the anointed
one," and the title given to Jesus, the Greek word *Christos*,
is only a translation of the Hebrew *Meshiah*; "Messiah"
signifies an office, not a man. Rabbinical teachings hold
Elijah to be the annunciator of Judgment Day, and the
Second Coming as Jews traditionally conceive it will be a
return of Elijah. He thus occupies a place in Judaic apo-
calyptic and messianic doctrine closely analogous to that
of Christ in the corresponding Christian doctrine, that of
the Anointed and the Deliverer. The Gospels reveal that
those among whom Christ preached so regarded Elijah,
and make a clear distinction themselves between Elijah and
the ordinary prophets.[7] Finally, medieval Church writers
saw every detail in the Old Testament account of Elijah
as prefiguring a detail in the New Testament account of
Christ.[8]

   The basis on which Bloom is associated by the author
with the dominant messianic figures in western civilization
is made plain in the foremost work of messianic prophecy,

the Book of Isaiah. The prophet Isaiah, author of the first thirty-nine chapters, calls the Messiah the "Prince of Peace" and specifies that he shall be descended from Jesse, the father of David. The anonymous author (or authors) of the remainder of the book, called "Deutero-Isaiah," has a very different conception. For him the Messiah is the "Suffering Servant"; and as Bible commentaries point out, the slightest care in reading reveals that the Messiah is not one individual but all Israel, the Hebrew nation, and its mission is to deliver the Gentiles.[9] The fact that family Bibles identify this Messiah with Christ in chapter headings, just as they do the Prince of Peace descended from David, is the result of the same misconception by which the lines in Deutero-Isaiah:

> O Zion, that bringest good tidings
> O Jerusalem, that bringest good tidings (Isaiah 40:9)

became:

> O thou that tellest good tidings to Zion,
> O thou that tellest good tidings to Jerusalem

in the first part of Handel's *Messiah*.

Although not in the genealogical sense, Bloom is ethnically of the house of David, of course. And his conduct in the present chapter conforms to that prescribed by Isaiah in the central "Prince of Peace" passage:

> But with righteousness shall he judge the poor, and reprove with equity for the meek of the earth: and he shall smite the earth with the rod of his mouth, and with the breath of his lips shall he slay the wicked. (11:4)

But Deutero-Isaiah describes Bloom even more closely. He represents the Lord as saying to the Hebrew people that He will make them "a light of the Gentiles; to open the blind eyes . . . "; and his familiar personified description of the Suffering Servant:

he hath no form nor comeliness; and when we shall see
him, there is no beauty that we should desire him.

He is despised and rejected of men; a man of sorrows,
and acquainted with grief; and we hid as it were our
faces from him; he was despised, and we esteemed him
not (53:2-3)

is plainly applicable to Bloom's character and behavior and
to the treatment of him. Bloom is one of those whom God
has anointed, given the office of reprover with equity for
the meek of the earth—Mrs. Breen and suffering cattle,
as well as all persecuted victims of "hatred among nations."
He smites the earth with the rod of his mouth, although
he fails thereby to open the blind eyes and make the Gentiles receive the light he embodies. The citizen's "—That's
the new Messiah for Ireland!" is as ideal an example of
the consistent dramatic irony of that character's remarks
as the chapter contains.

The representation of Bloom as literally a messianic figure
is a complete innovation in the novel. The association of
him with Odysseus and Shakespeare, and even with Christ
and Elijah before this chapter, has been essentially functional, for the purpose of unfolding the story. However, in
this chapter something has been indicated about Bloom's
actual self: here, association with Christ and with Elijah is
not a narrative device but characterization. The colloquial
wording at the end of the chapter, and the instrumental
role of the popular evangelist Dowie, even if they add a
minor ironic coloration—and they do not necessarily—
can hardly outweigh in significance all the elements of a
direct and unqualified association carefully laid out in the
eighth, ninth, eleventh, and present chapters and, with
respect to the horserace tip, as far back as the fifth chapter,
the second in which Bloom appears. Furthermore, this
carefully prepared disclosure about Bloom is an important
element in the rest of the novel.

In presenting a serio-comic account of a messianic figure,
a deliverer of the people, who is tried and rejected or
destroyed by them, Joyce is actually in a tradition; and

this fact also substantiates my assertion that Bloom is presented as in some sense a bringer of light and deliverer. Synge, before Joyce, in Christy Mahon, his playboy of the western world (precisely what Christ was as Synge uses the term "playboy," and as we normally understand "western world"), and Shaw, after Joyce, in his Joan, join with him to make the theme central to three masterpieces by modern Irish writers.

Incongruous as it may seem, then, Leopold Bloom's character, deportment, and circumstances combine at this point in *Ulysses* to indicate that he is not only Jew-cuckold-salesman but Messiah as well. Nevertheless, he seems to be unconscious that he possesses any such power. He did so in ignorance when he provided Bantam Lyons with the tip on Throwaway; in the eighth chapter, in which the messianic association is first developed, he debated whether or not to pass on Lenehan's tip for the race, Sceptre, which he overheard in the preceding (newspaper) chapter, and saw nothing personally significant in the Dowie "throwaway"; when he passed between Stephen and Mulligan at the end of the ninth chapter, it was the author who attributed to him the "step of a pard"; and in the present chapter, when the citizen offers him a perfect opportunity to declare himself by asking him if he is "talking about the new Jerusalem," he answers only, "I'm talking about injustice." The reader knows more about him than he knows about himself.

He does come to an understanding of the Throwaway affair and, to some extent, of the relationship between that and the handbill, in the last section of the novel. Reading a newspaper account of the race in the sixteenth chapter (shelter), he reveals that he was attentive not only to Lenehan's description of it in the fourteenth chapter (hospital) but also to the one Lenehan gives the others in the present chapter while Bloom himself and O'Molloy are arguing with the citizen; thus he comments on Boylan's bet on Sceptre "for himself and a lady friend," disclosed by Lenehan: "Different ways of bringing off a coup. Lovemaking damages," illogically (but significantly) involving himself in Throwaway's victory. He then reveals that he understands Lyons' behavior in the morning, and finally that he understands the reason for the animosity of the group at the bar (632-33). In the next chapter, the seventeenth, he sees the torn scraps of two betting tickets, and his "brow" is "corrugated" by:

> Reminiscences of coincidences, truth stranger than fiction, preindicative of the result of the Gold Cup flat handicap. . . . (659)

Thus, by the end of the day, he fully understands. And when he reflects on the occasions on which "previous intimations" of the race result had come to him, his list includes the initial offer of the newspaper to Lyons, Lyons' pointing him out as the originator of the tip in the eighth chapter (176), the incident at Kiernan's, *and his receipt of the Christ-Elijah "throwaway"*; he sees himself when he offered Lyons the newspaper as

> with the light of inspiration shining in his countenance and bearing in his arms the secret of the race, graven in the language of prediction.

Impressive as Bloom's hearing, memory, and powers of deduction are, they are not awareness of a truly messianic nature. He has no such awareness in the novel. His "inspiration" has no significance for him, and the whole matter resolves into resignation regarding his failure to take advantage of his "prediction" and satisfaction at having brought "light to the gentiles" (he is unaware that Lyons was dissuaded from following his tip by Lenehan). Still, his ignorance of his special endowment is no refutation of the fact. His very name (Leopold: "bold for the people") harmonizes with it. And the Homeric correspondence confirms it at a glance.

The "crucifixion" incident corresponds to Odysseus' boastful disclosure of his true name to the Cyclops from the safety of his escaping ship and the consequently enraged Cyclops' hurling the second and far greater of two rocks, which barely misses its mark: the biscuit tin barely misses Bloom's escaping carriage (not Bloom but the sun has "blinded" the citizen) after Bloom says, "Christ was a jew

like me." The exactness of the correspondence makes
Bloom's statement a similar revelation of identity, one element in the association of him with Christ, and an assertion
of the messianic concept of Deutero-Isaiah: Christ was
"like me," of Israel, God's Servant, bearer of light to
the gentile.

The Homeric correspondence is much more precise, however, and, for that reason, more important than it appears
at first glance. The incident is one of the critical points
of the *Odyssey*. Because Odysseus reveals his identity, the
Cyclops can appeal to his father, Poseidon, who condemns
Odysseus both to his decade of wandering and to his eventual return home "in evil case, with the loss of all his
company . . . and [to] find sorrows in his house." Butcher
and Lang say in the introduction to their translation that
Homer "has made his whole plot turn on the injury to
the Cyclops."[10] The correspondence in *Ulysses* follows the
original even to the element Butcher and Lang call "the
punning device by which the hero escaped."[11] In order
to ensure that the Cyclops will be unable to marshal help
after he has blinded him, Odysseus gives his name as
'Outis (literally, "no one")—in English translation, "Noman." The Cyclops then tells the Cyclopes who rally outside
his cave that "Noman" is assailing him. In fact, Odysseus
does not coin a pseudonym but suppresses half his name,
and, at the same time, literally suppresses half his identity;
for his name, *'Odusseus*, is composed of close puns on the
words "no one" (*'Outis*) and "God" (Zeus). When, because of vanity, he announces his name, reveals his full
identity, he precipitates the change in his fortune.

The application of recondite Homeric scholarship to
Ulysses has not been very fruitful. But the etymology of
Odysseus' name is familiar enough for the casual reference
to the "punning device" made by Butcher and Lang; it
is consistently mentioned in Greek editions of the poem;
and most important, it was known (and pointed out in
conversation) by Joyce himself.[12] As in the case of Odysseus, Bloom reveals to the citizen that he is not merely
the "no one," the Mister Nobody he is perceived as, but
a being in close relation to God as well. And as in the

case of Odysseus, the incident is significant for Bloom's destiny. The important difference between their cases is that Bloom's conduct, as worthy of praise as Odysseus' deserves criticism, would justify a favorable result.

Although the present chapter focusses on his ministry to the wayward about him, Bloom's apotheosis is also important for himself. In the opening paragraphs of the eighth chapter, at the point at which the Elijah-Christ association is introduced and is linked by the handbill to Bloom's horserace prophecy, his situation respecting his wife and the craving he has for a son are also brought up. The Bible elucidates the relationship between Bloom's exalted power and his personal problems. The one messianic prophet whose work conforms closely to the teachings of the Book of Isaiah,[13] who accepts the messianic role of Elijah, and who wants the Suffering Servant to forget about the gentiles and put his own house in order so that he himself may escape destruction, bears the name, prominent in *Ulysses*, of Malachi.

Malachi, a prophet of "the new Jerusalem," is the only Old Testament prophet to represent Elijah, who had risen four centuries before, as the Messiah promised by the Lord. Most of his scripture is in the form of a statement by the Lord to His people. The Lord reviews the history of His favor toward Israel, condemns their sins, describes the day of His coming, promises punishment for the wicked and triumph for the righteous on that Judgment Day, exhorts a return to the Law of Moses, and promises to send Elijah to lead the people to the right. Placed last in the Authorized Version of the Old Testament, the Book of Malachi is very short, and largely either petty or conventional in its preaching. Two interesting elements, however, are: its attack on divorce, and its promise of the return of Elijah on a mission of deliverance.

The first of these begins with a discussion of the sacredness of marriage. The lines that follow are cryptic; most Bible commentators regard them as a statement that men and wives are joined ("And did not he make one?") for the purpose of having offspring ("That he might seek a godly seed"). The conclusion is unequivocal, however:

> For the Lord, the God of Israel, saith that he hateth
> putting away. . . . (2:16)

The passage has been called "the most outspoken condemnation of divorce" ("putting away" one's wife) in the Old
Testament.[14]

The promise of Elijah's return is the conclusion of the
Book, and thus of the Old Testament in the Authorized
Version. It reads:

> Behold, I will send you Elijah the prophet before the
> coming of the great and dreadful day of the Lord:
> and he shall turn the heart of the fathers to the children
> [the Hebrew word almost always means "sons"] and
> the heart of the children to the fathers, lest I come and
> smite the earth with a curse. (4:5-6)[15]

There is no equivocation in this combination of promise
and threat which constitutes the final word of God to Israel.
Bloom must reunite with his wife, and he must "turn"
his "heart" to a son. And according to the prophecy of
Malachi, he is potentially capable of realizing those goals,
for he has the powers of Elijah within himself.

Furthermore, although rejected by the citizens in
Kiernan's, he may yet bring light to a gentile, may be
the Elijah who turns the heart of an unreconciled son to
his Father. When he crossed Stephen's path at the end
of the ninth chapter, there was a prefiguration of his
future importance to the young man. A few pages before
that incident, Mulligan announced, "The Lord has spoken
to Malachi" (211). The incident itself was the first climax
in the action of the novel, the end of the third chapter
following the two introductory sets of three. The final
incident of the present chapter is the second climax, and
again it is a prefiguration of a deliverer in the person of
Bloom. The third chapter after this takes place in nighttown and contains the ultimate climax of the novel; the
form of the ultimate climax and resolution and the role
of Bloom with respect to both his own story and that of
Stephen seem to have been indicated to us.

ONE fundamental question about the twelfth chapter of *Ulysses* has been hitherto avoided, for its answer becomes clear only when the theme and basic elements of the chapter are clear: Why is the action proper presented as a vituperative narrative in colloquial language, an anecdote by a far from admirable figure? The reason is provided by the narrator himself—the coiner of the punning designation of Bloom as "Cod's eye"—in his "I'll be in for the last gospel" when the citizen is about to "crucify" Bloom with the biscuit tin. "Gospel" is a contraction of "God spell"—story about God. One commentary on the gospels says:

> the main interest of the writers is biographical, not theological. Their aim is to place before the reader a vivid picture of the historical Jesus of Nazareth "in fashion as he lived. . . . "

Another points out that they are not complete biographies, but attempts "at producing faith by describing a few significant incidents taken out of a much larger whole."[16]

Of course, the narrator does not, in his "vivid picture of the historical [Bloom] of [Dublin]," "aim at producing faith" or even at increasing Bloom's popularity. However, he does in fact create a "gospel." The three synoptic gospels are accounts of Jesus the man "going about doing good, teaching . . . advising, guiding, rebuking," and of his trial, crucifixion, and resurrection. These are precisely the subjects of the narrator's account of Bloom—which, it must also be noted, he considers significant enough to tell. And although he is mainly critical, in some respects he is almost "really a great admirer of Bloom," as Joyce has characterized him.[17]

The Gospel According to Saint Mark is generally agreed to be the first of the gospels; it is the most colloquial in idiom and vituperative enough to attack many of the apostles; and it alone of the gospels has the Aramaic word *"Abba,"* which appears untranslated in both the Greek and English texts, a word that also appears untranslated in the Biblical parody that concludes the present chapter of *Ulysses* ("And he answered with a main cry: *Abba! Adonai!"*).

Joyce not only presented the revelation of Bloom's spiritual identity in the most appropriate form possible, he even had a model for his gospeller's very idiom and character.

1. L. A. G. Strong mentions *Martha* when discussing the "overture" (Strong, p. 33).

2. The popular assertion, based on Joyce's notes and declarations, that the "form" of the chapter is (in his phrase) a "fuga per canonem," with the "overture" the initial statement of fugal themes, has been very neatly disposed of by Harry Levin (Levin, pp. 98–99).

3. This translation is based on the text in the libretto published by the Academy of Music (New York, 186[?]).

4. See Mary M. Colum, *Life and the Dream* (New York, 1947), p. 386.

5. Gilbert, p. 255.

6. Roger McHugh, "The Passing of Barney Kiernan's," *Envoy*, I (December, 1949), 9–14.

7. See, e.g., Matt. 17:9–13, and Mark 9:9–13.

8. See, e.g., *Glossa Ordinaria*, vols. 113–14 in the Abbé Migne's *Patrologiae Latinae Cursus Completus* (1844–55), under "*I Libre Regum* XVII–XVIII."

9. "Let us now inquire who is this Servant? . . .
"The connections before and after show that it is Israel . . . idealized as they should be, as God in the beginning meant that they should be. To be such a people—such a Servant—is and always was their divinely appointed mission."—*The Abingdon Bible Commentary*, ed. F. C. Eiselen *et al.* (New York 1929), p. 656.

10. Butcher and Lang, pp. 151 and xv.

11. *Ibid.*, p. xiv.

12. Padraic Colum, Stuart Gilbert, and Aldous Huxley all write that Joyce told them of it. See Colum, *The Road Round Ireland* (New York, 1926), p. 328; and *James Joyce*, pp. 372 and 786, n. 6.

13. In Handel's *Messiah*, lines are drawn from Malachi rather than from the corresponding section of Isaiah. See, e.g., Malachi 3:2 and Isaiah 30:14, which have essentially the same burden and use much the same imagery.

14. Arthur S. Peake, *A Commentary on the Bible* (London, n.d.), p. 587.

15. Mr. Damon quotes this passage in the revised version of his article (Givens, p. 241), as does R. P. Blackmur in his "The Jew in Search of a Son," *Virginia Quarterly Review*, XXIV (1948), 96–116, 116. Messrs. Damon, Blackmur, and Levin all point out that Joyce is identifying Bloom and Christ in this chapter; see the two articles and Levin, p. 116.

16. The first quotation is from *A Commentary on the Holy Bible by Various Writers*, ed. J. R. Dummelow (London, 1910) p. 617; the second is from *Dictionary of the Bible*, ed. James Hastings *et al.* (New York, 1909), p. 304.

17. See Budgen, p. 165.

chapter eight

13 *the strand (bloom)*

It is during the half dozen pages at the precise center of
this chapter that a girl about twenty years old (the grand-
daughter of the owner of Garryowen, and so, if she really
existed, distantly related to Joyce) first swings one leg back
and forth in time with the music emanating from a church
service, then gradually reveals more and more of her thighs
to a dark stranger, whom she regards as romantic and
suffering, and who responds to the stimulation by masturbating. The attitudes and conduct of Gerty MacDowell and
Bloom at that point constitute the thematic center of the
chapter as well as the middle of the action.

The significance of Bloom's act is clear in terms of what
has been shown about him. The ultimate expression of his
attempted "lotus-eating" in the fifth chapter was his plan
to masturbate in his bath (83). The act he contemplated is,
as mere passivity or the endeavor to ignore his situation
by skirt-chasing and letter-writing is not, a precise symbol
of total betrayal of his aspirations as both husband and
father. He did not fulfil that intention, however, as he reveals
in the present chapter (362). And although the subject
came up again at the Ormond Hotel, when Miss Douce
caressed the beer-pull, Bloom's gratitude for what he regarded as a proffer to him did not prevent him from leaving
the Ormond and thereby rejecting it along with the other
"siren songs" in the chapter.

In the present chapter, despite his recent examples of resolution and "heroism," Bloom himself (although under provocation) commits the consummate act of negation. It has a moral as well as a symbolic significance. In a quasi-Biblical recapitulation of the day's experiences in the seventeenth chapter, the encounter with Gerty is referred to as "rite of Onan" (713):

> And Onan knew that the seed should not be his; and . . . he spilled it on the ground. . . .
> And the thing which he did displeased the Lord: wherefore he slew him also. (Genesis 38:9-10)

The Code of Jewish Law (*Shulhan Aruch*) says: "It is forbidden to cause in vain the effusion of semen, and this crime is severer than any of the violations mentioned in the Torah."[1] And when the admonition of the Lord through the prophet Malachi is recalled, Bloom's "spilling" of his seed in the great sin of Onan is seen to be also that turning away from Molly and his unborn son which is the path to destruction.

The masturbation at the center of the chapter is not merely a pathetic and sordid act but a representation, on every level of meaning, of Bloom's self-defeat and self-destruction. Following it and Gerty's immediate departure, the author presents, in a union of Bloom's natural physio-psychological reaction to his act and the significance that act has for the novel, a long passage of inner monologue in which Bloom is far more pathetic than when he feels frustrated, ashamed, and helpless; for he is depressed, resigned, and spiritually broken.

His thoughts follow a now familiar pattern: they revert again and again from the immediate subject, in this case the girl whose name he never learns, to Molly and her affair with Boylan. At one point he decides that Boylan should give Molly money for her favors because she is "worth" it, and then has an even more masochistic train of thought:

> Funny my watch stopped at half past four. Dust. . . .
> Was that just when he, she?
> O, he did. Into her. She did. Done.
> Ah! (363)

Although sordid, the reversion to the incident with Gerty
that directly follows these manifestations of pandering and
masochism intensifies the pathos:

> Mr Bloom with careful hand recomposed his wet shirt.
> O Lord, that little limping devil. Begins to feel cold and
> clammy. After effect not pleasant. Still you have to get
> rid of it someway.

Again and again the pattern is repeated. Bloom thinks of
Gerty, her two companions, Martha Clifford, the neighbor's
maid, the woman he saw accompanying A. E., Nurse Callan,
the novice in the Tranquilla convent, the "girl in Meath
street," the "high class whore in Jammets," Mrs. Breen,
Mrs. Duggan, the aristocratic woman he'd seen in the fifth
chapter, and Mrs. Dignam, from whose house he has just
come. The catalogue is long, but Molly eclipses the other
women right up to his somnolent last thoughts in the
chapter, which begin as a tribute to Gerty:

> O sweety all your little girlwhite up I saw dirty brace-
> girdle made me do love sticky we two naughty Grace
> darling she him half past the bed met him pike hoses
> frillies for Raoul to perfume your wife black hair heave
> under embon *senorita* young eyes Mulvey plump years
> dreams return tail end Agendath swoony lovey showed
> me her next year in drawers return next in her next her
> next. (375)

Combined with thoughts of Molly's tryst with Boylan is
another version of Bloom's revery of her return to him:
"years dreams return" and the Zionist (return) motif,
"Agendath," are augmented by "next year," a fragment of
a Passover Seder catechism expressing the exile's hope of
return. Thus the pronoun in "next in her next her next"
with which Bloom's long inner monologue ends refers not
to Gerty but to Molly.

The irony of Bloom's undiminished ardor for Molly lies
in the conclusions at which he arrives before this final paragraph. In the paragraph just preceding, in fact, he decides
that he will not accompany Boylan and Molly to her concert
at Belfast and categorically assents to being supplanted.

Prior to this, he thinks of the hill of Howth and the consummation of their love there, on which he dwelt so fully
in the eighth chapter. Only now he concludes, not with a
reflection on how far he has fallen ("Me. And me now"),
but with the thought that he is foolish to persist in his
unrequited love for Molly, that Boylan "gets the plums and
I the plumstones" (370). Yet, persist he does. And he does
not hesitate to blame himself for having recourse to masturbation because he lacks the simple courage to make love
to his wife (367).

The author shows Bloom's love for Molly to be a fundamental theme of the chapter with the help of "Love's Old
Sweet Song." By this point in the novel, the association
between the song and the tryst of Molly and Boylan has
been exploited twice (in the fifth chapter and the eleventh).
Now the song is no longer simply alluded to by its title;
phrases from it are woven into the narrative. The time of
the action is "twilight," and at four separate points that
term is used to indicate the time. There is repeated mention
of the bats, "flickering shadows," and their coming and
going occupies Bloom's thoughts at two points. Finally,
Gerty makes the association almost explicit by observing
of Bloom: "Perhaps it was an old flame he was in mourning for from the days beyond recall" (358). Although in
the most immediate sense Bloom is paralleling the "rehearsal" of it by Molly and Boylan in his own ignominious
way ("Still to us at twilight comes Love's old song"), the
song is even more significant of his awareness that they
have passed the vital point of their "rehearsal" and, as the
end of the chapter so sardonically and insistently states,
made him "*Cuckoo. Cuckoo. Cuckoo.*" This awareness combines with the depression that follows his masturbation to
bring him to his despondency of spirit.

The song is most significant, however, of his persisting
love for Molly. Gerty points out that he is mourning for
"an old flame," a "flame" of days that he now feels are
definitely dead and beyond recall. As the song itself states,
Love's "old sweet song" is the song Love sang to the lovers'
hearts. Now one of those lovers is deaf to it and to the
other lover:

> Tho' the heart be weary, sad the day and long,
> Still . . . at twilight . . . comes Love's old
> sweet song.

The second of the song's two "verses" describes Bloom's devotion:

> Even today we hear Love's song of yore,
> Deep in our hearts it dwells for ever-more.
> Footsteps may falter, weary grow the way,
> Still we can hear it at the close of day.
> So till the end, when life's dim shadows fall,
> Love will be found the sweetest song of all.

The impressive fact about Joyce's use of the song in the present chapter is that at the same time that its lines and his treatment of it represent Bloom's love for Molly and consequent suffering, the associations it brings to the chapter invoke the two specific causes of Bloom's extreme despondency—the lovemaking of Molly and Boylan and his own pseudo-lovemaking.

The first part of the chapter, from its beginning to the point where Gerty leaves the scene and the novel, is very different in both style and subject from Bloom's inner monologue. Characterized by critics as "dime-novel" or "penny novelette," and plainly a parody of pretentious sentimental fiction, its style suits a point of view very close to and sympathetic with Gerty.

The style is not merely suitable however; it is the author's vehicle for delineating Gerty's character and the significance of her principal action. In the first place, she is a pathetically obnoxious girl. The technique employed to show this is precisely that employed in portraying Father Conmee and the anonymous narrator of Barney Kiernan's: ironic touches in her speech or thoughts and in the language of the sympathetic narrator. Thus, her

artificial coyness is revealed simply in the way she is introduced; she is mentioned by one of her companions and
the narrator asks, "But who was Gerty?" The narrator
then speaks of her "winsomeness," but the specific description contains details like:

> Her figure was slight and graceful, inclining even to
> fragility but those iron jelloids she had been taking of
> late had done her a world of good much better than the
> Widow Welch's female pills and she was much better of
> those discharges she used to get and that tired feeling.
> (342)

And criticism can be little more overt than that contained
in the description of Gerty's eyes:

> Why have women such eyes of witchery? . . . It was
> Madame Vera Verity, directress of the Woman Beautiful
> page of the Princess novelette, who had first advised her
> to try eyebrowleine which gave that haunting expression
> to the eyes . . . and she had never regretted it. (342-43)

Her vanity, hinted at here, is revealed again and again.
She cries before a mirror "nicely," in moderation; and
"You are lovely, Gerty, it said." She has "a languid queenly
hauteur," and feels that one of her "innate refinement" was
wronged for not being born a noblewoman. She uses oint-
ments, cosmetic preparations, and treatments of every kind
for every part of her body.

More objectionable than her vanity are Gerty's spite-
fulness and jealousy. Her companions twit her about having
lost the interest of a neighborhood boy, and her thoughts
about them are painstakingly vindictive (343, 344). She
accuses Cissy Caffrey of vying with her for Bloom's attention, although Cissy's attitude toward Bloom is clear:
"—Wait, said Cissy. I'll ask my uncle Peter over there,
what's the time by his conundrum."

In contrast to Cissy during that incident, Gerty "could
see him take his hand out of his pocket" as the other girl
approaches, and observes that he changes from a "passionate nature," "fascinated by a loveliness that made him gaze,"

to a "distinguishedlooking," grave gentleman, and that his
voice has "a cultured ring."

Not only interested in Bloom, Gerty is clearly fully aware
of what she is about with him from the moment she lifts
her skirt in order to kick the ball to the twins (350). She
is a mildly libidinous girl, as Joyce suggests early in the
chapter with smiling irony:

> As for undies they were Gerty's chief care and who that
> knows *the fluttering hopes and fears* [italics mine] of
> sweet seventeen (though Gerty would never see seventeen
> again) can find it in his heart to blame her? (344)

And as Bloom correctly infers, she is approaching her menstrual period. Because of a combination of nature and circumstances, she undertakes her inversion of Nausicaa's
modest confrontation of Odysseus' nakedness. She finds
satisfaction in the fact that he is looking at her legs and
not those of her companions. She puts on her hat in order
to be able to observe him from beneath the brim:

> And swung her buckled shoe faster for her breath caught
> as she caught the expression in his eyes. . . . Her
> woman's instinct told her that she had raised the devil
> in him. . . . (354)

She sees him remove his hand from his pocket when Cissy
Caffrey approaches and return his hand to his pocket. And,
as soon as the others leave, she accelerates her performance:

> She looked at him a moment, meeting his glance, and a
> light broke in upon her. Whitehot passion was in that
> face. . . . At last they were left alone . . . and she
> knew he could be trusted to the death, steadfast, a sterling
> man, a man of inflexible honour to his fingertips [!]. *irony*
> His hands and face were working and a tremor went over
> her. She leaned back far to look up where the fireworks
> were . . . and there was no-one to see only him and
> her when, she revealed all her graceful beautifully shaped
> legs like that . . . and she seemed to hear . . . his
> hoarse breathing . . . because Bertha Supple told her
> once in dead secret and made her swear she'd never
> about the gentleman lodger . . . that had pictures cut

> out of papers of those skirtdancers and highkickers and
> she said he used to do something not very nice that you
> could imagine sometimes in the bed. (359)

Finally she limps off to join the others, and Bloom recom-
poses his wet shirt. She is exactly like "those skirtdancers
and highkickers" for whom she has contempt, and her hero,
her ideal lover, is exactly like the lodger.

Gerty is fully aware of what she is doing and what
Bloom is doing, yet her awareness is of a strange order.
She succeeds in filtering from it every element of reality
she finds unpalatable, in deluding herself about herself and
the world about her. Thus, when she mentions the "highkickers" and the man masturbating in the bed, she also says:

> But this was altogether different from a thing like that
> because there was all the difference because she could
> almost feel him draw her face to his and the first quick
> hot touch of his handsome lips. Besides there was abso-
> lution so long as you didn't do the other thing before
> being married. . . . (359)

There is no difference, and Bloom has done nothing to
cause her to think he would so much as speak to her. She
is able to make such assertions to herself because she is a
sentimentalist, because as the very style of the narrative,
which does not paraphrase Gerty's thought but renders its
essential characteristic, indicates, she sentimentalizes reality,
distorts it into a form she prefers. After kicking the ball,
and before deciding to swing her legs for Bloom, that is,
begin her exhibition, she observes:

> Yes, it was her he was looking at and there was meaning
> in his look. His eyes burned into her as though they
> would search her through and through, read her very
> soul. Wonderful eyes they were, superbly expressive, but
> could you trust them? (351)

Following this transparent combination of romanticizing
about Bloom and worrying about her reputation, she begins
to swing her legs (to show him "the bright steel buckles of
her shoes") and decides:

Here was that of which she had so often dreamed. It was he who mattered. . . . The very heart of the girl-woman went out to him, her dreamhusband. . . . If he had suffered, more sinned against than sinning, or even, even, if he had been himself a sinner, a wicked man, she cared not. (351-52)

Having identified her ideal lover, betrothed herself to him, and even decided to accept his wickedness, she needs to take only one more step, in time with the development of her exhibition, to the conclusion:

If she saw that magic lure in his eyes there would be no holding back for her. . . . She would make the great sacrifice. . . . There was the allimportant question and she was dying to know was he a married man or a widower who had lost his wife. . . . But even if—what then? Would it make a very great difference? From everything in the least indelicate her finebred nature instinctively recoiled. They would be just good friends like a big brother and sister without all that other. . . . (358)

The ridiculousness of Gerty's solution to the problem of an adulterous triangle (which would be so much less "indelicate" than what she is doing) is dwarfed by the ridiculousness of her fabricating a problem in the first place.

The whole combination of Gerty's actions, her misrepresentation of them, and Bloom's simple relationship to Gerty is manifested in the climax of the scene:

She was trembling in every limb from being bent so far back he had a full view high up above her knee where no-one ever . . . and she wasn't ashamed and he wasn't either . . . and he kept on looking, looking. She would fain have come to him chokingly, held out her snowy slender arms to him to come, to feel his lips laid on her white brow. . . . And then a rocket sprang and bang shot blind and O! then the Roman candle burst and it was like a sigh of O! . . . (360)

Gerty has succeeded, by a continual process of sentimentalizing, in turning black into white. Almost nothing she believes is true. She is not beautiful, she is not refined, her

companions are not jealous of her, the neighborhood boy
does not love her, Bloom does not love her, she is not
experiencing a romantic courtship, and she is not pure and
virtuous (although she probably is physically a virgin);
she is a libidinous girl whose persistent sentimentalizing
keeps her from the proscribed normal sexual activity and
yet causes her to act scarcely less immorally. Growing
older, deluding herself about her own charms, the attitude
men have toward her, and the things she does, Gerty seems
to have in store for her the emptiness and sterility indicated
for Bloom by his masturbation.

The attention given to a vain, petty, and self-deluding
girl would hardly be justified were Gerty herself the sole
subject of Joyce's parody. He is not breaking a crippled
insect on a wheel, however. "Love's Old Sweet Song" is one
of the two principal allusive elements in the chapter; the
other is the style of Gerty's section. In that style Joyce is
parodying not just a general kind of writing but a specific
model; and he did his best to identify it when he had
Gerty think that

> soon the lamplighter would be going his rounds . . .
> like she read in that book *The Lamplighter* by Miss
> Cummins, author of *Mabel Vaughan* and other tales.
> (357)

Turning to *The Lamplighter* of Maria S. Cummins, first
published in 1854, one finds the exact prototype of the
style and the charming little character it represents:

> It was a stormy evening. Gerty was standing at the
> window, watching for True's return from his lamplighting.
> She was neatly and comfortably dressed, her hair smooth,
> her face and hands clean. She was now quite well,—
> better than for years before her sickness. Care and kind-
> ness had done wonders for her, and though still a pale
> and rather slender-looking child, with eyes and mouth
> disproportionately large to her other features, the painful
> look of suffering she had been wont to wear had given
> place to a happy though rather grave expression.

Miss Cummins' verbal gifts are suited to her subject and the view of life manifested in the novel. Her style is turgid, coy, pretentious, with at times an almost obscene lack of taste. Joyce's parody is satiric, of course, but it is more a crystallization of the faults of the original than an exaggeration of them.

The faithfulness of Joyce's parody of *The Lamplighter* is important because of the importance of that novel, the first work of a highly successful American writer. A reprint published forty-eight years after the original publication is prefaced by the following information:

> Here is an American story for young people which has been in constant demand for almost half a century. At the time of its publication, in 1854, it enjoyed an immediate popularity second only to "Uncle Tom's Cabin" and "The Scarlet Letter." . . . Edition followed edition, in this country and in England . . . and how many "Lamplighters" have been issued in the unauthorized and mutilated forms in which the book has too often appeared can be only a matter of conjecture.[2]

The extreme popularity of *The Lamplighter* is a fact of social history. A very large number of people had sufficiently poor taste and poor judgment to embrace both its prose and its treatment of reality. By showing the insidious quality of sentimentalism in a parody of that book rather than in a general parody of the style of its genre, Joyce has made more pointed his statement about those people. Gerty Mac-Dowell is the ultimate popular development of Flaubert's Emma Bovary, the product of the degeneration of romantic idealism into sentimental wish-fulfilment and self-delusion. She is the representative of all those who, like her, read and enjoyed *The Lamplighter*. And this audience, large enough in itself, is representative of the mass of people blighted by self-deluding sentimentality. It is to make this criticism, familiar in his work, that Joyce parodies *The Lamplighter* and concerns himself with Gerty.

The criticism is levelled not only at individuals, but at their principal institution as well. The chapter has three subjects, not two, which are recapitulated at the end to stress that fact. In the order presented there they are Bloom, Gerty, and, between them, the Star of the Sea Church.

Simultaneously with Gerty's exhibition, the "Lamplighter" narrative presents phases in an evening service at the church. The service is the conclusion of a day-long "men's temperance retreat." At the point in the chapter where the parody ends, all mention of the church service ends. This is a significant association of the two, but there are more significant ones.

The patron saint of the church is the Virgin Mary, and most of the service appears to consist of prayers to the Virgin for deliverance from bibulousness:

> They were there gathered together without distinction of social class (and a most edifying spectacle it was to see) in that simple fane beside the waves, after the storms of this weary world . . . beseeching her to intercede for them, the old familiar words, holy Mary holy virgin of virgins. (347-48)

The satiric tone of this first description indicates the subject of Joyce's indictment. Most of the other passages about the church service reiterate the theme of supplication of the Virgin:

> And still, the voices sang in supplication to the Virgin most powerful, Virgin most merciful. (348)
> And care-worn hearts were there and toilers for their daily bread and many who had erred and wandered, their eyes wet with contrition but for all that bright with hope for the reverend father Hughes had told them . . . the most pious Virgin's intercessory power. . . . (350)
> Refuge of sinners. Comfortress of the afflicted. *Ora pro nobis.* Well has it been said that whosoever prays to her with faith and constancy can never be lost or cast away. . . . (352)
> Queen of angels, queen of patriarchs, queen of prophets, of all saints, they prayed, queen of the most holy rosary. . . . (353)

Joyce is attacking the popular cult of the Virgin. He sees it as that seeking after indulgence of weakness, after feminine, which is to say amoral, intercession with the masculine Godhead, which most of its critics say is behind the development into the second object of worship in the Roman

Catholic faith of a figure mentioned three times in the Gospels. The charge levelled is sentimentalism. The supplication of the Virgin is most insistently associated with Gerty by the repeated blending in one passage, in the same cloying narrative, of the church service and the action involving Gerty (who is a "daughter of Mary"). And Joyce's indictment points not only at the Church but also at the people, who required the cult and nurtured it, and who, as the passages suggest, delude themselves just as Gerty does about the significance of their actions. They have been willing to believe that however they sin, they "can never be lost"; thus, Gerty is certain that "there was absolution so long as you didn't do the other." Stephen speaks in the librarian's office of "the madonna which the cunning Italian intellect flung to the mob of Europe" (205).

During the morning, Stephen paraphrases an epigram from Chapter XXIV of Meredith's *The Ordeal of Richard Feverel* for the message of his telegram to Mulligan and Haines. Mulligan reads the telegram in the librarian's office "joyfully" (197), although he is really annoyed (418): "—*The sentimentalist is he who would enjoy without incurring the immense debtorship for a thing done.* Signed: Dedalus." Stephen's use of the moral apothegm is, like Meredith's, witty, for he is expressing his refusal to meet Mulligan and Haines and pay for their drinking. The serious application of it is made by Joyce in the present chapter. Those who pray to the Virgin for indulgence for petty weakness, like Gerty who romanticizes herself, her actions, and their objects, seek to enjoy the fruits of their frailty without incurring the immense debtorship of moral responsibility for their every act. Joyce has, in the "Lamplighter" part of the present chapter, castigated a fundamental fault of his fellow men.

What the sentimentalism Joyce sees as so pervasive in society has to do with Bloom is not difficult to determine. The first clue is that Bloom's part of the narrative is in his characteristic idiom, not in the sentimental style. The distinction is stressed at the point of transition:

> She walked with a certain quiet dignity characteristic
> of her but with care and very slowly because, because
> Gerty MacDowell was. . . .
>   Tight boots? No. She's lame. O! (361)

In contrast to the periphrasis, the attempted avoidance of
the unpleasant fact, is Bloom's direct statement. It is followed by a frank analysis of what has transpired, one that
sees clearly Gerty's motivations ("Thought something was
wrong by the cut of her jib. Jilted beauty," "Near her
monthlies I expect, makes them feel ticklish"), her ruses
("Will she? Watch! Watch! See! Looked around," "Wait.
Hm. Hm. Yes. That's her perfume. Why she waved her
hands"), and her character ("Hot little devil," "Go home
to nicey bread and milky and say night prayers with the
kiddies"). Far more important, Bloom correctly judges the
situation and his role in it ("Anyhow I got the best of
that," "Suppose I spoke to her. What about?", "you have
to get rid of it someway," "Did me good all the same");
it is principally in this respect that he is contrasted with
the sentimentalists. He knows that he has failed Molly in
"getting rid of it" in meaningless eroticism. He decides that
Molly is lost to him, and correctly blames himself for lacking
the courage to attempt to win her back by making love to
her. He acknowledges that he has incurred the immense
debtorship for the thing done. In eschewing sentimentalism,
Bloom is in direct contrast to the two other principal
elements in the chapter and is superior to them.

It is to Bloom's credit that he is ashamed to return
home (373); but his surrender in thought and act to his
predicament affirms that despite his apotheosis he is no
less the old Bloom, that the revelation at Barney Kiernan's
was an elaboration of his character and not the uncovering
of a disguise.

His surrender is accompanied by undiminished devotion
to Molly and suffering over the loss of her, and by a clear
sense of his culpableness in having lost her. For these
reasons, it may be premature. He remembers, for the first
time in the novel, a dream of the night before which corresponds closely to one twice recalled by Stephen—first in
the morning at the very same place, on the beach, and

then, in a context suggesting that Bloom would rescue him from his plight, at the end of the ninth chapter.

In an almost exact duplication of phrases in Stephen's first remembrance of his dream ("In. Come. Red carpet spread"), Bloom articulates the memory of his own: "Come in. All is prepared. I dreamt. What?" (364). He remembers it again just before the end of the chapter, this time recalling Molly's appearance in it:

> Dreamt last night? Wait. Something confused. She had red slippers on. Turkish. Wore the breeches. Suppose she does. Would I like her in pyjamas? (374)

The fact that Bloom remembers a dream involving himself and Molly which is plainly analogous to Stephen's dream predicting deliverance suggests, at any rate, that Bloom's love for Molly and his willingness to face reality may enable him to escape the fate to which he sees himself condemned, that his potential power of deliverance of himself and the young gentile has not been dissipated by the behavior of his lower self.

14 *the hospital*

The chronological sequence of parodies of English prose styles that constitutes the body of this chapter makes reading difficult, and the difficulty has no apparent purpose. If Joyce were merely trying to make the form of the chapter correspond to the birth of the new Purefoy baby, that would be scant justification for the device. In the first place the baby is a minor figure in the novel at best, certainly not worth such elaborate treatment. Secondly, birth is not gestation, which is what the device suggests; and not only does the chapter present less than one hour in the ninth month of the baby's pre-natal period, but he is born half-way through the progression of parodies. Any attempt to validate Joyce's stylistic device in this chapter on so tenuous a basis might more aptly turn to the labor of the infant's mother.

Readers willing to accept a labored association will accept labored art with equal readiness. And, unfortunately, Joyce himself encouraged a painstaking Alexandrian criticism of the chapter by providing an elaborate description of his intentions. In a letter to Budgen he said:

> Am working hard at *Oxen of the Sun,* the idea being the crime committed against fecundity by sterilizing the act of coition. Scene: lying-in hospital. Technique: a nineparted episode without divisions introduced by a Sallustean-Tacitean prelude (the unfertilized ovum), then by way of earliest English and . . . Anglo-Saxon . . . then by way of Mandeville . . . then Malory's Morte D'Arthur . . . then the Elizabethan chronicle style . . . then a passage solemn uses Milton, Taylor, and Hooker, followed by a choppy Latin-gossipy bit, style of Burton-Browne, then a passage Bunyanesque . . . after a diarystyle bit Pepys-Evelyn . . . and so on through Defoe-Swift and Steele-Addison, Sterne and Landor-Pater-Newman until it ends in a frightful jumble of pidgin English, Nigger English, Cockney, with Bowery slang and broken doggerel. This progression is also linked back at each part subtly with some foregoing episode of the day and besides this, with the natural stages of development in the embryo, and the periods of formal evolution in general. The double thudding Anglo-Saxon motives recur from time to time . . . to give the sense of the hoofs of oxen. Bloom is the spermatozoon, the hospital the womb, the nurse the ovum, Stephen the embryo.
> How's that for high?[3]

Most of the parodies "by way of" which the chapter is presented are good enough to be identified with reasonable accuracy independently of any testimonial by the author; some embody critical comments on the writer parodied; and some are among the funniest passages in the novel. Joyce's letter itself catalogues more than nine parodies, so that they are not the basis of the "nine-parted" structure of

the chapter. However, they are not the only allusive elements
in it. There is the maze of "links": back to nine of the preceding "episodes"; with embryonic and evolutionary
development; with oxen hooves; and with spermatazoon-
womb-ovum-embyro. He has built a labyrinth for his "Oxen
of the Sun" like that built by the first artificer, Daedalus,
for the minotaur. The slang expression which follows his
description, equivalent to "what do you think of that?", is
not the cap to a blatant mocking of his friend, but exultation
over having achieved a tour de force. It can be stated
categorically that he suggests no purpose for the tangle of
interrelations he created.

The labyrinth is even more complex. Hugh Kenner points
out that the forty paragraphs of English parodies correspond
to the forty weeks of gestation.[4] And perhaps the most detailed study of a part of *Ulysses* ever published begins with
Joyce's description of the chapter in his letter and proceeds
by close verbal analysis to a delineation of: the nine
divisions Joyce mentions; the references back to previous
chapters in each division; the correspondence between each
division and the foetus in the equivalent month of its
development; the recapitulation of the first six divisions-
months in the seventh, because in the seventh month "an
infant is likely to be born, and live"; and other elements
which its author finds, and which suggest to him the analogy
with the maze Daedalus built for the minotaur.[5]

However intricate the form of the chapter may be, and as
clever as its manifest intricacies are, its "technique" ought
ultimately to be functional. To argue that Joyce had to
fashion the chapter as he did is to offer an explanation and
no more; anyway, he is clearly proud of his links and
correspondences. With respect to some of them, the reader
has no alternative except to either charge the creator with
self-indulgence or admire the range and audacity of his
creation; but most of its complexities are, in fact, completely functional.

The action of the chapter begins after the two-page
"prelude" mentioned in Joyce's letter. On the beach Bloom
decided to inquire at the National Maternity Hospital about

Mrs. Purefoy (373), and the first incident is his arrival at the hospital, "stark ruth of man his errand." Nurse Callan, his landlady of nine years before, admits him; they talk; and Dixon, the interne on duty, who once treated a bee sting for him, invites him to join a party. Stephen, absent from the novel since the *"entr'acte,"* is one of the company and the most successful in realizing the intent "to be drunken an they might." The group is debating the Catholic prohibition against killing a child to save its mother.

Bloom is evasive when his opinion is solicited, and the "Elizabethan chronicle" parody begins with the example of it cited in Joyce's letter: "about that present time young Stephen filled all cups." Stephen takes the floor. He proclaims a doctrine presented in the librarian's office: that as a poet he is a creator and, therefore, is like God Himself:

> Mark me now. In women's womb word is made flesh but in the spirit of the maker all flesh that passes becomes the word that shall not pass away. This is the postcreation. (385)

He follows this with a characteristically scholastic blasphemy: that either the Virgin knew Christ, in which case she denied Him, or she did not, in which case she was spiritually ignorant. And he concludes his discussion of the Virgin with a criticism of the Virgin Birth:

> A pregnancy without joy, he said, a birth without pangs, a body without blemish, a belly without bigness. Let the lewd [ignorant] with faith and fervour worship, with will we withstand, withsay.

Stephen's open attack on a fundamental doctrine of the Church, the value of the Incarnation, prompts Dixon to ask facetiously, "why he had not cided to take friar's vows." Completely humorless, "he answered him obedience in the womb, chastity in the tomb but involuntary poverty all his days." His attitude toward the *"dio boia"* has not changed. He still chooses to "with will . . . withstand, withsay," and to suffer the consequent punishment "all his days."

More bawdy revelry leads into the topic of cuckoldry, which impels Stephen to echo the betrayal motif of his Shakespeare talk: "Bring a stranger within thy tower it will go hard but thou wilt have the secondbest bed." In a parody of a rebuke to His people by the Lord, in the idiom of the Authorized Version, he makes it clear that he is not speaking of sexual betrayal:

> Remember, Erin . . . how thou settedst little by me and by my word and broughtest in a stranger to my gates. . . . Therefore hast thou sinned against the light and hast made me, thy lord, to be the slave of servants. Return, return, Clan Milly: forget me not, O Milesian. Why has thou done this abomination before me that thou didst spurn me for a merchant of jalaps [medicine man"] and didst deny me to the Roman [Englishman] . . . ? (387)

As with his claim to semidivinity as "the maker," the absense of capitalization in the repeated "me" reveals that the pronoun is indeed personal. And Stephen's appeal to his people to "return" to him, the poet-prophet and their true ruler, is followed by a bitter and despairing complaint:

> But thou hast suckled me with a bitter milk: my moon and my sun thou hast quenched for ever. And thou has left me alone for ever in the dark ways of my bitterness. . . .

He attempts to paint over his blatancy with talk of the failure of "the wit of the septuagint" to describe the darkness referred to in the ostensible Bible passage (which does contain echoes of passages in Deuteronomy). His deception leads him to observations on another darkness, the state of man before birth and after death (388); and at that point in his stream of defiance, blasphemy, and criticism, a long roll of thunder is heard. The author, Lynch (facetiously), and Stephen himself all agree about its significance. Although unnerved and frightened by the "anger awful" of the "hammerhurler," Stephen plucks up his courage: borrowing a term from a fellow-rebel, Blake, "the braggart boaster cried that an old Nobodaddy was in his cups." But the author declares that "this was only to dye his desperation as cowed he crouched in Horne's hall."

Having taken the depiction of Stephen out of his hands, the author presents a moral analysis of him in the idiom of John Bunyan, complete with catechism and allegory:

> . . . he had in his bosom a spike named Bitterness. . . . But could he not have endeavoured to have found again as in his youth the bottle Holiness that then he lived withal? Indeed not for Grace was not there to find that bottle. Heard he then in that clap the voice of the god Bringforth or, what Calmer [Bloom] said, a hubbub of Phenomenon? Heard? Why, he could not but hear unless he had plugged up the tube Understanding (which he had not done). . . . And would he not accept to die like the rest and pass away? By no means would he and make more shows according as men do with wives which Phenomenon has commanded them to do by the book Law. (388-89)

It is the familiar picture: Stephen will not accept God, although he has the "Understanding" to acknowledge His power; the divinely created reality, Bloom's "Phenomenon," is the "throb always without" him with which he must live, but against which he will continue to struggle. However, the picture has been augmented. In the first place, the author suggests that to escape from his suffering and ultimate destruction Stephen must find "Holiness," *and to find holiness he must be accorded "Grace,"* the mercy of the God he defies. Secondly, Stephen's refusal to accept the world created by God and lead a normal life is here identified as sin. Finally, to lead a normal life is described as to "make more shows . . . as men do with wives." Although it is far more important in the present chapter than in the whole story of Stephen, fornication is an aspect of his sin against God.

The sentences describing Stephen's "Carnal Concupiscence" and the paragraph that follows them are among the funniest passages in the book. But their context reveals that the author is in complete earnest. Stephen's sin includes not only blasphemy, criticism, and open defiance of God, but a refusal to lead a normal life, to have a wife and children. And the others in the company are equally guilty in this. In the paragraph following the sentences concerned with Stephen, the last paragraph in the moral Bunyan's manner, the author adverts to them and declares:

> This [Carnal Concupiscence] was it what all that company that sat there at commons . . . the most lusted after. . . . For regarding Believe-on-Me they said it was nought else but notion and they could conceive no thought of it. . . .

The three reasons given for the sinfulness of the group are that "Two-in-the-Bush . . . was the very goodliest grot," that they are protected against "that foul plague Allpox" by a "stout shield of oxengut," and that they need not worry about "Offspring that was that wicked devil by virtue of this same shield which was named Killchild"—that fornication is enjoyable and they can "shield" themselves against both disease and the conception of a child. "Bunyan" concludes with an unequivocal statement about the nature of their attitude and its consequences:

> So were they all in their blind fancy, Mr Cavil [Lynch] and Mr. Sometimes Godly [Madden], Mr Ape Swillale [Costello], Mr. False Franklin [Lenehan], Mr Dainty Dixon, Young Boasthard [Stephen] and Mr Cautious Calmer [Bloom]. Wherein, O wretched company were ye all deceived for that [the thunder] was the voice of the god that was in a very grievous rage that he would presently lift his arm and spill their souls for their abuses and their spillings done by them contrariwise to his word which forth to bring brenningly biddeth. (389-90)

All those at the table have sinned by "their spillings," that is, committed the sin of Onan, in direct defiance of the divine ordinance to bring forth young, "as men do with wives."

"Bunyan's" statement cannot be dismissed as irony or verbal play, for it is an exact reiteration of the threatening injunction of healthy conjugality of the Book of Malachi, whose relevance to the novel has already been demonstrated. And it is a reflection of the theme of the present chapter as well. The chapter has been said to correspond to the incident in the *Odyssey* of the slaughter of the sacred "oxen" of the sun (Helios). The key to the correspondence is the symbolic use of light. The invocation which opens the chapter is to "bright one, light one," and asks for "quickening and wombfruit"; there is mention of "bigness wrought by wind of seeds of brightness" (383); and Bloom's first sexual experience, that with Bridie Kelley, is described in terms of light and the lack of it:

> They are entwined in nethermost darkness . . . and in an instant (fiat!) light shall flood the world. . . . In a breath 'twas done but—hold! Back! . . . She is the bride of darkness, a daughter of the night. She dare not bear the sunnygolden babe of day. (406)

Light represents fertility and procreation, against which the group in the chapter (including "Ulysses") has sinned by its "spilling." And the use of "Killchild" by Bloom's companions is analogous to the killing of the oxen ("cattle" is both more precise and more meaningful) of the god of light by Odysseus' crew. It is the light and darkness symbolism that both creates the Homeric correspondence and gives it the thematic function announced in Joyce's letter: "Am working hard at *Oxen of the Sun,* the idea being the crime committed against fecundity by sterilizing the act of coition."

That the author's Bunyanesque statement is a reflection of the theme of the chapter is indicated not only by the Homeric correspondence but by the two-page "Sallustian-Tacitean prelude" with which it opens as well. By virtue of its "Latin" idiom, this passage introduces the parodic delineation of the development of English. Actually, its Latinism is only a matter of words of Latin origin, a few Latinate neologisms, and the simulation of the inflected character of Latin by an almost impossibly compounded involution, phrase within phrase. It is much less important as a representation of the alien demi-source of English than as a means of making extremely cryptic (by its involute syntax) an open declaration, on the first page, of the theme of the chapter. It is, in other words, a "scrambling" device.

The page is almost taken up by the initial paragraph of the "prelude," which contains only one sentence and one question. Unscrambled, its word-order rearranged, the sentence begins:

> Universally that person's acumen is esteemed very little perceptive concerning whatsoever matters are being held as most profitably to be studied by mortals endowed with sapience who is ignorant of that which the most erudite in doctrine (and certainly by reason of that high mind's ornament in them deserving of veneration) constantly maintain when they affirm, by general consent, that (other circumstances being equal). . . . (377)

And with the excess verbiage eliminated, this becomes merely: "He is not very wise who is ignorant that the wisest and most worthy men affirm that. . . . " The sage affirmation, which is the important part of the sentence and a key passage in the "prelude," is more straightforward:

> by no exterior splendour is the prosperity of a nation more efficaciously asserted than by the measure of how far forward may have progressed the tribute of its solicitude for that proliferant continuance which of evils the original if it be absent when fortunately present constitutes the certain sign of omnipollent [all-potent] nature's incorrupted benefaction.

Both the principal social concern and the supreme moral good is "that proliferant continuance," procreation. The viewpoint is that of Malachi: the greatest evil is the breakdown of the family and the familial line, the greatest good is its preservation. The question that follows is rhetorical. It begins by asking who is unaware that any "exterior splendour" may merely mask a dark degeneration, and that "every most just citizen" must "become the exhortator and admonisher of his semblables." Joyce is presenting an *apologia;* he has put on the mantle of Malachi, and he is justifying himself. Thus, it concludes with the observation

that the "most just citizen" may well tremble for the future
if the present state of things is so degenerate that a man
would be:

> audacious excessively . . . to rise affirming that no more
> odious offence can . . . be than to consign to oblivious
> neglect *that evangel simultaneously command and promise*
> [italics mine; compare the Book of Malachi] which
> irrevocably enjoined that exalted function of . . . pro-
> creating [,] with prophecy of abundance or with diminu-
> tion's menace [,] on all mortals?

Despite the manifest strain of irony in both the form
and the burden of the "prelude," there is no doubt that the
exaltation of "that proliferant continuance" is sincere within
the limits of the chapter; Joyce speaks in his descriptive
letter of the *crime* "against fecundity" of "sterilizing the
act of coition." And it may be sincere beyond those limits.
Joyce said to one of his sisters, "The most important thing
that can happen to a man is the birth of a child," and told
a friend that he could not "understand households without
children. . . . To leave nothing behind, not to survive
yourself—how sad!" [6] Another friend describes how he
"wept in his cups when telling of the fertility of his fore-
fathers . . . [and swore that] . . . he was still a young
man and he would have more children before the end." [7]
Even if this is embroidered, it must have some basis in
truth. And so Joyce's personal attitude would seem to be
in sympathy with the simple and old-fashioned values asserted in the Homeric correspondence, the cryptic "prelude,"
and the Bunyanesque moral denunciation of the whole group
at the table. In any case, the theme of the chapter is
literally that having a family is an exalted thing and man's
cardinal responsibility, just as Malachi said.

There is no doubt that the revellers violate this moral
imperative. As soon as Bloom joins the company, he hears
a cry of pain from above, expresses his concern for Mrs.
Purefoy to Lenehan, and observes that she will, however,
be rewarded "by God His bounty." Lenehan's response is,
"Expecting each moment to be her next," the quip he made
in Kiernan's during the discussion of the desire of Jews

for male children. In the debate about the Roman Catholic injunction against killing a child to save its mother, the attitude of the company belies any concern for mothers and infants. At one point the drunken colloquy falls into hot controversy, "but the franklin Lenehan was prompt each when to pour them ale so that at the least way mirth might not lack." Stephen breaks in with a protest against the use of "Killchild," and his view is summarily rejected. Costello sings a snatch of a song mocking illegitimate pregnancy (385). When the others upbraid Costello (and Stephen for his judgment on the Virgin Birth, it is suggested), their epithets ("thou got in the peasestraw . . . thou dykedropt [born in a ditch], thou abortion thou"), are the true blasphemy in the context of the chapter. After more of such talk, the author condemns the "carnal concupiscence" of the company, but his statement is addressed to the reader, and the characters continue as they are. Mulligan is portrayed on his way from George Moore's soirée; he meets Bannon, Milly's inamorato, who speaks of her as "a skittish heifer," and they proceed to the hospital in the rain which has followed the thunder of God's voice. (Of this rain, the author remarks ominously that "those in ken say after wind and water fire shall come for a prognostication of Malachi's almanac.") When they arrive, Mulligan becomes once more in the novel the completely negative figure. His cynical joke about setting himself up as a *"Fertiliser and Incubator"* on a small island is a direct negation of the fundamental principle of procreation for the preservation of the family and the familial line. Then members of the company discuss girls and sexual escapades, Nurse Callan enters to announce the birth of the Purefoy baby and is accused of being pregnant, Mulligan "postulates as the supremest object of desire a nice clean old man," and there are pages devoted to discussion of abnormal births and infants. The predominant characteristic of the conversation throughout the chapter is its persistent correspondence to the slaughter of the sacred cattle of the sun.

Stephen and Bloom are not exempted from the condemnation of the company. It has been pointed out that Stephen protests against the use of contraception. He and Bloom do not laugh with the others at the bawdy humor that

follows the rejection of his protest. However, the reason
he will not mock mothers and maternity is probably his
sense of guilt with respect to his own mother; and although
his protest against "spilling" by the use of "Killchild"
explicitly calls it a sin against "the Holy Ghost, Very God,
Lord and Giver of Life," he is as guilty of that sin as
the others.

Bloom's reason for going to the hospital is "stark ruth of
man," pity for Mrs. Purefoy, a reflection, not only of his
mercy, but of his persistent concern throughout the novel
with maternity. Upon arriving, he feels "with wonder
women's woe in the travail that they have of motherhood"
and expresses sympathy for Nurse Callan because her
fiancé has died and she is still childless; then he declares
his concern about Mrs. Purefoy to Lenehan and seats himself, "Woman's woe with wonder pondering"; when the
Purefoy baby's birth is announced, he expresses his happiness, and the lack of reverence of the others shocks him.
Nevertheless, he is the cardinal sinner among them. Not
only has he just come from his "spilling," but it is more
significant than any mere sexual escapade of one of the
others: it represents surrender of his responsibility to maintain "that proliferant continuance," of his identity as husband and potential father. The others are sinning, but their
lives are before them and they are losing no tangible good.
Even Stephen's sin against fecundity is only one aspect of
his defiance of God. Bloom loves only Molly and "Soon
[he is] old." Furthermore, he not only, like Stephen, sins
with full knowledge; he sins while exalting maternity and
fecundity. Odysseus regards the sacred cattle of the sun
with the proper reverence and is innocent of their slaughter.
Bloom shares Odysseus' reverent attitude, but acts like the
Achaean's sinful, and, consequently, destroyed, crew.

With the thematic burden of the chapter delineated, it is
possible to reconsider its formal singularities more favorably. Its correspondence with the cattle of the sun episode
of the *Odyssey,* the first item in Joyce's descriptive letter, is
more obliquely drawn than most of the Homeric parallels in

the novel, but is a definite and fundamental vehicle of its theme. The letter speaks of it as "a nineparted episode without divisions introduced by a . . . prelude." If the "episode" indeed has a tenuously drawn representation of each of the nine months of pregnancy, it has quite meaningful "parts" as well, because, following the Latinate "prelude," its action has nine distinct phases. The first is Bloom's arrival at the hospital on Holles Street and the invitation to the party. The second is a description of the party. The third is devoted to Stephen and his pronouncements and ends with the Bunyanesque condemnation of him and all the others. The fourth is a short recapitulation of the situation in the language of "Pepys-Evelyn." The fifth is the "bull" discussion.

Mention of Mr. Deasy's letter on the hoof-and-mouth disease and its successful publication through the agency of Stephen, the "bullockbefriending bard," leads to a spirited and witty discussion of the Papal Bull of the English-born Adrian IV authorizing Henry II to "pacify" Ireland. This first English invasion (1169-1172) is the one spoken of by Mr. Deasy and the occasion of the defeat of Rory, the last High King. The "bull" is described in terms of its bovine homonym—as powerful, tyrannical, and extremely attractive to the Irish women; finally, all the Irish men leave for America in protest. The theme is the familiar one of the oppression of Ireland by England and the Church, and the cowardice of the people (the "women") in the face of it. The theme is not incongruous in the present chapter because the oppressor is unfruitful (the bull is really an ox), and because the discussion is an oblique reinforcement of the Homeric correspondence.

The sixth "part" of the action is the flippant and therefore blasphemous talk about sex, and is appropriately initiated by Mulligan's arrival at the gathering. The seventh is the discussion of childbirth and of abnormal infants and is initiated by the announcement of the birth of the Purefoy baby. The eighth deals with Mrs. Purefoy and her baby and Bloom's memory of Stephen as a little boy. The last begins with Stephen's shouted "Burke's!" and comprises the departure for Burke's public house, the drinking and conversation there, and the dissolution of the group after the bar closes. Mulligan sneaks away from Stephen (419) to keep a rendezvous with Haines "at Westland row station at ten past eleven" (405), and Stephen facetiously asks for a "plais whear to lay crown off his bed 2 night." When the bar closes at eleven and most of the revellers pursue a fire brigade, Stephen arranges with Lynch to go to "night-town," the brothel district. Bloom has not gone off either, for Lynch asks who he is. Stephen answers him with a flippant blasphemy and, spotting an announcement of Dowie's forthcoming visit, ends the chapter with a colloquial homily parodying the American evangelist.

As Joyce's letter says, the nine "parts" of the chapter proper are not created by arbitrary physical "divisions." Instead, they are a natural delineation of its action. The thematic significance of the number is obvious: the chapter is a celebration of human procreation.

Also functional, both thematically and in terms of the action, is the sequence of parodies of English prose styles. Following the prefatory passage, appropriately in "Latin," the action begins, narrated "by way of" a parody of Old English verse. The sequence ends with Carlyle during the last part of the action, and is followed by the actual conversation of the group, which ends the chapter. It is the talk of well-educated and very drunk young men in 1904, full of slang, imitations of Negro, Scottish, Jewish, and Chinese speech, ellipsis and abbreviations; and it contrasts strikingly with the long series of parodies of earlier and more pleasing forms of English. This contrast is pointed out occasionally in the body of the chapter; for example, the Elizabethan railing against Stephen's blasphemies concludes "to shut up his drunken drool out of that like a curse of God ape." It is the contrast of stark reality. Thus it follows the (infant's) cry "Burke's!" in the ninth "part" (month), and is the language of the emergence of the group from the hospital (womb) into the world outside. The Latinate "prelude," sequence of parodies, and final conversation represents human conception, embryonic development, and birth. The chapter is structurally, and stylistically, a celebration of procreation. In his Homeric analogy, his disposition of the action, and his narrative "technique" as well, Joyce has reiterated the theme of the chapter.

But as a representation of procreation, the parodic history of the language is not worth the fuss it has engendered,
and, perhaps, not even worth the effort. It accomplishes
a great deal more. Like the nine-part structure, it is a
functional element of the narrative itself. A critic has
observed that the parodies, unlike those of "a self-effacing
parodist—a Max Beerbohm," reveal primarily "himself—
Joyce the Jacobean divine, Joyce the Restoration diarist,
Joyce the Augustan essayist," etc.[8] They do so because, as
Joyce's letter states, the narrative is rendered *by way of*
each parody in turn. Like so much else he has brought into
the novel, Joyce is exploiting the subjects of his parodies
to tell his story.

On the simplest level, the appropriateness of a large
number of them makes a wedding of form and content.
The satiric "bull" discussion is couched in the idiom of
Swift both because of the Dean's advocacy of the Irish
cause and because one of his most scathing attacks on the
papacy uses the very same punning device (Section IV of
A Tale of A Tub). The account of the rainstorm and the
amatory gossip in the idiom of the Restoration diarists, the
raillery against Stephen in that of an Elizabethan pam-
phleteer, Stephen's complaint to his nation "by way of" the
Authorized Version, are similar examples of that appropriateness. Still, appropriateness is not necessity. The primary justification of the chapter's unusual principal device
is Joyce's special exploitation of the appropriateness of the
style of certain writers to certain subjects. A perfect example of this is the Bunyanesque denunciation of Stephen
and then of the whole group. The author achieves here
what he achieves in the involuted introductory passage:
direct statement. Only he does so smoothly and incon-
spicuously. In precisely the same way, he is able to
mockingly castigate Bloom "by way of" the pseudonymous
polemical satirist "Junius" (402-3), pay tribute to the family and to parental love "by way of" the sentimental
Dickens (413-14), and praise Purefoy as a father in the
boisterous idiom of Carlyle (416-17). Each of these direct
statements, judgments of Bloom, Stephen, the rest of the
company, familial devotion, and Purefoy, must be made
for the burden of the chapter to be communicated, just as

the introductory tribute to procreation and *apologia* for concern about it must be made. Joyce makes each statement through the mask of a style appropriate to it, and a style that is not only a ventriloquist disguise but integral to the chapter because it is an unobtrusive element in a chronological representation of English prose styles.

The cases of correspondence in the chapter enumerated toward the end of Joyce's description, beginning with "This progression is also linked back," warrant little attention. "The double thudding Anglo-Saxon motives [which] recur from time to time . . . to give the sense of the hoofs of oxen" is not only an unsuccessful device but a bit silly. Regarding the links with "foregoing episodes," "the natural stages of development in the embryo," and "the periods of . . . evolution": there are references to other chapters, not only in this, but in every chapter of the novel; babies and foetuses are constantly being discussed by virtue of the chapter's basic theme; and, except for a passing thought Bloom has of Darwin's "missing link" (400), there is no vestigial relic of a past anthropological age. The hospital is made to correspond to a womb, and Stephen's "Burke's!" at least permits Joyce's calling him "the embryo"; but in no meaningful sense is Bloom "the spermatozoon" or Nurse Callan "the ovum."

Nevertheless, the first part of Joyce's letter is a straightforward disclosure of the two important devices in the chapter. The sequence of parodies and the nine-part action are thematically functional, and, at the same time, they are essential elements of the narrative itself.

Although of secondary importance, the Purefoy baby is by no means irrelevant. His imminent birth is the reason for Bloom's presence, expressions of concern for the suffering mother, and praise of procreation. His ultimate advent is a reinforcement of the theme of the chapter. And it is the occasion of some important pronouncements by the author. The eighth "part" begins with a discussion of Mrs. Purefoy "by way of" an affectionate Dickens:

Reverently look at her as she reclines there with the motherlight in her eyes . . . in the first bloom of her new motherhood, breathing a silent prayer of thanksgiving to One above, the Universal Husband. And as her loving eyes behold her babe she wishes only one blessing more, to have her dear Doady there with her to share her joy. . . . But their children are grouped in her imagination about the bedside, hers and his, Charley, Mary Alice, Frederick Albert (if he had lived), Mamy, Budgy (Victoria Frances), Tom, Violet Constance Louisa, darling little Bobsy . . . and now this last pledge of their union. . . . And Doady, knock the ashes from your pipe . . . and dout the light whereby you read in the Sacred Book . . . and so with a tranquil heart to bed, to rest. He knows and will call in His own good time. You too have fought the good fight and played loyally your man's part. Sir, to you my hand. Well done, thou good and faithful servant! (413-14)

The satiric tone is apparent, but it is a genial and indulgent satire, with no trace of the undercutting irony which Joyce manages so well. Quite appropriately, for Dickens' sentimental idiom masks his own sentiments regarding the family; he himself commends the Purefoys ("pure in faith"), especially "Doady," who reads "the Sacred Book" and obeys its injunction.

Purefoy is the author's chief concern here because he and not Mina corresponds to the men in the chapter. The reader has learned already (401) of his devotion to Mina, mocked appropriately by one of the "slaughterers of the oxen," and of his paternal activity:

Her hub fifty odd and a methodist but takes the Sacrament and is to be seen any fair sabbath with a pair of his boys off Bullock harbour . . . trailing for flounder and pollock and catches a fine bag, I hear. (391)

The difference between Purefoy and the revellers is clear, and the contrast between him as a husband and father and Bloom's failure in both respects is pointed. Joyce presents a complete statement of his attitude toward Purefoy when he calls him the "remarkablest" father in the novel and accords him singular and enthusiastic praise, "by way of" the idiom of Carlyle:

> By heaven, Theodore Purefoy, thou hast done a doughty deed and no botch! Thou art, I vow, the remarkablest progenitor barring none in this chaffering allincluding most farraginous chronicle. Astounding! In her lay a Godframed Godgiven preformed possibility which thou hast fructified with thy modicum of man's work. . . . Thou art all their daddies, Theodore. Art drooping under thy load, bemoiled with butcher's bills at home and ingots (not thine!) in the countinghouse? Head up! . . . Dost envy Darby Dullman there with his Joan? A canting jay and a rheumeyed curdog is all their progeny. . . . Copulation without population! No, say I! Herod's slaughter of the innocents were the truer name. . . . Twenty years of it, regret them not. With thee it was not as with many that will and would and wait and never do. Thou sawest thy America, thy lifetask, and didst charge to cover like the transpontine bison. (416)

And in this pronouncement which concludes the progression of parodies there is no trace of even genial satire. Although the passage is a parody, the burden of "Carlyle's" panegyric is so clearly the culmination of Joyce's thesis that even Thomas Carlyle's characteristic enthusiasm may be said to be adopted with thorough sincerity. Explicitly condemning both the young men, who perpetuate Herod's slaughter of the innocents, and Bloom, who will and would and waits and never does, Joyce has made a final restatement of the chapter's theme.

Purefoy is all the author says. Unlike the young revellers, Boylan, Dollard, Power, and so many others in the novel, he has a family. And unlike Simon Dedalus, Richie Goulding, the sailor in the sixteenth chapter (shelter) who has not been home for seven years and does not know his son's whereabouts, the money-lender Reuben J. Dodd who gave a man two shillings for saving his son's life, Bob Doran, Denis Breen, the childless Mr. Deasy, Martin Cunningham, and Mr. Lyster, unlike even Dignam, who finally succumbed to alcoholic saturation, he fulfils his responsibility to his family. In fact, *Purefoy is the only character in the novel who does so—who is a good husband and father.*

In the Latinate "prelude" to the chapter, Joyce declares that each man's fulfilment of that responsibility is the sole basis for the prosperity of the nation. The fact that the men in the novel are the "citizens" of an impoverished captive country whose marriage and birth rates had been falling for half a century cannot be coincidental. Depicted again and again as without public courage, dignity, accomplishment, or hope, they also fail as fathers and husbands. The insistence on man's responsibility to effect "that proliferant continuance" is not merely an element in the present chapter. Philosophically primitive, theologically simplistic, and politically obvious, it is nevertheless the principal assertion about the nature and conduct of man made thus far in this highly sophisticated novel.

Incapable of the ideal conduct of Purefoy, Bloom nevertheless understands its value. This difference from the men of the decaying society about him is what makes him the chief subject of the novel: what happens to him is worth relating because his fate at least is still to be determined. Analogous to Bloom as a man, Stephen as an artist may or may not realize his desire. The destinies of both are clearly related; and the climax and resolution of their compound story follows the decisions they make in the present chapter. There are some good omens: Stephen is the "bullockbefriending bard"; Bloom's daughter works in Mullingar, a cattle-market town; and he himself worked in a Dublin cattle market, and has his scheme for a tramline for cattle; above all, the darkening sky which Stephen considered ominous during his meditation on the beach, and the "drouth" Bloom spoke of a few pages later, in his first moments in the novel, have been resolved in a fructifying rainstorm.

As the chapter opens, Bloom has just come from committing the consummate sin of onanism, his conduct on the beach after his apotheosis at Barney Kiernan's constituting an eloquent statement that he is indeed "no one" as well as "Zeus." His reverence for maternity and procreation is revealed as early as the sixth chapter (cemetery) to be a reflection of his awareness of his situation. Estranged from Molly, cut off before and behind, he must win back his wife and effect "that proliferant continuance" to save himself. His love for Molly and desire for a son, which have persevered until now, are undiminished. Nothing "could ever efface the image of that voluptuousness," the author says during this chapter; and on the very next page, Bloom expresses bewilderment that:

> a child of normally healthy parents and seemingly a healthy child and properly looked after succumbs unaccountably in early childhood (though other children of the same marriage do not). . . . (412)

Nevertheless, on the beach he surrendered to his predicament and relinquished his aspiration. Thus, when he expresses inwardly his objection to the derisive treatment of maternity by the others, the author roundly denounces him "by way of" the scathing Junius:

> But with what fitness . . . has this alien . . . constituted himself the lord paramount of our internal polity? . . . It ill becomes him to preach that gospel. Has he not nearer home a seedfield that lies fallow for the want of a ploughshare? . . . The lewd suggestions of some faded beauty may console him for a consort neglected and debauched but this new exponent of morals and healer of ills is at his best an exotic tree which, when rooted in its native orient, throve and flourished and was abundant in balm but . . . its roots have lost their quondam vigour. . . . (402-3)

The cause of Bloom's outrageous conduct, his alienation from Molly, is the chief subject of attack. Her adultery is excused if not justified, and he is mocked again and again for pretending to be a messiah, to regenerate others ("a censor of morals," "pelican," "preach that gospel").

Despite his sinfulness, Bloom is still messianic. The concern for Mrs. Purefoy that takes him to the hospital is called "stark ruth of man"; entering the room, Mulligan notices the sardines and bread on the table and him simultaneously, and they are called "loaves and fishes"; less overt is the suggestion of the Last Supper in his pouring ale for Lenehan who, having directly caused his "crucifixion," is analogous to Judas.

It has been pointed out that, in the context of the Book of Malachi, Bloom as Messiah should lead himself to a reunion with his wife and "turn his heart" to his son. Shortly after Junius' denunciation, he faces his predicament. "Ruminating, chewing the cud of reminiscence," he "beholdeth" himself as a boy, and as a young salesman for his father bringing home "many a commission to the head of the firm seated . . . in the paternal ingle." Then "the young knighterrant recedes"; "Now he is himself paternal and these about him might be his sons."

The passage is a reiteration of the idea of the familial line, the "proliferant continuance," which is presented in the sixth chapter in Bloom's thoughts about Rudy's coffin and his father's deathbed. His father is dead, and the young men are not his sons. He is neither the son nor the father of his vision. In the phrase used when he recognized his situation in the earlier chapter, "nobody owns" him. By now, he has become fully aware of the relationship between his familial isolation and his alienation from Molly (onanism), for his "rumination" continues with the prostitute Bridie Kelly, his first sexual partner:

> Together . . . they hear the heavy tread of the watch as two raincaped shadows pass the new royal university. Bridie! Bridie Kelly! He will never forget the name, ever remember the night, first night, the bridenight. They are entwined in nethermost darkness, the willer with the willed, and in an instant (fiat) light shall flood the world.

But his youthful relationship with "the whore of the lane" (as he called her at the end of the eleventh chapter) was "Carnal Concupiscence," and so:

> Did heart leap to heart? Nay, fair reader. . . . She is the bride of darkness, a daughter of night. She dare not bear the sunnygolden babe of day. No, Leopold! Name and memory solace thee not. . . . No son of thy loins is by thee. There is none now to be for Leopold what Leopold was for Rudolph. (406-7)

The next paragraph depicts the journey of Bloom's soul "over regions of cycles of cycles of generations that have lived," to a view of Molly and Milly. But there is no re-union: "They fade, sad phantoms: all is gone. Agendath is a waste land. . . ." And the paragraph ends with a depiction of the "murderers of the sun" tramping to the Dead Sea, the symbol in the fourth chapter (kitchen) of absolute sterility, to attempt to slake their thirst.

Feeling so powerfully the bleakness of his situation and prospects, Bloom does not reassert his claim on Molly, but instead gives up any hope of having a son; he understands that the way of Bridie Kelly is fruitless, onanism, and sees Molly as lost to him. And overtly, although not con-sciously, he seeks a substitute in Stephen. During the ride to the cemetery, he thought of Dedalus as "Full of his son" and envied him. At the beginning of the present chapter, he gives three reasons for staying with the boister-ous company: he is tired, they are treating him well, and "he bore fast friendship to sir Simon and to this his son Stephen." Two pages later, his attitude is more manifest. Rudy is mentioned, then:

and now sir Leopold that had of his body no manchild for an heir looked upon him his friend's son . . . and as sad as he was that him failed a son of such gentle cour-age (for all accounted him of real parts) so grieved he also in no less measure for young Stephen for that he lived riotously with those wastrels and murdered his goods with whores. (384)

This passage at the beginning of the chapter joins with one at the end, which expresses the crystallization of Bloom's attitude toward Stephen, to straddle the chapter. He is thinking of a party attended by himself and Molly during their youth:

And yonder about that grey urn where the water moves . . . you saw . . . Floey, Atty, Tiny, and their darker friend with I know not what of arresting in her pose then. . . . A lad of four or five in linseywoolsey . . . is standing on the urn secured by that circle of girlish fond hands. He frowns a little just as this young man does now. . . . (415)

Bloom's bald association of the young Stephen and Molly
is followed almost immediately by Stephen's cry "Burke's!"
and the exodus of the revellers from the hospital. At the
bar, Bloom witnesses Mulligan's sneaking away and Steph-
en's inquiry about a berth for the night. When the other
revellers chase the fire brigade and Stephen and Lynch
arrange to visit a brothel, Lynch notices a third party:

> Whisper, who the sooty hell's the johnny in the black
> duds? Hush! Sinned against the light and even now that
> day is at hand when he shall come to judge the world by
> fire. Pflaap! [The fire brigade.] *Ut implerentur scrip-*
> *turae.* (420)

Stephen has mentioned both aspects of Bloom's identity.
Bloom has, in terms of the symbolic meaning of "light" in
the chapter, "sinnned against the light," and he is the messiah come "in order that the scriptures may be fulfilled."
The combination of phrases from Isaiah 66:15 and 16
("the Lord will come with fire," "by fire will the Lord
judge") in Stephen's statement reinforces the messianic
identification.

Bloom has sinned against the light, and his attitude toward
Stephen does not affect his sin. Stephen is not his son.
This is a simple fact, and an uncompromising one. If he
is to implement the fulfilment of the scriptures, the promise
of Isaiah and Malachi—if he is to rescue both Stephen and
himself—he must turn Stephen's heart to his "father" and
reunite himself with his family.

Regarding Stephen, the author has presented in the chapter a concise recapitulation of the "father" aspect of his self-
destroying dilemma: Stephen's complaint against his country and his Church, and his defiance of God. He has also
explicitly stated that Stephen can achieve the "flight" that
will save him only by worshipping God (finding "holiness"), and that he can do so only with God's grace. This
is not a surprising religious doctrine but, introduced in a
novel, it prescribes a surprising development in the action
—the dramatic representation of the granting or withholding of grace. Such a representation is possible in *Ulysses*,
however, because its principal character has been identified

as the Messiah, the agent of God's grace. That Bloom is on a messianic errand in his pursuit of Stephen is indicated ironically, not only in Stephen's flippant identification of Bloom, but in the parody of Elijah-Dowie with which he ends the chapter. Stephen's mock-sermon is inspired by an inquiry from Lynch about Dowie, one that echoes the inquiry about Bloom that directly precedes it. In the context the "Elijah" of the last words of the chapter can only be Bloom, and the sinner addressed in the sermon can only be Stephen himself, the rebel against God. The italics are my own:

> Christicle, who's this excrement yellow gospeller on the Merion hall? Elijah is coming. Washed in the Blood of the Lamb. . . . *Come on, you triple extract of infamy!* . . . The Deity ain't no nickel dime bum-show. *I put it to you that he's on the square and a corking fine business proposition. He's the grandest thing yet and don't you forget it. . . . You'll need to rise precious early, you sinner there, if you want to diddle the Almighty God.* . . . He's got a cough-mixture with a punch in it for you, *my friend,* in his backpocket. *Just you try it on.* (420-21)

Neither deliverer nor infidel is aware that Stephen's flippant blasphemy is the exhortation of the one to the other. But the chapter ends as Bloom, conforming to the prediction of Malachi Mulligan at the end of the first part of the novel, covets Stephen, and prepares to follow him to nighttown.

Bloom has achieved understanding of the interrelation of the two elements of a man's family. His unconscious substitution of Stephen for the son he has lost hope of having, the product of desperation, is a bizarre manifestation of yearning for the family he sees denied him, of undiminished service to the absolute value that constitutes the chapter's thematic burden. This aspiration to the good on the part of the sinner Bloom, which distinguishes him from the other sinners in the chapter (and in the novel), may have its reward, for his pursuit of his projected foster-son takes him to nighttown. And since the familyless man who has put away his wife and spilled his seed is also the bearer of divine grace, the desperate impulse of the one Bloom to create a false family is the instrument for advancing the action to the critical point in the novel at which the other Bloom, potential deliverer of both familyless man and "fatherless" boy, contends with the place of sterile brothels, the city of the night.

1. *Shulhan Aruch*, chap. cli. Quoted from the Goldin translation (New York, 1929), IV, 17.

2. Maria S. Cummins, *The Lamplighter* (Boston, 1902), p. iii. The passage from the novel is on p. 26 in this edition.

3. *Letters*, pp. 138–39.

4. Kenner, *Dublin's Joyce*, p. 19.

5. A. M. Klein, "The Oxen of the Sun," *here and now*, I (January, 1949), 28–47.

6. Quoted from *James Joyce*, p. 212. The sister is Eva Joyce, the friend, Louis Gillet.

7. Robert McAlmon, *Being Geniuses Together: An Autobiography* (London, 1938), pp. 14–15.

8. Levin, p. 106.

chapter nine

15 *nighttown*

This chapter extends over almost as many pages as do all the nine chapters that constitute the first part of the novel. It has excited more interest and praise than any other part of the novel except Molly's soliloquy, and that has the advantage largely because it is apparently less difficult to read. The appearances are deceptive. The last chapter's seemingly unconstrained and clear flow of language conceals qualities essential to understanding the chapter and the novel as a whole; and in contrast, the seemingly chaotic present chapter develops clearly and directly to portray the dramatic climax in the story of Stephen and Bloom.

In the discussion of "Style in *Ulysses*" in Chapter Four, its basic narrative device was characterized as a "quasi-dramatic format": the chapter is nominally a play, complete with speech-designations, and stage directions italicized within parentheses. However, much of the action is fantastic in nature, and the stage directions are generally disguised fictional narration, or descriptions of fantastic phenomena. Of the many analogues and possible sources of the chapter suggested in Chapter Four, the closest is Strindberg's *Dream Play*. One of his late "expressionistic" works, it is characterized throughout by illogicality, fluidity of transition, overt symbolism, and fantasy. The characters even speak like the unreal characters in Joyce's chapter.

Despite its unusual qualities, however, Strindberg's play is internally consistent. It has one locus of action, the mind of "The Poet," its protagonist; and it exists on one plane, the dream-world of that mind. Joyce's chapter is much more complicated. It portrays its subject, the experiences of Bloom and Stephen in the brothel district, on two planes, the physical and the psychological; and there are three loci, the external natural world of the brothel district, the mind of Bloom, and the mind of Stephen. The three are interinvolved, and, as a result, certain natural elements of the situation, such as the passage of time, are distorted. But the emotions, the attitudes, and the spiritual experiences of the two characters are rendered with consummate faithfulness.

The psychological plane is the dominant one. It dictates the character of the chapter and contains the significant action. It comprises a series of fantasies in the minds of Bloom and Stephen, varying in length from six lines to twenty-six pages, and, in addition, countless incidental hallucinatory metamorphoses of people, things, and events of the lurid section of the city in which the characters find themselves.

The fantasies are apparently made possible by mild drunkenness. Stephen has visited a number of bars during the day and evening; and for Bloom the "second drink does it" (444). However, drunkenness does not cause them. Some are invoked by the world around the characters; the great majority are the expression of preoccupations of their minds which are sufficiently powerful that almost anything will serve to set them off. Obviously these revelatory fantasies are the most important to the action. The other fantasies, like the innumerable metamorphoses that dot the chapter—speaking doorknobs, materializing kisses, oriental music—build and maintain the device which is exploited, whose *raison d'être* actually resides, in these.

The first fantasy in the chapter, although very short, is such a revelatory one. It begins with a "stage direction":

(A sinister figure leans on plaited legs against O'Beirne's wall, a visage unknown, injected with dark

mercury. *From under a wideleaved sombrero the
figure regards him with evil eye.)*

BLOOM

Buenos noches, senorita Blancha, que calle es esta?

THE FIGURE

(Impassive, raises a signal arm.) Password. *Sraid
Mabbot.*

BLOOM

Haha. *Merci.* Esperanto. *Slan leath.* *(He mutters.)*
Gaelic league spy, sent by that fireeater. (429)

Probably a figure was leaning "against O'Beirne's Wall";
and with equal probability, it was a woman. However,
although her face might have been sinister, it is highly
unlikely that she was wearing a sombrero or that they had
the polyglot colloquy represented. The scene depicted as
Bloom walks past the leaning figure occurs in his mind;
and it is the product of his fear, as a Jew, of the chauvinistic forces represented by the citizen.

Nothing in this first fantasy is physically impossible—
fantastic in the literal sense. Subsequent creations of the
fatigued and tormented minds of Bloom and Stephen are
less restrained, however; and the natural circumstances
from which they proceed, which they incorporate in themselves, and to which they return the two characters, contrast
sharply with them. A "reminder" with which Strindberg
prefaces *The Dream Play* is also a close description of
Bloom's and Stephen's fantasies:

Anything may happen; everything is possible and probable. Time and space do not exist. On an insignificant
background of reality, imagination designs and embroid-
ers novel patterns: a medley of memories, experiences,
free fancies, absurdities and improvisations.

The characters split, double, multiply, vanish, solidify,
blur, clarify. But one consciousness reigns above them
all—that of the dreamer; and before it there are no se-
crets, no incongruities, no scruples, no laws.[1]

It is not a precise description because in *Ulysses* the "dreamer" does not create all out of his consciousness— natural circumstances and "dream" are intimately related. The relationship is one of reciprocal influence: a fantasy departs from, incorporates, and returns to the physical reality in which the character experiencing it simultaneously exists; on the other hand, it can change his conduct, and thereby change that reality.

This complex and difficult relationship, however, does not justify a refusal to distinguish between the quality of fantasy and that of reality in the chapter—a conception of the world of the chapter as a magical one in which the impossible becomes real, as one of secular miracles—on the grounds perhaps that Joyce believed in the occult. On the basis of that view, for example, when Bloom, turned into a grovelling woman by the "Bello" of his fancy, becomes a man again—

(Bloom half rises. His back trousers' button snaps.)

THE BUTTON

Bip!

. . . .

BLOOM

(Coldly.) You have broken the spell   (539-40)

—the situation is construed as simply that "Here a button breaks, 'Bip,' from Bloom's trousers and restores to him his manhood." [2] But the snapping off of a trousers button (which actually happened, Bloom discovers in the next chapter) cannot arbitrarily accomplish such a result in fiction any more than in life. And Joyce has not tried to arrogate to this particular snapping the functions of action and character-motivation. The return of Bloom to manhood in his fantasy of transformation is in fact fully motivated; it is a conclusive development of the action on the psychological plane, the dominant plane in the chapter. The dramatic "Bip!" of the button and the fact that it is a trousers button announce that development in the story very nicely.

but it exists, Bloom's attitude has changed. His "half" rising from his grovelling position in his fantasy is what causes the button to give way, and that fancied change of position is tangible indication of the real change of attitude. The snapping off of the button is not merely an arbitrary symbolic announcement, but is a natural consequence of the movement which expresses the development of a manly attitude in one who has been grovelling. And so it marks precisely that outcome of the psychological action, that change motivated by what happened before it in the fantasy —that change motivated, conventionally enough, by the character's experience. The fantasies are not magic but fiction, representations of part of what happens in the novel.

The trousers-button incident exemplifies one frequently bewildering quality of the fantasies which has led to talk of mysticism and magic, the relationship of the novel's fact and the characters' fancy. Another frequently bewildering quality which has done so is the presence of things that cannot be known by the character experiencing the fantasy, such as the word "Nebrakada," taken from the love charm Stephen found in an occult book during the tenth chapter (city), which Bloom speaks in two of his fantasies, and statements made by an accuser of Bloom called "the Nameless One" which echo private phrases of the narrator of the incident in Barney Kiernan's. The first of these qualities, the relationship of novel's fact and characters' fancy, is implicit in one of the two principal meanings of the term "fantasy," the psychological: the fantasies of Bloom and Stephen are daydreams and, as such, admit and transmute elements of reality. (The term commonly used in critical discussion of this chapter of *Ulysses*, "hallucination," is inaccurate, for a hallucination is totally a product of the imagination.) And the other principal meaning of the term, the literary, implies the second quality: the fantasies are literary artifacts, not case reports. They are artistic representations rather than precise records of psychological phenomena; and, as such, they can contain things for the sake of effect that Bloom and Stephen themselves cannot possibly know. Like the anecdote of a vindictive gossip, the thoughts of a self-deluding girl, and the conversation of drunken revellers in the three preceding chapters, the daydreams of Bloom and Stephen are not simply communicated naturalistically but represented in terms dictated by the author.

That they are daydreams is the most illuminating fact about the fantasies. More precisely, they are what psychologists call daymares, nightmares experienced while awake, the nightmare being defined as a dream motivated by anxiety. As in the case of the *Portrait,* Joyce's knowledge of the work of Freud and other early students of the psychology of dreams is uncertain. It was probably greater at this later time, but dream literature has existed for thousands of years, and the analogues of the chapter, especially Strindberg's play, could have provided sufficient inspiration for the fantasies. The important thing is that, perhaps because of Joyce's perceptiveness, they conform to the descriptions of dreams published by psychologists since the turn of the century.

One of their most obvious dream characteristics is their relationship to natural time. A long dream really takes place in a matter of seconds (or, according to some very recent theories, of minutes). Fantasies extending over many pages occur between a comment and a response, or an entrance and a salutation. In the process of enticing Bloom into Bella Cohen's brothel, Zoe asks him for a cigarette. Bloom says, "The mouth can be better engaged than with a cylinder of rank weed." Zoe mockingly tells him, "Go on. Make a stump speech out of it," and in a fantasy he does. After a rapid rise and decline in public position, he is "carbonized" in a fiery immolation, the assimilation into the fantasy of Zoe's very next sarcasm (which appears nineteen pages later), "Talk away till you're black in the face."

That assimilation is another dream characteristic. As the dreamer preserves his dream by accommodating it to a noise in the street or a disturbing bright light, so when a bit of reality penetrates a fantasy, it establishes itself within it while remaining part of the natural plane of action. During the chapter every possible variety of interrelation of the two planes of action occurs, with the result that an almost kaleidoscopic blending of them is achieved. However, given the way in which dreams, and the fantasies, work, there need be little confusion regarding whether a passage be actual or imagined. For example, when the speech of two spectators at Stephen's row with the British soldier undergoes a shift of style—

BIDDY THE CLAP

Did you hear what the professor said? He's a professor out of the college.

CUNTY KATE

I did. I heard that.

BIDDY THE CLAP

He expresses himself with much marked refinement of phraseology.

CUNTY KATE

Indeed, yes. And at the same time with such apposite trenchancy (574-75)

—what has happened is that the real speech of the women has penetrated the fantasy Stephen is experiencing at the time and promptly established itself as an element of it.

One can speak of elements of the fantasies because, again like dreams, they are relatively whole constructs: in the very short fantasy quoted above, Bloom sees the "Gaelic league spy," addresses her, is answered, makes a final statement and a remark *sotto voce*, and "escapes." The fantasies are of a sufficiently organic nature to be susceptible of interpretation, just as most dreams are.

Instantaneous, responsive to external reality, and meaningfully unified, the fantasies are finally like dreams in developing their meaning largely by way of grotesque symbols. However, these symbols present nothing like the problem with which psychoanalysts wrestle. They are never arbitrary and cryptic like most dream symbolism, and they are generally prominent elements in the fantasies, fully described in Joyce's "stage directions." For example, when one of the prostitutes mentions an item in the newspaper to the effect that "the last day is coming this summer," then mentions Antichrist, Stephen makes a significant discovery. Thereupon, a "hobgoblin" appears to him and says:

> *Il vient! C'est moi! . . . Sieurs et dames, faites vos jeux! (He crouches juggling. Tiny roulette planets fly from his hands.) Les jeux sont faits! (The planets rush together, uttering crepitant cracks.) Rien n'va plus. (The planets, buoyant balloons, sail swollen up and away. He springs off into vacuum.)* (496)

The dream-like quality of the fantasy is apparent. Furthermore, the symbolic "hobgoblin" is described, and identifies himself, as the precipitator of the "end of the world" spoken of by the prostitute. Despite the manifest whimsy in the "roulette planets" and "balloons," their significance as minor symbols is apparent. They contribute to the depiction of a view of the ruler of the universe as an arbitrary, capricious, and callous monster—Stephen's view—at a place in the action where such a depiction is needed.

Other symbols are merely fantastic extensions of synecdoche: Zoe's dress-buckles, Bella's fan, Lynch's cap, speak for, and otherwise represent, the respective individuals. Still others are simple and clear representations of other kinds.

Although the effect of the natural world on the fantasies is significant, the influence of fancy on fact, of the imagined on the real, is ultimately the vital thing. The change wrought on the actual language of the two nighttown ladies is not real but a product of Stephen's fancy; and if it were real, it would be insignificant. But the change the fantasies do work in the real world, the alterations of attitude that result from Bloom's and Stephen's experience of them, the alterations which constitute the effect they have on the story of Bloom and Stephen, constitute the only possible reasons for their presence in the novel. It is in connection with their function that the similarity of the fantasies to dreams is most important.

The psychological force that engenders the daymare is anxiety. In the fantasies of Bloom and Stephen, guilt, fear, and apprehension are its ingredients. And each fantasy,

even at its funniest—for they are shot through with zany
humor—both projects and intensifies the motive force for
the character to perceive it clearly and feel its effect strongly.
Bloom's fantasies about his sexual perversions and the marital situation that engendered them and Stephen's about his
"mother" and "father" are more powerful experiences than
any previous thought either character has had about these
preoccupations. It is this fact about the present chapter
that is announced toward the end of the preceding one:

> There are sins or (let us call them as the world calls
> them) evil memories which are hidden away by man
> in the darkest places of the heart but they abide there
> and wait. He may suffer their memory to grow dim, let
> them be as though they had not been and all but per-
> suade himself that they were not or at least were other-
> wise. Yet a chance word will call them forth suddenly
> and they will rise up to confront him in the most various
> circumstances, a vision or a dream, or while timbrel and
> harp soothe his senses or amid the cool silver tranquil-
> lity of the evening or at the feast at midnight when he is
> now filled with wine. Not to insult over him will the
> vision come as over one that lies under her wrath, nor
> for vengeance to cut him off from the living but shrouded
> in the piteous vesture of the past, silent, remote, re-
> proachful. (414)

Not for denunciation or vengeance, but to reproach him
does the vision or dream come to the sinner at the feast at
midnight.

The fifteenth chapter of *Ulysses* is less long than its dramatic format makes it appear, but it is very long nevertheless. And it clearly owes its length to the fantasies, for the
natural action is both simple and brief. Stephen and Lynch
enter nighttown and are accosted by a bawd. Bloom enters
in pursuit of them, meets the same bawd, hears a piano,
and guesses that the player is Stephen. The piano-player
is in Bella Cohen's brothel and Zoe, standing on the doorstep, induces Bloom to accompany her inside. In the parlor
Bloom sees Stephen and Lynch with two of Zoe's associates.

After some desultory talk and licentious flirtation, Mrs. Cohen enters the room and demands payment from the men. Stephen carelessly throws money on the table, but Bloom saves him from being cheated. After some more badinage, they begin to dance. Stephen dances frenziedly, finally stops, strikes the ceiling lamp with his "ashplant," and runs out of the brothel. Bloom adroitly quiets Mrs. Cohen's protests and follows Stephen, who has become involved with two British soldiers. Despite Bloom's remonstrances, one of them knocks Stephen down. Corny Kelleher, the undertaker, arrives just in time to save Stephen from arrest, and the chapter ends with Bloom standing guard over the unconscious young man.

Aside from incidental figures, the natural action has only seven characters: Bloom, Stephen, Lynch, Bella Cohen, and her three girls: Zoe Higgins, Florry Talbot, and Kitty Ricketts. Lynch, described in the *Portrait* as resembling a hooded reptile (p. 205), was portrayed in the preceding chapter as mocking and baiting Stephen. When distinguished from Bloom's fantasy of her, Bella Cohen is a contemptible person—vulgar, pretentious, and avaricious. The three prostitutes have been said to symbolize animal, vegetable, and mineral, but Joyce is not being so pompous. Zoe ("life" in Greek) is alert, lively, frankly carnal; Kitty is thin, pretentious, mannered, cold—feline; Florry, fat, stupid, good-natured, slothful, is a vegetable. The names are significant of the girls' characters as the chapter reveals them. Thus, when in one of Stephen's fantasies they confess the beginning of their waywardness, Kitty is full of excuses and claims of high social connection, Florry says that she had become drunk, and Zoe, in a statement characteristic of her sympathetic nature throughout the chapter, announces, "I let him larrup it into me for the fun of it."

Some of the fantasies in the chapter occur in fragments, with part of a fantasy experienced by Bloom, for example, separated from the next part by both a bit of natural action and part or all of one experienced by Stephen. (A fair idea of the way in which the simple natural action combines with the elaborate fantasies to form the chapter is provided in the appendix, which precedes the notes to this chapter.) Bloom's fantasies begin soon after the chapter opens; and, although its final paragraph is one of them, his critical psychological experience ends during the scene in the brothel. Stephen's fantasies begin after Bloom joins him in the brothel, about halfway in the chapter, and his critical psychological experience occurs as the chapter nears its conclusion. The respective psychological actions develop organically. Although the body of Bloom's fantasies extends through three-fourths of the chapter, one source of guilt or anxiety will be elucitaded in a fantasy and another broached; then that other will be the principal subject of the next fantasy; and this process continues until he faces every aspect of his problem and condition. Furthermore, the sequence of his fantasies follows a classical psychological pattern, which will be described below. Stephen's two last and most affecting fantasies, that involving "the mother" and that which he experiences in the street, in combination with the physical action relevant to each (respectively his striking the brothel parlor lamp and his argument with the British soldiers), are similarly unified.

In view of these facts, it is possible to discuss the earlier part of the chapter, devoted primarily to Bloom, separately from the later part, devoted primarily to Stephen. After the effect of his psychological experience on each has been examined, a third and more fundamental question can be considered: the significance of the chapter's action in the composite story of Stephen and Bloom.

Bloom's first extended fantasy comes immediately after his vision of the "Gaelic league spy." His father appears to him and berates him for being in the brothel district and for having "left the house of his father and left the god of his fathers Abraham and Jacob" in his youth and spent his time with gentiles. His mind is being more than fair to the memory of his father, for Rudolph nee Virag had changed both the family's name and religion. But Rudolph's Jewish chauvinism has a non-religious element; his concern about the presence in the brothel district, the center of "spilling," of his "son, Leopold, the grandson of Leopold" (Rudolph's father), that is, the descendant of their "fathers," is in part a concern for the breakdown of the familial line. (When Bloom's comically distressed mother joins his father, she drops among other possessions, "a shrivelled potato," referred to by Bloom three pages earlier as "poor mamma's panacea"; this potato is also related to the theme of Bloom's responsibility toward "that proliferant continuance.")

One aspect of Bloom's waywardness having been castigated, his conscience turns to the other: suddenly the place of his parents is taken by Molly:

A VOICE

(Sharply.) Poldy!

BLOOM

Who? *(He ducks and wards off a blow clumsily.)* At your service. (431-32)

The two lines of dialogue fully depict the familiar situation: Molly's imperiousness, Bloom's subservience, and his willing acceptance of that state. Molly is in Turkish costume, a fact significant first because she is so dressed in the dream, analogous to Stephen's, that Bloom recalled while on the beach, and secondly because the costume includes trousers and a yashmak. The trousers symbolize her domination; the yashmak suggests inaccessibleness, and recalls an observation Bloom made earlier in the day: "Her eyes over the sheet, a yashmak. Find the way in. A cave. No admittance except on business" (277). The rest of the exchange elaborates the point of Bloom's neglect of Molly and the fear from which it stems. After demanding that he call her "Mrs Marion," she says, "*(Satirically.)* Has poor little hubby cold feet waiting so long?"; and although he denies this, he has admitted it before, and his causing her to mention it is another admission. She suggests that she is pregnant, reflecting Bloom's disturbance about that possible result of her liaison. Finally, she asks him, "*Ti trema un poco il cuore?*", and walks away "*in disdain*," "*humming the duet from* Don Giovanni." The question is formed from one of Zerlina's verses, and expresses her trepidation about accompanying the Don into his castle. In Molly's parting words, Bloom likens himself to the timid maiden, climaxing his self-reproach for lacking the courage necessary to make love to and thus win back his wife.

Coincidental with, and probably causing, Molly's departure is the appearance of the bawd who a few pages earlier approached Stephen and Lynch. Obtruding on the fantasy with her wares, she diverts it to what in the preceding chapter was called Carnal Concupiscence. The girl she offers materializes as Bridie Kelly, Bloom's partner in his "bridenight," described in that chapter. The first accessory to his sinful onanism is succeeded by the latest one, Gerty MacDowell, who in turn is replaced by a more subtle manifestation of Bloom's "putting away" of Molly—Mrs. Breen, the former Josie Powell, in their youth the companion of Molly and her competitor for Bloom's attention. After a flirtatious exchange culminating in her fervent repetition of "yes," she "fades" to end the fantasy.

This fantasy, which presents Bloom's fundamental problem and the sin related to it, is followed very shortly by another, which expands his self-indictment. It probes Carnal Concupiscence more deeply, especially the furtive and shameful pseudo-sexual activities to which he has descended. The rising "up to confront him" of "sin or . . . evil memory" here is appropriately precipitated by the passing of the routine police patrol, for the patrol, "*two raincaped watch*," is a specific recall of "the watch . . . two raincaped shadows," who came upon and abruptly ended his first youthful essay into sexual sin.

The fantasy begins with apparent irony: the watch accuse him of wrongdoing because he is feeding meat he has bought to a stray dog. However, the pig's foot and sheep's foot he gives over to the beastly creature are phallic emblems—the action is a symbolic one. And so the watch are not simply agents of feared victimization. They express Bloom's sense of being, as another of his fantastic creations describes him, a "street angel and house devil," and his consequent fear of justice, punishment for his real sins, as well as of injustice, persecution by society.

Although he protests "I am doing good to others" and enumerates acts of kindness to animals, and although the gulls he fed Banbury cakes during the eighth chapter appear to bear witness for him, Bloom's sense of guilt is not assuaged. For the watch are adamant, and soon the accusers appear, led by Martha Clifford. He lies desperately, misrepresents himself, and courts the favor of the watch, with indifferent success. The first watch calls the first formal witness at what is now a trial, Mary Driscoll, the Blooms' former maid, who complains that Bloom accosted her "in the rere of the premises." With the legal aid of J. J. O'Molloy, he undertakes a protracted defense. This is interrupted by: "Mrs Yelverton Barry," wearing a "sabletrimmed" cloak, who orders his arrest for epistolary indecencies; and another gentlewoman, "Mrs Bellingham," dressed entirely in furs, who makes similar charges and discloses that in his letters he referred to her as a "Venus in furs."

Venus in Furs is the title of a well-known short novel of the nineteenth century, by Leopold von Sacher-Masoch von Lemberg, an Austro-Hungarian, whose name provided Krafft-Ebing with the term "masochist." Its title figure is a woman who dresses in furs like Mrs. Bellingham, and in "sabletrimmed" garments like Mrs. Yelverton Barry, and it is about the love affair of a masochist. The thinly-disguised autobiographical hero insists on serving his mistress as a bonded slave and being cruelly treated, stipulating only that she always wear furs in his presence, for he associates furs with the imperiousness he craves in a mistress. The woman complies because of her love for him and, as she fears, her morality is corrupted and their relationship ruined. He is cured only when, as a final gesture before abandoning him, she pretends to love him still and to wish to whip him, but after binding him has her new lover flog him mercilessly.

While shopping at the book stall in the tenth chapter (232), Bloom revealed that he is familiar with the work of Sacher-Masoch, his namesake and his father's countryman, co-religionist, and contemporary. And although *Venus in Furs* is referred to only obliquely in the present chapter, there is no doubt of the relevance of the book whose masochistic hero reads excitedly "in the Odyssey about the beautiful witch who transformed her admirers into beasts":[3] Molly's sharpness in the previous fantasy echoes the fur-clad "Venus'" insistence on deference; there are the allusions in the present fantasy; and Bloom's daymares of self-reproach draw again and again upon Sacher-Masoch's book.[4]

When the two society ladies are joined by a third, "The Honourable Mrs Mervyn Talboys," dressed "in amazon costume," who testifies that Bloom "implored" her "to give him a most vicious horsewhipping," "as he richly deserves," the parallel with *Venus in Furs* becomes most pronounced. The fur-clad ladies reveal that Bloom also asked them to whip him, the Honourable Mrs. Talboys prepares to "scourge the pigeonlivered cur as long as I can stand over him," and his response is delighted terror (459).

Bloom has not suddenly become pathological. His guilt-ridden mind simply expresses the truth in an extreme and therefore distorted form. He does crave punishment, but not to any important extent for sexual gratification (the strict meaning of masochism). He conforms to the pattern of the hero of *Venus in Furs,* the desire to be made to suffer by a woman to whose service he is dedicated (he serves Molly, accepts her domineering manner, and panders for her), because of his sense of guilt for failing to be that woman's true husband. And the fact that his craving for punishment so extremely represented in the fantasy derives from guilt rather than sexual perversion is shown by his earlier characterizing of Martha Clifford's letter, which speaks twice of "punishing" him, as "her silly I will punish you letter" (362).

Although Bloom desires punishment principally because of his neglect of Molly, the specific reason for his guilt in this fantasy is his furtive pseudo-sexual activities. Further-more, the indictment his fancy attributes to the three imag-inary ladies is harsher than those it attributes to the servant girl and Martha Clifford, and the desire of those ladies to punish him is so strong because his advances to them were neither manly as in the one case nor welcome as in the other. They represent the respondents who were not like Martha to his advertisements in the *Irish Times* for a typist (448), and all other unwilling subjects of his perverted thoughts and activities.

When the ladies call Bloom "a wellknown cuckold" and the "jury," whose spokesman is the "Nameless One," agree about his reputation, the focus shifts from his sexual sins to society's injustice to him. The watch accuse him of being an anarchist, and Sir Frederick Falkiner orders the "wellknown dynamitard, forger, bigamist, bawd and cuckold" to be hanged. Rumbold the master barber appears, but he is saved just in time when Dignam comes from the grave to confirm that he is in black, not because he is an anarchist, but because of Dignam's funeral. And on this burlesque note the fantasy ends.

Bloom's significant experience in nighttown comprises six consecutive closely-related fantasies and the natural action connected with them. The first of these six is the fantasy in which his parents invoke his familial responsibility, and Molly his connubial; and then, presumably because of the real bawd who obtrudes, Bridie Kelly, Gerty, and Mrs. Breen appear in rapid succession to represent his Carnal Concupiscence. The second, just discussed, grows out of this last element of the first: it develops from Mary Driscoll, the maid, to Martha, to the three imperious but also truly indignant women, to the trial of the privately guilty but publicly persecuted Bloom. Each of the remaining four fantasies in the series similarly expands an element in the preceding one. The third presents the career of the public Bloom, ending in his immolation. In it "Dr Mulligan" and "Dr Dixon" defend him on the grounds that he is "bisexually abnormal," "the new womanly man," and finally, "about to have a baby"; and the fourth, precipitated by the opportunity for masculine sexuality offered by Zoe, elaborates the point made by the ostensible defense witnesses. The fifth, Bloom's climactic psychological experience, presents the transformation and domination of him by "Bello," the correspondingly transformed Bella Cohen, who is the blatant Circe of the correspondence with Book X of the *Odyssey*. It also presents the consequence of that transformation, and prepares for the sixth, which sums up Bloom's situation. In his *Psychopathia Sexualis*, Krafft-Ebing delineates a classic development of male perversion from passivity to masochism to feminization. This is precisely the pattern in Bloom's psychic drama: the first of the series of six fantasies, aside from recapitulating his failings and predicament, represents his submission to Molly; the second develops this characteristic, and the second and third represent his masochism; the third, fourth, and fifth are primarily about the final stage in Krafft-Ebing's description, Bloom's inadequate manliness. However, the pattern is not so much fact as plot. Because the drama is psychic, all that really happens is that Bloom tells himself about himself, probes and suffers over the depths of his perversion until his experience motivates the climax and resolution of the unified psychological action.

The first three fantasies of the six all occur in rapid succession; and, to the point where the second one ends, the natural action is slight. Bloom has done little but walk in pursuit of Stephen. As the fantasy involving the three ladies and the trial ends, he hears the sound of a piano in one of the brothels and astutely observes that the music played would be characteristic of Stephen. Zoe, stationed on the doorstep, indicates that his observation is correct. She then makes a physical advance and discovers his mother's potato ("poor mamma's panacea"), which in the morning is the only thing aside from his latchkey for which he checks his pockets before leaving the house. The latchkey is already "in the trousers I left off," and so he does not demur when Zoe insists on keeping the potato and puts it "greedily" in her pocket. They flirt, and Zoe asks him for a cigarette; whereupon he makes the sententious remark that goads her to the sarcastic "Go on. Make a stump speech out of it," which precipitates the third fantasy in the sequence.

While in the preceding fantasy he manages to escape execution, in this third one his position in society and his guilt-motivated masochism produce the logical results. First he becomes "alderman sir Leo Bloom" and makes his "stump speech," a caricature denunciation of the rich. He is promptly lauded and rises to "emperor president and king chairman." His imagination permits itself to improve on this orgy of wish-fulfilment: he "repudiates" his *"former morganatic spouse"* and takes a princess; John Howard Parnell acclaims him as the successor to his brother; and finally the citizen, choked with emotion, says, "May the good God bless him!" But he is too aware of his real social situation and his character to be able to maintain the vision of acceptance and recognition. Appropriately, Lenehan

initiates his downfall by heckling him; with equal appropriateness, Purefoy accuses him of using a masturbating
device; and before long the "mob," reflecting the perfidy
attributed to the Irish in the novel, says, "Lynch him!
Roast him! He's as bad as Parnell was." He attempts to
save himself by calling on Mulligan, Dixon, and the other
medical students in the preceding chapter. The result of
their testimony that he is an epicene and pregnant and of
his corroborating delivery of seven more than the one male
child he craves is his wishful and under the circumstances
ironic conception of himself as the most exalted mortal a
Jew can conceive of. The miraculous multiple birth stays
the "mob," and he is asked, "Bloom, are you the messiah
ben Joseph or ben David?" (God or man). In a direct
echo of Christ, he replies "You have said it." Then he per-
forms a series of miracles, the papal nuncio recites a mock
genealogy beginning with Moses and ending "and Virag
begat Bloom *et vocabitur nomen eius Emmanuel*," and he
has reached the pinnacle of the eminence which he (like
most men) craves. It lasts only for an instant before he
is denounced as the false Messiah, again largely for his
personal sins (for example, his tailor presents a bill "To
alteration one pair trousers"), and set afire (in a *"garment
marked I.H.S."*). In conjunction with Zoe's "Talk away
till you're black in the face," which immediately follows
her invitation to him to "Make a stump speech out of it,"
he becomes "mute, shrunken, carbonised," and the first
half of the sequence of six fantasies ends.

He discloses his state of mind at this point immediately,
telling Zoe that "Patriotism, sorrow for the dead . . . future
of the race" are all "insanity" and expressing a desire to
commit suicide by taking aconite, just as his father did.
However, she restores his spirits and induces him to accompany her into the brothel. Inducement is necessary although
he is eager to join Stephen, and it promptly becomes clear
that this is because of his personal sexual problems. After
being reminded of the situation at home by a man's hat
and waterproof on the antlered hatrack, he follows Zoe into
the parlor, where Stephen sees him and experiences the
fantasy involving "The End of the World." He, however,
only stands and watches Zoe. When she stretches to light

a cigarette from the ceiling lamp, Lynch raises her dress, and her body *"bare from her garters up"* is exposed. She addresses a lewd remark to Lynch and then:

> *(Squinting in mock shame she glances with sidelong meaning at Bloom. . . . Bloom stands, smiling desirously, twirling his thumbs. . . .* (500)

Bloom's attitude is symbolic. He desires, yet twirls his thumbs. At this point the fourth fantasy in the sequence begins, and its chief subject is Bloom's failure to be unequivocally masculine, which is the extreme development of his eleven-year-old inability to make love to Molly.

To flay him for this fundamental failing, Bloom's fancy conceives the consummate old lecher who is a bizarre mutation of his grandfather. Virag discusses the prostitutes one by one, expressing a simply carnal view of women and enjoining Bloom to "tumble" one of them, with equal emphasis. Bloom interrupts the appraisal of Florry to explain his situation with a transparent hunting metaphor: *"(Regretfully.)* When you come out without your gun," but does not deter the old man, who ultimately sums up:

VIRAG

> *(Severely, his nose hardlumped, his side eye winking.)* Stop twirling your thumbs and have a good old thunk. See, you have forgotten. Exercise your mnemotechnic. *La causa è santa.* Tara. Tara. *(Aside.)* He will surely remember. (503)

The cause is indeed—ultimately—holy. Virag's reference to the loss of manliness as "forgetting" how to act like a man and the consequent use of "memory" and "remembering" to signify return to manly behavior are understandable in terms of the long history of Bloom's debility: he has "forgotten" a formerly familiar aspect of his life. Thus, in testifying about Bloom's epicene nature in the preceding fantasy, Mulligan says, "In consequence of a family complex he has temporarily lost his memory" (483). Bloom responds to Virag's appeal sufficiently to say inquiringly,

"Mnemo?", and Virag answers *"(Excitedly.)* I say so. I say so. E'en so. Technic." He continues his exhortation, refers caustically to Bloom's submission to female domination and to "Gerald," a homosexual with whom Bloom was involved as a youth, and departs.

As in the "Venus in furs" passage in the second fantasy of the series, Bloom's guilt-ridden imagination has caricatured the situation. Virag is not an embodiment of his conception of proper sexual behavior but an exaggeration of it. He need not be as lecherous as Virag in order to accept the validity of the old man's injunction. What he does is to offer a bar of chocolate to Zoe, who playfully gives some to Lynch and, saying "Do as you're bid. Here," offers some to him as well. *"(A firm heelclacking is heard on the stairs.)"* announces the approach of Bella Cohen. The owner of the hat and waterproof on the antlered rack in the hall has just gone out. He is presumably her lover, who, according to Zoe, "gives her all the winners and pays for her son in Oxford." She has been "working overtime [because] her luck's turned today" (possibly she too bet on Sceptre); but now she is free to attend to the business of her establishment. Bloom hears the man in conversation on the doorstep, thinks of Boylan, and in a brief fantasy conjures his departure. Before Bella has entered the parlor, he meditates on the chocolate:

BLOOM

(Takes the chocolate.) Aphrodisiac? . . . Mnemo. Confused light confuses memory. . . . Eat and be merry for tomorrow. *(He eats.)* . . . But it is so long since I. Seems new. Aphro. . . . Better late than never. (515)

Thus, as a result of the fantasy in which his recreation of his grandfather exhorted him to "remember," to act like a man again, he decides to attempt to have normal sexual relations with Zoe. However, at this point:

(The door opens. Bella Cohen, a massive whoremistress, enters. . . .)

BELLA

My word! I'm all of a mucksweat.

Bella does nothing, and makes only this one vulgar remark, but the submissiveness, masochism, and lack of manliness which Bloom has just suppressed make her the vehicle for a reassertion of their sovereignty. He begins to undergo the fifth in the series of six fantasies, the climax of the psychic drama and of his experience in nighttown. The fantasy brings to a head his sense of his failure to be the man he must be in order to regain Molly and stop his perverse practices and his sense of guilt regarding that failure. It is the longest one in the chapter, and proceeds uninterrupted through more pages than are taken up by any of the first five chapters.

Bella's fan, a synecdoche for the "whoremistress" herself, begins the fantasy with some trenchant observations:

THE FAN

(Flirting quickly, then slowly.)   Married, I see.

BLOOM

Yes. . . Partly, I have mislaid. . .

THE FAN

(Half opening, then closing.)   And the missus is master. Petticoat government.

BLOOM

(Looks down with a sheepish grin.)   That is so.   (515-16)

He is "partly" married because he has "mislaid" his key; it is in the trousers he "left off," and he will not disturb "the missus" to recover it. Knowing this, the fan very quickly asserts its domination over Bloom, who actually confesses: "Enormously I desiderate your domination." When he obeys the fan's command that he fasten Bella's shoelace, Bella's *"eyes strike him in midbrow. His eyes grow dull, darker and pouched, his nose thickens"*—he is transformed to an epicene swine-like creature by a quasi-Circe, who becomes correspondingly semi-masculine. "Bello" now berates him for his sexual and marital sins and abuses him physically. Finally, the beating ceases and Bello declares:

No more blow hot and cold [act like both a man and a woman]. What you longed for has come to pass. Henceforth you are unmanned and mine in earnest, a thing under the yoke. . . . You will shed your male garments . . . and don the shot silk. . . . (523)

The apparent correspondence between Bloom's humiliating subjugation and that of the hero of *Venus in Furs* is actually insisted upon. In both, the man ties the woman's shoe; in both, she places her foot on his neck; and Bloom's fantasy contains many verbal echoes of the novel. The correspondence is meaningful because Bloom identifies his Bella-Bello with Molly. "Embonpoint," a word applied to Raoul's adulterous mistress and to Molly, is applied to Bella when she first appears; kneeling to lace her shoe, he observes that he knelt to search beneath their bed for Molly's novel in the morning; and while lacing it, he mentions his lacing of Molly's shoes the night she met Boylan. He sees his relationship with Molly as the abject one of the hero of *Venus in Furs*, and himself as too weak (womanish) to upset it. He recognizes the justice of the humiliation and pain inflicted on him by the creature of his fancy.

After forcing the "unmanned" and "enslaved" Bloom to confess various homosexual and womanly acts and upbraiding him further, Bello makes an explicit announcement of the essential nature of the fantasy: "The sins of your past are rising against you"; whereupon "The sins of the past," in a medley of voices, catalogue additional examples of his perverted sexual behavior. The sequence of confession and castigation continues until Bello specifies Bloom's new duties, all menial womanly chores, and finally puts "her" up for sale at auction. The slave is instructed to commit sodomy with "her" prospective buyers, and on complaining is explicitly challenged, in a passage that dramatically intensifies Bloom's self-castigation:

BELLO

What else are you good for, an impotent thing like you? . . . Where's your curly teapot gone to or who docked it on you, cockyolly? . . It's as limp as a boy of six's doing his pooly behind a cart. Buy a bucket or sell your pump. *(Loudly.)* Can you do a man's job? (528-29)

He responds "Eccles street," but Bello says "there's a man
of brawn in possession there," enlarges upon Boylan's sexual vigor, and then expresses Bloom's acute fear of losing
irrevocably the wife he loves and the family he craves by
stating as fact that Boylan has impregnated Molly—something which Molly herself had only suggested in Bloom's less
tormented imaginary encounter with her early in the chapter. Bello's observation, "That makes you wild, don't it?
Touches the spot?", is apparently sound. At any rate, with
his fear of total and irrevocable loss invoked for him to
confront squarely, following hard upon his harrowing self-
castigation, Bloom's suffering reaches a climax:

BLOOM

To drive me mad! Moll! I forgot! Forgive! Moll!
. . . We. . . Still. . . (529)

But the creature of his self-reproach, unaffected, declares the
situation to be indeed irrevocable and his lapse of
"memory" to have been the sole cause of it:

BELLO

(Ruthlessly.) No, Leopold Bloom, all is changed by
woman's will since you slept horizontal in Sleepy Hollow
your night of twenty years. (529)

Bello continues to ridicule Bloom's perversions and condemn
his neglect of Molly, and then describes at length the spolia-
tion of his possessions by Molly's lovers. In response to
this, he declares, with the resolution of his Achaean analogue, that he will "return" and "prove"; but Bello repeats
that he is "too late," and then articulates the one "decent"
alternative left to one who has done what he has done and
must endure his future existence: death. Bloom had
thought of his dismal prospects during the day, but he had
not regarded them as his just deserts. Now he does so, and
his guilty exaggeration brings him to a distinct, conscious
revelation:

BLOOM

(Clasps his head.) My will power! Memory! I have
sinned! I have suff. . .

(He weeps tearlessly.) (531)

Unfortunately, however, he does not resolve to exercise
his will and his "mnemotechnic" to become husband and
marriage partner. Despite the validity of the revelation, his
mind entertains an alternative view of his condition, and
that view is expressed now. The "nymph" in the picture
over the Blooms' bed, "The Bath of The Nymph," an illustration from the salacious magazine *Photo Bits*, appears and
comforts him in Bloomian archaism: *"(Softly.)* Mortal!
(Kindly.) Nay, dost not weepest!" She will accept the
mortal as he is, ignores his apology for his abject position
to thank him sentimentally for having taken her out of
"evil company" and framed and admired her. Then, alternately placing her fingers in her ears and covering her face
because of shamed propriety, she criticizes the activities in
the Blooms' bedroom. It soon becomes plain that she
objects not to perversion but to sexuality itself; and her
only response to Bloom's discussion of a youthful experiment in sodomy and his private life with Molly is a boast:

THE NYMPH

(Loftily.) We immortals, as you saw today, have not
such a place and no hair there either. We are stonecold
and pure. (538)

She is alluding to his visit to the "naked goddesses" in the
National Museum on his way to the adjoining Library. His
revery during lunch of his experience with Molly on Howth,
and his concluding observation, "Me. And me now" (173),
motivated the visit, for "They don't care what man looks."
Identifying herself with the lifeless statues ("immortals" in
that sense too), she also recalls the perverse Marthas and
sentimental Gertys who deny normal sexuality, the fully
"mortal" condition. She accepts the Bloom denounced by
Bello for the reason his partners in perversion accept the

Bloom rejected by Molly: because she prefers him in his present unmanned state. Ironically, the monstrous Bello is an expression of Bloom's healthy impulses and the pretty goddess of his corrupt ones. The nymph of the picture over the disused marriage bed, she and not Molly is the analogue in Bloom's first chapter to Homer's Calypso. While he has served Molly, he has also neglected her for the past eleven years. And the reason for his decade of absence from her as a husband and marriage partner is that he has been in thrall to the "immortal" nymph, unable to act like a proper "mortal." Here, in his fantasy, the correspondence is completed. At the end of ten years' imprisonment, Calypso offered Odysseus immortality as her mate, and he rejected both the goddess and her great gift in order to attempt to return to his (mortal) wife Penelope. In asserting the value of the "stonecold and pure," escape from "mortal" sexuality—which is the logical extension of his unmanly perversions—the nymph of Bloom's fancy is making a corresponding offer.

This alternative view of his condition entertained by Bloom's mind, in terms of which he can escape the choice between suicide and the attempt to restore his "will power" and "memory" and return home as "mortal" husband, entails his rejection of the healthy values upon which Bello's denunciation is based: connubial love, manly conduct (and self-respect), children. The crucial opposition that has cropped up so often in the novel, between his desire to reform and change his situation and his desire to abandon himself to it, has come to a head in this fantasy. And it is resolved in the remainder of it, in two stages. First: as a result of the nymph's contemptuous treatment of sexuality, Bloom becomes defensive, elaborating on the strong sexual attraction women and especially Molly have for him; the nymph, in the white habit of a nun, reproves him with her example, saying, "No more desire. . . . Only the ethereal"; at this he *"half rises"* from his prostrate position, his trousers button snaps off, and he reveals the symbolic significance of his movement by declaring *"(Coldly.)* You have broken the spell."

Bello's Circean "spell" (her prostrating and transforming him at the beginning of the fantasy), which expresses

Bloom's self-reproach for inadequacy as a man and a husband (for his long years in the cave of the nymph), is
actually an acute and dramatized version of the goddess'
depraved "spell." When the goddess appears in his mind
and reinforces the "spell" by approving of him in precisely his prostrate "unmanned" position, he is happy because she has provided an alternative to his painful (and
true) view of his condition. When she goes on to denounce
his sexual activities, he is explanatory and even apologetic.
But, when she asserts what her initial approval has implied,
the final development in the attitudes and impulses she represents, she violates too radically his conception of the
nature and duty of man, and his common sense.[5] His
assumption that nuns cannot successfully deny their sexuality, articulated earlier in the novel (152-53, 362), is not
only relevant to the fantasy but expressive of this conception.
When she asserts that "desire" should be eliminated and
that she as a (mortal) nun was able to eliminate it, she
adds self-ridicule to Bloom's self-castigation; ironically, she
actually intensifies his repugnance for all those of his attitudes and impulses which she represents to such a point
that he rejects them—to the point of breaking her "spell."
And so he "half-rises" to manhood, responds to her assertion with his "cold" declaration, and asks, echoing the
theme of the preceding chapter, "If there were only ethereal
where would you all be, postulants and novices?"

Freed from the "spell," Bloom proceeds to the second
stage of his return to manhood: a new access of self-doubt
and weakness is expressed as a savage attack on his re-
surgent sexuality by the nun-nymph, who declares that he
wishes to "sully" her "innocence"; but as she *strikes at
his loins*" with a *"poniard,"* he:

> *(Starts up, seizes her hand.)* . . . Fair play, madam. No
> pruning knife. The fox and the grapes, is it? . . . Cruci-
> fix not thick enough? . . . A holy abbot you want.
> . . . (540)

He completely routs her. And he exposes her "ethereal"
pretentions as well, for when she flees it is: *"unveiled, her
plaster cast cracking, a cloud of stench escaping from the*

cracks." As a final gesture of mastery, he calls after her the remainder of his contemptuous debunking of her celibacy, provoking her to an Irish keen of lamentation.

Bloom's firm action is accompanied by his "starting up" —standing fully erect. And the rest of the fantasy bears out the suggestion that he has become fully a man again. Immediately he is required to face his former master, whose "You'll know me the next time" echoes the "You shall know me!" with which the despotic woman in *Venus in Furs* prepares to flog the hero, and is an exact repetition of Zoe's (actual) remark when she took the shrivelled potato from an unwilling intimidated Bloom many pages, but only a few minutes, before; the statement is intended as a reassertion, therefore, of power over an unmanly Bloom. However, Bello has become Bella again, and Bloom, correspondingly "remembering" the full manhood of earlier years, subjugates her as easily as he routs the nymph. "Composed," he speaks contemptuously of her age and appearance. She tries harder to regain the upper hand, but in vain. Bloom has become master of the situation. He has, that is to say, rejected shabby prurience, unmanly submissiveness, masochistic pandering, and so dispelled the guilty self-reproach that they engendered.

Bloom's fantasy over, the real Bella is permitted to finish the statement which begins with her vulgar complaint about the heat. She turns to the piano and asks, "Which of you was playing the dead march from *Saul?*", pointing up the difference between the fantasy and reality and posing the obvious question: "Is the long 'daymare' really significant in the novel?" It is the manifest climax in the series of six fantasies that embody the psychological drama of Bloom's self-reproach; furthermore, the state of mind that caused his degeneration from proper man and husband is, along with its consequences, the central fact of Mr. Leopold Paula Bloom's character and story. If his triumph over that state of mind has no effect on his actual behavior, it is an ephemeral or illusory triumph; and the fantasies are not true fictional action but *outré* exposition.

The effect is made unmistakable. Bloom does not go upstairs with Zoe, as he had almost decided to do when Bella entered the room a moment before and precipitated the fantasy. But that exercise of "mnemotechnic" would also be "spilling"; what he does is less dramatic but really no less revelatory: immediately, as his very first act, he goes to Zoe and asks for the return of his potato.

When the fan commanded his subservience at the beginning of the fantasy, he said, "I should not have parted with my talisman," and spoke of that "parting" as a "peccadillo" "at dewfall on the sea rocks"—linked the potato with his masculinity by reference to the incident with Gerty. His attitude toward the potato was very similar in the morning, when he was concerned to make sure that, although he was not in possession of the latchkey to the door of his house, he still had the potato. And the significance he attaches to it is discreetly reinforced by the author: it is shrivelled and black—old, not renewed; Zoe mistook it for his testicles (467); although she realized her error, she seized it "greedily"; a potato is both a seed and a root.

Thus, when at the very end of the fantasy Bella tried to reassert Bello's former domination of Bloom, she spoke the exact words with which Zoe had secured the potato. And now, a moment later, insisting that Zoe return it to him despite her reluctance, he uses a word that has been charged with meaning; he says: "There is a memory attached to it." The return of the potato to Bloom's possession is symbolically significant, but Joyce is neither being highhanded nor sharing literally Bloom's superstition about it: its return symbolizes precisely Bloom's capacity to effect that return.

Other indications of the change in Bloom occur in the remainder of the chapter. *"Two raincaped watch"* who came on him near the beginning recalled the similar police patrol which had interrupted his first sexual experience, and so they precipitated a guilt-ridden fantasy; near the end appear *"two raincaped watch, tall,"* drawn by the street fight just after Private Carr has knocked Stephen unconscious. In pointed contrast, Bloom is not disturbed, nor does he leave (although Lynch does) or cringe, but orders them to take Carr's regimental number and otherwise represents Stephen's interest with vigor. A few pages before, when Carr's blow is still impending, Bloom experiences the execution of the croppy boy in a fantasy; and the behavior of the three *"highly respectable Dublin ladies,"* who, in the

fantasy precipitated by the "watch," were indignant about
his carnal overtures, is another pointed contrast between
Bloom as he was and his new masculine self-confidence:

> *(A violent erection of the hanged sends gouts of sperm
> . . . to the cobblestones. Mrs Bellingham . . . rush
> forward with their handkerchiefs to sop it up.)* (578)

Most significant of all, however, is his treatment of the
madam, Bella Cohen, who simply by her appearance was
able to precipitate and become the dominating figure in his
climactic psychological experience in nighttown. He is no
less firm with her than he finally succeeded in being with
his mental projection of her. When she complains to him
about the lamp Stephen has struck, he asks impatiently,
"What lamp, woman?" When she demands ten shillings
in damages, he protests indignantly. When she tries to
extort the money by intimidation, he calmly shows her that
the lamp works, and asserts that the damage amounts to less
than sixpence. Finally, because she persists in threatening
to report Stephen to the police, he mentions that he knows
of her son at Oxford and cows the tough and cynical woman.
Then he runs out to assist the young man, who has gotten
into his new trouble on the street. Edmund Wilson says:
"And he emerges finally a man again from the brothel of a
Circe who had transformed him into a swine." [6]
    Actually, the Homeric correspondence is not very close.
Odysseus was never transformed; Bloom was the agent of
his own transformation; above all, it has extended over a
period of more than a decade, so that he emerges from the
brothel not simply "a man again," but the man he has not
been in all those years.
    However, Bloom's problems are not automatically solved
by his recovery of his manhood. The necessary complement
to it, without which it is meaningless, is return to Molly;
and the "man again" is still sonless and wifeless—he
"emerges . . . from the brothel" with his predicament unchanged. The last fantasy in the series of six, which occurs
immediately after his psychological battle back to manhood,
reveals that he is fully conscious of the fact.
    He has secured his potato from Zoe, and she is reading
his palm. She divines that he is "henpecked." The word

causes a momentary fantasy of unmanliness and subservience in which a black rooster lays an egg. Then the girls begin to whisper and giggle; and Bloom, too self-conscious about the Boylan matter not to react, experiences the extremely painful sixth fantasy, of the tryst of Molly and Boylan. Not only does Boylan address him *"loudly for all to hear,"* but he greets his wife's visitor dressed as a flunkey. Boylan tips Bloom and announces the purpose of his visit. Molly emerges from her bath, calls Boylan "Raoul" after the lover in *Sweets of Sin,* and asks him to dry her. Although she threatens to have her contemptible husband whipped, Boylan generously invites him to observe them through the keyhole, and he is grateful. The situation recalls that at the end of *Venus in Furs* which reforms the masochist; however, Bloom's imagined ignominy is much greater than that to which Sacher-Masoch's hero would submit.[7] Not only is he aware of the lover's presence, but the sexual activity he witnesses is vigorous, and his enjoyment is frenetic.

What Bloom's feelings of guilt and shame, perhaps intensified by his return to manhood, have done, is to create the most extreme exaggeration of any in the chapter's fantasies. In eloquent testimony of his self-reproach for permitting the affair and his suffering because of it, he represents himself as acquiescing in it, implementing it, and even deriving great enjoyment from watching through a keyhole, by permission. But unlike Bloom's deficient masculinity, Boylan is not a psychological problem, and he can do nothing in nighttown about his predicament except reproach himself and suffer.

Bloom's painful fantasy of Molly and Boylan does not affect the others, and the giggling around him continues until Lynch points to the mirror and laughs. Stephen and Bloom "gaze at" the mirror together and have simultaneous visions of the face of Shakespeare crowned by the antler hat rack in the hall.

Bloom's psychic drama of six fantasies has just ended, and the two related fantasies which constitute Stephen's significant psychological action are about to begin. With characteristic audacity, Joyce presents a transition. It is not, however, one fantasy magically involving both characters; it comprises two fantasies caused by the same stimulus and with the same general subject. The simultaneous similar fantasies of Bloom and Stephen may suggest future communion or understanding, but they can be explained naturally and need no magical rationalizations.

To begin with, the context indicates that one real head is accidentally reflected in combination with the hat rack in such a way as to appear horned, and that the head is Bloom's. Zoe's charge that he is "henpecked" is followed directly by her whispering about the reflection to Florry (549), to begin the whispering and giggling in the room which invokes Bloom's fantasy of Molly and Boylan; the joke is imparted to everyone but Bloom and Stephen; and while there would be nothing funny about the irrelevant accident of horns on the reflected head of an unmarried Stephen, in the case of Bloom it is not irrelevance but very funny coincidence. The fantasies Bloom and Stephen simultaneously experience confirm that both of them, as well as all the others, see Bloom's face. Bloom's is more elaborate. Stephen only envisions the face of Shakespeare, beardless because the actual face of the less famous bawd, cuckold, and commercial traveler who was so closely associated with Shakespeare in the ninth chapter (library) is beardless, hears a Shakespearean comment on Lynch's laughter, and praises just men abused by women. Between his fantasy and his statement, which appears a page and a half later (554), Bloom's fantasy occurs. When he looks in the mirror, Shakespeare says explicitly *"(To Bloom)"* in Bloomian archaism, "Thou thoughtest as how thou wastest invisible," a reference to Zoe's discovery moments before of his henpecked state. Then Shakespeare laughs like *"a black capon,"* recalling the black rooster of the brief fantasy invoked by the word "henpecked" before the giggling invoked Molly and Boylan, and the reflection in the mirror invoked Shakespeare. Bloom returns to the natural world to ask Zoe with feigned ignorance, "When will I hear the joke?" Zoe's response, "Before you're twice married and once a widower," precipitates the rest of the fantasy. "Mrs Dignam, widow woman" appears, and Shakespeare says in garbled

form, "None wed the second but who kill the first," a line
from *Hamlet*,[8] a play Bloom knows, which reflects not only
Zoe's remark but his domestic situation. Still in Bloom's
mind, *"The face of Martin Cunningham, bearded, refeatures
Shakespeare's beardless face,"* reflecting his thought on the
way to the cemetery that Cunningham looks like Shakespeare. And the fantasy ends after Mrs. Cunningham appears and sings a snatch of a song Bloom recalled her
singing during that train of thought (95).

No mystical communion but a point at which the fantasies of Bloom and those of Stephen coincide and roughly
concur, the mirror incident marks that place in the chapter
where the locus of its significant psychological action
ceases to be the mind of the novel's older protogonist and
becomes the mind of its younger one.

Although Stephen appears briefly at the very beginning,
the natural as well as the psychological action focusses
on Bloom until he and Zoe join the group in Bella Cohen's
parlor about half way in the chapter. At this point Stephen
becomes as prominent as Bloom in the natural action and
experiences fantasies, mostly in brief installments, some of
which are important in the novel; but Bloom remains the
central figure until he has undergone the three fantasies
involving respectively Virag, Bello and the nymph, and
Molly and Boylan. When the shift of focus occurs following
the mirror incident, only a small part of the chapter remains. Stephen dances frenziedly, has his first major
fantasy, strikes the chandelier, and rushes out to the street;
there he gets into the altercation with the British soldiers,
has his second major fantasy, and is knocked unconscious.

Stephen's long declamation in the maternity hospital, a
complaint against his nation for abandoning him, rejection
of Christianity, and open defiance of God, indicated that
his attitudes had not changed during Bloomsday afternoon.
He still defies the claim on him of God and His cardinal
manifestations—country, religion, and family—and simultaneously both acknowledges that his defiance is futile, on
the one hand, and, on the other, "broods," reproaches himself for feeling as he does. His contradictory attitudes are
possible because he separates God in his thinking into the
Omnipotence whom he defies and a "mother," a source and

protector whom he has wronged. He acknowledged in the "battle against hopelessness" of his Shakespeare theory that he cannot deny either the Father or His principal manifestation—"history," circumstances, Bloom's "Phenomenon" —that the "nightmare from which I am trying to awake" is reality and so his attempt to escape from it is futile. And he has been no more successful in his efforts to salve his "brooding." In his own words, he is harried by the "Throb always without [him] and the throb always within." His predicament fills him with remorse while it keeps him wracked with anger and fear; he does not leave Catholic Ireland and attempt to fulfil the destiny he envisions; and remaining, he is impaled, adamantine, and desperate. The source of the predicament that has brought him so close to breakdown is his inability to accept the oneness of Father and "mother"—to accept that God is not a merciless *"dio boia"* and His world not nightmarish.

Stephen's defiance of God took him to Bella Cohen's parlor, for his setting out for nighttown at the end of the last chapter was a clear flouting of the divine injunction against "Carnal Concupiscence." Before the present chapter focusses on him, different aspects of his predicament are represented. He cannot sing "Love's Old Sweet Song" for Florry because he is "a most finished artist." The antipodal self-images he creates in a fantasy express his view of the source of his trouble by modifying a blasphemous French joke about the Virgin that he recalled in the morning (42):

PHILIP DRUNK

(Gravely.) Qui vous a mis dans cette fichue position, Philippe?

PHILIP SOBER

(Gaily.) C'était le sacré pigeon, Philippe. (509)

When it is pointed out that whiskey cannot be provided because "it's long after eleven," he remembers the riddle of the "fox burying his grandmother"; he recites it with minor changes appropriate to the brothel and then makes explicit what was only implied in the   second chapter (school): that he is the fox and his mother the grand-mother, and that he is burying her because "Probably he killed her" (545). When Zoe is about to read his palm, she remarks that he has the brow of "Mars, that's courage"; Lynch mocks him for his fear of manifestations of God's wrath, such as the thunder of the last chapter, then mentions "pandybat" and invokes out of Stephen's childhood Father Dolan, who had pandied him at Clongowes (and whom he associates with the *dio boia*), and the reconciling Father Conmee. His loneliness and yearning for love, expressed while he was on the beach and in the librarian's office, are represented in his murmuring, while Zoe examines his hand, "Continue. Lie. Hold me. Caress."

At that point, in order to protect Stephen from an un-pleasant prognostication, Bloom turns Zoe's attention to his own hand, and the simultaneous visions of Shakespeare occur. The significant relationship between Bloom and Stephen in the novel is established during this episode, from Bloom's entrance into the brothel parlor to the begin-ning of the action devoted to Stephen, but the episode is best deferred until that later action is discussed.

The action devoted to Stephen begins when the company in the parlor hears the discordant singing of "My Girl's A Yorkshire Girl" by the two British soldiers and their female companion (whose name, apparently by coincidence, is "Cissy Caffrey"), who are passing in the street. Stephen and Zoe are seized by a desire to dance; and Zoe starts the player piano, which plays "My Girl's A Yorkshire Girl" in waltz tempo. Stephen makes Zoe dizzy, and Florry and Kitty in turn. Then he dances with his stick ("ashplant") until his frenzy, which seems a pure expression of suffer-ing, causes him to say "Dance of death," whirl giddily and experience, pale and tottering, a vision of his dead mother similar to the dream of her which he recalled on the third page of the novel (7). Mulligan appears to announce that she is "beastly dead" and that "Kinch killed her dogsbody bitchbody," and she tells Stephen that some day death will come to him also. But he is preoccupied with his wrong to her. He protests that cancer killed her, "not I." "The" mother's only answer is the statement that he sang to her during her final illness Yeats' "Who Goes

With Fergus" (the song Mulligan brought into the first chapter). Satisfied that this is a sympathetic response, he asks a question of importance to him. At the end of his meditation on the beach, when he expressed his sorrow and loneliness, he asked, "What is that word known to all men?" (49). Feeling that it is known to the mother because in his dream she had "bent over him with mute secret words" and now she has appeared "uttering a silent word":

STEPHEN

(Eagerly.) Tell me the word, mother, if you know now. The word known to all men. (566)

The mother's answer is:

Who saved you the night you jumped into the train at Dalkey with Paddy Lee? Who had pity for you when you were sad among the strangers? Prayer is all powerful. . . . Repent, Stephen. (566)

That is to say, the word is the Logos, the Word of God, His manifestation and His Self. "The mother" asserts what Stephen has been unwilling to accept: she, loving and protecting, is one with "the father," simply an aspect of God—He is merciful and deserves Stephen's reverence. In telling him that he shall die and that he sang to her of submitting to the omnipotent Fergus, she has made the point that his defiance is futile; her response to his "eager" inquiry about "the word" is a more blatant expression of an evangelism which in fact subsumes everything said by this creation of Stephen's conscience. (It corresponds to, and perhaps was inspired by, the unconscious evangelism of Bloom, which has already occurred.)

But Stephen is unyielding. Given the answer to his question—acknowledging to himself that the Word and the mother who utters it are aspects of the hated Father—he exclaims "The ghoul! Hyena!" When the mother again asks him to repent and reminds him of "the fire of hell," he responds "*(Panting)*" with a more explicit and thus more defiant epithet: "The corpsechewer!" The mother warns him to beware of God's hand and raises her hand toward him, whereupon a green crab (cancer) attacks his heart. But he has faced the threat of God's wrath before in his thoughts, and in response he curses and declares *"Non serviam!"* The mother implores Jesus to "have mercy on him" and "save him from hell"; and enraged at her soliciting mercy for him, he expresses his defiance of her and every other manifestation or agent of God who might press him to devotion: "Break my spirit all of you if you can! I'll bring you all to heel!" In response, his impulse to reverence, which he denied for so long and against which he is now struggling, takes its most extreme form. The mother has asked Jesus' mercy; her next and final speech is as Him, interceding with His Father, reminding Him: "Inexpressible was my anguish when expiring with love, grief and agony on Mount Calvary."

This is the point at which Stephen's psychological struggle and the natural action of the chapter reach a joint climax, which is also the major dramatic climax of the novel. He cannot reconcile his intellectual view of a cruel God with the reproachful insistence of part of his mind that God is merciful. In bold and angry defiance of "all" the agents of a Deity Whom he sees as wishing to "break" his "spirit," he strikes at the lamp. Then, "abandoning his ashplant, his head and arms thrown back stark," he rushes out into the street, where he meets Private Carr in the real world and, in the second of his two major fantasies, "Old Gummy Granny," his mind's version of the "poor old woman" *(Sean Van Vocht)*, symbol of Ireland.

The lamp is a common type of the turn of the century, a chandelier with one gas jet around which is an incandescent mantle or hood. A shaped glass tube, the chimney, encloses the source of light. About the chimney of Bella's lamp has been placed a "shade of mauve tissuepaper." It apparently has no other unique characteristic, but much is made of it during the chapter. When she and Bloom first enter the room, Zoe turns the flame up full; later the gas jet goes out; Zoe adjusts it and lights a cigarette by it; on separate occasions Bloom and Virag stare at the lamp. The reason for all this attention is that the lamp is a light.

"Light" has already been used in the novel to represent divine power, both traditionally (Bloom as bearer of "light to the gentiles") and in a special sense ("light" as fertilization, an analogy with the cattle of the sun). But the original and enduring Old Testament concept of God as "like unto a light in the heavens" is more directly relevant. One of the few things Stephen does at the beginning of the chapter is to punctuate a blaspheming conversation by waving his stick under a street lamp, *"shivering the lamp image, shattering light over the world."* And a fantasy he experiences in which Mananaan MacLir claims to be "the light of the homestead" (a pun on the *Irish Homestead* connection of A.E., whom the god resembles) is ended when a *"judashand strangles the light,"* suggesting the ritual, during the singing of the Tenebrae on Holy Thursday, of extinguishing the altar candles to symbolize the death of God. With his harmless waving of his stick spoken of as "shattering light over the world," his association of Mananaan with a lamp, and his play on the Holy Thursday ritual, the symbolic significance to Stephen of Bella's lamp is clear when the climactic action, foreshadowed in the first of these, occurs. And that action is the climax of his rebellion—an attempt to destroy God and His creation.

As he *"smashes the chandelier"* with it and achieves, in his mind, the total destruction of God's dominion (*"Time's livid final flame leaps and, in the following darkness, ruin of all space, shattered glass and toppling masonry"*), Stephen calls his stick *"Nothung,"* which is the name of the miraculous sword in Wagner's version of the Germanic legend of the *Götterdämmerung.* In *Siegfried,* Wagner's hero broke the staff of rule of Wotan (Odin), chief of the gods, with his sword Nothung, and thereby put an end to Wotan's power over men and initiated the destruction of the gods. Stephen asserts that he is repeating Siegfried's feat.

Given his intoxication and emotional state, it is impossible to say to what extent Stephen views his intention and action literally. But whatever his hope the novel makes plain that he has achieved very little. Although there was never any question of his literally destroying God and His world, by asserting an analogy with Siegfried's exploit he ironically undercuts his act even as symbolic gesture.

Despite his conception of it at the critical moment, Stephen's weapon is not a great sword but a wooden stick: it is analogous not to Siegfried's sword but to Wotan's spear-staff—which is also made of ash. In the phrases of his own imitation of "Elijah" Dowie at the end of the last chapter, he has not risen early enough to diddle the Almighty God. And Joyce's irony persists. "Nothung" is obviously similar to the word "nothing." Appropriately: the lamp Stephen "smashes" lights again with no trouble when Bloom pulls the chain; the tissue paper shade, which is dented, can be undented; there is no toppling masonry; and the shattering glass, the only achievement of his brave and violent attack, is a standard lamp chimney valued at sixpence. The climax in the action of the novel is a representation of the futility of Stephen's struggle to defy God.

This representation and the fantasy that precipitates it constitute the first part of the significant action devoted to Stephen in the chapter. That action is completed when Stephen himself comes to recognize what is clear to the reader with the abortive attack on the lamp—when he encounters Private Carr and Gummy Granny.

That Stephen's altercation with Carr begins over a "shilling whore" is appropriate to its setting. But it is also significant. In the librarian's office Stephen represented Ireland as a wanton ("Gap-toothed Kathleen") who is easily seduced by England; and the sexual metaphor is the basis of the two principal representations in the novel of the Irish people's betrayal of their country, that of the spinsters and Nelson's Pillar and that of the English bull and the Irish women. The two British soldiers and their wanton Irish girl are a literal embodiment of the metaphor. Thus the song they sing is that played during the viceregal procession in the afternoon.

Stephen's habit of seeing Irish girls and women as symbolic of Ireland (in both the *Portrait* and *Ulysses*), his regarding the Irish as having sold themselves, and his attitude toward his country's conqueror—all indicate that he will be brought into the symbolic relationship. The first words he addresses to the soldiers are, "You are my guests. The uninvited. By virtue of the fifth of George and seventh of Edward." And he has already asked the girl to leave

them for him, the Irish bard and her true mate, only to be
told, appropriately, "I'm faithful to the man that's treating
me."

Stephen's invitation to the girl only starts the trouble,
and he is unwilling to give the chivalrous Private Carr
satisfaction. But he makes the situation irrevocable by a
reference to his method of solving his predicament. He
ran out of Bella Cohen's "abandoning his ashplant," as
though in acknowledgment of the quixotic nature of his
attempt to destroy God by force. When Bloom tries to
give it back to him, he says, "Stick, no. Reason. This
feast of pure reason." However, as "Lord Tennyson" says
of the soldiers in one of Stephen's fantasies, "Their's not
to reason why." And so his very declaration that he will
use his more characteristic weapon for dealing with the
divinely-created reality around him which Carr and his
comrade embody—"(*He taps his brow.*) But in here it is
I must kill the priest and the king"—is misconstrued by
Carr as the expression of a desire to assassinate Edward
VII; and his fate is sealed. At the same time, he recognizes
that an important reason for the soldiers' hostility is his
nationality; and playing on the "bull" metaphor, he says,
"I seem to annoy them. Green rag to a bull." Where his
fragmentary fantasies have been mocking ones of Tennyson
in a Union Jack blazer and of Edward VII, he is visited
now by Kevin Egan and other "wildgeese," who encourage
him to represent Ireland against the Sassenach. He does
not do so, but he does not deny his nationality to the
soldiers, and the bystanders insist upon the representational
character of the principals and of the situation itself.

By the time Bloom experiences his fantasy of the martyrdom of the croppy boy, Stephen has only become bored
with Carr's repeated threats and annoyed with the representational situation. However, in the midst of his objections, he exclaims, "But by Saint Patrick!", for Old Gummy
Granny suddenly appears to him. He calls her by a favorite
metaphor for Ireland ("The old sow that eats her farrow!")
and reveals that he knows what she wants of him ("Hamlet,
revenge!"). She bemoans the "strangers in my house";
he reviles her; and an onlooker, seeing his countryman
back away from the Englishman, says, "Our men retreated."

Carr gets more vociferous and obscene in his threats, Bloom becomes more desperately placatory, and Stephen recites amatory gypsy poetry to Cissy.

At this point shouts of "Police" change Stephen's mood abruptly, and he experiences a fantasy which begins with the firing of Dublin prior to a big battle (Bloom has been experiencing a fantasy involving Irish forces under the citizen and British forces under Molly's father, Major Tweedy). As it develops, Irish national heroes duel with each other, representing the futility and bumbling of Ireland's efforts to win independence, and finally a camp mass is celebrated. It is a black mass, because Stephen has been and is battling against God. Not only is there a human sacrifice, but she is *"Mrs Mina Purefoy, goddess of un-reason"*—pure faith, in contrast to his own weapon against God, faithlessness, reason. The celebrant is the pseudo-Catholic Mulligan, and he is assisted by a pseudo-Protestant combination of Haines and the landlord-minister Love, Father Cowley's evictor. Following the elevation of a symbolic and bloody host by the pseudo-Catholic, and a realistic translation by the pseudo-Protestant, the praise of God after His destruction of Babylon in the Revelation of St. John is intoned in reverse by "The Voice of All the Damned." As they deserve, Adonai's response is correspondingly reversed: "Dooooooooooog!" When "All the Blessed" render the praise correctly, they receive the correct response.

Preparing to give Stephen his just deserts, Private Carr outdoes all his previous essays in obscenity. Gummy Granny thrusts a dagger toward Stephen's hand and says, "Remove him, acushla. At 8.35 a.m. you will be in heaven and Ireland will be free." Stephen does not respond to his country's plea, but he does stand his ground against the Sassenach, despite a last attempt by Bloom to take him to safety. Finally, Carr knocks Stephen unconscious with one clumsy blow—the rapid victory of brute British power. Bloom's fantasy ends with a cease fire called by the victorious Major Tweedy. After the soldiers, the crowd, the watch, and Corny Kelleher leave, Bloom hears the half-conscious Stephen murmur parts of the first and last couplets of "Who Goes With Fergus?" With his recital of (apparently) all of Yeats' song, the chapter's significant action

devoted to Stephen comes to an end. The chapter itself
ends on the next page, with Bloom's vision of a senti-
mentalized eleven-year-old Rudy.

What happens in that significant action is: (1) Stephen's
conscience ("unreason") confronts him with an appeal to
revere God (he experiences the fantasy of the evangelical
mother), and he responds by physically striking at God,
unsuccessfully; (2) the other "whirr," the world without
him, confronts him with Private Carr, he responds with
his customary weapon, reason, and it strikes at him, successfully. The fantasies that cause the two blows are similar
not only in their personae but in their subjects: The mother
reproaches him for his lack of faith, Gummy Granny for his
lack of patriotism. Furthermore, both women are manifestations of the same abiding object of his self-reproach,
so that it is completely appropriate for Gummy Granny,
as the last thing she does, to pray, "O good God, take
him!", just as the mother does. The blows that follow the
two parallel fantasies are even more plainly complementary
events. Finally, the singing of the soldiers and girl as they
passed by the brothel caused the first part of Stephen's
significant action, for it precipitated the dancing which led
to his fantasy of the mother and blow to the lamp—the
fantasy and action in the street are tightly linked to the
fantasy and action that precede them in the parlor. The
part of the chapter devoted to Stephen is a unity as much
as the part devoted to Bloom, the sequence of six fantasies
and interplay between those fantasies and real events which
portray Bloom's recovery of his manhood.

The end of Stephen's part is not Carr's blow but the
effect it has on him, the outcome of that unified psychological and physical action. Its pattern is too symmetrical
not to be meaningful. Stephen is struck by Carr because
he has struck the lamp. This could be explained naturalistically (if he had not struck the lamp he would not have
run out to the street and met Carr), were it not for the
place in the pattern of Stephen's two parallel fantasies, the
symbolic significance created for the lamp in the chapter,
and the fact that the actions are *reciprocally* causative (if
Carr had not been in the street to inspire him to dance he
would not have struck the lamp). The complex pattern

Joyce has presented has only one reasonable explanation, and Stephen's situation and preoccupation to this point in *Ulysses* insist on it: he has struck at God and God has struck him back. This is not a case of *deus ex machina* but —like Raskolnikov's overhearing a conversation in a crowded market that tells him when he can murder the pawnbroker, only more pointedly so—a dramatic representation of the working of divine will in human affairs.

God is not being vindictive, confirming Stephen's view of Him, for Stephen has committed a great offense. And, for the same reason, the blow is not simply punishment; no mere blow with a fist could be suitable punishment. God is granting Stephen a revelation of the absolute futility of his defiance. When Stephen begins to recover from the revelatory blow, he discloses how much he understands, what effect his experience in nighttown has had on him.

What he says at that point would have to be heavily qualified, since he is only partly conscious, were it not true that he understands quite a lot before the blow is struck. When Carr and his companions were first heard singing outside Bella's parlor window, he said, "Hark! Our friend, noise in the street!" At that point he was being flippant, and the remark is significant only as a hint to the reader. However, in his first speech to Carr and his companion, he tells them, regarding their presence in Ireland, "History to blame": he has just come from his futile violent blow at God, the "nightmare" of reality within him, has rushed into "the street," only to be made to realize that that reality ("history") is all about him. And so he attempts, as he always has done, to contend against it with the aid of his reason. But this time he fails dramatically even to escape his place in it, for everyone in the street—the soldiers, the spectators, even Bloom and he himself (as their respective fantasies show)—perceives him as The Irishman; and, although he rejects the active patriotism urged on him by his national feeling (Gummy Granny), he stands his ground as an Irishman; to that extent, at least, he is knocked down as an Irishman. Indulging in a habit of thinking familiar in both the *Portrait* and *Ulysses*, he likens himself to Christ (the novel always does that *for* Bloom, a meaningful difference), and so he alludes to Judas when Lynch abandons him. But he is submitting to an Irishman's martyrdom.

In other words, Stephen's familiar weapon has proven as futile as his brief essay into violence—so futile indeed that he has been unable to make not only Carr (a foregone conclusion) but himself participate in his proposed "feast of pure reason": he does not leave the scene, cannot avoid being part of the brawl, of the "noise in the street," of the creation and manifestation of God. And the black mass that takes place in his mind just before Carr's blow fells him reveals that he realizes all this and understands what it signifies.

The crucial fact about the black mass is that "Adonai" answers the praise of "The Damned" who participate in it as well as the subsequent praise of "The Blessed" who do not. The sacrificial murder of Mina Purefoy ("pure faith": "unreason") by the "beastly" (materialistic: rationalistic) celebrants is appropriate to a diabolical rite; so is the reversing of the praise of God from Revelation by "The Damned" as a means of praising the antithetical master to whom their black mass is dedicated. And the meaning of the reversed response is apparent: as the beastly is the opposite of the spiritual, so "Dog" is the opposite of "God." However, the fact that Adonai ("The Lord") and not Satan makes that response signifies something equally apparent about the opposed "Dog" and "God": that they are the same substance in different forms. Just before he is felled, Stephen's mind tells him that God contains the beastly as an opposite manifestation of Himself—that He is "all in all," the Lord of "The Blessed" and "The Damned" both, answering each in their own terms. In other words the unfaithful, who invoke the dominion of Satan, who like Stephen hope to escape from God in a Manichaean world, receive a response that merely follows the perverse form of their invocation. And if they take comfort in it, they do so because they are blinded by their perverse point of view; for it signifies that the Lord of the faithful is their master as well, that there is no escape from Him.

Stephen is expressing the effect of his psychological and physical experiences in nighttown when he lies semi-conscious in the street, recovering from Carr's blow, because the blow is only the final confirmation of that which he recognizes before it strikes—the absolute futility of trying to defy God when he is one of His creatures living an existence willed by Him in His world. He had told himself all day that it was so; and in nighttown, God has demonstrated the fact to him. He only does two things: he "*doubl*[es] *himself* together," curls into the form of a foetus; and he recites Yeats' song. The position he assumes suggests dependence, and the song makes it plain that he is acknowledging his dependence on God. When Mulligan told him, in a snatch from the song, to "turn no more aside and brood," he stimulated his "brooding"; the mother" did so as well by mentioning the song; but now he himself recites the lyric that instructs the young man to no longer stand alone and despond, to acknowledge his subjection to the conditions of life, "go with" "Fergus."

There is nothing in Stephen's experience, from the moment the discordant singing by the soldiers and the girl is heard in the brothel parlor to his recital of "Who Goes With Fergus?", to indicate that his conception of God has changed. Rather, he has acknowledged the dominion he formerly fought so painfully and frantically, will no longer "battle against hopelessness" with sophistical heresies and artificial distinctions between a "father" and a very different "mother." He does not recognize that God is not the corpsechewer conceived by his reason but merciful, and so he has not come to the reverence for God that would liberate him. But if he has not yet been enabled to "fly" any more than Bloom has restored his family, like Bloom he has made his salvation possible. The preceding chapter made the point that Stephen Dedalus must receive divine grace before he can achieve "Holiness"; having accepted God's dominion, he has put himself in a position to accept His grace.

The manifestation of that grace is the Jew who has followed Stephen from the maternity hospital to Burke's tavern, from Burke's to Stephen's unsuccessful argument with Mulligan and Haines at Westland Row Station over the key to the tower (apparently he and Lynch ran into them there by accident), and from the station to nighttown. Although most of the chapter is devoted to the private experiences of each of the protagonists, a significant fact of the novel is that Stephen is the reason Bloom is in a position to experience and then act as he does; and Bloom becomes, by the time the singing soldiers appear in the street, just as instrumental in Stephen's story.

From his agitated pursuit of the young man to the end of the chapter, Stephen remains the object of Bloom's inchoate project for adopting a son; and his actions when they concern Stephen are consistently and blatantly those of a father. Minutes after his discovery of Stephen in Bella Cohen's brothel, Bella enters the parlor (precipitating the fantasy by which he restores his manhood) in order to demand payment. Capable of asserting himself at just that moment, he rescues the excess money Stephen gives Bella and gains, in addition to her admiration, an opportunity to suggest to Stephen that he care for Stephen's money. Stephen acquiesces and he rounds out the sum in Stephen's favor (545). Immediately after, when Stephen drops his cigarette, he throws it in the grate, says, "Don't smoke. You ought to eat," and asks Zoe for some food. When Zoe sees something disturbing in Stephen's palm, he substitutes his own hand. When Stephen strikes the lamp, he not only protects his money and his reputation but pays the damages out of his own pocket, like the father of any wayward boy (at the end of the chapter he still refers to Stephen's money as "One pound seven"). When he learns of the trouble in the street, he rushes out, and he remonstrates not only with Stephen but with Carr and even with the girl. When a bystander examines the prostrate Stephen, he *"(Glances sharply at the man.)* Leave him to me." When the watch of whom he was so terrified an hour earlier arrive, he challenges Carr *"(Angrily)"* and instructs the watch to report him. Finally, when Kelleher abandons him with the prostrate young man, he stands guard, thinks of Stephen's welfare, pledges himself to secrecy, and has the psychological experience that expresses what he has been about. This same vision of Rudy which appears to him at the culmination of his pseudo-paternal activity and concludes the chapter is, however, proof to the reader of the futility, the pathetic sentimentality, of his project. Stephen cannot truly mean for Bloom what Bloom wishes.

And yet Bloom truly has for Stephen the no less singular significance of emissary of Stephen's Father, bringer of the light to one in shadow. This fact, which is apparent at the end of the last chapter, when the Messiah-sinner follows Stephen because of an impulse to "turn his heart" to a son, is stressed at the very beginning of the present one, at the point at which the focus shifts from Stephen and Lynch to Bloom. The young men pass a street lamp which is then carried by a drunken day-laborer to a tram siding; and *"On the farther side under the railway bridge Bloom appears."* On the next page, Bloom sees the "light-bearer" and suddenly remembers his mission ("I'll miss him. Run. Quick").

During the body of the chapter, this relationship is developed. An instance of the symbolic use of light occurs in the fantasy Stephen experiences when he first sees Bloom in Bella's parlor. Lyster the librarian's injunction, "Seek thou the light," is Stephen talking to himself about Bloom, not about "Mananaan MacLir." His eventual acknowledgment of subservience to God follows, not only the meaningful sequence of fantasies and blows in parlor and street, but also his recognition of God's emissary, already identified for the reader, who carries "light to the gentile" unawares.

The recognition occurs in the period between Bloom's entering the parlor and the singing in the street which begins the action devoted to Stephen. This part of the chapter contains, along with all the natural action involved, the last three in Bloom's sequence of fantasies (those concerning Virag, Bello and the nun-nymph, and Molly and Boylan), various other fantasies experienced by both characters, and the simultaneous fantasies of Shakespeare. However, it begins and ends with—is framed by—two brief fantasies experienced by Stephen. When Bloom enters, Stephen envisions "The Hobgoblin" and the auditors of his Shakespeare talk; when his vision of his winged father and of a horserace ends, he hears the passing soldiers and their girl. The fantasies occur only minutes apart despite all the pages that separate them, and they are related. Their

subject, and the subject of most of the action involving
Stephen framed by them, is his recognition of Bloom's
significance for him.

When Bloom and Zoe enter the brothel parlor, Stephen
is arguing with Lynch (in his drunken imagination, with
Lynch's cap), toying with the piano, and apparently discoursing on the diatonic scale. But his statement that "the
fundamental and the dominant [tones] are separated by
the greatest possible interval" "Consistent with. The ultimate return" to form "The octave," is in reality a reassertion of the conclusion of his Shakespeare talk. He had
said that in trying to escape from himself, a man "going
forth" only meets himself, that the "battle" against the
identity willed him by God is "hopeless"; as with the
octave, no variation from the fundamental can be great
enough to violate the pattern that leads to the "ultimate
return." While he makes his comment on his "battle" in
this new guise, a phonograph in the street begins to play
an evangelical song, the first element in the evangelism to
which he is to be subjected, and:

> STEPHEN
> *(Abruptly.)* What went forth to the ends of the world to
> traverse not itself. God, the sun, Shakespeare, a com-
> mercial traveller, having itself traversed in reality itself,
> becomes that self. . . . Damn that fellow's noise in the
> street. Self which it itself was ineluctably preconditioned
> to become. *Ecco!* (494)

This passage deserves quotation in full for three reasons:
it reiterates more explicitly Stephen's belief in the "hopelessness" of his "battle" when the action that ends in his
capitulation—when his story in nighttown—has just begun;
it discloses that Stephen regards the evangelical music as
an expression of God; and it shows Stephen characterizing
God in terms applicable to Bloom, before he is aware of
Bloom's presence ("the sun [a light], Shakespeare, a commercial traveller").

The fantasy develops out of Florry's comment on his
proclamation. She says, "They say the last day is coming
this summer." Zoe expresses Stephen's feelings, saying
laughingly, "Great unjust God!", and Florry responds

"*(Offended.)* Well, it was in the papers about Antichrist."
At this, he envisions newsboys announcing the "Safe arrival
of Antichrist" and, apparently simultaneously, "*(Stephen
turns and sees Bloom).*" He says, "A time, times and half
a time," and experiences the fantasy presenting, in order:
"*Reuben J. Antichrist, wandering jew*" bearing on his
shoulders his near-drowned son; the "Hobgoblin" who so
ghoulishly juggles worlds and causes them to explode; "*the
End of the World*" and the "*second coming of Elijah*";
finally, Mananaan MacLir—A.E., demigod of Stephen's companions in the librarian's office, Lyster, Best, and Eglinton,
who is announced by them.

The *dramatis personae* of Stephen's fantasy are all variations on one familiar theme, his conception of God. What
is significant is that Bloom is implicated. The conjunction
of Stephen's first sight of Bloom and the announcement in
his imagination of the "safe arrival of Antichrist" invokes
the fantasy, and Bloom is (consequently) related to its first
figure. Stephen knows that Bloom followed him and Lynch
from Burke's, and he knows that Bloom is a Jew. Thus
"Reuben J. Antichrist" is rescuing the drowning (with the
special significance of the term to Stephen) young man for
the hangman God (anti-Christ) whose agent he is. Bloom
is almost as certainly the inspiration for the hobgoblin.
When he and Zoe enter the parlor and Zoe (significantly)
turns the chandelier light up full, Lynch says, "Enter a
ghost and hobgoblins." Stephen knows that Zoe has entered,
because she speaks a number of times before the fantasy;
but he is not aware that Bloom is with her. The sight of
Bloom identifies Lynch's hobgoblin as his own "Reuben
J. Anti-Christ," and so the hobgoblin is the next divine
agent in his fantasy. Of the remaining three figures, only
the End of the World is not recognizable as part of the
identification of Bloom by Stephen's imagination as an
emissary of the unjust God; and that apparition is accompanied by an Elijah who talks like the parody of the evangelist Dowie which Stephen created at the end of the last
chapter, when Bloom and Dowie were brought to his attention together. Following the pattern set up by Reuben J.
Antichrist's rescue of his drowned son and Elijah's evangelical appeal ("God's time is 12.25 [the actual time]. Tell

mother [!] you'll be there. . . . Join on right here!"),
Lyster tells Stephen to "Seek . . . the light"; and here,
too, Bloom is suggested, for Mananaan MacLir has not
appeared yet, and Lyster also says ambiguously, "He is our
friend. I need not mention names."

The ridiculousness of Mananaan and the fact that a
"judashand strangles the light" and ends the fantasy
promptly suggest that Stephen remains defiant. Furthermore, there is no indication that he consciously accepts the
identification of Bloom made in his imagination, even
though Bloom invoked the fantasy in the first place. However, the irony at Stephen's expense that results later on
from his striking the lamp is anticipated here. "A time,
times and half a time" occurs twice in the Bible, both times
in the Book of Daniel. Its first occurrence is a description
of the length of the reign of Antichrist, and this is apparently the object of Stephen's allusion when he sees Bloom
and the fantasy begins. Subsequently, however, the phrase
denotes the period, following the destruction of Antichrist,
during which salvation is awaited.[9] The irony that the
unintended product of Stephen's erudition confirms the
beneficence of Bloom's mission and defeats his own blasphemy is yet another example of his folly in defying God.

Stephen's fantasy, and all the natural action that leads
to and accompanies it, occurs before Bloom does anything
in the brothel parlor; he has followed Zoe in, and he merely
stands. After the manner of the daymare, the end of
Stephen's fantasy coincides with a malfunction of the
chandelier which causes it to dim. Zoe goes to adjust it,
Lynch exposes her lower body, and Bloom is visited by his
"Granpapachi," Virag. Bloom's mind remains the focus
of the narrative until (many pages but mere minutes later)
the real Bella demands payment and a manly Bloom begins
to confirm Stephen's inchoate belief about him by his
protectiveness and ministrations. When he substitutes his
hand for Stephen's during Zoe's palm-reading and explains
about a scar on it, "Fell and cut it twenty-two years ago.
I was sixteen," Stephen reflects on the conjunction between
Bloom's history and his own and calls it a confirmation of
Mr. Deasy's definition of history ("All history moves
towards one great goal, the manifestation of God"): "See?

Moves to one great goal. . . . Sixteen years ago I twenty-two tumbled" (549).

Having identified him consciously, although perhaps whimsically, as someone divinely linked to himself, Stephen implicates Bloom in his paradigm for God ("the sun, Shakespeare, a commercial traveller") by seeing him in the mirror as Shakespeare. And moments later, Stephen remembers his dream of the previous night, in which he "flew," and in which a Levantine man ("Haroun al Raschid") had held a melon "against my face" and invited him "in." The dream had been interrupted by the "unfaithful" Haines' nightmare of a panther; and at the very end of the first part of the novel, as the two protagonists met in front of the library, Bloom (who had had a dream that corresponds to Stephen's) was identified for the reader as the "pard" who is Stephen's destined host and deliverer.

The talk of cuckoldry in the parlor leads Stephen to entertain the company by imitating a French guide conducting a tour of the Paris demimonde. When he mentions two combined forms of the word "water," "Waterloo. Watercloset. *(He ceases suddenly and holds up a forefinger.)*" and says, "Mark me. I dreamt of a watermelon." The others chide him, but he continues:

STEPHEN

(Extending his arms.) It was here. Street of harlots. In Serpentine Avenue Beelzebub showed me her, a fubsy widow. Where's the red carpet spread?

BLOOM

(Approaching Stephen.) Look. . .

STEPHEN

No, I flew. My foes beneath me. And ever shall be. World without end. *(He cries.) Pater!* Free!

BLOOM

I say, look. . .

STEPHEN

Break my spirit, will he? *O merde alors!* . . . Hola! Hillyho! (557)

Were his opposition to God not so adamantine, this incident would be the resolution of Stephen's story. He remembers the principal details of the dream, and remembers that the stranger in it frees him from his predicament. The "melon" is now also a "fubsy widow," and it has not been offered him; but Bloom does approach and directly, although unwittingly, answer his question. In a sense, their encounter in the "street of harlots" is even a fulfilment of Stephen's adolescent quest of "the unsubstantial image" which "would, without any overt act of his, encounter him" in a "secret place" and enable him to be "transfigured"; for his dream of a meeting that will accomplish his deliverance is a dream of meeting the agent of that once-sought transfiguration—not a woman, not even simply Bloom, but Bloom as that unsubstantial image, agent of the grace of God.

However, Stephen looks to Satan's minion Beelzebub, not to the minion of God, for help. The man in the dream delivered him, and he thinks he needs deliverance from God. So when Bloom answers his question, he says, on some level rejecting Bloom's unwitting identification of himself as that man even if only ignoring it consciously, "No, I flew. My foes beneath me. And ever shall be. World without end." He distorts the *Gloria Patri* into a statement that he spurns not only the emissary of God but God himself, says not "Glory be to the Father and to the Son and to the Holy Ghost as it was in the beginning, is now and ever shall be, world without end," but "I flew," beyond the reach of his foes, the Father, the Son, and the Holy Ghost, and that he ever shall be, world without end, beyond their reach. Then, with the voice of Icarus (215), he calls on his consciously adopted forebear.

He is more vehement when Bloom reiterates, still unwittingly, the answer to his question: "I say, look." And hilloeing, he calls again on "Pater," the fabulous artificer who flies above the dominion of God. Immediately he experiences the second of the two significant fantasies that frame the portrayal of his recognition of God's emissary. Dedalus appears, but turns out to be his own father. Characteristically, the genial Simon delivers himself of comforting words, snobbish complaints about his son's associations, and empty encouragement. Stephen is telling himself that he cannot call on or emulate the "fabulous artificer" he designates as his spiritual father. That ancient Greek who was able to devise and effect his flight was indeed "fabulous," and his father is really and merely Simon Dedalus. The remainder of the fantasy presents what must happen if Stephen is to be delivered: a fox who has just "buried his grandmother" is pursued by dogs and hunters *"hot for a kill,"* when suddenly by the kaleidoscope of the daymare the chase becomes a horserace, won by *"a dark horse riderless,"* whose field includes *"Sceptre, Maximum the Second, Zinfandel"*—horses that ran in the Ascot Gold Cup (632). Both at the hospital and at Burke's, Lenehan spoke in Stephen's presence about Bloom's tip on the "dark horse" Throwaway and the outcome of the Gold Cup. The two things Stephen's fantasy signifies are his awareness that a fabulous pagan cannot help him "fly" from his plight, and his recognition that "the johnny in the black duds" can rescue him from it. In other words his imagination asserts, as it did in the fantasy that stands opposite this one in the episode, that he should recognize that Bloom is God's emissary sent to save him; only now there is no condemnation of a Reuben J. Antichrist or hobgoblin, or mockery of a Dowie or Mananaan, to qualify his portrayal of Bloom to himself and exhortation of himself.

But he has no chance to reconsider God, Bloom, and the deliverer of his dream. The fantasy is ended precisely when the singing of Private Carr and his companions is heard through the window, and the narrative moves from the story of Stephen's recognition of Bloom's significance for him to the story of Stephen's submitting to God.

The novel emphasizes the principal elements of Bloom's significance for Stephen at the climax of that story of his submission. When Stephen strikes the lamp and runs out into the street and Bloom tries to pacify Bella, he raises Stephen's stick in order to demonstrate what Stephen did; and Bella cries, "Jesus! Don't!" Just before he rushes out to aid Stephen, Bella asks, "Who are you incog?"; and, as though in answer, he is described a few lines below, with the same abbreviation, as *"incog Haroun al Raschid"* hastening *"with fleet step of a pard"* to Stephen's rescue.

But Stephen does not accept that Bloom is either a true deliverer or the Levantine man. When he bends over the prostrate young man and calls his name:

STEPHEN

(Groans.) Who? Black panther vampire. *(He sighs and stretches himself then murmurs thickly with prolonged vowels.)*
　　Who. . . drive. . . Fergus now.
　　And pierce. . . wood's woven shade? . . . (592)

Aroused by Bloom, Stephen for the first time explicitly identifies him with God—as the agent of the "corpsechewer." Stephen's grogginess is not material, for just as he understood the significance of his argument with Carr before he was struck down, so he understood (imaginatively at least) the significance of Bloom's presence and ministrations before Carr came along. Therefore, finding that the rescuer sent by God revives him from the demonstration of God's omnipotence, he sighs, the common expression of resignation. And then he declares his submission by reciting Yeats' poem. The passage is the dénouement of his adventure in nighttown.

Ironically, Stephen's harsh description of Bloom includes a reference to the traditional symbol for Christ which has been used so frequently in connection with Bloom in the novel, and which, in fact, was invoked when the "incog Haroun al Raschid" ran to Stephen's rescue a few minutes before. But his view of Bloom is clear; and in keeping with it, he will tolerate the company of the older man because to defy God's will is futile, but he will be inclined to be less than friendly.

God's grace has been extended to Stephen, as the conclusion to the "Telemachia" (the three-masted schooner incident) and the conclusion to the first part of the novel (his meeting with Bloom on the library steps) forecast; not Kelleher, but Bloom, a minister to the living, is to undertake the care of him. But he fails to apprehend God's true nature, considers Bloom, whom he recognizes as His emissary, his enemy for that very reason. And so he continues to hate the God he has ceased to defy.

Bloom's attitude toward women and toward his relations with them has changed dramatically. Because he turned his own heart to his son in obedience to the injunction of Malachi with such intensity that he followed a drunken and arrogant near-stranger to the brothel quarter, he is brought closer to the salvation promised by the prophet. But he fails to apprehend the fatuity of his adoptive intentions toward Stephen. And so he continues in his dogged and futile attempt to simulate a family.

The pattern is the same for both characters. Bloom has routed the nun and Bello, restored himself to manhood, but has not resolved the root problem of his estranged wife and nonexistent son. Stephen has submitted to God's dominion, ceased his futile and wracking defiance, but has not resolved the root problem of his misunderstanding and consequent bitterness. In the seventeenth (house) chapter of *Ulysses,* the present chapter is called "Armageddon," an indication that it contains the critical action in the novel and that that crisis is the battle between Good and Evil which prepares the way for the Kingdom of God. Bloom and Stephen have fought the battle; and although one of them went there to commit Carnal Concupiscence and the other has recovered his ability to do so, they turn their backs on nighttown and proceed to the next chapter: "atonement."

appendix

The following is a sketch of the disposition of the fantasies in the fifteenth chaper. Most run their course uninterrupted by the natural action; when interruptions occur, they are brief, and it is generally clear which fantasies are fragments of larger wholes.

Stephen and Lynch enter nighttown and are accosted by an old bawd. The focus shifts to Bloom. He follows their route, buys a pig's foot and a sheep's foot, and is almost run down by a streetcar.

[Bloom, 429: *He exchanges words with a sinister woman, assumed to be spying for the citizen.*]

Bloom alerts himself against pickpockets.

[Bloom, 430-34: *His parents appear and chastise their wayward son, Molly her negligent husband.*]

He is approached by the bawd who accosted Stephen and Lynch

[Bloom, 434-42: *Three former objects of his amatory endeavors confront him*]

and by prostitutes. He reviews the occurrences between the departure of the group from Burke's and his arrival in nighttown in pursuit of Stephen, then feeds the two animals' feet to a stray dog. The watch pass.

[Bloom, 445-66: *He is tried and almost hanged for a number of offenses.*]

He hears Stephen playing the piano. Zoe accosts him, tells him that Stephen is inside, and takes from him a shrivelled black potato. He makes a bombastic remark about cigarettes, and she replies, "Go on. Make a stump speech out of it."

[Bloom, 469-88: *He makes his speech, becomes the successor to Parnell, is rejected, then becomes the Messiah, is rejected and immolated.*]

He feels the effect of disappointment and expresses his feeling to Zoe. She solicits him again

[Bloom, 490: *He is a baby. The buckles of Zoe's slip entice him on*]

and they enter the brothel. In the parlor they find Stephen, Lynch, Kitty, and Florry. Stephen asks Lynch, "Which side [of Lynch's cap] is your knowledge bump?"

[Stephen, 493-94: *He denounces Lynch's cap. He reasserts the impossibility of escaping oneself.*]

Florry makes her first contribution of the evening: "They say the last day is coming this summer." Zoe and Kitty respond curtly and Florry *"(offended)"* says, "Well, it was in the papers about Antichrist." At this, *"(Stephen turns and sees Bloom.)"*

[Stephen, 495-99: *A hobgoblin appears. Elijah-Dowie and Mananaan Maclir–A.E. make proselytizing speeches.*]

Lynch lifts Zoe's slip. The sight of her naked body and a subsequent look "with sidelong meaning" from the prostitute excite Bloom.

[Bloom, 500-506: *His grandfather, Lipoti Virag, discusses sex and women and prods him to take one of the prostitutes.*]

Stephen plays a piece on the piano.

[Stephen, 506: *Almidano Artifoni reproaches him.*]

Florry asks Stephen to sing a song, suggests "Love's Old Sweet Song." He refuses.

[Stephen, 507: *Philip Sober and Philip Drunk argue.*]

Florry repeats her request and Stephen again refuses.

[Stephen, 508: *Philip Sober and Philip Drunk speak in unison to him.*]

Florry suspects Stephen of being a priest. Zoe mentions that a priest has been to her.

[Bloom, 508: *His grandfather renews his lecherous patter.*]

Bloom, Lynch, and Zoe discuss the priest.

[Bloom, 509: *Virag recounts various theories denying the existence or divinity of Christ.*]

Kitty mentions the misfortunes of an associate.

[Stephen, 509-10: *Philip Sober and Philip Drunk blaspheme against the Holy Ghost.*]

Lynch teases the prostitutes.

[*Bloom, 510-11: Virag , Ben Dollard, and "Henry
Flower" express characteristic attitudes toward love and
lust.*]

Stephen makes remarks that cause Florry to call him "a
spoiled priest. Or a monk." Lynch replies, "He is. A cardinal's son."

[*Stephen, 512-13: "Simon Stephen Cardinal Dedalus"
appears and sings a bawdy song and a love song.*]

Bloom wonders if a man on the doorstep is Boylan.

[*Bloom, 514: "In Svengali's fur overcoat," he exorcises
the man on the doorstep.*]

Bloom mutters "Thanks." Zoe offers him some of the chocolate he had previously given her. He associates eating it
with determining to have normal sexual relations with Zoe
and decides in favor of the chocolate "aphrodisiac," when
Bella enters the room.

[*Bloom, 515-41: "Bello" compels his servitude, then
torments him about the consequences of his neglect of
Molly. The nymph of the Blooms' bedroom picture replaces Bello as the dominant figure, tries to brand Bloom
a lecher, and fails. Finally he is able to assert his masculine power over the once more feminine chief antagonist,
Bella.*]

Bloom retrieves his potato from Zoe. Bella asks for payment, and Stephen produces money with drunken indifference. Bloom rescues some of it and convinces Stephen to
let him hold his money. Zoe offers to read Stephen's palm.
Lynch, teasing her, mentions the word "pandybat."

[*Stephen, 547-48: Father Dolan appears, to unjustly
pandy the child Stephen.*]

Zoe suddenly looks at Stephen's palm closely and asks him
if he wants to hear "what's not good for you." Bloom tells
her to read his palm instead. Zoe almost immediately observes "Henpecked husband. That wrong?".

[*Bloom, 549: A black rooster lays an egg.*]

The girls giggle.

[*Bloom, 550-53: Boylan makes love to Molly. A lackey,
he watches them with great pleasure.*]

The constant whispering and giggling are explained by a reflection in the mirror in which the hatrack antlers appear to be on Bloom's head.

> [Bloom and Stephen, 553: *The face of Shakespeare appears to both Stephen and Bloom in the mirror.*]

Bloom asks, "When will I hear the joke?"

> [Bloom, 553-54: *Mrs. Dignam and her brood and the Martin Cunninghams appear.*]

Stephen imitates a French guide for lecherous English tourists. While the others laugh, he mentions the dream he'd thought of twice before. He gets excited, cries *"Pater! Free!"*

> [Stephen, 557-59: *A winged Simon Dedalus appears. "A dark horse" wins a horserace.*]

They hear Private Compton, Private Carr, and "Cissy Caffrey" pass by in the street, singing "My Girl's a Yorkshire Girl." Zoe, from Yorkshire, shouts "That's me. Dance! Dance!" Stephen seizes her and they dance to the pianola.

> [Bloom 560-64: *Professor Goodwin plays for and Professor Maginni directs a "dance of the hours."*]

Stephen makes Zoe dizzy, dances with Florry and Kitty in succession. Then he cries *"Pas seul!"* and, with his ashplant, dances fiercely. The others are all dancing now as well. Suddenly he stops.

> [Stephen, 564-67: *"The mother" comes to implore him to reform and God to save him.*]

Stephen shouts *"Non Serviam!"* and "Break my spirit all of you if you can." Then he strikes the "chandelier" and runs out. Lynch, Kitty, and Zoe chase him. Bella demands that Bloom pay her for the lamp even after he proves that it is only slightly damaged. Bloom finally chastens her by revealing that he knows of her son at Oxford. At this point Zoe announces, "There's a row on," and Bloom rushes out. On the steps he sees Corny Kelleher approaching in a cab accompanied by two strange men and averts his face.

> [Bloom, 570-72: *He becomes Haroun al Raschid, incognito. He is chased by a great mob.*]

Bloom goes over to the "noisy quarrelling knot." Stephen addresses the two soldiers as "my guests. The uninvited." Because of Stephen's supposed insult to Private Carr's girl, Private Compton suggests that he "biff him one."

[Stephen, 573: *Tennyson appears, representing England.*]

Stephen rambles on drunkenly. Bloom tries to draw him away. He refuses to leave and provokes the simple-minded Private Carr further by an innocent reference to "the king."

[Stephen. 575-76: *Edward VII appears.*]

Bloom tries to mollify the soldiers' anger, without success, and Stephen says, "I seem to annoy them. Green rag to a bull."

[Stephen, 577: *Kevin Egan and a composite of wild geese appear.*]

Bloom tries again to get Stephen to leave. Different members of the crowd make remarks supporting Stephen, as an Irishman, or the British soldiers.

[Bloom, 578-79: *Rumbold hangs and draws the croppy boy.*]

Carr again challenges Stephen, who is less willing to brave him than a moment before.

[Stephen, 579-80: *"Old Gummy Granny" appears.*]

Private Carr's belligerency increases, and Bloom *"(Terrified),"* intercedes again.

[Bloom, 580: *The citizen and Major Tweedy prepare for battle.*]

Private Compton incites his comrade to "Do him one in the eye," and Bloom speaks of the service of the Irish in the British army.

[Bloom, 580: *Major Tweedy orders a charge.*]

Private Carr prepares to act. Bloom turns in desperation to the girl. She cries "Police!", and other voices take up the cry.

[Stephen 582-84: *There is a general holocaust, and a unique "camp mass" is celebrated.*]

Private Carr continues to threaten Stephen.

[Stephen, 584: *"Old Gummy Granny" commands him to "remove" the British soldier.*]

Lynch refuses Bloom's appeal for help and drags Kitty away. Stephen refers to him as Judas. Bloom makes a last desperate effort to get Stephen to leave. "Cissy Caffrey" does the same with Private Carr. But the soldier breaks away from her and knocks Stephen down.

[Bloom, 585: *Major Tweedy orders his victorious men to cease fire.*]

Bloom pushes the crowd back, and "two raincaped watch, tall," question them. Bloom orders the watch to take Carr's regimental number. The watch refuse and ask Stephen's name and address. Bloom tries to avoid giving them the information, and just in time Corny Kelleher arrives and gets them to leave. Kelleher goes off, Bloom attempts to wake Stephen and then, holding his hat and ashplant, stands guard over him. He recites the masonic oath.

[Bloom, 593: *"A fairy boy of eleven" appears.*]

Bloom addresses the boy "inaudibly" as "Rudy."

1. *Plays by August Strindberg,* tr. Edwin Bjorkman (New York, 1912), p. 24.

2. Budgen, p. 252.

3. Leopold von Sacher-Masoch von Lemberg, *Venus in Furs* (New York, Sylvan Press, 1947), p. 29.

4. Mr. Ellmann reviews in detail the parallels between *Venus in Furs* and Bloom's fantasies. See *James Joyce,* pp. 380–81.

5. Joyce said that among the "many leaves" of Bloom's "moly," the plant which protects Odysseus from Circe's spell, is "laughter, the enchantment killer." See *Letters,* p. 144.

6. Wilson, p. 196.

7. Sacher-Masoch himself, however, observed through a keyhole his mistress and the second lover he induced her to take. See James Cleugh, *The Marquis and the Chevalier* (New York, 1952), pp. 186–87. The incident may have been Joyce's source.

8. *Hamlet,* III, ii, 183.

9. The two occurrences of the phrase are in Daniel 7:25 and 12:7.

chapter ten

The concluding part of the novel begins immediately after
the events of nighttown. It presents the resolution of
Stephen's story in action involving Stephen and Bloom, then
does the same for Bloom's story in action involving Bloom
and Molly. The first action extends through the sixteenth
chapter and to the point in the seventeenth, just past the
middle, where Stephen walks out of number 7 Eccles Street
and the novel. In the remainder of that chapter and in the
last one, Bloom and Molly end *Ulysses*. The form of Section III, with a chapter and a half (ninety-two pages)
concerned with Stephen's story followed by a chapter and
a half (eighty pages) concerned with Bloom's, seems almost
laboriously symmetrical when described abstractly, but it
is merely simple and logical. Furthermore, there is no
sharp dichotomy between the two resolutions, as there
should not be in a single action: Bloom's relationship with
Molly is a reciprocal of his relationship with Stephen. In
keeping with the attempt being made in this study to represent the phases of the action of *Ulysses* in successive
chapters, this chapter deals with the first part of III, and
Chapter Eleven with the second, the conclusion of the novel.

16 *the cabmen's shelter*

The sixteenth chapter begins only a few minutes after Bloom has the vision of his dead son, which, if anything, reinforces his paternal intention toward Stephen. Thus: upon Stephen's request for something to drink, he guides him toward "the cabman's shelter, as it was called"; after Stephen lends a half crown to "Lord" John Corley (title figure, with Lenehan, of the *Dubliners* story "Two Gallants"), whom they meet on the way, he asks, "how much did you part with . . . if I am not too inquisitive?", and lectures Stephen about living away from his family and associating with Mulligan; when they have arrived at the shelter, and Stephen is unable to drink the coffee or eat the roll Bloom has ordered and is unwilling to engage in conversation, Bloom reflects that he is "already several shillings to the bad," has "in fact, let himself in for it," but concludes that "to cultivate the acquaintance of someone of no uncommon calibre who could provide food for reflection would amply repay any small. . . ." And "the elder man who was several years the other's senior or like his father," in the narrator's words, continues his cultivation through the discovery that Stephen has had no dinner, an invitation to his home for something to eat and lodging for the night (this has another motive as well), and payment of Stephen's check. The chapter ends with the two of them walking toward Eccles Street.

The essential action of the sixteenth chapter is Bloom's concentrated endeavor to achieve a quasi-paternal relationship with Stephen. The preoccupation of both characters and the circumstances prevented him from pursuing his intention in nighttown, but the circumstances in the present chapter—the two of them alone, Stephen tired and resigned to his company, the absence of distraction—provide his **opportunity.**

The strange style of the narrative has been generally characterized as "fatigued," in representation of the "fatigue" of the protagonists.[1] However, although Stephen is tired, there is no indication that Bloom is so; and although the situation is relaxed and the conversation desultory, nothing in the style itself provides a basis for describing it in that way. It is neither monotonous in its rhythm nor heavy in its sound. It is pretentious. And it is clichéd. In fact, the clichés are precisely the pretentious kind resorted to by a speaker striving for an impressive eloquence, and are combined with a more plebeian level of diction to achieve a result that, although ludicrous, is energetic rather than weary. The lack of sophistication, the silly pretension, the diffuse, verbose quality—all seem characteristic of Bloom; and a close look at the dialogue identifies the narrator's voice plainly; for example, when Stephen is questioned by Bloom about a favorite subject, the soul:

> —They tell me on the best authority it is a simple substance and therefore incorruptible. It would be immortal, I understand, but for the possibility of its annihilation by its First Cause, Who . . . is quite capable of adding that to . . . His other practical jokes. . . .
> Mr Bloom thoroughly acquiesced in the general gist of this . . . still he felt bound to enter a demurrer on the head of simple, promptly rejoining:
> —Simple? I shouldn't think that is the proper word. Of course, I grant you, to concede a point, you do knock across a simple soul once in a blue moon. (618)

The style of the narrative is neither "fatigued" nor related in any way to Stephen's condition. Its characteristics are those of Bloom's speech. And so, suggesting (like that speech) the attempt of a poorly-educated man to impress by discoursing with sophisticated eloquence, it is a representation of the chapter's essential action, Bloom's endeavor to win Stephen.

That conscious endeavor fails and yet Bloom succeeds. He fails to win Stephen as he wishes for his own advantage, but unknowingly succeeds in winning him as he must for Stephen's salvation.

Bloom's decisive gesture as both aspirant father and unwitting messiah is his invitation to Stephen to accompany
him home. It is the result of a line of thought which begins
early in the chapter, and which discloses that the advantage
he has in mind is more than quasi-adoption—that his motive
is neither simple nor wholly above reproach. During their
conversation, Corley tells Stephen that Bloom knows Boylan
and gets Stephen to ask Bloom to solicit a menial job for
him. Bloom's distress when Stephen casually passes on Corley's petition (603) serves as prologue to that line of
thought; and it then begins with some observations on the
nature of return. Shortly after their arrival at the shelter,
the red-headed sailor W. B. Murphy (from the "Rosevean,"
the three-masted ship that appears at the end of the third
chapter) remarks that he is about to return to his "own
true wife" after seven years of roving; Bloom pictures the
homecoming in a pessimistic light ("there sits uncle Chubb
or Tomkin . . . in shirtsleeves, eating rumpsteak and
onions. No chair for father. . . . Her brand new arrival is
on her knees, *post mortem* child"), even though the gregarious Murphy seems far from the type to be broken-
hearted by a wife he is plainly in no hurry to see. Thereafter, the difficulty or impossibility of return recurs in
Bloom's thoughts sufficiently often to indicate that his interest is not academic. When the possibility that Parnell has
escaped death is broached, he thinks, "Still, as regards
return, you were a lucky dog if they didn't set the terrier
at you directly you got back." After some thought about
the role of Parnell's relationship with Kitty O'Shea in his
downfall and subsequent death, he decides that "the coming
back was the worst thing you ever did because . . . you
would feel out of place."

Coupled with Bloom's trepidation about effecting a return—as proper husband—to Molly is his devotion to her.
And the combination produces an interesting result. Prior
to the discussion of Parnell, Murphy describes a knifing by
an Italian in Trieste. Among extensive comments to Stephen
about the sailor and his stories, Bloom speaks of the Italian
assassin, generalizes about the "passionate temperaments"
of "Spaniards, for instance," and then says:

> My wife is, so to speak, Spanish, half, that is. . . . She has the Spanish type. Quite dark, regular brunette, black. I, for one, certainly believe climate accounts for character. (621)

His observations on Molly's passionate Spanish character are accentuated during the Parnell discussion. The keeper of the shelter, "Skin-the-Goat," makes a contemptuous remark about the cuckolded Captain O'Shea which elicits general laughter. Bloom, "without the faintest suspicion of a smile, merely gazed in the direction of the door and reflected upon the historic story" of Parnell and the O'Sheas, in terms that apply transparently to his own "historic story":

> Whereas . . . it was simply a case of the husband not being up to the scratch with nothing in common between them beyond the name and then a real man arriving on the scene. . . . The eternal question of the life connubial, needless to say, cropped up. Can real love, supposing there happens to be another chap in the case, exist between married folk? (635)

The question is one of direct personal relevance. But Bloom is not concerned with reconciling himself to Boylan; that vulgar dandy's injury to him is plainly too great (at one place in the chapter the name "H. du Boyes" in the newspaper gives him "a bit of a start"). Having made the point about his wife's "passionate Spanish temperament" to Stephen earlier, he directly associates Molly and Kitty O'Shea in his thoughts: "she also was Spanish or half so . . . passionate abandon of the south, casting every shred of decency to the winds," and then does so openly:

> —Just bears out what I was saying, he with glowing bosom said to Stephen. And, if I don't greatly mistake, she was Spanish too. (636)

His wish to adopt Stephen is subconscious, so that he is aware only of a strong attraction to the young man, respect and admiration for his accomplishments, and the desire to

form a lasting and intimate relationship with him. In
addition, he wants to regain Molly's love, and fears simply
"returning," storming her couch to win her back from
Boylan and thereafter keep her securely to himself. Bloom
is seeking a *modus vivendi* with Molly that will not require
of him what is clearly his responsibility; and his bosom
"glows" as he draws the analogy for Stephen because he is
subtly offering Molly to him.

An affair between Molly and Stephen would bring about
the desired relationship between himself and Stephen, eliminate Boylan, and keep Molly happy, which Bloom desires
at least as much as he does the pseudo-paternal relationship
itself. The motivation for his invitation to Stephen is, as
has been said, neither simple nor above reproach. And his
private philosophizing just before he extends it does not
vindicate him, although it clarifies his scheme and the
reasoning behind it:

> He personally, being of a sceptical bias, believed . . .
> that . . . men . . . were always hanging around about
> a lady, even supposing she was the best wife in the
> world . . . when . . . she chose to be tired of wedded
> life . . . to press their attentions on her with improper
> intent . . . the cause of many *liaisons* between still at-
> tractive married women getting on for fair and forty
> *and younger men* [italics mine]. . . . (639-40)

Near the beginning of the chapter, when he thinks of organ-
izing a summer concert tour in obvious opposition to Boylan's Belfast tour, Bloom decides that such an enterprise
would require "puffs in the local papers . . . managed by
some fellow with a bit of bounce. . . . But who?" He
mentions no prospect at that point, but he seems to know
that it was Stephen who got Deasy's letter into the evening
paper (632); and during the chapter, he prods Stephen to
what he calls "literary labour": "writing for newspapers."
The young man he has seen in Crawford's and Lyster's
offices, writer and friend of editors and literary men, is an
obvious candidate.

Bloom's scheme to use Stephen to rid himself of Boylan
is fully formulated and intently pursued by the time the

Parnell discussion occurs toward the end of the chapter. Immediately after making "with glowing bosom" his point about the significant similarity between Molly and Kitty O'Shea, he places before Stephen a flattering portrait of his wife "in evening dress cut ostentatiously low for the occasion" and asks, "—Do you consider, by the by . . . that a Spanish type?" He bends over to look at the photograph himself, discusses the proficiency as a singer of "my wife the *prima donna*, Madam Marion Tweedy," and complains that the photograph fails to do justice to her figure, "not to dwell on certain opulent curves of the. . . ." He then deliberates leaving the picture with Stephen "for a very few minutes to speak for itself," but decides with unwitting irony that "it was scarcely professional etiquette" and only "looked away thoughtfully with the intention of not further increasing the other's possible embarassment while gauging her symmetry of heaving embonpoint." After "viewing the slightly soiled photo creased by opulent curves, none the worse for wear," and deciding that "the slight soiling" is in fact "an added charm," a hardly disguised testimonial of the adulterous Molly's attractiveness to him, he moves on to thoughts about Stephen which lead into further apparent observations about the Parnell-O'Shea affair:

> The vicinity of the young man he certainly relished, educated, *distingué*, and impulsive into the bargain . . . though you wouldn't think he had it in him. . . yet you would. Besides he said the picture was handsome. . . . And why not? An awful lot of makebelieve went on about that sort of thing . . . instead of being honest and aboveboard about the whole business. How they were fated to meet and an attachment sprang up between the two. . . . (638)

Bloom's concern about whether or not "he had it in him," and the "And why not" which links the thoughts about the appealing young man and the adulterous couple, following as they do his association of Molly and Kitty O'Shea and proffer of Molly's photograph, signify clearly what he is about. Thus, the very next page presents his already-quoted philosophizing about the inclinations of married

women, which concludes that they will inevitably seek to
be soiled, preferably through the agency of "younger men."
That even more overt suggestion that Stephen would be
a suitable lover for Molly is followed immediately by a
disturbed meditation on Stephen's association with "pro-
fligate women, who might present him with a nice dose to
last him his lifetime," and disapproval not only of prostitutes but of the virtuous "Miss Ferguson" of whom Bloom
thought so highly at the end of the last chapter. He then
reflects on his sympathy and affection for the young man,
asks when he had dinner, and, learning that he had none at
all, broaches to himself the possibility that he take him
home and feed him. His motivation for doing so is manifestly a combination of fatherly solicitude and the desire
to use Stephen as a bait for luring Molly from Boylan.

He does not extend his invitation without weighing the
consequences. "To think of him house and homeless" prods
his interest in both Stephen's practical need of a roof over
his head for the night and his own more ambitious design;
on the other hand, Molly might object and therefore "spoil
the hash altogether." Finally, he cannot guess what Steph-
en's attitude toward the "hash" might be: "he mightn't
what you call jump at the idea." Despite the possibility
that neither Molly nor Stephen will co-operate with his
ultimate design, he decides to take the step that will initiate
it and also give Stephen the immediate help he needs—
"eschewing for the nonce hidebound precedent, a cup of
Epps's cocoa and a shakedown for the night." And "while
prudently pocketing her photo," he extends his invitation
to "just come home with me and talk things over."

Preparing to pay the bill for Stephen's untouched coffee
and bun, he spins "Utopian plans," not only for "education
(the genuine article), literature, journalism," but also for
the concert tours he thought of at the beginning of the
chapter: "turning money away, duets in Italian with the
accent perfectly true to nature." A particular question of
Italian "accent" has dogged him during the day: the pronunciation of *"voglio,"* the indicative word for "I will"
which he has subconsciously substituted for the conditional
"I would" in the line *"Vorrei e non vorrei,"* which Zerlina
sings in *"La ci darem"* from *Don Giovanni,* one of the

two pieces Molly is rehearsing with Boylan. In his first and third chapters (kitchen and cemetery) he wondered about it; in the next chapter (newspaper), he debated asking Nannetti the printers' foreman about it; and in the fantasy in nighttown in which she appeared in Turkish costume and hummed a snatch of the duet, he does ask Molly about it. His concern would disappear if the Don to whom she consented so unhesitatingly were replaced by Stephen—with Stephen she might sing "duets in Italian with the accent perfectly true to nature." Unable to tolerate the contemporary who invades his house and takes his wife from him, he anticipates with increasing excitement the domestic, social, and (with the musical possibilities in the association) material advantages that would result from his giving her to the younger man.

Thus, as they walk to his house, he talks with Stephen about music, praising Molly's singing ability, and, in a final revelation of what he has in mind as both husband and impresario, interrupts Stephen to say that Molly is "passionately attached to music of any kind," even while he wonders about the young man's suitableness: Stephen is "not quite the same as the usual blackguard type they unquestionably had an indubitable hankering after." Still, he is confident that Stephen has "his father's gift" as a tenor; and during the time Stephen is confirming his confidence by singing, according to the narrator, "an old German song of *Johannes Jeep*," [2] he plans for him a brilliant concert career which would provide wealth, fame, social position, and amorous success, and yet allow "heaps of time to practise literature in his spare moments when desirous of so doing."

Bloom's revery is an extreme indication of the inseparable gulf between them. His misunderstanding of Stephen is revealed constantly (he even calls him "a good catholic"). He is always literal and concrete, Stephen metaphorical and abstract. The difference between his statements and Stephen's in their conversation about the soul, quoted above, or between his advocacy of inspection and licensing for prostitutes and Stephen's complaint about the spiritual prostitution of some of their countrymen, is precisely that between the lamp image employed by Stephen in the *Por-*

trait in discussing the wisdom of Aristotle and Aquinas and the literal conception of Stephen's metaphor by the dean of studies (pp. 187-88). As he himself observes, Stephen is "a bit out of his sublunary depths." And his ultimate misunderstanding is his belief that the young man needs or wants to become a prosperous and socially prominent Dublin concert tenor. His scheme is not only as it concerns Molly a sordid and hopelessly artificial substitute for the course of action required of him, it is equally hopeless with respect to Stephen.

This fact is made clear on the last page of the chapter. First the author comments on Bloom's plans for his prospective pseudo-son: at the point at which Bloom finishes his long revery on Stephen's future as a concert tenor, the horse of a street-sweeping car is said to have "reached the end of his tether," and to that revery the horse "added his quota by letting fall on the floor, which the brush would soon brush up and polish, three smoking globes of turds." In the remainder of the page, the car's driver becomes more prominent. The narrator has already called him "the lord of [the horse's] creation" and Bloom has said of his sweeper, "—Our lives are in peril tonight. Beware of the steamroller"; now it is "his scythed car." Although the sweeper's rotary brushes are the pretext for the metaphors "steamroller" and "scythed car," the driver in his car is made to represent a divine being reminiscent of Fergus, ruler of the brazen cars, and particularly associated with death. His attitude toward the protagonists bears out the suggestion. The final paragraph of the chapter begins as Stephen concludes his "song of *Johannes Jeep*":

Und alle Schiffe brücken

The driver never said a word, good, bad or indifferent. He merely watched the two figures, as he sat on his low-backed car, both black—one full, one lean—walk towards the railway bridge, *to be married by Father Maher*. As they walked, they at times stopped and walked again, continuing their *tête à tête* (which of course he was utterly out of), about sirens, enemies of man's reason, mingled with a number of other topics of the same category, usurpers, historical cases of the kind while the man

in the sweeper car or you might as well call it in the
sleeper car who in any case couldn't possibly hear because
they were too far simply sat in his seat near the end of
lower Gardiner street *and looked after their low-backed
car.* (649)

The situation provides no reason for a street cleaner to
speak to two total strangers, so the narrator's remark directly following the last line of the song is part of the
symbolic treatment of the driver. The juxtaposition of the
line which declares that by some unmentioned agency "all
ships" are "bridged" and the narrator's remark indicates
that the driver refrains specifically from commenting on the
suggestion embodied in the line that Stephen and Bloom
are no longer isolated "ships." The italicized phrase "to
be married by Father Maher," the description of the
sweeper car as a "lowbacked car," and the final phrase, also
distinguished by italics, "looked after their lowbacked car,"
are from a popular Irish romantic song, "The Low Backed
Car" (by the novelist and poet, Samuel Lover), with the
phrases in reverse order. The song tells of the admiration
and longing of various men as they "look after" "Peggy," a
peasant girl, driving by in her low-backed car; the singer
finally declares that he yearns to be driving with Peggy "in
a low-backed car, / To be married by Father Maher."
Bloom and Stephen are here specifically referred to as "to be
married by Father Maher." *Maher* is German for "reaper,"
and the suggestion is that they are, despite appearances and
whatever either may think, to join only in death. Thus
the last words of the chapter are the innocent line that
appears early in the song, with the pronoun "her" made
plural: the driver of the "scythed car," the perilous "steamroller," "looked after their lowbacked car," not simply
observed Bloom and Stephen from behind but tended the
car in which they, in a manner different from Lover's
singer and Peggy, are to be joined by a different Father
Maher—"the sweeper car or you might as well call it . . .
the *sleeper* [italics mine] car."

Near the beginning of the present chapter the statement
was made that Bloom's endeavor to win Stephen for his own

advantage fails; motivated as it is, it deserves to fail, and only its failure could make any worthwhile success for him possible. The complementary statement made there was that he succeeds in winning Stephen as he must for Stephen's salvation. The passage just discussed, the last page of the sixteenth chapter of the novel, which indicates the futility of Bloom's hope for a relationship with Stephen except as all men come together, in death, at the very same time indicates his success in this other, unwitting, endeavor: it concludes a chapter whose action presents simultaneously Bloom's sordid wooing of Stephen and his divine ministry to him.

Stephen needs the grace of God if he is to find faith; and although that grace was extended to him in nighttown in the person of Bloom, he spurned it. He recognized that Bloom is God's emissary and therefore, despite Bloom's unwitting overtures when he remembered his dream of the nature and agent of his salvation, rejected Bloom: he expected that agent to be, not a Messiah sent by the *dio boia*, but "Beelzebub." His fantasy of the fox and the racehorse told him that God's emissary could truly rescue him, but at that point the "noise in the street" of the soldiers and the girl began the action that ended with his prostration by Private Carr. As the present chapter begins, he only suffers Bloom's company because he has acknowledged the futility of defying God.

Blithely unconscious of the fact, Bloom pursues his messianic mission in the chapter assiduously; for example, while they are walking to the shelter, he asks not why Stephen lives away from home but "why did you leave your father's house?" The special significance of his nominally paternal ministrations, although "a bit out of his sublunary depth," is not lost on Stephen; and when they arrive and he orders the coffee and bun for him, the reader is pointedly reminded of it. The italics are mine:

> The keeper . . . put a boiling swimming cup of *a choice concoction labelled coffee* on the table and a rather antediluvian specimen of a bun, *or so it seemed.* . . . Mr Bloom . . . *encouraged Stephen to proceed . . .* by surreptitiously pushing the cup of *what was temporarily supposed to be called coffee* gradually nearer him.

—Sounds are impostures, Stephen said. . . . Like
names, Cicero, Podmure, Napoleon, Mr Goodbody, Jesus,
Mr Doyle. Shakespeares were as common as Murphies.
What's in a name?
—Yes, to be sure, Mr Bloom unaffectedly concurred.
Of course. *Our name was changed too,* he added, *push-
ing the so-called roll across.*   (606-7)

Bloom's ordering the coffee and bun and his insistently
pressing Stephen to partake of them can be understood in
purely naturalistic terms. Even the systematic suggestion
that the drink and bread only appear to be coffee and bun
might also be explained as a comment on their quality in
the narrator's characteristic style, were it not that the liquid
is *"temporarily* supposed to be called coffee." For the narrator has gone to lengths to indicate that the "concoction
labelled coffee" and the "so-called roll" are wine and wafer,
the Eucharist in disguise—that the messianic Bloom is unwittingly urging Stephen to accept Communion with God.
Thus, when Stephen names Shakespeare, Jesus, Podmore,[3]
and others associated with God—including the enigmatic
sailor,[4] who uses Stephen's remark about "Shakespeares"
and "Murphies" to initiate conversation—Bloom makes the
comment on his family's name which is simultaneously a
statement that the Messiah has appeared among men as
different mortal individuals ("our name was changed too"),
and "pushes" to Stephen the dry and stale "so-called roll,"
almost as close a representation of the unleavened bread
at the Lord's Supper as is the ritual wafer used by the
Church.

Stephen declines the nourishment Bloom presses upon
him, however. When Bloom again urges Stephen to partake of it later, he reveals how completely unaware he is
of its significance and his mission, for he does so while
he is concluding an argument against "the existence of a
supernatural God"; and he compounds the irony: "[The
bun is] like one of our skipper's bricks [i.e., from the cargo
of the 'Rosevean,' symbol of Calvary] disguised. Still, no
one can give what he hasn't got. Try a bit" (618).
Stephen declines, Bloom solicitously stirs the coffee and
proffers it again, and "thus prevailed on to at any rate
taste it," Stephen does that and no more.

This second attempt by Bloom to get Stephen to eat and drink occurs during their discussion of the soul and almost directly follows Stephen's bitter remark that the "First Cause" "is quite capable of adding" annihilation of the soul to "His other practical jokes." Stephen "couldn't" partake of God's Sacrament at this point because of his unrelenting hatred of Him. But a few minutes later, the hatred is modified. The men in the shelter have begun prating chauvinistically, and Bloom is reminded of the incident at Kiernan's. He tells Stephen of his contention with the citizen, concluding:

> So I . . . told him his God, I mean Christ, was a jew too, and all his family, like me. . . . A soft answer turns away wrath. . . . Am I not right?
> He turned a long you are wrong gaze on Stephen. . . .
> —*Ex quibus,* Stephen mumbled in a noncommittal accent, their two or four eyes conversing, *Christus* or Bloom his name is, or, after all, any other, *secundum carnem.* (627)

Stephen is alluding to Paul's Letter to the Romans; in the Vulgate version of Romans Saint Paul says of the "Israelites," "Et ex quibus est Christus secundum carnem" (9:5), identifies them as the people to which Christ belonged as a mortal ("as concerning the flesh" in the Authorized Version). Stephen's statement is more than a reiteration of his recognition that Bloom is analogous to Christ. In contrast to the occasions in nighttown when he rejected Bloom forcibly, or used epithets like "vampire," he here echoes Bloom's earlier "our name was changed too" in an "accent" that is explicitly "noncommittal." Bloom has just told Stephen a story illustrating his advocacy of love, his innocence of any wrong, and his subjection to unwarranted rejection and contempt, and has concluded by unwittingly but explicitly stating the association between himself and Christ that his experience of the afternoon plainly suggests and the author took pains to establish. He may not have intended any chastisement of Stephen, but he has also said "A soft answer turns away wrath," and bestowed on him "a long you are wrong gaze"; and so, "their two or four eyes conversing," Stephen relents partially, modifies his extreme position.

He is still unable to relent completely, however; and when, on the next page, he is pressed about one aspect of his apostasy, he expressly rejects the communion that has been sitting before him. Bloom tries to induce him to go to work, in the process making of the cynical Latin proverb "Ubi bene, ibi patria" a lofty one (*"Ubi patria, vita bene"*) by means of his blessed ignorance. Stephen looks at "the eyes that said or didn't say [four lines below Bloom is 'the person who owned them pro. tem.'] the words the voice he heard said—if you work," objects, and is told that Bloom is speaking of Stephen's own work, that the "philosopher" belongs to Ireland as much as, and is as important as, the peasant. Characteristically, he says, "I suspect . . . that Ireland must be important because it belongs to me." Bloom is shocked, protests that he must have misunderstood or misheard him, and asks for clarification, until he loses patience with Bloom's evangelism:

> Stephen, patently crosstempered, repeated and shoved aside his mug of coffee, or whatever you like to call it, none too politely, adding:
> —We can't change the country. Let us change the subject. (629)

Bloom has succeeded neither in filling his companion's stomach nor in saving his soul.

However, the fact that Stephen's soul is ripe for saving after his experience in nighttown has been suggested by the first substantial action of the chapter, his meeting with Corley. Except in one respect Corley is no worse off than himself, and this fact is accentuated by a carefully drawn correspondence between their situations: Corley is out of a job; he has no place to sleep; "His friends had all deserted him. Furthermore, he had a row with Lenehan [his closest companion]" (601). Stephen does not exchange whines with Corley, only says "I have no place to sleep myself" as an explanation for not offering to put him up, and then shares equally with him the single temporary advantage he has—the two half-crowns in his pocket (he seems to have forgotten that Bloom rescued some of his final salary).

The "loan" to Corley not only contrasts with Father Conmee's denial of silver (a crown) to the beggar in the tenth chapter (city), but reveals a developed capacity for pity. Unlike Stephen's pupil Sargent in the second chapter, Corley is in no way similar to himself, and he is pointedly no more well off, all in all, than Corley.

At this point near the beginning of the chapter, Stephen still condemns the God to Whom he has submitted. In a little while, he modifies his attitude, at least becomes "noncommittal" toward God's emissary. But then Bloom appeals to his patriotism and he "shoved aside" the Communion that has been offered him. It is after this event that the discussion of Parnell, Bloom's final formulation of his sordid scheme, and the "unprecedented" invitation occur. Stephen's certainly no less unprecedented acceptance is motivated by desire neither for food nor for Molly. But Molly is its instrumental cause. Between Stephen's summary rejection of the "concoction labelled coffee" and his agreement to accompany Bloom home for cocoa, one (and only one) significant action occurs: Bloom's implementation of his scheme, by talking of Molly's beauty and "passionate Spanish temperament" and showing Stephen her picture. As a result of this action, Stephen comes to understand what his fantasy of the fox and the racehorse tried to tell him, that God's emissary has been sent out of His mercy and can truly save him: he recognizes that the genuine deliverer promised him in his dream of the night before is Bloom.

When in the preceding chapter Stephen recalled his dream for the third time, Bloom approached him and unconsciously identified himself in a parlor overlooking the "street of harlots." But Stephen expected genuine aid only from an agent of Satan: "Beelzebub showed me her, a fubsy widow." More important than that, he failed to see the fulfilment of any of the details in his dream. This is because their fulfilment had not yet come. It began when he made his climactic gesture of defiance of God and ran out of the brothel, and Bloom, after interceding with Bella Cohen, hurried out *to the street itself* to aid him in the brawl. At that point the identity of Bloom and the deliverer of Stephen's dream was established for the reader beyond any doubt. The "stage direction"—"*(He hurries out through the hall. The whores point. . . . Incog Haroun al Raschid, he*

. . . hastens . . . with fleet step of a pard . . ." (570)
—conforms exactly to the relevant part of Stephen's first
and fullest recollection of the dream, while he was sitting
on the beach in the morning—"Open hallway. Street of
harlots. Remember. Haroun al Raschid" (47)—and incorporates the significant pard-panther motif of his second
recollection, at the library entrance at the end of the first
part of the novel. Following the fight, Bloom led Stephen
to the shelter for rest and nourishment. The remainder of
the dream as Stephen recollected it in the morning is:

> That man led me, spoke. I was not afraid. The melon
> he had he held against my face. Smiled: creamfruit
> smell. That was the rule, said. In. Come. Red carpet
> spread. You will see who. (47-48)

And when Bloom has performed the acts of the dream-
deliverer in every detail, Stephen himself realizes that they
are one.

From the antler incident in the brothel, he knows that
Bloom is probably a cuckold; in the librarian's office he
spoke of the supplanted Shakespeare as "dead" and the
grass widow Ann Hathaway as a "widow." With Bloom's
description of his wife's passionate temperament, exhibition
of the "photo showing a large sized lady, with her fleshy
charms on evidence," discourse on Molly's pulchritude, and
invitation home, Stephen recognizes in Molly the "fubsy
[plump] widow"; and in her husband, who has so blatantly
held "the melon" before him, spread "the red carpet," and
said, "In. Come. . . . You will see who," the man who
followed him out of an open hallway to a street of harlots,
stood by him, and finally led him away, he recognizes the
deliverer of his dream.

A common question in Catholic catechisms asks why man
was created, or how he is to earn the ultimate happiness
of heaven—in one form or another, what his basic purpose
in life is. The answer has three elements, always in the
same order: man's purpose is to know God, love God,
serve God. In his talk with Cranly at the end of the *Portrait*, Stephen said, "—I will not serve" (p. 239) and "—I
tried to love God. . . . It seems now I failed. It is very

difficult" (pp. 240-41). Stephen reversed the order prescribed in the catechism: he would not serve God because
he could not love Him; but he could not love Him, Joyce
has pointed out from the first chapters of *Ulysses*, because
he did not know Him. Bloom is not the Messiah for the
men in Kiernan's or for himself, but only for Stephen.
God announced his coming and sent him to Stephen alone.
And the salvation of Stephen is the result of the compassionate and concerned man's advent, not of anything super-
human about him (indeed Bloom does not even begin to be
aware of the significance Stephen perceives in their relationship). For that salvation Stephen needed, and the fact
of Bloom provides, a revelation about the God Who ordained
it. What Stephen realizes is that the God he called *"dio
boia"* and "corpsechewer" promised in a dream and then
sent His servant to a miserable sinner, sent him following
that sinner's climactic sin, the sin of Satan, which He knew
the sinner would commit—for He announced in the dream
the intercession of His emissary on the street of harlots, that
is, *immediately following* the commission of it. Stephen
finally understands that he never knew God, that God is
Love as well as Power.

The sixteenth chapter of *Ulysses* is called "Eumaeus" in
Joyce's schema, after the loyal swineherd in whose hut the
disguised Odysseus establishes himself on his return to
Ithaca. The Homeric correspondence boasts the usual number and variety of elements, but the purpose for which it
exists is illustration of the chapter's most significant development, Stephen's recognition of his dream-deliverer and consequent realization about God. Odysseus' identity is neither
discovered by his old nurse nor revealed to Eumaeus and
Penelope until he makes his way to his palace ("home")
later in the poem; but he discloses it to Telemachus upon
Athene's instructions when they are in Eumaeus' hut, in
Book XVI. For the purpose, the goddess temporarily
changes the shabby clothes and haggard physical condition
which disguise him (increases his "bloom" in the phrase
of Butcher and Lang). When Telemachus says that the
stranger must be a god, he protests that he is only his
father *(Outis-Zeus)*, explains the changes, and says that the
gods can bestow any mortal form they wish. Although the

Father whose true nature is made known to Stephen in the corresponding hut of "Skin-the-Goat" is not Bloom but the One he represents—although Stephen can never acknowledge the unimposing stranger whom *he* meets to be his father—like Telemachus, he has seen the stranger temporarily transformed by God, and like Telemachus he has come to know his Father at the divinely-appointed time.

And so Stephen accepts the invitation of "L. Boom" (a noise in the street), as Bloom shows him he is called in the newspaper list of Dignam's mourners. Bloom uses a word from Stephen's dream (while the narrator suggests the supernatural), "—Come, he counselled, to close the *séance*," and they rise to leave. At the door of the shelter Stephen pauses, and the abstract thinker asks a question which does not tax the concrete wisdom (wisdom about the created world) of his new mentor:

> —One thing I never understood, he said . . . why they put . . . chairs upside down on the tables in cafes.
> To which impromptu the neverfailing Bloom replied without a moment's hesitation, saying straight off:
> —To sweep the floor in the morning. (644)

And they leave for Bloom's house, Bloom putting his arm through Stephen's and saying, "Lean on me," Stephen thinking he "felt a strange kind of flesh of a different man."

When Bloom begins to discuss music, Stephen, so taciturn and grudging throughout the chapter, describes for a whole paragraph the music he likes and then proceeds to sing. His singing is doubly significant. The very fact that he does so for the first time in a novel filled with song and singers is noteworthy enough; in the afternoon he rejected Almidano Artifoni's appeal that he use his voice to derive some satisfaction from life, and during the last chapter he stubbornly refused Florry's request for just one song. But his selections are also significant.

First he renders, presumably by humming, "exquisite variations . . . on an air *Youth here has End* by Jans Pieter Sweelinck," a theme and variations for keyboard written by the Dutch composer for a German Protestant hymn. The hymn is sung by a dying youth, a fact obscured in Joyce's translation of its title, which is *"Mein junges Leben hat ein End."* Stephen's "describing" variations on the tune only of a song identified by the significantly distorted translation of its title, following as it does his recognition of Bloom as the man promised in his dream of deliverance, would seem to indicate that he is announcing that his youth, that painful part of his life, precisely "here" has ended. Now, he is saying, he has come to know God, which he did not do when young, and having achieved understanding of Him he has been delivered—from his awful disabling hatred of Him and His creation—can love God, and even serve Him in his own way: the artist as a young man can become an artist. He would find "Holiness" through "Grace" if at all, the fourteenth chapter (hospital) declared; the embodiment of that grace, of the revelation that delivered him from his mind's bondage, is now leading him, and he sings for joy which is also partly joyous anticipation. As "Armageddon" occurred in nighttown, this is the chapter of "atonement."

Stephen's second song is that by the extremely obscure Johann Jeep. Only the opening couplet and the final verse (already quoted) appear. Although *"Und alle Schiffe brücken"* is an ironic comment on Bloom's plan to adopt Stephen, and although all Bloom's far-fetched plans with regard to Stephen (which Joyce has characterized by his cloacal pun) will be swept away, the verse also suggests a passage out of danger. The sweeper is called a "ship of the street" (647), and Bloom has pointed out that it "imperils" their lives; "side by side" the two men succeed in making their way past it ("bridging" it) and past the chains significantly beside it, while Stephen sings the words *"Und alle Schiffe brücken."* The opening couplet, which Stephen has already sung:

> *Von der Sirenen Listigkeit*
> *Tun die Poeten Dichten*

and "translated *extempore*" for Bloom, is illuminated by the final paragraph of the chapter. The narrator says that Bloom and Stephen talk as they walk toward Bloom's house "about sirens, enemies of man's reason." Bloom's unwitting advocacy of faith—"unreason"— and his tempting Stephen with the singing Molly identify him as Stephen's siren, although *"Listigkeit"* ("cunning") dignifies an endeavor that is partly unwitting and partly crude: he has been the agent of the artist's deliverance, has enabled one particular poet to "do" his work. That is what Stephen proclaims, and while Bloom's schemes involving Stephen seem slated for failure, that is what the novel suggests at this point about the outcome of Bloom's divinely-inspired endeavors on Stephen's behalf.

17 *the house (to stephen's departure)*

The action moves without interruption to the presentation of that outcome in the first half of the next chapter; and by the middle of it, the story of Stephen Dedalus, child, adolescent, and young man, ends. The "form" of the seventeenth chapter was designated by Joyce a "mathematical catechism,"[5] and he called it "arid" and "very strange" on some occasions, on others "the ugly duckling of the book" and his favorite chapter.[6] If he was using the term "mathematical" as a synonym for "scientific" or "mechanistic," the designation is appropriate. His other comments concern the substance and style of the series of questions and responses; pedantic encyclopedism expressed in a prose that is abstract, dull, cacophonous, and awkward —that is in fact the prototype of current social science and military English—should be arid indeed. But that prose achieves a fresh, albeit precious, charm, the charm of harmonious unfailing wrongness that an occasional almost impossibly Victorian house possesses. While the Victorian architect did not share our pleasure, however, Joyce's way of saying that Milly has inherited Bloom's Jewish nose (677) or of describing Bloom's vision of himself as a country gentleman (699) is analogous to the burlesque of the seemingly inept clown in a tumbling or skating troupe: as the rich pattern of neologism, inverted word order, and other verbal tricks employed in achieving the effect of unfailing wrongness suggests, it is the work of one who has mastery over his medium.

This narrative manner is unique in the series that began following the *"entr'acte,"* because it alone of all those Joyce creates from chapter to chapter does not seem to have any special fictional work to do: it neither makes a point about the theme nor implements the unfolding action of the chapter. Nevertheless, it is functional. In addition to the particular special function of each of the other varieties of narrative, all of them work to remove the author's voice from their respective chapters, to make the work more dramatic. The present chapter avoids even the identifiable narrator, as distinct from author, of the chapters that rely on stylistic parody, for the burlesque prose is not merely the disguise of style but the denial of it; and the combination of that grotesque with the parody of catechism and the pedantry achieves almost complete objectivity, presents the concluding action of the novel's two protagonists in, to use Joyce's phrase, "the baldest and coldest way."[7]

The "bald" "cold" objectivity of Joyce's narrative stance in the chapter seems also to have two special functions. The major one is to reinforce at its conclusion the whole portrayal of the two characters and their one-day action by asserting (through the hypernaturalism) the authenticity of that portrayal, and even more by providing it (in the course of the apparently promiscuous factualizing) with vital, previously undisclosed, information about the characters, especially Bloom, and with a fuller context and setting. The other purpose is to effect the pretense of belittling Bloom and Stephen and their interinvolved stories, principally through the encyclopedic irrelevance and a broadest possible ("cosmic") frame of reference, a pretense which evokes for them, as does the sarcasm in John Crowe Ransom's poems about the deaths of children, a final active sympathy from the reader.

In the final paragraph of the chapter before this, the paragraph which intimates that Bloom and Stephen cannot sustain a meaningful relationship, they also are said to be discussing "sirens" and "usurpers," subjects close to the hearts of both men. And the intimation of failure is seemingly contradicted by a good deal else in the chapter, not the least of which is its action: Stephen goes from taciturn resentment of Bloom to accompanying him home and singing for him. Like that final paragraph, the initial unit of question-and-response in the present chapter represents the fate of Bloom's association with Stephen ambiguously:

> WHAT PARALLEL COURSE DID BLOOM AND STEPHEN FOLLOW
> returning?
>   Starting united. . . . (650)

While the first explicit statement in the chapter is that they are "starting united," the term "parallel" injects the suggestion that the courses Bloom and Stephen follow to Bloom's house, being parallel, shall never meet. But like so much of the preceding chapter, the subsequent units of question-and-response during the walk tend to contradict the intimation of failure. There is even a list of the similarities in their "reactions to experience" deduced by Bloom (throughout this part as well as in the latter part of the chapter, Bloom's thoughts and actions are its major subject).

When they arrive at the house, Bloom discovers anew the symbolically significant fact that had slipped his mind during the conversation with Stephen—that he lacks his key; it is no less significant that he achieves an unconventional entry. Letting Stephen in by the front door, he takes him to the kitchen, where they drink cocoa and their conversation resumes.

They discuss meetings when Stephen was a child and another "connecting link," Mrs. Riordan, "Aunt Dante" of the *Portrait,* who received Bloom's attentions a decade before because of his hope of benefit from her will. They inquire into possible similarity in "their educational careers," and both avoid "openly allud[ing] to their racial differences," while they make various comparisons of Irish and Hebrew. Stephen does not patronize Bloom, and grad-

ually they cease to be curiosities to each other and become
companions. Echoing the action, the interlocutor asks questions that result in a long exposition of the analogy that
"existed between their ages," the revelation that both were
baptized by the same priest at the same church, and an account of the "points of contact" between the Irish and Hebrew languages "and between the peoples who spoke
them." [8] While, before drinking the cocoa, Stephen con-
verses freely with Bloom because of his recognition of the
deliverer promised in his dream, afterwards he shows himself not only also willing but almost equally eager to explore
every possible similarity, increase the understanding, and
so establish a basis for a relationship between them.

After Stephen sings of *"Little Harry Hughes"* in his
modernized version of the medieval ballad about Jewish
ritual murder, "Hugh of Lincoln," Bloom takes the critical
step in his scheme, invites Stephen to spend the night "on
an extemporised cubicle." His thoughts about the "advantages" for each of the three people involved that "would
or might have resulted from a prolongation of such extem-
porisation" (679) come as no surprise. The advantage for
"the host" of "vicarious satisfaction" is an apparent reference to "security of domicile and seclusion of study" for
"the guest," but clearly ambiguous in view of Bloom's
scheme and of his impulse to offer Stephen one of Molly's
handkerchiefs (661). Thus the advantages for "the hostess"
are "disintegration of obsession" and "acquisition of correct Italian pronunciation," which have been shown to be
the same thing.

However, "promptly, inexplicably, with amicability, gratefully," Stephen rejects the invitation; whereupon, pausing
only to return Stephen's money, Bloom quickly, and one
feels with a note of desperation, makes "counterproposals"
for Stephen to give Molly Italian instruction, Molly to give
Stephen voice instruction, and the two men to have a series
of meetings for the sake of "intellectual dialogues" (680).
Stephen accepts these, but Bloom recognizes that their
"realisation" is "problematic" for two reasons: "the irre-
parability of the past" and "the imprevidability of the future." His illustration of the first truth is an incident at a
circus in which a clown "had publicly declared to an exhila-
rated audience that he (Bloom) was his (the clown's)

papa," that of the second an instance when he marked a
florin with three notches "for circulation on the waters of
civic finance, for possible, circuitous or direct, return."
The relevance is plain: no more than in the case of the
clown can kinship between himself and Stephen be simply
declared or created spontaneously and immediately; once
released into the world, Stephen is likely to fail to return,
just as the coin did.

Bloom has finally come to understand the impossibility of
realizing his scheme. Their paths are parallel. A son
cannot be fabricated. And Stephen's "inexplicably" rejecting his largesse (actually because the response Stephen
had to his offer of Molly does not extend to Molly herself)
also ruins his plan for effecting a "disintegration of obsession." He is, the reader is told (681), dejected by this
conclusion to a colloquy that had begun to be so promising
toward the end of their visit to the cabmen's shelter. Nevertheless, he accompanies his guest into the garden and there
dejectedly, but impressively for a layman, meditates about
the universe and discourses on "various constellations." At
Stephen's suggestion they urinate together, demonstrating
(as Stephen apparently intended) that a fundamental relationship as men does exist between them. Finally, they join
hands across the garden doorway, and Stephen walks away.

As they are clasping hands, the author presents a final
reiteration of the futility, now recognized by both characters, of any attempt to develop an intimacy between them.
The bells of Saint George's Church toll two o'clock. The interlocutor asks "what echoes of that sound" are heard by
each and is told that Stephen "hears" the snatch of prayer
from the Extreme Unction which he associates with his
mother's death, and that Bloom "hears," "*Heigho, heigho, /
Heigho, heigho,*" the sounds he "heard" at the end of his
first chapter (kitchen), when he was thinking of Dignam's
funeral and the church bells rang. The last words of that
chapter are "Poor Dignam!", preceded by a cluster of
"heighos." Thereafter the church bells–"heigho" conjunction occurs twice in the novel (274 and 463), both times
signifying death. The parting of Bloom and Stephen actually completes a pattern of references to death and the dead
which was begun when they joined company. At that point,
the beginning of the preceding chapter, the narrator men-

tioned gratuitously that their path to the cabmen's shelter
took them past the morgue (598); thereafter, dead men,
murder, Digman's funeral, return from the dead, and similar
subjects arose; and the chapter ended with Stephen's talk of
sirens, which he also called "murderers of men," and with
the "scythed car," imperiling "our lives," of "Father
Maher." The motif persists in the present chapter, through
thoughts and conversation about dead people and Stephen's
ballad of the murdered child to the simultaneous tolling
church bells and handclasp of the two men, the final blatant
statement of what is intimated constantly throughout the
period of their association and pointedly at the end of the
preceding chapter—that (as both now realize) they shall
join only in death.

The second intimation with which the preceding chapter
ends, that by Bloom's agency Stephen shall achieve atonement with God and be free of the oppressions that constitute his story in *Ulysses*, is also fulfilled in the first part of
the present one. Knowing that his dream had foretold the
ministry of a deliverer immediately after his futile gesture
of consummate defiance of God, and that Bloom, God's
emissary, has fulfilled the dream, Stephen recognizes God's
true mercy and the adolescent folly of his condemnation of
Him. Consequently, one of the subjects about which the
two men disagree in a list at the very beginning of this
chapter (651) is the cause for the near-collapse which followed Stephen's frenzied whirling in nighttown. Characteristically, Bloom ascribes it to physical conditions, "gastric
inanition," excessive drinking, the whirling, and Stephen
sees its spiritual origin: "the reapparition of a matutinal
cloud (perceived by both . . .) at first no bigger than a
woman's hand." The cloud Stephen refers to is described
as beginning "to cover the sun" in the respective chapters
introducing the two characters, and is one of the devices
used to establish their simultaneity. His phrase, "at first
no bigger than a woman's hand," is an allusion to "the
mother," who appeared to him at his "collapse," pointed
her accusing and punishing finger, and revealed herself to
be a manifestation of God; and this allusion plays off and

reinforces the primary one, which is to the "little cloud out of the sea, like a man's hand" described by Elijah's servant in I Kings 18:44. The climax of Elijah's mission among Israel is the outcome of his challenge to four hundred and fifty priests of Baal that they test the relative strength of Baal and Jehovah on Mount Carmel. The pagan priests supplicate their god to set a sacrifice afire, without success; then Elijah builds a similar pyre to Jehovah, soaks it with water, and surrounds it with a water moat. In answer to his prayer to "turn [Israel's] heart back again," pyre, moat, and even the stones of the altar are consumed by flames, and the people return to God. Then Elijah prays for deliverance from the drought. The prayer is answered by the little cloud out of the sea, and rain soon follows. Stephen is not only associating his "cloud" with "the mother" but also suggesting that in the morning the promise of deliverance was hard to perceive ("a woman's hand").

Because of his new knowledge, Stephen not only drinks cocoa with Bloom when they enter the house but understands the significance, as always a bit out of Bloom's sublunary depth, of their action. This significance is first indicated by the treatment of Bloom's thoughts about his unwitting prophecy of Throwaway's victory and its consequences during the day, which occur when he sees Molly's and Boylan's torn betting tickets. Directly after he concludes that he is satisfied "To have sustained no positive loss. To have brought a positive gain to others. Light to the gentiles," the interlocutor asks, "How did Bloom prepare a collation for a gentile?" The common final word links his preparation of cocoa with his messianic function, and this link is reinforced by the fact that for Stephen, at least, he is a successful bearer of the light among the gentiles. When to these facts are added: his first washing his hands, as the celebrant does in the Mass before preparing the Communion; the use of "collation," a theological word and one signifying a light meal during days of general fast, to describe the hot cocoa; the reference to it as "Epps's massproduct, the creature ['of the Creator'] cocoa"; and the fact that it is a solid whose botanical name is *Theobroma* ("god-food" in Greek) *Cacao*[9] combined with a liquid— the significance of the "collation" is apparent. It was after he found himself "unable" to partake of the "concoction labelled coffee" and the "so-called roll" that Stephen recognized Bloom as the deliverer of his dream and accepted his invitation to go home with him, "talk things over," and, by implication, drink something more palatable, which Bloom had already decided would be the cocoa. On the way he sang "Youth Here Has End"—"atonement" has followed "Armageddon." And atonement is the preparation for Holy Communion. Now Stephen "seriously," in serious "silence" that Bloom "erroneously," the narrator takes the trouble to say, ascribes to "mental composition" (661), drinks the "massproduct."

Not only Stephen and the narrator but also Joyce himself insist that Stephen has in this episode accepted the sacrament proffered by God's emissary. The conjunction of details confirms this, and the preceding action carefully prepares for it. Receiving Holy Communion, Stephen is returning to what in the fourteenth chapter was called "Holiness," reverence of, and acceptance by, God.

Thus, for the remainder of his presence in the novel, he talks freely, listens attentively, sings, and writes in Gaelic, showing ease, warmth, interest. And he dwells, as though to express his wonder, on various aspects of his deliverance. He has a "quasisensation" of Bloom's concealed identity as "the traditional figure of hypostasis" (the Trinity, or Christ alone). He comments on "Little Harry Hughes" in terms that identify himself as the Christian child and embody that wonder:

> One of all, the least of all, is the victim predestined. Once by inadvertence, twice by design he challenges his destiny. It comes when he is abandoned and challenges him reluctant and as an apparition of hope and youth holds him unresisting. It leads him to a strange habitation, to a secret infidel apartment, and there, implacable, immolates him, consenting. (676)

He was "predestined" to be "immolated" (consecrated to God), "consenting," by a Jew in that Jew's house, for the deliverance articulated by his dream was precisely that event; and he challenged" that "destiny," "by inadvertence" when Bloom crossed his path and invoked the dream at the library entrance, and "by design" first when he spurned Bloom in nighttown and struck at God and then when he rejected the coffee and bun Bloom offered him.

Stephen's ostensible commentary on his ballad is really a celebration of his deliverance. And although both are unaware of this, his commentary is almost as fully applicable to Bloom. The linked modifiers in the phrase "an apparition of hope and youth" describe both Stephen as Bloom saw him in the maternity hospital and Bloom's vision of Rudy, while only "hope" describes what Bloom's display of Molly's picture signifies for Stephen; thus the interlocutor promptly calls Bloom not only "secret infidel" but also "victim predestined." If Bloom's "destiny" was articulated in his corresponding dream of the night before, first recollected at twilight on the beach (364)—in which Molly, dressed in Turkish ("infidel") costume (374), "which is thought by those in ken to be for a change" (391), invited *him* into *her* "apartment" (364)—then he certainly shall be as "consenting" a victim as Stephen. He "challenged" that particular destiny inadvertently, perhaps, when he did nothing to stop Boylan from leaving the Ormond for his rendezvous with Molly, and by design, certainly, in his various shoddy sexual activities and his attempt to involve Stephen with her. Approaching the outcome of Stephen's story, Joyce is introducing the question of the outcome of Bloom's, which will be the subject of the rest of the novel.

Following the song and commentary, Bloom makes his offer of asylum, is disappointed, and comes to understand the futility of his endeavor. The interlocutor asks if Stephen shares Bloom's "dejection," and is told:

> He affirmed his significance as a conscious rational animal proceeding syllogistically from the known to the unknown and a conscious rational reagent between a micro- and a macrocosm ineluctably constructed upon the incertitude of the void. (682)

What Stephen affirms is exactly what he presumptuously proclaimed at the end of the *Portrait*, but his attitude now is sober, qualified, and realistic. His proceeding "from

the known to the unknown" (going "to encounter the
reality of experience") is a departure from familiars and
home: the snatch of Irish he sang (672) is from *"Shule
Aroon"* (*"Shule Agra"*), the song of a girl whose lover
has gone to fight in France; he has been given abundant
proof that Ireland and her *literati* do not want him. His
function as "reagent," a chemical term signifying a substance used in detecting, examining, or measuring other
substances, "between a micro- and a macrocosm" is that
of maker of a work from reality, the created world—
that of the artist; freed to accept and deal with reality,
the "macrocosm" within and about him, to be the "reagent"
between life and his art, he can now try to forge his race's
conscience.

Having replaced the foolish proclamation of his premature and abortive "flight" with this sober "affirmation"
of his intentions as a man and as an artist, Stephen begins
to go forth once again in his life. As he leaves Bloom's
house, he intones privately a psalm, "the 113th [Vulgate
numbering], *modus peregrinus: In exitu Israel de Egypto.
. . .* " The interlocutor calls Bloom's house "the house of
bondage" and points out that the psalm is appropriate for
a man sojourning in foreign lands (*"modus peregrinus"*),
but what Stephen suggests by his singing contradicts the
first assertion and extends far beyond the second. It is
from "his mind's bondage" that the grace of God has
delivered him—"the house of bondage" is his miserable
former self. And with that self analogous to Egypt, the
valid significance of the psalm pointed out by the interlocutor is eclipsed by the relevance to Stephen's new situation of its title and its text, which is a glorification of God
and a mocking of the earthly obstacles He dispelled in
effecting the deliverance of Israel (Bloom has already
chanted for Stephen part of the Zionist anthem, "Hatikvah,"
whose title means "hope"). Stephen is probably suggesting
even more by the psalm he intones *"secreto"* in Latin.
By ancient Catholic custom, the priests sing it while the
dead are carried into church, a signification that they have
been delivered from "the bondage of sin" into the grace
of God.[10] Dante, in Canto II of the *Purgatorio*, depicts
the souls being brought to purgatory by an angel (messenger of God) as singing it in thankfulness at having

been saved from eternal damnation; and his famous letter
to Can Grande, cited in the Introduction, which uses this
very psalm to illustrate the four-fold meaning in his poem,
asserts that "allegorically" it signifies man's redemption
by Christ, and "in its moral sense" it portrays "the con-
version of the Soul from the plaint and misery of sin to
the state of grace."[11]

Stephen's expression of awareness of, wonder at, and
thankfulness for what has been granted him is eloquent.
But the psalm is even more significant than he knows.
Associating himself as he now has become with dead souls,
he causes the psalm to be linked to the whole death motif
that began with the beginning of the last chapter. The
incident involving the sweeper car at the end of that
chapter signified, simultaneously, that Bloom and Stephen
would join permanently only in death and that Stephen
would be delivered. The second, positive, intimation was
made largely through the nature and placement of the
songs Stephen sings there; and of these, the more pointedly
suggestive one plays precisely, as does the biblical psalm,
on the idea of Stephen's dead youth. As Sweelinck's hymn
title, mistranslated, informs the sweeper incident with its
very different second meaning, the biblical psalm informs
the tolling of the church bells with this same signification
of deliverance. On the simplest level of analogy, the psalm
is appropriate to one who will be staying in a foreign
country and who has been delivered by God from bondage.
The Church and Dante see in it an expression of the Pauline
doctrine of achieving eternal life through death, and Stephen
plays on this concept of it to say that self-bound youth
has died and a new man been born in his place by the
grace of God. Finally, *Ulysses* exploits Stephen's metaphor
to invoke again the very different significance of the persistent death motif. And so the sounding of the church
bells as Stephen departs culminates the death motif in a way
that signifies one thing about the two men's shaking hands
and something very different about Stephen.

As they urinate in the garden before Stephen departs,
Bloom thinks on his material level of "problems" related
to Stephen's lack of circumcision (a final reflection of
his recognition that Stephen cannot be his son) while

Stephen mulls over a theological problem with respect to
Bloom, "the problem of the sacerdotal integrity of Jesus
circumcised" (a final reflection of his deliverance, the
other main element of the action). The bells sound, they
clasp hands, and Stephen walks away "on the heaven-born
[God-created] earth." He has gone from the mock-mass
of the false prophet-priest that opened the novel to the
Communion provided by the true deliverer, from near
breakdown to salvation, on Bloomsday. And from his
Good Friday mortification in nighttown, whose streets he
entered chanting "the *introit* for paschal time" (424),
through Holy Saturday atonement in the shelter, to Communion and spiritual rebirth in Bloom's kitchen, chapter
for day, he has at long last done his Easter duty! The
snatch from "Shule Aroon" which he recited for Bloom,

suil, suil, suil, arun, suil go siocair agus, suil go cuin
(walk, walk, walk your way, walk in safety, walk with
care) (672),

is an index of the future life of Mister Stephen Dedalus,
artist. The story of the artist as a young man is complete.

1. See, e.g.: Gilbert, p. 351; Golding, p. 135; Tindall, p. 46;
Wilson, p. 208.

2. "*Johannes Jeep*" is listed with a query in the exhaustive study
of Matthew J. C. Hodgart and Mabel P. Worthington, *Song in the
Works of James Joyce* (New York, 1959); and I have been unable
to locate a song of that title. Joyce's italicization seems to be wholly
misleading, and the reference seems to be to a German composer of
religious and secular songs who was a later contemporary of Sweelinck (1562–1641), composer of Stephen's "air *Youth here has End.*"
Johann Jeep was born at Dransfeld near Göttingen in 1585 and died
about 1650. Very little of his work is extant and very little is known
about his life. See *Musikalisches Conversations-Lexicon*, ed. Her-
mann Mendel (Berlin, 1869), V, 373–74.

3. Frank Podmore was a contemporary spiritualist (1865–1910).

4. His name is linked with Shakespeare's: he is from the "Rosevean," whose masts symbolized Calvary and therefore Christ; he
knows a Simon Dedalus who turns out not to be Stephen's true
father; he has left his wife a grass widow, like Bloom and Shakespeare; he is referred to as a "*soi-disant* sailor" (614); he is associated with Odysseus; he has a tatoo on his chest bearing, without

apparent reason, the number 16, which corresponds to the date of the novel; his postcard is addressed not to "W. B. Murphy" but to an "A. Boudin." The association with God is disturbing because it has no apparent function or significance.

5. In a letter to Frank Budgen (*Letters*, p. 159).

6. The positive remarks were made to Frank Budgen; see Budgen, p. 258. In a letter to Claud W. Sykes, he complained of "the aridities of Ithaca" (the word is transcribed "acidities" by Stuart Gilbert: *Letters*, p. 164; the permission of the Society of Authors, the literary representative of the Joyce Estate, to reproduce my reading of this passage is gratefully acknowledged); in a letter to Harriet Shaw Weaver, he spoke of its "dry rock pages" (*Letters*, p. 173); he called it "very strange" in letters to Robert McAlmon (*Letters*, p. 175) and Valery Larbaud (*"très étrange"*), (*Letters*, p. 169).

7. See *Letters*, p. 159.

8. Joyce himself is said to have regarded the modern Irish and Jews as similar types with similar destinies.

9. Tindall, *Reader's Guide*, p. 222. Mr. Tindall sees the cocoa as representing the Eucharist, although he looks on the incident as more symbolic than literal in import; see also Tindall, p. 29.

10. Dummelow, p. 371.

11. Emelia Russell Gurney, *Dante's Pilgrim's Progress* (London, 1897), p. 101.

chapter eleven

Bloom's Hebrew counterpart to Stephen's snatch of verse
is indicative of his future, also. Following Stephen's
account of a romantic tryst and his "Parable of the Plums"
(featuring the one-handled adulterer), Bloom meditates on
his most preoccupying "domestic problem," which he prefers to generalize as "What to do with our wives" (670).
And following that they recite their verses. From the
Song of Solomon, Bloom's line occurs twice. The first
occurrence (4:3) is in the famous rhapsody of the singer
on the beauty which has "ravished my heart" of "my sister,
my spouse," the passage drawn upon so heavily by Stephen's
boyhood prayer book; the second (6:7) is followed directly
by, "There are threescore queens, and fourscore concubines,
and virgins without number. My dove, my undefiled is
but one." Bloom's "domestic problem" is vitally important
because his future holds undiminished love for Molly
which no queen, concubine, or virgin can divert.

The pointed irony that Molly is not undefiled is also a
reminder that although Bloom has acknowledged his responsibility for her adultery, and although he decided even
as Boylan was setting out from the Ormond bar that the
important thing was reconciliation (280), he has no basis
for assuming that Molly will relinquish her defiler, that

she requites his desire and his devotion. Stephen shall make his way, with care, but with God's love. When Stephen rejects Bloom's invitation and "affirms" that he has been enabled to go forth, "proceed . . . from the known to the unknown," Bloom is "comforted" by the awareness "that as a competent keyless citizen he had proceeded energetically from the unknown to the known. . . . " In contrast to Stephen, his problem has been to effect a return, and he congratulates himself on having done so. However, he is still "keyless," has only gained an undignified entrance to his house, not effected a true return to Molly's side. He shall love and desire Molly always; but this fact can portend sterility, frustration, misery, and ultimately, in terms of the morality postulated in the novel, spiritual damnation, as readily as happiness and fulfilment.

Bloom's capacity for achieving the favorable alternative is a consequence of his manhood, restored in nighttown as the indirect result of desire for a son and the direct result of conscience, self-respect, and good sense. This capacity continues to express itself; for example, when Bridie Kelly attempted to solicit in the shelter, he not only avoided her but recalled that once in approaching him she "begged the chance of his washing," and reflected, "Still, candour compelled him to admit that he had washed his wife's undergarments . . . and women would and did too a man's similar garments . . . if they really loved him, that is to say," a conception of his distorted relationship with Molly that would have been impossible before night-town. But he is unaware of the salutary change in his attitude and has refused to attempt to recover his family, first developing his thesis that true return is impossible, then formulating his scheme involving Stephen.

A mitigating fact about this scheme is that it is not like Bloom's former guilt-motivated inclination to pander. He wants, not to give Molly away, but to take her from Boylan, to effect "For the hostess, disintegration of obsession, acquisition of correct Italian pronunciation," and eventually to retrieve her himself. The outrageous last refinement he develops for the scheme shows clearly that he would not be satisfied merely to keep her content with him by

means of Stephen, and Stephen content wih him by means
of her:

> Why might these several provisional contingencies
> between a guest and a hostess not necessarily preclude
> or be precluded by a permanent eventuality of recon-
> ciliatory union between a schoolfellow and a jew's
> daughter?
> Because the way to daughter led through mother, the
> way to mother through daughter. (679)

"Schoolfellow" and "jew's daughter" derive from "Little
Harry Hughes," and refer to Stephen the scholar and Milly.
The reconciliation their union would effect is not between
them, clearly, for they have never met; it is a reconciliation
of Bloom and Molly. Bloom's sordid scheme is "provi-
sional," directly leading to his "permanent" reunion with
Molly and the acquisition of Stephen as a son-in-law,
Stephen's way to Milly being through Molly, and his own
way back to Molly, consequently, being through (Stephen's
transfer of affections to) Milly.

It is after this final outrage is disclosed to the reader
that Stephen rejects Bloom's invitation, and the "keyless
citizen" takes comfort from having "proceeded energetically
from the unknown to the known." As unwarranted as his
comfort is, it nevertheless indicates that he has reacted well
to the disappointment: finally required to face squarely
his twofold problem of Molly's estrangement and his
sonlessness, he makes a beginning with the thought that
he did well, and acted with some resourcefulness besides,
in entering his locked house. Any symbolic significance
in his undignified but "energetic" action may be a bit out
of his sublunary depth, but he is promptly given more overt
encouragement to act like the man he has become. Immediately, Stephen intoning the psalm, the two men go
into the garden, and he discourses on constellations for
Stephen's edification and meditates on the cause and nature
of the universe around him for his own. Following his
"logical" conclusion that it is not divinely created and
yet that it is unknowable, he turns back from the "Utopia"
to consider the "affinities . . . between the moon and

woman," all of which apply to Molly. The general similarity
is represented and one element of it, "her isolated dominant
implacable resplendent propinquity," emphasized by the
round projection (721) of the light of the lamp upon the
windowshade of an upper window. He draws Stephen's
attention to it and speaks of Molly, they "contemplate" each
other, and "at Stephen's suggestion, at Bloom's instigation
both," they urinate. Then, "their gazes, first Bloom's, then
Stephen's" fasten on Molly's window. It is disclosed that
the "trajectory" of Bloom's urination extends further, and
Bloom's boyhood superiority in urination contests is
mentioned.

Their urination, preceded by Bloom's drawing Stephen's
attention to Molly's window, suggested by Stephen and in-
stigated by Bloom, accompanied by their gazing at the
window, reported by the narrator in competitive terms, is
represented as a contest, much like the urination contest
to win a woman in Pope's *Dunciad* and the one in which
Emer is said to have won the ancient Irish hero Cuchulain.
Freud points out, with erudite allusion to Swift and Rabelais, the basis for the contests in Joyce, Pope, and Irish
legend: a human tendency to associate urinary power with
sexual potency.[1] Even if Bloom and Stephen are not aware
of their contest, they have brought Molly into the situation,
and the author suggests that if he is being whimsical about
the contest in part, he is also partly serious. For while they
urinate (and reflect in characteristic ways on questions of
circumcision), they see:

> A star precipitated with great apparent velocity across
> the firmament from Vega in the Lyre above the zenith
> beyond the stargroup of the Tress of Berenice towards
> the zodiacal sign of Leo. (688)

They see a falling star (a sign of good luck), caused to fall
("precipitated") from the constellation Lyra, pointedly
called the Lyre, which is "beyond" the constellation named
for the hair dedicated in a temple by a faithful wife to the
safe return of her husband, "towards the zodiacal sign of
Leo." With this "celestial sign," Joyce is once again using

the same elements to suggest two different things. The instrumental element is the Berenice referred to. Berenice II, wife of Ptolemy III, not only made the gesture on behalf of her husband's return, but also killed her suitor, and finally was murdered by her son, Ptolemy IV. Exploiting this last aspect of his allusion, Joyce is saying that Stephen has been caused to go from self-centeredness (Lyra) and a "flop" (the etymology of "Vega" derives it from the Arabic for "falling"), past the condition precipitated by the death of his mother and in which we find him at the beginning of the novel, to his deliverance through the meeting with "Leo" Bloom.[2] The application of the passage to Bloom is simpler. Vega is a star of the first magnitude; Molly, the light in the window, has during the urination contest been caused to go from the poet (the lyre), in the direction of the constellation celebrating a loving and loyal wife eager for her husband's return, "towards," although not fully to, Leo. Bloom has won the contest.

The novel has pointed out repeatedly and, at this point, demonstrated at length Bloom's adeptness at identifying stars and constellations; and his youthful participation in and winning of urination contests has just been mentioned. If Stephen has deduced nothing from the falling star, that is not necessarily the case with Bloom. After they clasp hands to the tolling bells and Stephen leaves, Bloom thinks of his ostensible friends (Simon Dedalus, Joe Hynes, John Henry Menton, *et al.*), hears the departing feet of the one man with whom he has truly had "interindividual relations" in eleven years (651)—since the death of Rudy—feels, "alone," "the cold of interstellar space, thousands of degrees below freezing point," and reflects on "companions now . . . defunct." What impresses itself on him now is the terrible state of isolation; once more he recognizes the necessity that he return to his family. And in view of this sentiment, and of the astronomical comment on his urinating farther than the young man whom he has considered a much more likely attraction for Molly than himself as they "gazed" at Molly's window, it is no surprise that to the question, "Did he remain?", the narrator replies, "with deep inspiration he returned. . . ."

17 *the house (from stephen's departure)*

Although it is accompanied by deep inspiration, Bloom's "return" is still not the essential one that is necessary, and this is pointed out immediately. When he re-enters the house, he does not go again to the kitchen, which is in the basement and a servant's room; he goes directly to the parlor, and there "his ingress" is "suddenly arrested": he bumps his head against a corner of a sideboard which has been moved. There is no indication that Bloom understands the significance Joyce gives the rearranged furniture; but the Bello of his fancy had mentioned just such an alteration when she taunted him with being supplanted (530). The point is elaborated by the description of two chairs, re-disposed to face each other, one with an "amply upholstered seat," the other with a "seat . . . of white plaited rush," like Boylan's hat. The symbolic play is then made explicit: the chairs are said to have "Significance of . . . circum-stantial evidence, of testimonial supermanence." And fin-ally Joyce's point about the nature of Bloom's "return" is reinforced by the last exploitation of "Love's Old Sweet Song" in the novel, mentioned in the discussion of "Style in *Ulysses*": the score is on the piano, "open at the last page with the final indications [to the accompanist, Boy-lan] *ad libitum*, forte, pedal, *animato*, sustained, pedal, *ritirando*, close." Bloom is painfully and rudely confronted with the fact that he cannot simply return because his home is no longer that; his own Bello had said, "all is changed by woman's will since you slept . . . your night of twenty years. Return and see."

The action of *Ulysses* now has only its principal subject, the story of Leopold Bloom. That story begins with Bloom's condition in the morning. It includes certain singular events that occur as the action develops and that have a potential effect on his predicament: his following Boylan to the Ormond, opposing the citizen, pursuing Stephen to

nighttown, among others. And the novel as it nears its
end reveals that these events have had certain significant
consequences: his recovery of the manhood he began to
lose with his sexual neglect of Molly following Rudy's
death more than a decade before, and his friendly conversation with Stephen, the first such "communion" in the
same period of time. The novel has presented Stephen's
predicament as it was on Bloomsday morning and certain
singular events of the day that led to the conclusion of his
story; the conclusion of Bloom's similarly presented story
will be, correspondingly, his ultimate success in escaping
from his predicament by the end of *Ulysses*, or his failure to
do so. Whichever alternative it be, Bloom's success or
failure *within the scope of the novel* in effecting a reunion
with Molly constitutes the resolution of the fully developed,
singular (not "typical") action; and as such, that success
or failure is the conclusion of the story of Leopold Bloom.

The present episode, the portion of the seventeenth chapter between Bloom's return from the garden and his falling
asleep at the end of the chapter (690-722), presents his last
thoughts and acts in the novel. These constitute his contribution to the resolution of the action, and their sequence
is vitally significant; for that reason they must be examined
closely in sequence. (Page references are reserved for major
points.)

If not to the literal blow as well, Bloom explicitly (691)
reacts to the figurative blow inflicted on his "return" by
the rearranged furniture: "His next proceeding" is to burn
incense. None of the many uses of incense in Church
ritual with which his action has been associated enlightens
it. The secular Bloom burns incense precisely at this point,
not for some sort of consecration, but for the purpose for
which he has it in the house, fumigation. He is attempting
to erase the evidence of Boylan's presence.

But incense cannot rid Bloom's home of the usurper,
or return his wife to him. Joyce is making an ironic contrast with the corresponding incident in the *Odyssey*. After
his needlessly bloody but thoroughly effective restoration
of authority over his home, Odysseus arranges for the
killing of the household women and Melanthius, after which
"all the adventure was over." Then Odysseus immediately

tells his faithful old nurse Eurycleia to bring him "sulphur . . . that cleanses all pollution and bring me fire, that I may purify the house," and to summon Penelope to him. After he "thoroughly purged"[3] the defiled rooms, Book XXII of the *Odyssey* ends. Book XXIII presents the return of Odysseus to the side of Penelope, their love, and their pillow talk. Bloom would effect the purging of the pollution, and the subsequent full repossession of his home and reunion with his wife without first undertaking the "adventure" of eliminating the defiler. His burning of incense signifies as much wish and as little accomplishment as his gaining entry to the house without a key.

Nevertheless, his situation is represented optimistically. He observes in the mirror the reflections of three "homothetic objects" on the mantelpiece below—three wedding gifts. He then looks at his reflection, described at length as:

> The image of a solitary (ipsorelative) mutable (aliorelative) man.
>
> Why solitary (ipsorelative)?
> *Brothers and sisters had he none.*
> *Yet that man's father was his grandfather's son.*
>
> Why mutable (aliorelative)?
> From infancy to maturity he had resembled his maternal procreatrix. From maturity to senility he would increasingly resemble his paternal creator.   (692)

The first proposition is simple: considered by himself, Bloom is alone, although he descended from a familial line. The second is more complex; it states a general perception about men as they develop to and beyond maturity. But it also relates to the one above it and to the action of the novel. The mirror has shown Bloom the wedding gifts. The final thing it reflects for him is his bookshelf, with the books inverted and "improperly arranged," a testament of Molly. "Mutable," he has been able to change from resembling his mother to resembling his father. In the context, "aliorelative" means not only "in comparison with others" but also "in his relationship to another." The narrator is stating that Bloom's behavior toward Molly shall change because he has recovered his manhood.

Bloom rearranges the books, seats himself, and is specifically afforded not aesthetic pleasure but "consolation" by the characteristics, including its "youth, grace, sex," of a small statue of Narcissus. The two immediate sources of need for consolation are the loss of Stephen and the usurpation of Molly by Boylan; these and the long-term disappointment to which they relate, his lack of a son, indicate what the consoling statue suggests to him. After contemplating it, he partially undresses; the interlocutor asks: "In what ultimate ambition had all concurrent and consecutive ambitions now coalesced?", and the long account of his material and social desires is presented. It is a brilliant document in social history, an accurate representation of the taste, social values, aspirations, economic activity, customs, and material trappings of the western European petit bourgeoisie at the beginning of the present century. His ivy-covered cottage, its furnishings, its grounds, his dress, and recreational activities are described in an ascending scale of affluence. He "would" become justice of the peace, register a coat of arms, and dispense justice principally "against . . . all perpetuators of international animosities, all . . . recalcitrant violators of domestic connubiality" like the citizen and Boylan. Following a discussion of his intellectual and political integrity, his schemes for providing the necessary lacking element are reviewed: discovering a precious postage stamp, being informed of hidden Spanish treasure, then more and more elaborate industrial development projects until he decides that he needs a large bequest to undertake any moneymaking project and, coming full circle, concludes that he "would" succeed otherwise by "The independent discovery of a goldseam of inexhaustible ore." Whereupon the seven-page revery collapses from the weight of its vanity, and the interlocutor asks, "For what reason did he meditate on schemes so difficult of realisation?", and is told that it is because: "similar meditations . . . when practised habitually before retiring for the night alleviated fatigue and produced as a result sound repose and renovated vitality." The passage illustrates not only Bloom's thoroughly secular and bourgeois Weltanschauung but also his great resource, his rare good sense.

After the characterization of Bloom is further amplified, the interlocutor proposes a hypothetical reversal of the process of self-aggrandizement that characterized his "ambition"; this describes a "reduction" through the "mendicancy" of "nocturnal vagrant [Corley], insinuating sycophant [Lenehan], maimed sailor, blind stripling," to a "nadir of misery." However, in making his proposal, the interlocutor states that Bloom's financial assets protect him from such "reverses of fortune," and that in addition, certain "positive values" would keep him from ever emulating Lenehan or Corley. While Bloom's "ambition" is an extreme standard against which to measure his social and material success, the "reduction" is also extreme. And just as he has a reason for the former, he has a reason for thinking of himself as reduced to an "aged impotent disfranchised ratesupported moribund lunatic pauper." It is the principal "attendant indignities" of that condition: "the unsympathetic indifference of previously amiable females, the contempt of muscular males." This and the next two items in the catechism reveal the true nature of Bloom's concern for the future: "such a situation" could "be precluded," "By decease (change of state), by departure (change of place)"; and "The latter, by the line of least resistance" is "preferable." His fear of attempting to return to Molly is reasserting itself against both his "inspiration" and his understanding of the necessity that he do so. His economic decline is as irrelevant as it is unlikely; Molly's "unsympathetic indifference" and Boylan's "contempt" he sees as accompanying not a far-fetched future destitution but a present "situation."

In this way Bloom comes to consider "departure"—the abandonment of his responsibility—and the question of return and its alternative is broached for the final time in the novel. The "siren" lure wins out at first, as the sequence of questions indicates: "What considerations rendered it not entirely undesirable?"; "What considerations rendered it not irrational?"; "What considerations rendered it desirable?" The answer to the first question is that domicile with Molly has impeded "mutual toleration of personal defects" and that a temporary "sojourn" would at least end the present situation. The answer to the second is more important. Bloom considers "departure" "not irrational" because of the demands of that present situation, which are both "absurd" and "impossible." He and Molly had united, "increased and multiplied," and their child has matured; yet they

> if now disunited were obliged to reunite for increase and multiplication, which was absurd, to form by re-union the original couple of uniting parties, which was impossible. (711)

Bloom's truly rational argument against return is twofold: reunion to effect "that proliferant continuance" would be "absurd," and, as he said in the last chapter, absolute return to a past condition is "impossible." Thus he con-siders the "desirable" aspects of "departure"—the ad-vantages of travel.

This discouraging rationalism does not long prevail in Bloom's irregular internal debate. He soon imagines that Molly would miss him and advertise in an effort to find him, and then decides that after a time he would "return an estranged avenger, a wreaker of justice on malefactors . . . a sleeper awakened, with financial resources (by suppo-sition) surpassing those of Rothschild." No longer sleeping his "night of twenty years," and with the wealth to realize his "ambitions," he would return, despatch Boylan, and win back Molly. Outlandish as this is, it signifies a healthy change of direction. And the very next question and answer present the basis on which Bloom dismisses his plan to conquer the world before conquering his predicament. The plan is "irrational" because, while the "space" through which the "exodus and return" would occur is "reversible," the "time" is "irreversible" (713); the plan would cost time, and as he has come to realize, "Soon I am old," and he may already have "slept" too long. Thus, he considers different "forces, inducing inertia," beginning with trivial-ities but finally mentioning as reasons for his wish to remain where he is: "the anticipation of warmth (human) tempered with coolness (linen), obviating desire and rendering de-sirable" (Molly's presence, in company with bedsheets, which will dissipate any unrequited desire); and "the statue

of Narcissus, sound without echo, [which] desired desire"
(the image of a quasi-son which "wanted to be wanted").
And after considering the "advantages . . . possessed by
an occupied . . . bed" and reviewing his day, he prepares
"to rise in order to go so as to conclude, lest he should not
conclude": he decisively puts an end to his equivocating
deliberation. The judgment is against departure and a
possible later triumphant return and for persevering in
an immediate return of some kind.

However, his conclusion is very limited in scope. While
he is walking to his room to complete the change to his
nightgown and to go to bed, he "enumerates" the "imper-
fections" in what is actually called "a perfect day"; and,
as this phrase suggests, he completely passes over Molly's
adultery. This limitation is challenged immediately when
he enters his bed: he encounters "the imprint of a human
form, male, not his." His reaction is to "reflect" that Boylan
and every other man, including himself, is one of "a
series originating in and repeated to infinity." His amusement belittles Boylan and Boylan's exploit, but it is hardly
conducive to reconciliation. And he cannot persist in his
attempt to ignore what has happened: he begins an inquiry
into the nature, and the significance for any future reunion
between Molly and himself, of her infidelity.

The starting point is a naming of the "series" of Molly's
lovers; the list enumerates a farmer, a Lord Mayor, an
organ grinder, a priest, and others, to Boylan, for a total
(to date) of twenty-five men. Only Boylan concerns him,
however; and after thinking about the rake, he develops
"antagonistic sentiments" of "Envy, jealousy, abnegation,
equanimity." His "envy" is of Boylan's sexual vigor and
"jealousy" of his relations with Molly. The opposing two
"sentiments" are less forthrightly explained. His "abnegation" is ascribed to previous pleasantries between Boylan
and himself, Boylan's "comparative youth," and similar insufficient causes. He bases his "equanimity" on the proposition that what Molly and Boylan have done is "natural"
("nature" and "natural" are repeated eight times in one
sentence), on the irrelevant observation that it is "not as
calamitous as" collision with the sun, and then on the
absurd claim that it is "less reprehensible than" crimes

ranging from murder to malingering and contempt of court. Only after these rationalizations does he disclose the true reasons why he is not irate about the adultery. He considers it "As not more abnormal than all other altered processes of adaptation to altered condition of existence. . . . As more than inevitable, irreparable": Molly adapted herself to his neglect of her—it is his fault; it is done, and cannot be undone by any amount of distress or anger. And for the first of these two reasons he decides that he feels "more abnegation than jealousy, less envy than equanimity"; he "the matrimonial violator of the matrimonially violated had not been outraged by [Molly] the adulterous violator of the adulterously violated." As a result he rejects conventional "retribution." "If any," his can properly be no more than taking Molly away from Boylan. That must be done, he decides, by direct competition with her lover and manager, "emulation" (718). And since he can no longer count on Stephen, he must do it, if at all, by himself: the "separator" must become the "successful rival agent of ['moral'] intimacy" as well as rival impresario.

Having definitely decided in the garden that he wants to return to Molly and in the parlor that he shall attempt to do so in some way immediately, Bloom has now, in Molly's very bed, established his attitude toward her and her adultery: he has no right to blame her, nothing is to be accomplished by dwelling on what is irrevocably done, the only proper course of action is to take her back from the usurper.

However, his lack of vindictiveness against his wife and her lover disturbs him. And with respect to Boylan, it disturbs some critics even more, for it constitutes a pointed contrast to Odysseus' slaying of the suitors who established themselves in his home. The situations are not directly analogous. While Homer's Odysseus was blamelessly wronged by the suitors, Joyce has both confirmed in the action of the novel and explicitly endorsed, "by way of" Junius, Bloom's repeated declarations that his behavior toward Molly is fully to blame for her conduct. Furthermore, Boylan is not a suitor but a lover; the returning husband's efforts must be directed to actually winning back his wife, for to kill the lover and the adulteress, or even

just the lover, is to leave his problem fundamentally un-
solved. And, of course, as well as for these two reasons,
because he is no bronze-age warrior but a modern Dubliner
and a notably pacific and humanitarian one, there is no
question about his exacting any "retribution" from Molly,
or any from Boylan other than that he has a right to exact,
the recovery of Molly. The critics Bloom disappoints force
an analogy, and also ignore his eminently sound thinking
on the matter.

His own disturbance over the "equanimity" and "abnegation" he has achieved is more understandable. It is
apparent only because directly following his decision about
"retribution" the interlocutor asks, "By what reflections
did he, a conscious reactor against the void of incertitude,
justify to himself his sentiments?" The long list of those
"reflections" ranges from "the preordained frangibility of
the hymen," through "the variations of ethical codes," to
"the apathy of the stars." With less justice, this paragraph
rather than the preceding one is sometimes linked to
Odysseus' slaughter of the suitors, either as pointed irony
at Bloom's expense or directly, with Bloom achieving the
bloody homicide through a cosmic indifference that con-
signs Boylan, Molly, and necessarily himself as well to
meaninglessness. Far from having such vital importance, it
is a jumble of superfluous rationalizations. It is a list of
the "reflections" with which Bloom, explicitly "a conscious
reactor against the void of incertitude," *tries to* "justify to
himself his [tractable] sentiments" about Molly's affair. It
is artificial and useless.

But it is unnecessary in the first place—that fact about
Bloom's whole "conscious reaction" is indicated by the
next question and answer in this significant passage which
begins with his entering his and Molly's bed and extends
to the end of the chapter and of his role in the novel (716-
22). Furthermore the question and answer suggest that
even his sound thinking on the matter is not terribly
important:

In what final satisfaction did these antagonistic sentiments and reflections . . . converge?

> Satisfaction at the ubiquity . . . of adipose posterior
> female hemispheres . . . expressive of mute immutable
> mature animality. (719)

It is immediately made clear that the general "ubiquity"
satisfies him because Molly's particular behind is there,
that the sole fact of Molly's presence at his side eclipses all
deliberation and rationalization: he kisses each "hemi-
sphere" in turn as a tribute to the essential animal woman-
ness of which they are "expressive," something he is in
the habit of doing, her soliloquy reveals, possibly because
he is unable to render the more appropriate one. His
tribute is presented in neat parallelism suggestive of an
elaborate ritual, from "antesatisfaction" to the kiss of
tribute to "postsatisfaction." In the first stage he has an
incipient erection, turns to Molly, raises himself, uncovers
her, and contemplates her "adipose . . . hemispheres." The
result is the abstract "satisfaction at the ubiquity" of
those expressions of femaleness which the narrator has
already mentioned, which in the sequence is represented
by his kiss of tribute. Then, in the third stage ("postsatisfaction"), he exactly reverses the procedure: contemplation,
recovering, and so on.

The significance of the symmetrical little pattern lies in
the insubstantial nature of Bloom's "satisfaction," which
in its concrete form is not the action that should follow
the procedures of "antesatisfaction" and be followed by
those of "postsatisfaction," but instead a mere kiss, of
recognition of the possibility of love and adoration of the
object of love. In this case, nothing in the situation in
Ulysses restricts comparison with the *Odyssey*. Odysseus
and the chaste Penelope went to bed together as man and
wife after twenty years; Molly lies asleep in bed sated by
her lover, and Bloom, no less devoted or desiring than
Odysseus, does as he does.

Thereafter the contrast becomes correspondence. After
the consummation of their reunion, Penelope and Odysseus
talk in bed. Bloom's pointed failure to consummate his
return nevertheless wakens Molly. She experiences "incipient excitation," but only questions him about his day.
His "modifications" of his experiences with the citizen

and Gerty and of Stephen's fight with Carr are motivated by prudence. If his accounts of his "promptitude of decision and gymnastic flexibility" in entering the house and the "eldest surviving son of Simon Dedalus" (who "emerged as the salient point of his narration") are for the purpose of impressing Molly with his intrepidity in returning home and preoccupying her with Stephen, whether as lover or son-figure, they have no immediate effect. Molly reflects on them in the next chapter along with his escapade with Gerty, which she has apprehended, although in a form distorted in his favor.

While Bloom talks, each of them thinks of a major defect in their present relationship. Molly is troubled by the eleven-year-old "limitation of fertility" (since November 27, 1893, "carnal intercourse had been incomplete . . ."); she craves a child, as Bloom has been shown to do throughout the novel, and that is at least part of her reason for resenting his sexual neglect of her. Bloom is troubled by the complete breakdown of "mental intercourse between himself and the listener," the final degeneration of their relationship, since Milly's reaching puberty almost a year ago; as the narrator said earlier in the chapter, "offspring produced and educed to maturity," they have nothing to hold them together, neither children nor the promise of children. Thus at this point in the novel Bloom and Molly are concerned about the breakdown of their family, both in the relationship between them and in the "proliferant continuance."

Nevertheless they maintain their habitual positions, Bloom with his head at the foot of the bed, curled up, much as Stephen was at the end of the nighttown chapter. After asking Molly to serve him eggs for breakfast in bed (a fact not fully revealed until the beginning of the next chapter), he falls asleep. Molly, who craves a child and has just had sexual intercourse, lies awake "in the attitude of Gea-Tellus, fulfilled, recumbent, big with seed," to conclude the novel.

In the sixteenth chapter Stephen recognized Bloom as the deliverer of his dream and then accepted Bloom's shab-

bily motivated invitation to his home; the chapter's significant action was the basis for the resolution of Stephen's
story, his deliverance, which actually occurred in the first
part of the seventeenth chapter. The part of the seventeenth
chapter under discussion has a corresponding place in the
structure of the novel. The resolution of Bloom's story, his
success or failure in reuniting with Molly, occurs in the
final, eighteenth, chapter; and it is based on the developed
and unresolved significant action of the latter part of the
seventeenth.

The episode begins with Bloom alone in the garden, desiring reunion but ignoring the change in his home with
which he must contend if he is to achieve it; in the parlor
he is painfully confronted by that change and cannot fully
refute the proposition that reunion is "impossible," yet
recognizes the need to come to a decision and decides to go
to his wife's bed; there, he is obliged to deal with the
situation squarely, resolves his feelings about it in a
reaffirmation of his love, tries to impress Molly, and finally
asks her to reverse their normal routine by serving him
breakfast. But although he has made a decision and has
acted on it in certain ways, he has not reunited with
Molly. On the other hand, although he has not made love
to her and is not aware that he is no longer "unmanned"
(perhaps the reason for the first fact), he has not failed to
achieve the saving reunion, for the resolution of his story
has not occurred when he leaves the novel.

The preparation for that resolution, his coping with the
problem of reunion, which is the central action of this
second of the chapter's two episodes, occurs in the context
of certain significant prior developments. One of the unique
events of the day of the novel, one which, as in Stephen's
case, occurred before he awoke in the morning, Bloom's
dream, is strikingly like Stephen's dream of deliverance.
The ambiguous treatment of Stephen's "commentary" on
his ballad of "the victim predestined," just before Stephen
left the novel and the preceding episode ended, suggested
that Bloom's dream was also prophetic of the salvation he
craves even if it is not to be similarly instrumental. And
although when Bloom first remembered it on the beach
(364), he guilty regarded the Turkish costume in which
Molly had been dressed as signifying that she "wore the

breeches" (374), the author later indicated that she simply wore Near Eastern dress as Bloom himself did in Stephen's dream and, furthermore, that her "Turkey trunks . . . is thought by those in ken to be for a change" (391).

Also significant are the manifestations of Bloom's metamorphosis. A number of times during the day he abandoned his formerly characteristic cowardice, began to act like the "unconquered hero" hailed by the author; and finally he recovered his dissipated manliness. His request for breakfast is the last manifestation of that promising develvelopment in the novel. It is in direct line with his firm dealing with Bella Cohen in nighttown, his opinion expressed in the shelter that a wife properly did domestic chores for her husband, his decision to take Stephen home despite Molly's possible objection, and his use in the cocoa of "her cream" as he called it in the morning (63), the cream which she drank while the maid and he drank milk, which he habitually purchased (174) for the breakfast that is her normal daily prerogative. His request for breakfast is a reaction against the normal situation and an unconscious declaration of the change in himself that would make possible a change in it.

The basis for the resolution of Leopold Bloom's story comprises, on the one side, all the reasons for optimism, such as those discussed above, which are the context of Bloom's final episode (for example, the falling star just before the episode begins), his ultimate decision and actions in that episode itself, and the mutual concern of husband and wife about their broken family; and, on the other side, it comprises the sordid devices implicating Stephen and even Milly, the lack of decisive manly action, and the possibility that Molly is pregnant by Boylan, that she is like "Gea-Tellus" in more than "attitude." That resolution itself is the business of the last chapter, of Molly's thoughts.

In addition to preparing for the resolution of Stephen's story, the sixteenth chapter presented, at its end, an intimation of what that resolution should be. The latter part of the seventeenth chapter is like the sixteenth in this respect as well. And the intimation is that Bloom shall succeed, that he has achieved what he himself called "impossible."

It begins a half-page before the end of the episode and chapter, with the paragraph describing Bloom's curled position, symbolic of the ultimate return. The last words in that paragraph are "the childman weary, the manchild in the womb," and they are followed by:

Womb? Weary?
He rests. He has travelled.   (722)

He rests in his ultimate home, is weary because he has travelled: again return is intimated. And it is intimated in the next question and response also:

With?
Sinbad the Sailor and Tinbad the Tailor and Jinbad the Jailer. . . .

The series of plays on "Sinbad the Sailor" seems to be a list of Bloom's companions in his "travels": the sailor, W. B. Murphy; the tailor, his friend George Mesias, in whose shop he met Boylan (717); the jailer, Alf Bergan the court clerk; the nailer, Corny Kelleher, the undertaker; the failer, Simon Dedalus; the bailer, Martin Cunningham, who twice during the day saved him from predicaments; the hailer, Lenehan; the railer, the citizen; the "phthailer," a friend who died of "phthisis" (689). But the most important name is the initial one. Both literally and figuratively it reiterates the motif of return: Sinbad returned, and Murphy is about to do so. Furthermore, Sinbad is a mythical and literary figure analagous to Odysseus, who even has similar adventures, including a narrow escape from a Cyclops; and Murphy is explicitly called "friend Sinbad" by Bloom (620) and is thought by him to "draw the long bow" of Odysseus. Above all else, the fundamental similarity among the three is that they return from extended travels. And Bloom—Odysseus' analogue, who has "travelled" with "Sinbad-Murphy," who has "travelled" for almost eleven years as "Sin-bad," who was to have written a song about the return of an Irish hero ("If Brian Boru could but come back and see old Dublin now") for a per-

formance of the Christmas pantomime, *Sinbad the Sailor*
(662)[4]—is linked to them by a web of associations. The
link to his Homeric analogue could not be much stronger,
since his narration of his day's "odyssey" to Molly and
subsequent falling asleep directly parallel Odysseus' actions
in Book XXIII.

The next, and last, two sets of question and answer complete the pattern intimating Bloom's return. He rests, for,
the childman weary, he has travelled; he has travelled
"With" Sinbad and the others; furthermore, the manchild
in the womb, he rests, *returned* to the womb-bed from his
travels; he rests:

> When?
> Going to dark bed there was a square round Sinbad
> the Sailor roc's auk's egg in the night of the bed of all
> the auks of the rocs of Darkinbad the Brightdayler.
>
> Where?
>
> ●

Bloom is said to rest, returned, explicitly *when* the "roc's
auk's egg" of Sinbad is in his bed; and that time has come,
for the large black dot, which is the last statement in the
chapter, represents the egg. The roc's egg, which figures
twice in the tale of Sinbad, is the manifestation of the
miraculous giant bird which unknowingly rescues Sinbad
with his first fortune from the Valley of the Diamonds.
And containing the embryo of another roc, the egg is itself
miraculous. The nineteenth-century English expression,
"a roc's egg," meaning something marvelous or unattainable,[5] reinforces the point of the allusion. Joyce is saying
that Sinbad-Bloom in fact has the unattainable roc's egg,
for it is in the bed (Molly's and his bed) that Bloom has
achieved what he himself regarded as "impossible" minutes
earlier. Thus the egg is called "square-round": he has
squared a circle, the impossible feat mentioned during the
chapter as one means he might employ to realize his
"ambition" (703).

In a pattern of symbols, allusions, and word-plays similar to, but more intricate than, that at the end of the six-

teenth chapter, Joyce has intimated the outcome of Bloom's story. And the intimation is not of success for one party and failure for the other, as it was in that case, but of success for both.

18 *the bed*

The final chapter of *Ulysses* is a representation of Molly Bloom's thoughts for a period of about a half-hour, the uninterrupted ultimate form of inner monologue properly designated "stream of consciousness." It seems to be a naturalistic slice of life, lacking real beginning and end; and it seems to have no more argument than form, to fail to advance the narrative of the novel or even to relate more than incidentally to it. Critical descriptions of the chapter make both these points [6] and liken it (admiringly) to the flowing river of life and the endless gyrations of the earth. Joyce himself asserted that the chapter has four "cardinal points" of meaning and that this argument is "expressed" in a form based on four recurring words, one for each "point." But the two critics of the novel to whom he apparently made his disclosure [7] were not given identical lists of words; and when he made it to the first of them, he wrote to his patron, Harriet Shaw Weaver, "Penelope has no beginning, middle or end." [8] Furthermore, not content with contradicting the assertion to the others that it has a coherent form and argument (achieved by means that are suspiciously both mechanical and ineffectual), he also denied in the letter to Miss Weaver that the chapter functions in the action and called the seventeenth chapter "in reality the end" of the novel.

Although statements Joyce made about *Ulysses* have been quoted a number of times in this study, they were selected because they confirm conclusions based on the text itself

and were selected from among countless others. It is well
known by now that he not only received invaluable help
from friends and admirers who served as readers and
scribes when his eyes were failing, but also shrewdly pro-
moted publicity about himself and his works as soon as he
had a following willing to be exploited toward those ends.
The assistance provided by his friend Claud W. Sykes (who
typed the completed parts of the manuscript of *Ulysses*
when a professional English-language typist could not be
found in wartime Zurich), his unstinting patron Miss
Weaver, and the selfless friend and aide of his last ten
years, Paul Léon, was in every case vital to his work and
career. But the reviewers, critics, memoirists, and biog-
raphers whom he encouraged and in some cases induced to
serve his reputation were not in this category, although
some of them were close companions. And it seems that he
reacted occasionally to their humorless adulation of his art,
and to the constant soliciting of "clues" and "hints" by
some of them, by making misleading, even outlandish, assertions. This situation is mentioned here because he made a
number of such assertions—which have become much too
well known—about the present chapter of *Ulysses,* and
simultaneously made some truly revealing remarks, sometimes to the same persons.

As the novel itself has been the corroboration for Joyce's
statements already quoted in this study, the eighteenth
chapter itself reveals which statements are sound and which
facetious or insignificant (that anything this most self-
conscious of writers said about what he was doing was
simply mistaken is unlikely). And what the chapter reveals
is that all the statements quoted above deserve to be disre-
garded as at best unimportant. There is no rendering of
form and theme through four "cardinal points," each "expressed" by its own word. Furthermore, although Joyce
was most revealing to Sykes and Miss Weaver about
Ulysses,[9] unless he simply misjudged his work both statements made in his letter to her are untrue. The chapter
does have "beginning, middle [and] end," in argument and
form both. It is no appendix but quite properly itself "in
reality the end" of the novel. It is not a "stream" in the
sense of formless psychological naturalism, although on
that presumption the chapter has been praised for forty

years and on that presumption about the novel as a whole
Wyndham Lewis denounced *Ulysses* in *Time and Western
Man*; rather this very chapter triumphantly refutes Lewis'
charge, for it embodies itself and completes for the novel
precisely that articulation, that formal pattern, which Lewis
justifiably insisted on in art.

My assertion that the chapter is both coherent and functional can be confirmed only by a full discussion of it.
However, the latter is suggested by two circumstances. The
first is the apparent similarity, so far borne out, between
the relationship of the sixteenth chapter with the first part
of the seventeenth, and that of the second part of the seventeenth with the eighteenth. The second circumstance is the
unresolved state of the novel's major action when Bloom
falls asleep—after he has raised certain issues which are
directly related to the resolution, and which are about to be
considered by Molly in its sole remaining passage.

This suggestion that the chapter is functional is reinforced by a more extensive consideration of the other assertion, that Molly's "unpunctuated monologue"[10] is coherent
in form and substance. The difference between stream of
consciousness and the more common inner monologue which
occurs in combination with dialogue and exposition is embodied in the word "stream": it is the verbal representation
of the pure, uninterrupted thought of a single character.
Molly's thoughts are rendered in simple language with the
phrases tumbling after one another in apparent near chaos,
and the chapter wholly lacks capitalization and punctuation
of any kind (controversy over whether or not it has a period
before the end is pointless, and those variously placed
in various editions are typographical errors). The typographical innovations are not capricious but justified. A
writer would only create an impediment to the literary
representation of pure thought if he employed along with
the words, which are unavoidable, the special symbolic
characteristics of written language. And the near chaos of
the discourse is only apparent. For example, the chapter
begins with a capital letter and ends with a period. In addition, it has eight parts, each indicated by a break in the
line (the erroneous periods in different editions occur at
these points) followed by an indentation **at the beginning**
of the next line, as with a paragraph of conventional prose.

Certainly, were Molly's thoughts truly haphazard, there would be little reason to divide them into clearly distinguished sections.

These facts, and Joyce's repeated mention of the chapter's eight "sentences" to friends[11] as well, point to some sort of definite organization of material—and so signify that the chapter contains meaningful material to organize. The tumbling stream of phrases is very simple reading except for one characteristic. As unconcentrated thought late at night well might be, Molly's is easily deflected from a particular subject, to return to it only after having explored the diversionary tangent. Thus, the chapter begins:

> Yes because he never did a thing like that before as ask to get his breakfast in bed with a couple of eggs since the *City Arms* hotel when he used to be pretending to be laid up with a sick voice doing his highness to make himself interesting to that old faggot Mrs Riordan that he thought he had a great leg of and she never left us a farthing . . . (723)

And Stephen's "aunt" Dante continues to occupy Molly until, halfway down the page, she returns to Bloom's one-time pretensions of illness: "if ever he got anything really serious the matter with him. . . ." However, the fact that she does make such returns suggests that her thought has specific subjects, is not simply the mental wanderings of an insomniac. For example, Bloom's request for breakfast has clearly puzzled her, and she reverts to it a number of times. It is only one step from the plain fact that she is not thinking about nothing in particular to the proposition that those particular things about which she is thinking are meaningful related.

Molly's wakeful state is caused by, is her response to, her husband's tribute, which awakened her with a feeling of "incipient excitation"; his late arrival; and his account of the day's activities. Her wakeful thought is dominated by these happenings and by the fact that Bloom has, for the first time since their residence in the City Arms hotel, a period during which Rudy died and their estrangement began, asked her to bring him breakfast in bed. A verbal representation of the thoughts with which Molly reacts to and reflects on her situation, the chapter is very properly called "Molly's soliloquy." And Molly's soliloquy is as functional in the novel as the stream of consciousness by which it is achieved, for the conclusion of *Ulysses* is whatever happens to be the estranged wife's attitude—positive, negative, or undecided and therefore negative by default—toward her husband's behavior and his attempted return.

The present chapter has structural integrity and a meaningful development because through it, from beginning to end, Molly *arrives at* her attitude—her stream of consciousness is not merely content but process. The content may be wandering and even contradictory, but the process of her uninterrupted thought endows it with relevance and meaning in the action. Actually, the chapter is a debate within her mind, between contending pro and contra elements. And much as the auto-debate that constitutes Hamlet's most famous soliloquy, with its conflict and resolution, is an action, so is Molly's.

Its popularity with people who regard the rest of the novel as too difficult—like the critical concensus that it is simple, chaotic, and, in any real sense, extrinsic—attests the subtle quality of the chapter's true nature. The historical result has been distortion of it into a highly spiced tour de force combining characterization of Molly with a vague affirmation of life, or sex, or womanhood, and into a source of emphatic statements by Molly's supporting almost any point of view on almost any subject, principally the subject of Leopold Bloom, with both fervent praise of him indicating that the novel ends happily and withering condemnation indicating that it ends unhappily—and with neither indication more than merely that. It has been distorted into a poor conclusion to a very long book.

Although less explicitly than "To be, or not to be, that is the question," Molly's deliberation begins, like Hamlet's, by a statement of the question being considered:

Yes because he never did a thing like that before as ask to get his breakfast in bed with a couple of eggs since the *City Arms* hotel when he used to be pretending to be laid up with a sick voice . . .

Bloom "never did a thing like that" since their estrangement began; and, furthermore, he had not even before then simply (manfully) asked her outright, but had feigned illness as a pretext. Should she honor this unusual, unexplained, and, in view of their relationship and Bloom's responsibility for it, wholly unjustified request, foregoing in the process the same matutinal pleasure, which she enjoys daily as a result of his guilty subservience, or should she not; that is the question.

Can this truly be the central subject of a meaningful final chapter of *Ulysses?* As a number of critics have pointed out, the serving of breakfast in bed on one morning is not itself sufficiently significant to indicate a fundamental change in the relationship between a man and a woman. But Molly, far from certain that she will honor Bloom's request, is concerned about more than her next morning's pleasure, for her deliberation involves every fundamental aspect of her relationship with her husband. Furthermore, there is a close correspondence between the status of his request at any point in the soliloquy and his own standing in her eyes, an indication that the matter of his breakfast is at least related to her attitude toward him and toward his assault on their relationship (for he does not want simply to be released from servitude, he wants uxorial service from her).

In fact, not only the action in the novel motivated by Bloom's request, that of the present and final chapter, but also the action which motivated it, signifies that the breakfast matter cannot be considered in isolation. He decided to attempt to return to Molly, expressed the belief that wives properly do domestic chores for husbands they love, used Molly's breakfast cream, and gave his distorted narration of the day's events before he finally "did . . . that." He probably remembered that one of Bello's dire threats had been that she "shall sit on your ottomansaddleback every morning after my thumping good breakfast." And although apparently unaware that he had recovered his manhood, he was undoubtedly fully aware of the change he was asking his wife to submit to in his final action of the novel, from the habitual morning routine which is a direct expression of their blighted relationship and by which he is introduced to the novel.

The result of important developments in the story of Bloom on Bloomsday, the motivation for the concluding episode in his story, and a pointed contrast to his first action in the novel, Bloom's last action is shown to raise a significant issue by two other facts. The first of these is that before the present chapter, except for the brief episode in the tenth chapter (city) in which she extended her arm out the window and threw a penny to the crippled sailor, Molly has appeared in the novel only as a virago who reclines in bed while her breakfast is brought her, and who orders imperiously:

> —Hurry up with that tea. . . . I'm parched.
>
> . . . .
>
> —Poldy!
> —What?
> —Scald the teapot.   (62)

The second is that the end of the last chapter both does not reveal Bloom's request and does intimate that he shall succeed in returning to Molly, using as the final element of that intimation the roc's egg, the big black dot. The withholding of knowledge of Bloom's action only to disclose it, by Molly's opening words about "breakfast in bed with a couple of eggs," as the subject of her deliberation links the unresolved matter in the novel—his return—to her soliloquy through the issue of his breakfast; furthermore, her words themselves link the breakfast to the roc's egg, symbol of his achievement of the impossible return. It would appear that Bloom, Molly, and the author all consider her decision vitally significant.

The request for breakfast in bed is both the principal manifestation of Bloom's attempt to win Molly back and the principal issue in the resolution of her attitude toward him and his attempt. But although the present chapter begins with the posing of the issue and ends soon after it is decided, it arises explicitly in only a few places; and although it is the most important element of the preceding action of the novel which is resolved in the chapter, there are many others. In other words, while it has been made a symbol and an index of the outcome of the story of

Leopold Bloom, it is quite properly not the sole meaningful subject of the deliberation that determines that outcome.

Molly's deliberation discloses that she too craves a return to the Blooms' former relationship and that she will honor his first essay in effecting that return. Before arriving at her conclusion, however, she deliberates vigorously, if unintentionally. Faring rather well at the beginning of the soliloquy, Bloom and his request are progressively eclipsed. Then certain of his positive characteristics occur to her, Stephen enters her thoughts in a significant way, and Bloom's breakfast and his destiny are secured. As this brief outline indicates, the soliloquy develops, *mutatis mutandis*, along a parabolic line. In terms of the chapter's eight divisions, Bloom's fortunes are fairly secure through much of the first section but progressively falling in the second to reach their nadir during the third, fourth, and fifth, and then rising again. One of Joyce's complaints about the seventeenth chapter occurs at the end of a letter to Sykes, in a passage which reads:

> Struggling with the aridities of Ithaca—a mathematico-astronomico-physico-mechanico-geometrico-chemico sublimation of Bloom and Stephen (devil take[?] 'em both) to prepare for the final amplitudinously curvilinear episode Penelope.[12]

The passage is interesting for a number of reasons. Sublimation is the chemical process of turning a solid directly into a vapor, and Joyce is using the term in its primary, technical sense to say that Bloom and Stephen are both dispatched from the novel and etherealized; he reveals a measure of weariness with their story; and he describes the manner of the seventeenth chapter. But its major point of interest is the words "amplitudinously curvilinear," which seem to allude to Molly but are explicitly applied to the "episode" itself: they indicate that he not only plotted a process of development for her thought, but plotted the parabolic development her chapter manifestly has.

This development of Molly's attitude toward Bloom from mild favor, through total rejection, to a crystallized full acceptance of him can be discerned from the following brief

résumé of the content of her soliloquy. At the same time
it presents in convenient form the larger contexts of specific
important passages discussed later. The eight sections of
the soliloquy are distinguished; their pages are indicated;
and each page of the chapter is represented (approximately)
by a full stop in the résumé, so that passages can be located
easily.

First section (723-29). Her surprise at Bloom's request
for breakfast in bed; the perverse behavior of old women,
and of men when they are ill; Bloom's having had a sexual
experience; his distorted account of his day's activities. His
extra-marital activities. Boylan's overture to her; the
pleasure of seducing a boy; Bloom's perverted questioning
of her "when I was knitting that woollen thing" (Rudy's
shroud); the joy of an intense kiss. Confession; Boylan
and their lovemaking. The trials of motherhood; the pleasure of having another child; the reasons for Bloom's apparent sexual ardor; a lovers' quarrel occasioned by Bloom's
attention to Josie Powell (now Breen). Possible rivals for
Bloom and the ease with which she could rout them; his
attractiveness to women; his extreme good looks when
young. His polite manner; the contrasting behavior of
Josie's husband, Denis Breen; the case of a woman who
had poisoned her husband for another man;

Second section (729-38). The first time Boylan saw her.
His admiration for her foot; Bloom's similar attitude; a
romantic incident involving Bartell d'Arcy, the tenor; her
intention "some day not now" to tell Bloom of this. An incident, before they were married, in which Bloom had im-
portuned her in the rain for sexual favors. An obscene letter
he had sent her following the incident; the impending tour
with Boylan. Bloom's association with the Sinn Fein; Lieutenant Gardner, a former lover. Shopping with Boylan in
Belfast; Boylan's affluence and handsome clothes. Their
own domestic indigence. Her meager wardrobe; prominent
femmes fatales. Bloom's poor job; a "rubbishy" dress she
bought because of him; her experience when trying to get
back for him a job he had lost.

Third section (738-39). Boylan's attentions to her breasts.
Nursing Milly; Bloom's manner and that of Boylan in con-

trast; her desire; her impatience for Boylan's next visit, three days away;

Fourth section (739-44). Bloom's sloppiness. Gibraltar; the goring of "those poor horses" at the bullfights. The departure of a family friend; the subsequent loneliness; her shabby nightclothes. Her father and his friend; boredom then and now. Thanksgiving to God for Boylan.

Fifth section (744-48). Her girlhood sweetheart, Lieutenant Harry Mulvey. Their lovemaking. More about Mulvey. Lieutenant Gardner. Favorable comparison of herself with a group of female singers;

Sixth section (748-55). Memories of childhood. Resentment of Bloom's request for breakfast in bed; plans for a picnic with Boylan and Mrs. Fleming (the domestic). Bloom's once swamping a rowboat; his grandiose promises before their marriage. Milly's behavior and habits (751-52). Bloom's bringing Stephen home unannounced. The advent of her menstrual period. Her removal from the bed and measures occasioned by her menstruation.

Seventh section (755-61). A pre-marital visit to the doctor indirectly caused by Bloom. Her first meeting with Bloom; his strange ways. Her return to the bed; their economic state; his vocational instability; his promiscuity and late return home. His request for breakfast in bed; the possible identity of his consort for the evening; his flirtatiousness; his social circle, and his superiority to the other members of it in familial responsibility. Ben Dollard's borrowing his dress suit; Simon Dedalus' singing; Stephen; Stephen as a child. Stephen's approximate age; Stephen and Bloom compared. The young poet, Stephen, as her lover; the question of Boylan;

Eighth section (761-68). Criticism of Boylan's crudeness and of his ignorance; partial amelioration of this criticism. Criticism of Bloom for neglecting to love her properly. Objection to his request for breakfast in bed; Rudy's death; the subsequent deterioration of their relationship. Gibraltar; plans for entertaining Stephen. Plans for serving Bloom breakfast; plans for tempting him, then telling him that Boylan completely satisfied her desires. Plans for allowing him to engage in his habitual sexual behavior as a reward for money and clothing; plans for marketing for breakfast and for flowers in anticipation of another visit by Stephen. The grandeur and beauty of nature; the contemptibleness of atheists; Bloom's proposal to her, and the first consummation of their love, on the Hill of Howth; Gibraltar. Gibraltar; the first consummation of their love, on the Hill of Howth, and her acceptance of Bloom's proposal.

Final confirmation rests with the chapter itself, but the evidence signifies that Molly's soliloquy is complete in itself, and that by representing her ultimate accession to her husband's attempt at reconciliation, it completes the novel. These facts were actually asserted by Joyce in a brief sentence in a letter to Frank Budgen: "[Molly's soliloquy] is the indispensable countersign to Bloom's passport to eternity." Budgen quotes Joyce in his book;[13] and elaborating upon Joyce's metaphor, he speaks of Molly as a passport officer who "retouches" Bloom's portrait, enumerates negative judgments she makes during the contra phases of her deliberation, and says, "Marion's visa on Leopold's passport will bring trouble on him in all the countries and mandated territories of eternity." However, the metaphor is to be apprehended as it stands. At the end of the seventeenth chapter, it declares, Bloom has secured a passport to eternity, has initiated a return to Molly and restoration of his family. But the passport is not valid as yet. A "countersign" (certification of authenticity) is "indispensable." In other words, Molly's endorsement of Bloom's final actions is necessary for the story to be complete: the last chapter of the novel is the cap to the action. Furthermore the requisite "countersign" is simply that, a signature, an endorsement, not a deposition; nothing less than the whole of Molly's numberless observations on Bloom and other thoughts—the coherent construct which is the chapter—is her "countersign."

My procedure in validating what has been asserted above about the novel's final chapter will be to discuss the significant developments in Molly's deliberation as they occur. Line as well as page references are given because of the crowded nature of the text; and because the meaning of individual passages is generally quite plain, where possible they are paraphrased and cited by page and line rather than quoted.

Ulysses is about the interinvolved stories of Leopold Bloom and Stephen Dedalus. But Molly, so instrumental in Bloom's—the major—story, dominating the conclusion of the novel, and elaborately portrayed through her soliloquy, is only slightly less important than the protagonists. Joyce uses much the same technique in portraying her as Chaucer does with such *Canterbury Tales* characters as the Prioress and the Wife of Bath. In the morning she is shown to be officious ("Poldy!"), vulgar ("having wiped her fingers smartly on the blanket, she began to search the text with the hairpin") and stupid ("—It must have fell down, she said"). This portrayal, which is sketchy, is not later refuted but, as with Chaucer's characters, is modified and augmented. Her officiousness is shown very soon to be a function of her relationship with Bloom and welcomed by him. At the end of the novel, her soliloquy reveals that although vulgar she is indeed, what has been taken for stupidity is a lack of education in a rather perceptive mind.

It also reveals that she is worthy of Bloom's devotion and of the fulfilment of a husband and son. Joyce's initial characterization of her is augmented significantly in his "portrait gallery" in the middle of the novel (city) in only one respect: he portrays her gesture of charity to the beggar refused by Father Conmee. Her kindness is revealed again and again in her soliloquy. Thinking about Gibraltar, for example, she is disgusted by the Spanish men and women who cheer as the bulls disembowel "those poor horses" at bullfights, and feels pity for a sentry, "poor devil halfroasted," and for "the poor donkeys slipping half asleep." This kindness, like her vulgarity and ignorance, is part of her dominant character trait, absolute naturalness, an almost ingenuous Weltanschauung that is nevertheless valid. She is thoroughly sensual, dwelling indiscriminately on details of Boylan's sexual efficacy and a fondly remembered dinner. And yet she is thoroughly devout. She says of her confessor, "what did he want to know for when I already confessed it to God," and recalls how Bloom made her cry "when he said about Our Lord being a carpenter." But her piety is made most clear when, thinking about details of her tryst with Boylan, she recalls falling asleep after his departure to be awakened by the thunder:

> God be merciful to us I thought the heavens were coming down about us to punish when I blessed myself and said a Hail Mary . . . and they come and tell you theres no God . . . (726:34-37)

In the fourteenth chapter (hospital) the thunderstorm was identified as:

> the voice of the god that was in a very grievous rage that he would presently . . . spill their souls for their spillings . . . contrariwise to his word which forth to bring brenningly biddeth. (390)

The rage of God at the spillers was unrecognized by Bloom and defied by Stephen. Only Molly, who had then just committed adultery and joined the ranks of the spillers, both recognized it and was contrite.

It is Molly's total naturalness that accommodates both carnality and piety, or both ignorance, dwelt upon at great length by Bloom in his last episode, and the perceptiveness he grants her even in the midst of his criticism. She is never out of the house during the whole novel; she is almost never out of her bed. She knows nothing of the world of men and values it at less than nothing. Politics, learning, medicine, metaphysics—all are summarily dismissed during the course of her soliloquy. Her conviction regarding the intellectual vanities of men, the wonder of nature (which includes the human body, emotions, and appetites), and the glory of God is eloquently expressed near the end of the chapter:

> all sorts of shapes and smells and colours springing up even out of the ditches primroses and violets nature it is as for them saying theres no God I wouldnt give a snap of my two fingers for all their learning why don't they go and create something . . . (767:5-9)

And the note of essential soundness that seems to persist in her ingenuous view of life indicates that Joyce holds her in high regard.

Ulysses concludes with Molly's "countersign" because it is "indispensable" to the completion of Bloom's story; that completion also depends upon a final disposition of both two general factors in his situation and the specific potentialities created in the latter part of the preceding chapter. The general factors are: his dream in which she is dressed in Turkish costume, invites his return, and announces a change; and the possibility that Boylan has impregnated her and reunion is therefore impossible. The unresolved elements of his final episode are: the indication in the urination contest that his attractiveness is superior to Stephen's and the accompanying astronomical representation of her gravitating from Stephen to him; the possibility, manifest in the list of lovers he draws up, that she cannot be monogamous, that he is one of "a series originating in and repeated to infinity" numbering twenty-five men besides himself to date; her apparent desire for a child (her reflection on the "limitation of fertility" imposed by him); the effects on her of his late return and distorted account of the day's events (which avoids mention of Gerty, exaggerates his "promptitude of decision and gymnastic flexibility" in entering the house, and focusses on Stephen and his invitation to him); finally, his request for breakfast in bed, the ultimate manifestation of his attempted return, representing all else that awaits final disposition in the novel.

Unless the sounding of the quarter-hours by the bells of Saint George's Church and the whistling of a passing train are so regarded, the only physical action of any kind in the chapter is the advent of Molly's menstrual period and its consequences: menstruation begins, she gets out of bed, she takes certain measures, and she returns to bed. By the very nature of Joyce's method in the chapter, some of her stream of thoughts must concern the church clock, the train whistle, and the menstruation. Some also touch on childhood, that is to say pre-pubertal, experiences. But all the rest, comprising a review she makes of aspects of her life as a nubile girl in Gibraltar, her life with Bloom and

the afternoon with Boylan, and her reflections on romantic
and sexual experiences and on the people closest to her,
father, daughter, husband—essentially the whole chapter
—belongs to its subject: Bloom's request and Bloom himself.

It has been pointed out that Bloom fares well at the
beginning of Molly's soliloquy. After her initial surprise
at his request for breakfast, Molly praises his politeness and
freedom from snobbery, and reveals that she is intensely
jealous of him. She infers that part of his account of his
day is "a pack of lies" fabricated to hide the fact that he has
had a sexual experience (723:40–724:2). Her deductions
fully establish her perceptiveness; but through them Bloom's
concealment of his sordid experience with Gerty works in
his favor, for she thinks that he has had normal sexual
relations with a woman and her jealousy is aroused. She
decides that he is not in love but has been with a "night
wom[a]n" or (correctly) "little bitch," and her perception
of "his appetite" for her (723:40-41) seems to reassure
her (that she should recognize this desire for her in the
present context is important); she recalls discovering him
in the act of writing his last letter to Martha and also mis-
conceives that sordid situation in his favor, saying "not
that I care two straws who he does it with . . . though Id
like to find out" (724:12-22); then turning to his relations
with Mary Driscoll, the oyster-pilfering former maid, she
says, "I wouldnt lower myself to spy on them the garters
I found in her room the Friday she was out that was
enough for me" (724:38-40). These manifestations of
jealousy, so positive in their significance, end temporarily
with another encouraging sign: her opinion that he was
attentive to the maid "because he couldnt possibly do
without it that long so he must do it somewhere" (725:6-7),
which reveals that she has been completely unaware of his
sexual debilitation.

At this point Molly turns to thoughts of Boylan, of the
possibility of seducing a boy, and of Bloom's perverted
sexual behavior with her. Still there is affection for Bloom,
because she wishes to spur his jealousy (725:39-40). After
recalling her fear when awakened by the thunderstorm that
it was God's judgment on her adultery, she reflects more
minutely on Boylan, principally on the size of his penis and

the possibility that he has impregnated her. She thinks of
the burdens of motherhood and then, having already observed that Boylan "hasnt such a tremendous amount of
spunk in him" (727:14-15), speculates on having another
child but "not off" him, assures herself that he "would
have a fine strong child," but concludes significantly: "but
I dont know Poldy has more spunk in him yes thatd be
awfully jolly" (727:29-32).

Following directly this new and highly germane expression of appreciation of Bloom, Molly experiences an access
of jealousy. He had told her during his distorted narrative of his meeting with Mrs. Breen, and she decides that the
former Josie Powell helped stimulate his sexual appetite
(727:32-34). After paying tribute to his knowledge
(728:3-6), she asserts her ability to effect a reconciliation
between them:

> I could quite easily get him to make it up any time I
> know how . . . I know plenty of ways ask him to tuck
> down the collar of my blouse or touch him with my
> veil and gloves on going out 1 kiss then would send
> them all spinning . . . (728:11-16)

She is right, of course. And although there are no mis-
tresses to send spinning, her knowledge that it is within her
power to reunite them is a promising fact. She proceeds
to thoughts about the possibility that his presumed affair
is with Josie, and as she is insisting on her indifference
states that she would searchingly inquire of Josie if she
loved him (728:16-20). She then thinks of an occasion on
which he almost, but not quite, proposed to her, expresses
approval of his self-respecting restraint, and thinks of the
attempts of other women, especially Josie, to win him from
her (728:21-38). This train of thought leads her to a reflection on his youthful handsomeness and Josie's envy of
her, and a comparison, which is to Bloom's complete advantage, with Josie's husband, Denis Breen (728:38–
729:22).

It is plain that Molly's attitude toward Bloom in this
first section of her soliloquy is distinctly positive. But this
is a far less stable basis for optimism than the things she

reveals. Her total ignorance of his sexual debilitation is chief among these.   Another concerns her romantic history and will be discussed below. Less reliable revelations, because like her attitude toward Bloom they are subject to change, are her expressed desire for a child, her jealousy, and the effect on her of his late return home.

Her attitude toward him is about to change.   The section ends on an ominous note: reflections on a woman who poisoned her husband, she presumes, because of another man; she feels that the threat of hanging was no deterrent because "if that was her nature what could she do," and that the authorities would not be "brutes enough to go and hang a woman" (729:26-38). The omen is immediately fulfilled. The second section begins with a review of her first meeting with Boylan and proceeds promptly to thoughts of two other lovers, Bartell d'Arcy, the concert tenor (730:29-36), and a person not mentioned before in the novel named Gardner (731:34-35), later revealed to be a British army lieutenant (733:40-41) transferred during the Boer war from Ireland to South Africa, where he died of fever (734:4-8).

Paradoxically, Molly's revelation of an additional man in her life discredits the general critical conception of Leopold Bloom's wife as a woman "of prodigious sexual appetite, who has been continuously and indiscriminately unfaithful to him." [14] That is based mainly on the catalogue of twenty-five former lovers which is one of the unresolved elements of Bloom's final episode (716); and the basis is a flimsy one, for the list was compiled *not by Joyce but by Bloom*. It is reasonable to simply accept the narrator's statement that in it he was presenting the "series" of lovers Bloom had in mind and that, as they did in so much of the chapter, his words communicated Bloom's thoughts. The reasonable assumption is confirmed by the existence of a lover not on the list, a lover of whom Bloom is ignorant but of whom an omniscient narrator, even a pedantic one, must be aware.

Bloom's list includes a bootblack, a farmer, two priests, and other unlikely paramours. It also includes people whose relationship to Molly is plainly disclosed during her soliloquy: Menton is a "babbyface" and a "big stupo" (724:4, 8), and he himself said earlier in the novel that he had danced

with her before her marriage (105) ; Pisser Burke is grouped
with Nosey Flynn as "that other beauty" (750:8) ; Pen-
rose is a medical student who boarded with a neighbor and,
on one occasion, "nearly caught me washing through the
window" (739:7-8) ; Mastiansky is a friend of Bloom
whom she mocks for his sexual perversions, revealed to her
by his wife (734:32-35) ; Lenehan, "that sponger," had
been "making free" with her (735:1-3) on various pretexts,
as he himself boasted early in the novel (231), during a
carriage ride; the occasion was the end of a dinner party at
the house of Valentine Dillon, the Lord Mayor, who was
"looking at me with his dirty eyes" (735:3-4) ; the "unknown gentleman in the Gaiety Theatre" had been looking
down from the dress circle into her low-cut gown while
Bloom discoursed to her on Spinoza, as Bloom recalled
early in the novel (280). Molly's soliloquy discloses various degrees of involvement with certain of the men listed.
For example, she had only pretended attentiveness to her
husband's disquisition at the Gaiety Theatre; as fully aware
as he of the stranger's interest, she had been cultivating
it (754:15-20). But most of them received an appreciative
glance or less.

This is not the case with three men in addition to Boylan,
the two who have entered her thoughts (d'Arcy and Gardner) and Harry Mulvey, the naval lieutenant whom she
had known as a girl in Gibraltar and whose name heads
Bloom's list. D'Arcy comes up in connection with one
incident; it is always possible that she had sexual relations
with him, but the incident was isolated and spontaneous,
she says of it only "he commenced kissing me," and it
occurred before Rudy and the deterioration of her marriage,
in a church after a concert (730:29-36). If Molly had any
real extramarital relationship in the past, it was with the
one man absent from Bloom's list and dates back from two
to five years. Furthermore, that relationship seems never
to have been consummated. She speaks of using the same
method to control Gardner's ardor that she had used with
Bloom during their courtship (731:34-35) ; although she
compares his ability to "embrace" favorably with that of
Bloom (732:15), the term is used literally; and in contrast
to her recollections of erotic experiences with Bloom, Boy-

lan, and Mulvey, she remembers nothing more intimate with him; she says of Boylan, "O thanks be to the great God I got somebody to give me what I badly wanted" (743:25-26); above all, she reveals on the third page of the chapter that that afternoon she committed adultery *for the first time:* reflecting on the frustration Bloom's perverse sexual activity with her engenders, she thinks, "anyhow its done now once and for all with all the talk of the world about it people make" (725:34-35).

Bloom's list of lovers is invalid, and one must turn to Molly's private thoughts for a true one. This would include Mulvey, d'Arcy, Gardner, and Boylan, if the word "lover" is used in the most inclusive possible sense. Of these her relationship with Mulvey antedates her marriage, that with d'Arcy was ephemeral and trivial, and those with Gardner and Boylan definitely occurred during the period of, and so were presumably the result of, Bloom's sexual neglect of her; finally, only with Boylan, a few hours before, did she commit herself to a full-fledged affair. To these facts, one more should be added: although her feelings for Mulvey had been intense, their love had never been consummated (746:5-7). Since she had married Bloom shortly after that girlhood romance and no man who might have entered her life during the brief intervening period is mentioned by her, it may reasonably be assumed that Bloom was the second man with whom she thought herself in love, and that the incident on the Hill of Howth during which he proposed and their love was consummated was a signal and unique experience in her young life.

Mulvey is gone, and Gardner dead, but Bloom is not therefore plagued by only one usurper. The point has been made that it is in Molly's mind that the suitors usurp his place and in her mind that they must be eliminated. However, the catalogue is much less extensive than it at first seemed, and Molly is by no means a promiscuous and insatiable whore but a robust woman "put away," as Malachi expressed it, by her husband. Bloom's "series" is invalid, and so is his belief that his wife cannot be faithful to one man.

At the end of the first section of her soliloquy, Molly thinks of the woman who poisoned her husband; and with the beginning of the second section and her thoughts about d'Arcy, Gardner, and Boylan, Bloom's standing diminishes markedly. She considers his petty lecheries (731:3–732:2) and, although she praises his courtship of her, compares him unfavorably with Gardner (732:10-15). Then she thinks of the tryst with Boylan and indicates in two ways that her lover is successfully displacing her husband: first, she expresses satisfaction that Bloom will not be going to Belfast for her concert because, should Boylan be in an adjoining room and Bloom press his perverted attentions on her, Boylan would object (732:35–733:2); then she associates the trip with the idyllic visit to Howth during which Bloom proposed and their love was consummated (733:15-19). Thus she entertains the idea of eloping with Boylan (733:21-22). Bloom enjoys some compliments for his cleverness, but Gardner reappears (733:40–734:9), and is followed by a long train of thought about Boylan, her tryst with him, and the finery which she will get him to buy for her in Belfast (734:16–735:27).

During this passage devoted to Boylan, Molly remarks that at one point he left her to buy a "stoppress" edition of the *Evening Telegraph* announcing the upset in the Ascot Gold Cup race. Bloom had heard the hawking of this edition just before being declared "cuckoo" at the end of the thirteenth chapter (strand-Bloom); and as Molly reveals, he had indeed already been cuckolded by Boylan. However, Molly's lover returned to her "tearing up the tickets and swearing blazes because he lost 20 quid he said he lost over that outsider that won" (734:40-41). Identified early in the novel with both Elijah and the racehorse in question, running the race in Stephen's fantasy as man, messiah, and horse combined, harshly affected by its outcome, Bloom is closely linked to the Ascot Gold Cup race. In the shelter he had remarked on the bet Boylan made for himself "and a friend of mine" (261) and lost, "Different ways of bringing off a coup" (633), and his connection with both further associates the race with the affair between Molly and Boylan: Throwaway's competitor, on which Bloom's competitor had bet, the phallic Sceptre represents not only Boylan's interest but Boylan himself. This passage in Molly's soliloquy is the final disposition of the

Throwaway-"throwaway" matter in the novel. She is speaking of Throwaway, but the horse was called an "outsider" a number of times before and is identified with Bloom; the word fits Bloom, not only in Molly's special racing sense, but also in the general one; and his social isolation was most fully manifest when the "throwaway" (messianic) and Throwaway (race) elements combined in Barney Kiernan's. As the Introduction to this study suggested, the totally unexpected victory of Throwaway over the favorite, which so enraged Boylan, signifies the ultimate victory of Bloom despite the heavy odds against him.

Furthermore, Bloom will win because of Boylan. The race was run at four o'clock, as Boylan was keeping his rendezvous with Molly but just *after* Bloom began to act in a unique way *in response to* that impending rendezvous. Ironically, Boylan never had a chance with Molly, the race had already turned in Bloom's favor; the phallic favorite cuckolded the dark horse but that very action was the immediate cause of the other's endeavor to win back his wife.

However, Molly is ignorant of the significance of the upset. Following her thoughts about Boylan's affluence and the things he will buy her, she thinks of the necessity for constant economy as Bloom's wife (736:8-16) and then thinks of his general lack of aggressive masculinity and business success and his inadequacy as a provider (737:8-16). These thoughts lead her directly to the conclusion of this second section, an account of her attempt to recover for him a job he had lost (737:16–738:3).

The tone of Molly's thoughts about Bloom at this point prepares the way for the very brief third section. It begins with examination of her breasts and reflections on Boylan's attentions to them (738:4-8), contains various indications of her years of sexual frustration, and concludes with an impassioned expression of sexual desire (739:20-22) and a paean to Boylan (739:32-33). Her fervid counting of the days to Boylan's next visit ends the section, and Bloom has been completely eclipsed.

The fourth section of the soliloquy centers on her childhood and adolescence in Gibraltar, and its principal motif is her present loneliness. Beginning with an expression of sympathy for the crew of the passing train, away "from

their wives and families" (739:37-38), it promptly turns
to a favorable comparison of Gibraltar with her subsequent
and permanent home (740:6-8). She thinks about her
father, a woman who mothered her (Mrs. Stanhope), the
woman's husband ("Wogger"), with whom she carried on
a childish flirtation, the bullfights, and stages in her physical growth. She observes sadly, "its like all through a mist
makes you feel so old" (740:40-41), recalls the departure
of the Stanhopes from Gibraltar, and reflects: "Lord how
long ago it seems centuries of course they never come back"
(741:31-32). As does Bloom, she associates happiness with
the past and with the East, and her sense of isolation is
similar to his. She complains of the lack of visitors and
mail (743:5-6) and even objects to Boylan's (probably
prudent) reticence in his letter of that morning. Nevertheless, she is able to forgive Boylan, and offers her thanks to
God for having, at long last, "somebody to give me what
I badly wanted" (743:25-26) just before the section ends.
Bloom is mentioned only twice in this section, first at the
beginning when she complains of his habit of saving old
periodicals, and then in connection with the lack of mail.
Neither occasion shows her attitude toward him, but his
absence from her thoughts and her vehement thanksgiving
to God for Boylan do so eloquently. At this point, midway
in the eight sections and almost the physical middle of the
chapter (741), the prospects for Bloom's breakfast and
destiny are at their nadir.

As the fifth section begins, Molly is still concerned with
letters (744:3-4), but she is immediately diverted to the
author of her first love letter, Mulvey. She reviews for
pages almost without interruption her meeting with him,
their romantic and sexual activities, his departure, and her
subsequent sadness. Then she thinks of the ring he gave her
as a keepsake, "that I gave Gardner going to South Africa
where those Boers killed him" (747:19-20). Following this
and another mention of Gardner (747:41), she thinks in
rapid succession about her husband, who is "fit to be looked
at" (748:5), Boylan (748:7), and d'Arcy (748:13-14).
Where Bloom stands in this roster of the men in her life
is indicated by one of the remarks with which the section
almost immediately ends, "I wish hed sleep in some bed by

himself with his cold feet on me" (748:20-21). Her unwitting pun on the "cold feet" with which his fantasy of
her mocked him in nighttown is directly relevant: he may
be presentable, but there is no point to his being in her bed.

Although Molly's remarks about Bloom in the sixth section are anything but complimentary, they are frequent—
he is returning to her thoughts—and they and a significant
occurrence signify together an upturn in his situation from
its depressed state in the past three sections. As soon as the
section begins, she complains about his nocturnal companions and exaggerates the lateness of his arrival home
(749:2-6). Then she comments sarcastically on his request
for breakfast and indicates the high regard which she has
for her matutinal privilege:

> then he starts giving us his orders for eggs and tea
> Findon haddy and hot buttered toast I suppose well have
> him sitting up like the king of the country pumping the
> wrong end of the spoon up and down in his egg wherever
> he learned that from and I love to hear him falling up
> the stairs of a morning with the cups rattling on the
> tray . . . (749:8-13)

Apparently, she would have to rise early and market in
order to honor his "orders"; and she is unwilling not only
to do that but to allow him to assume the pose of "the king
of the country," and forego her own privileges. She goes
on to plan a picnic for two couples, herself and Boylan and
her husband and Mrs. Fleming (749:28-29), and to think
of a relevant example of Bloom's bumbling (749:37—
750:4), regarding which she regrets—complementing his
guilt-motivated masochism—that she did not "flagellate"
him (750:4-6). She reflects, apropos of his new practice of
nocturnal carousing, that although she does not like being
alone in the house at night, "I suppose Ill have to put up
with it" (750:23-25), presumably because she cannot re-
strict his freedom in view of her own behavior. She thinks
of the grandiose promises he made her (750:29-35) and
expresses twice more her objection to his leaving her alone
and unprotected at night, "not that hed be much use"
(750:37-39; 751:6-12). Then, after a period of maternal

preoccupation with Milly, she remarks on his invitation and visitor and on his entry to the house, the very subjects exaggerated in his account (753:25-34).

It is at this point that the significant event occurs—the advent of her menstruation (754:6-11). She decides that it probably ruins her arrangement to see Boylan on Monday, but the fact of the menstruation itself overshadows this consideration: Boylan has not impregnated her, and she can accept Bloom back. A few moments later she expresses relief that "anyhow he didnt make me pregnant" (754:27-28), and although she turns to thoughts of her lovemaking with Boylan, the section significantly ends with her comments on the torrent of her menstruation.

As it has resolved the doubt about Molly's ability to love one man raised by Bloom's "series" in the last chapter, and as it has revealed the favorable effect (thus far) of his distorted narrative (suppression of his encounter with Gerty and extended discussion of Stephen and of his own "key-less" entrance) and late return in that chapter, Molly's soliloquy now also settles one general element of Bloom's situation, her possible impregnation by Boylan, again favorably. The other, his dream, has not yet come up in any way; nor have some of the unresolved specific elements of his final episode, which include, in addition to his late arrival and misrepresentations: his invitation to Stephen, the indication of the urination contest and the falling star that Molly shall prefer him to Stephen, her apparent desire for a child, and, of course, his request for breakfast.

But more important than either Molly's menstruation or the upturn in Bloom's status in this sixth section is the conjunction of these two facts. Molly says that Boylan's vigorous lovemaking induced her menstrual period (754: 7-8), and her thinking is physiologically sound. The causality is not only ironic but profoundly and significantly so. It was pointed out above, in the discussion of the association between the race at Ascot and the Blooms' domestic triangle, that Boylan's assignation with Molly precipitated the change in Bloom; now it has also precipitated Molly's menstruation, which not only is a good thing in itself but *marks the end of a cycle.* The fact that it is the only thing that happens to her in this critical final chapter of the novel, its intrinsic importance for Bloom's story, the fact that it ends a cycle, and the event that precipitated it—all suggest an analogy between the advent of Molly's menstrual period and the change in Bloom begun during the day by the same cause, and suggest that it symbolizes as well the end of a cycle of much greater duration. And that the symbolically significant occurrence coincides with renewed concern about Bloom confirms the suggestion.

The seventh section begins with Molly's fear that she has a genital disorder, which in turn leads to recollection of such a disorder before her marriage because of stimulation by Bloom and his passionate love letters (756:5-11). Her thoughts of Bloom's effective letters relate meaningfully to her reflections during the fourth section about the paucity of mail, her thoughts about Mulvey's love letter (her first), and Boylan's contrasting laconic note. She turns from his letters to Bloom himself, to the night of their meeting, recalled by him when Dedalus sang "M'appari" ("When first I saw thy form endearing") at the Ormond (271). Just as Bloom did, she confesses to having been attracted by him, "I dont know how the first night ever we met" (756:13-14). And the fact that her memory of her meeting with Bloom near the beginning of this next-to-last section of the chapter corresponds to her memory of her meeting with Boylan at the beginning of the second section indicates strongly that the chapter's "amplitudinously curvilinear" development is now an ascending one.

From these memories of her early love for Bloom, Molly returns to the jealous concern of the first section, his presumed amorous adventure of the evening (757:3-5). She follows this with a complaint like the extensive one in the second section—about their straitened circumstances and his lack of business success (757:12-26). However, there is a significant difference, another indication of a difference in the direction of his fortunes. Whereas in the second section she contrasted him to the affluent and commercially aggressive Boylan and thought of eloping with the usurper, here Boylan is not mentioned, and she again regards herself as Bloom's (neglected) wife: "God here we are as bad as ever after 16 years" (757:12). The church bells marking two forty-five cause her to revert to his late arrival and his

method of entrance, and her attitude toward his new social
habits undergoes a distinct change: she resolves to prevent
his nocturnal absence in the future and, mistakenly making
of Gerty and Martha one true mistress, to squelch his extra-
marital adventure (757:31-37). Her jealous resolutions
imply a willingness to adjust her own relationship with him,
and perhaps they are the cause of her turning immediately
to his request for breakfast:

> then tucked up in bed . . . then tea and toast for him
> buttered on both sides and newlaid eggs I suppose Im
> nothing any more . . . (757:39–758:5)

The tone of this third reflection on the request is not sur-
prised like that which began the soliloquy, or mocking like
that in the last section, but almost plaintive.

Following it, she expresses further the jealousy prevalent
at the beginning of the chapter and in the last few pages,
wondering once again if Josie is her husband's paramour.
She decides not and condemns his perennial skirtchasing
(758:14-24). Then she compares him favorably to his circle
of acquaintances, Kernan, M'Coy, Cunningham, Power,
Dedalus, praising him for his sense of responsibility to his
family in contrast to their sterile and alcoholic camaraderie
(758:35–759:4); in the process she expresses a perceptive
and tender concern for "my husband," vowing that the
others will not get him "again into their clutches if I can
help it making fun of him then behind his back." This train
of thought soon focusses on Simon Dedalus, and moves from
him to his son, the "salient point" of Bloom's "narration."
She first thinks of Stephen as a possible lover (759:29-35),
but then remembers that she last saw him as a boy when
she was mourning for Rudy, and recalls his appearance in
"his lord Fauntleroy suit" (759:35-42)—her thinking parallels Bloom's own view of him as both agent of "disintegration of obsession" for her and foster-son to himself. When
Bloom "narrated" about Stephen at such length before
falling asleep, he did not expect him to return, and he
apparently had no other purpose than to displace Boylan in
Molly's thoughts; but for her to be set thinking about a
possible son can only, in view of her resentment of the

"limitation of fertility" he has imposed and of her belief that he possesses virility surpassing that of Boylan, work in his favor.

However, Molly then settles on the view of Stephen Bloom had in mind for her. Stephen immediately begins displacing Boylan in her plans for a lover (760:1-11) and soon even eclipses Bloom himself in the area in which Bloom's standing with her was formerly secure, that of intellect (760:34-39). The section moves to its conclusion with excited speculation about an affair with Stephen, including plans to make herself deserving of him and reflections on their notoriety when he should become famous (761:14-22). Only with the very last words does she recall the virile lover who had been so prominent in the middle sections of her soliloquy: "O but then what am I going to do about him though" (761:22-23).

Bloom's status has distinctly improved in this seventh section. Molly's praise of his loyalty to his family, her jealousy, her memories of their early love, her plaintive comment on his request, the significant parallel to the second section—all indicate this. Stephen has become the focus of her thoughts, but this may be favorable too; the urination contest and falling star suggested that Bloom shall regain pre-eminence, and Stephen appears to be achieving the "disintegration of obsession" which Bloom had hoped to achieve with his sordid plot, and for which his extensive talking about Stephen was apparently a (not too promising) substitute.

The very beginning of the eighth and final section reveals that Stephen has indeed accomplished that disintegration, and one more element in Bloom's attempt to return has been resolved favorably. First Molly decides, with Stephen as her obvious standard, that Boylan has "no manners nor no refinement nor no nothing" and is an "ignoramus that doesnt know poetry from a cabbage" (761:24-27); then, unconscious of the pun being made on Bloom's name, she compares Boylan to a lion—facetiously (761:34-35); and after briefly tempering her condemnation on the grounds that his unrefined manner was caused in part by her own extreme desirableness, she dismisses consideration of the usurper completely from her thoughts.

At this point she launches an extended condemnation of Bloom, echoing the charge of "Junius" in the fourteenth chapter and Bloom's own acknowledgment of blame for their estrangement, and combines with it a declaration of her intention to have whatever relations she wishes with men (762:9-22); then she criticizes Bloom for his eccentric sexual behavior with her and speculates about approaching a sailor or a gypsy (762:22-42). Following these unfavorable developments, however, she once more mentions his request for breakfast. This time her attitude is neither surprise, nor scorn, nor plaintiveness, but a hollow-sounding bravado which also illuminates her talk of sexual license:

> and Im to be slooching around down in the kitchen to get his lordship his breakfast while hes rolled up like a mummy will I indeed did you ever see me running Id just like to see myself at it show them attention and they treat you like dirt . . . (763:15-19)

In keeping with this weakening of the forces within her opposing reconciliation with him, Molly now grants Bloom the victory portended in the urination contest and falling star: she begins to look upon Stephen exclusively as a son-figure, to think of Rudy, and to actively desire a son. She comments on Stephen's degenerate habits and observes, "well its a poor case that those that have a fine son like that theyre not satisfied and I none was he not able to make one it wasnt my fault" (763:31-33). Then she thinks of the death of Rudy and echoes in almost the same words Bloom's observation of the morning, "we were never the same since" (763:35-39). She continues to entertain the possibility of Stephen's staying with them (not in her own bed but in Milly's room), and even decides that Bloom might as well make Stephen's breakfast along with hers (764:41–765:4); but at this point her ostentatious resistance breaks down, and she indicates that she will accept his return. She decides to get his breakfast in the morning! Endowed with the significance delineated earlier, developed as it has been in her soliloquy, Bloom's breakfast, the central subject of the chapter, is now resolved in such a way that its meaning cannot be ignored—it is resolved in conjunction with the remaining unresolved general factor in his attempted return, his dream:

> Id have to get a nice pair of red slippers like those Turks with the fez used to sell ["he having dreamed tonight a strange fancy of his dame Mrs Moll with red slippers on in pair of Turkey trunks which is thought by those in ken to be for a change"] . . . Ill just give him one more chance Ill get up early in the morning . . . I might go over to the markets . . . who knows whod be the first man Id meet theyre out looking for it in the morning . . . then Ill throw him up his eggs and tea in the moustachecup . . . I suppose hed like my nice cream too . . (765:7-21)

Molly's talk of meeting men is only her pride tempering the fact of her compliance with Bloom's request. The important thing is that she will rise early and purchase, prepare, and serve his breakfast in bed, including the cream which had been her exclusive privilege until he manfully used it in his and Stephen's cocoa, and the moustache cup, the masculine utensil representing his "symposiarchal right" (666). Furthermore, she accepts the implications of her compliance, that getting his breakfast is giving him "one more chance" to be her proper husband, is extending her invitation to return and effect the "change" brought directly into the context by the author through her unwitting allusion to Bloom's dream. With the concurrent disposition of the breakfast matter and Bloom's auspicious dream all the elements of his attempted return have been resolved, and favorably in every case. The only possible improvement in the situation would be for Molly's "countersign" to his "passport to eternity" to be less grudging, for her guarded acceptance of him to become enthusiastic.

Immediately following her favorable decision, Molly experiences her bitterest resentment of Bloom's past sexual behavior toward her. She thinks of making plain to him that she has found satisfaction with, and he has been cuckolded by, Boylan. This she would do by "gayly" singing significant snatches from *"Là ci darem"*; the one she mentions, *"mi fa pieta Masetto"* ("I feel sorry for Masetto"), unlike the *"Vorrei e non vorrei"* of Bloom's *"Voglio"* and the other previous excerpt, *"Mi trema un poco il cor,"* occurs directly before Zerlina's capitulation to the Don. Then she would "start dressing myself to go out presto non son piu forte Ill put on my best shift and drawers let him have a good eyeful out of that" (765:21-25). At this point her righteous anger becomes vehement; she thinks of compelling Bloom to have intercourse with her (756:31) and declares bitterly, "its all his own fault if Im an adulteress" (765:33). Continuing her resentful planning for the morning, she determines to secure money for clothes from him and then gratify his customary perverse desires (756:38–766:11). When it occurs to her that she is menstruating, she decides that that is not unfortunate even though she will have to wear her old underwear, for he will be unable to know whether or not Boylan succeeded in cuckolding him (766:12-17), and concludes "so much the better itll be more pointed." However, the reader can hardly agree, can only deduce that the point she has just been planning so carefully to drive home will be blunted and that she is aware of this.

Furthermore, this thought marks the end of the bitter (and fully justified) resentment that accompanies her decision to "just give him one more chance" and get Bloom's breakfast. She decides that following his onanistic gratification, "Ill go out Ill have him eyeing up at the ceiling where is she gone now make him want me thats the only way" (766:19-20): she will leave the house abruptly, without indicating her destination, in order to "make him want me," *because* "thats the only way" to secure his complete return to her. And, as she has already decided, having mysteriously gone out and thereby begun to make him want her, she will return with the ingredients of his breakfast— will show him that he can have her.

She considers momentarily the possibility that Bloom may again bring Stephen home that day, makes her eloquent praise of nature and of God quoted from earlier, and begins the conclusion of her deliberation and the novel. That conclusion, about a page in length, first indicates what the precise agency of the Blooms' reconciliation will be, and then proclaims the fact and nature of Molly's desire for it.

The conclusion concerns Bloom's proposal of marriage to Molly and her response. It immediately follows her praise of nature and God:

> they might as well try to stop the sun from rising tomorrow the sun shines for you he said the day we were lying among the rhododendrons on Howth head in the grey tweed suit and his straw hat the day I got him to propose to me . . . (767:15-19)

And it is made a distinct unity by its symmetrical form: it proceeds from the fact of his proposal to a description of its circumstances, the idyllic situation on Howth hill on a day in June, from that description to one of Gibraltar in the spring, from that back to the idyllic scene of the consummation of their love, and finally to the answer to his proposal.

The agency by which the reunion of Bloom and Molly will be effected has actually been revealed already. She avers in the first section (728:11-16) that she "could quite easily get him to make it up any time" and mentions ways in which she could do so with such ease. And the reader knows even at that point, from Bloom's adoration of her and the change in him, that she is right. Now she asserts that she "got him to propose to me" on Howth and, elucidating his proposal, discloses that she always was able to exert the characteristic influence of the woman over her man:

> I knew I could always get round him and I gave him all the pleasure I could leading him on till he asked me to say yes and I wouldnt answer first . . . (767:25-27)

Furthermore, Joyce has shown us that she does not exaggerate her power by providing Bloom's account of the same incident:

> O wonder! Coolsoft with ointments her hand touched me, caressed: her eyes upon me did not turn away. Ravished over her I lay. . . . (173)

The conclusion indicates that the agency by which the Blooms' reunion will be effected is Molly's power over her adoring husband. It indicates this by focussing on the incident of the consummation of their love and by making plain that that significant event was caused by the same agency. Bloom has regarded the incident as the epitome of their past happiness, and his comparison of it and their present relationship has been an important source of his suffering. Now, having decided to effect a reunion with him, Molly thinks of it, concludes the novel with her thought of it and of how she brought it about. Finally, she reveals that it not only is associated with the idea of reunion with her husband, but for her, too, represents the ideal past.

That the incident on Howth is a symbol of a former happiness to which Molly as well as Bloom wishes to return is revealed by her association of it with that other ideal life in the past to which she has expressed a desire to return. Gibraltar, the East, has now become absorbed in her former happiness with Bloom, just as for him the Holy Land, the East, became so absorbed. Just as he does, she wishes:

> to reunite for increase and multiplication, which was absurd, to form by reunion the original couple of uniting parties, which was impossible. (711)

The roc's egg suggests that their mutual wish is not absurd, the formation by reunion of the original couple not impossible. And since a possible vehicle of "return" to that original couple is their respective memories of the couple's origin, and Molly has already resolved to effect a reunion with Bloom, the essential nature of this unified concluding passage of the novel is plain. Having progressed from her thought of Bloom's proposal to the circumstances of that proposal to Gibraltar, the passage develops from Gibraltar to the incident on Howth to her answer:

> and Gibraltar as a girl where I was a Flower of the mountain . . . and how he kissed me under the Moorish wall and I thought well as well him as another and then

I asked him with my eyes to ask again yes and then he
asked me would I yes to say yes my mountain flower
and first I put my arms around him yes and drew him
down to me so he could feel my breasts all perfume yes
and his heart was going like mad and yes I said yes I
will Yes. (768:10-18)

The conclusion is a *re-creation* of Molly's original passionate
acceptance of Bloom's love, a complete displacement of her
former grudging "countersign." She is saying an enthusiastic "Yes" to Bloom now as she did then, only while
then he was simply a desirable man ("and I thought well
as well him as another"), now she has to consider his bid
for reunion in the light of their long and mostly unsatis-
factory relationship and of her life before him and with
other men. Molly's soliloquy has resulted in the crystallization of her attitude toward Bloom, the arrival at "Yes" in
answer to his invitation: it has been the process by which
she realizes that she wants her husband back and decides, as
she did that June so many years earlier, to secure him for
herself. If *Ulysses* describes any cycle, the cycle is that of
the return of Bloom and Molly to the married state that
commenced almost precisely sixteen years before. And
Bloom's story ends with the imminent reunion of his family, ends, like that of Stephen, with his salvation.

This most important single fact in the novel is confirmed
in various ways, thoroughly removing any possibility of
ambiguity. First, the conclusion is introduced with what
turns out to be Molly's final observation on God and
nature, "they might as well try to stop the sun from rising
tomorrow," because that prompts her to remember a statement of Bloom's during the incident on Howth, "the sun
shines for you he said the day" (which she reconstructs
more fully a few lines down: "the sun shines for you
today"); the youthful Bloom's statement is directly echoed
in Molly's reverent declaration that the sun will surely
rise on the morrow, and the suggestion is that the explicit
"today," a day in June, 1888, of his proposal on Howth is
associated with her "tomorrow" (which has already arrived), with June 17, 1904. The sun will shine in the
morning as it shone upon their initial union.

Furthermore, having eliminated Stephen, whom he exploited to eliminate Boylan, Bloom combines with Molly's first love, Mulvey. It is he, not Bloom, who "kissed me under the Moorish wall." During the day, Bloom commented on the occasion and the effect on her of her first kiss: "Remember that till their dying day. Molly, lieutenant Mulvey that kissed her under the Moorish wall beside the gardens" (364). Now, as part of her revery of return which associates the two elements of the ideal past, Gibraltar and her early relationship with Bloom, Molly has confused her first love, at fifteen in May, with her second, that for her husband, only two years later in June. She both says that she was "a Flower of the mountain" in Gibraltar when actually Bloom had used the term on Howth and speaks of Bloom as the man whose kiss "under the Moorish wall" decided her "as well him as another." It is an understandable confusion, in view of the Gibraltar-Howth association she makes and the fact that she is now twice as old, but a significant one. D'Arcy, Gardner, Boylan, and Stephen have been displaced. With his absorption of Mulvey in the intensity of her memory of their early love, Bloom stands alone in Molly's thoughts at the conclusion of her soliloquy. Edmund Wilson says, "It is in the mind of his Penelope that this Ulysses has slain the suitors who have been disputing his place"; [15] and although there are fewer disputants than is generally thought, he is fundamentally correct. The point has been made that it is precisely in her mind that they had to be slain.

Finally, that Boylan, representing all future "suitors," has actually been conclusively vanquished by Bloom is indicated in the last words of the novel: "yes I said yes I will Yes." The repetition of "yes" has certain apparent significance: it is Molly's enthusiastic response to her vivid recreation of Bloom's proposal; it is, of course, expressive of affirmation, of a positive attitude toward life, although this point has been badly overstressed; it signifies sexual consent—the "yes" of a courted woman (in a fantasy in nighttown, the amorous apparition of Josie Powell leaves Bloom with a succession of yeses) ; her last word, Molly's "Yes" contrasts with her first word in the book, significantly

pronounced in response to Bloom's asking her if she wanted
anything special for breakfast, a muffled "No" (56)—and
the contrast recalls both the contrast between Bloom's first
and last actions and that between the mock Mass of Stephen's
opening scene and the true Communion at the end of his
story, and is, like those contrasts, significant of a total
change. What is less apparent, however, is that the last
words of *Ulysses* signify precisely that Bloom has displaced
Boylan as the Don Juan of "Zerlina." The transposition
Bloom enjoys from association with the betrayed to association with the beloved recalls his reading in *Sweets of Sin*
in the tenth chapter; significantly, the end of that novel
portrays an ambiguous "he" who complains to the adulterous heroine, so like Molly in appearance, "—You are
late," and its last words are, "An imperceptible smile played
round her perfect lips as she turned to him calmly"
(232-33).

At any rate, the beginning of the ubiquitous duet from
Don Giovanni is:

> *Là ci darem la mano,*
> *Là mi dirai di sì.*

"There," in his home, Zerlina will "give her hand" to the
Don, and there she "will say 'yes'" to him. Bloom had
been able to think of himself as Don Giovanni only in connection with Martha Clifford, had been obliged to fret
Masetto-like about the "pronunciation" of *"voglio"* with
respect to Molly. Now, however, Molly's projected singing
to him in the morning would seem to express not resentment but total capitulation to him as her Don: it is for
the jilted Boylan that she will have *"pieta."* The very last
words of *Ulysses* are: "I will Yes." Molly's capitalized
"Yes" is "sì," addressed to Bloom; and with "I will," she
discloses that she has learned to pronounce *"voglio"* correctly—to pronounce it to her husband. Although the race
on Bloomsday was a close one, the dark horse has secured
the victory.

1. Sigmund Freud, *Civilization and Its Discontents* (New York, 1930), p. 50, n. 1. Emer is supposed to have won Cuchulain by making the largest hole in the snow.

2. Indebted to Tindall, p. 30.

3. Quotations from Butcher and Lang, p. 374.

4. The narrator says the pantomime was "written by Greenleaf Whittier," but the reference is probably to one by E.L. Blanshard which was part of the standard Christmas pantomime repertoire; neither John Greenleaf Whittier nor anyone else of that name wrote a pantomime about Sinbad. Perhaps Joyce's erudition has failed him again.

5. See, e.g., Thackeray's *The Newcomes*, chapter xlvii.

6. See, e.g., Duff, p. 59, and Golding, p. 139.

7. Frank Budgen and Stuart Gilbert. Budgen quotes from a letter of Joyce's on pp. 262–63 of his book, and the complete letter is printed in *Letters*, pp. 169–70; Gilbert does not mention the source of his delineation of four "wobbling points" in Molly's monologue (Gilbert, p. 387), but the general and specific similarities indicate that Joyce was his ultimate, if not immediate, source.

8. The letter, dated July 10, 1921, is in the Yale University Library. The letter to Budgen is dated August 16, 1921. They were written while he was working on the chapter.

9. This conclusion is based on a reading of much of his correspondence, both published and unpublished. His reasons for sincerity are obvious: Sykes was typing the manuscript during the period he wrote to Sykes about *Ulysses*; and he was greatly indebted to Miss Weaver.

10. *Letters*, p. 206.

11. He made the point in letters to Miss Weaver, Valery Larbaud, and Frank Budgen. See *Letters*, pp. 168, 169, 170; and Budgen, p. 262.

12. See Chapter Ten, note 6. The word that Gilbert has transcribed from Joyce's difficult hand as "take" seems to be the meaningless (or portmanteau?) "fuke."

13. Budgen, p. 264. Budgen's comment is from the same place. The whole letter is in *Letters*, pp. 159–60.

14. Wilson, p. 195.

15. *Ibid.*, p. 202.

conclusion

Just as the form of *Ulysses* is not mechanically contrived, the audacities of its manner not arbitrary, and its characters and action not static and futile, so the import of the novel is not the pessimism or cynical disdain an art with such qualities would have expressed. Neither is it a simple optimism about the human condition and a genial affirmation of life. Furthermore, a reader of so rich and subtle a work of art, which implicates figures and situations from Hebraic, Christian, Celtic, and Hellenic myth as well as from high, folk, and popular culture, but which addresses itself directly only to what happens to two particular Dubliners, projects general conclusions about that work at considerable peril. For this reason I offer my conclusions in this last chapter with less confidence than I have in the specific observations of previous chapters, even though I believe them to be valid.

The most prudent starting point is the most appropriate, the two subjects of the novel themselves. The person named in its title is Bloom. A timid man mildly despised by his peers in a modern middle-class urban society, he nonetheless acts *mutatis mutandis* like Odysseus in pointedly corresponding situations. If he falls below the Achaean hero with respect to his cattle of the sun, he rises above him in dealing with his Cyclops. He is ultimately as resourceful and brave in the den of his psychological Circe and as successful in returning to his home and dispatching the usurpers of his place. Joyce insists by his method that *Ulysses* is a novel with a hero, in the fullest sense of that word.

The point must be emphasized because Bloom is so far from being a hero through so much of the book. At the end of the episode in the maternity hospital, the voice of "Carlyle" praises Doady Purefoy, the ideal father contrasted to Bloom, for acting ("With thee it was not as with many that will and would and wait and never do") not only to express the ventriloquist Joyce's approval of fatherhood with Thomas Carlyle's vigorous assertiveness but also to signify that Purefoy is in a sense the hero as citizen. In other words, the philosopher's style is not merely a useful mask; his thought is intrinsic to the point being made in the contrast drawn between the two men. Bloom must not only become a husband and father like Purefoy but must do as the "pure in faith" does in order to realize that end: he must act, assert himself, alter circumstances by his will. And that would be to affect history and so to become a hero in Carlyle's terms.

On the other hand, through most of the book, Stephen cannot—and his willingness to try right up to the climax contrasts exactly with Bloom's reluctance to do so—alter the circumstances that concern *him* by his will. Stephen is not loath to act, and he is courageous, but his proper course is not heroism: Carlyle's heroic philosophy is invalid for him. Although *Ulysses* has a true hero, it has only one. About the proclamations and deeds by which Stephen defies God, truly heroic actions, the significant thing for the story of Stephen Dedalus is that they are totally wrong. In his own words at the end of the first part of the novel, he must learn to "cease to strive."

S. Foster Damon's brilliant early essay contrasts Stephen's "*Non serviam!*", his "warring in vain against the Things That Are," with Bloom's attitude of submission.[1] And critics have asserted that Stephen "rejects the actual for daring to fall short of his vision," [2] and that "the man who will not assent to the conditions of life is damned." [3] However, the contrast between them is not to Bloom's advantage. Although it was on his brief youthful stay in Paris that Joyce copied into his notebooks the observation of Aristotle's, "That which acts is superior to that which suffers," he was not being puerile, for common sense says that submissiveness can be at least as much of a fault as its extreme opposite; and the novel itself makes clear that Bloom's benighted submission is by no means a standard against which Stephen is to be measured.

A more fundamental error in such judgments of Bloom and Stephen is that they are final ones, that they are based on a conception of the two characters as static: on a conception of the nature of each as it is through most of the novel as the total truth about him. In fact, the contrast between them does not prevail, precisely because they do change. The first of the general conclusions I have drawn from *Ulysses* is one about the significance of the changes in its two subjects.

That those changes have special significance is suggested by the fact that the whole novel really balances on them. Its action is, in the most basic sense, psychological. Boylan is no villain but merely the necessary third point of a triangle inevitably created by Molly because decreed by Bloom, his own villain. And however much Mulligan may be or symbolize the Villain, he is not Stephen's antagonist. As the novel begins, Bloom is an exile who wishes to return, Stephen a captive who wishes to escape. In nighttown, each comes to a realization of what he must do, how he must change. Thereafter the hero Bloom wins out against the villain Bloom in his inner conflict; and in contrast to the originally submissive Bloom's case, the captive hero Stephen achieves his good fortune by becoming a willing victim in the sacramental sense. Although with the manifest assistance of divine grace, at the end of the novel the captive submits and so is able to "depart," and the exile acts and so is able to "return."

Bloom's original benighted submission is not a standard against which Stephen is measured, yet it is a model for him. The actual case presented in *Ulysses*, its basic conceptual principle, is that both of its subjects are headed for catastrophe and that each must adopt as a model for correction the wrong conduct of the other. They are analogous to Othello and Hamlet. Had either of those contrasting characters been in the other's situation, he would have dealt with it easily; neither the warrior nor the intellectual is an ideal; and each in his situation brings catastrophe on himself. However, Joyce's characters correct their catastrophic faults during the novel and are saved.

Like *Crime and Punishment, Ulysses* is concerned with the classical polarity of will and circumstance or self and world in human existence, and presents characters who are living at one extreme or the other.[4] Reduced to simplest terms, the novel tells the story of the salutary and timely abandonment of his particular fateful extremity by each of its two subjects. Apparently, the basic conceptual principle of Joyce's long complex story of Bloom and Stephen was formulated and expressed by a saint of the Church three hundred years before Joyce created it. A prayer attributed to Francois de Sales, who happens also to be the patron saint of writers, runs:

> God grant me the serenity to accept the things I cannot change, the courage to change the things I can, and the wisdom to know the difference.[5]

Saint Francis' prayer expresses perfectly not only the design of, but also the primary moral embodied in, the careers Joyce created for the two subjects of his novel. And my beginning this chapter with Bloom and Stephen is not only prudent and appropriate, but for this reason convenient as well. Through the agency of the prayer, my second general conclusion about *Ulysses* gains credence from the first—and it is not easily made credible.

There is a sense in which every major work of art may be said to be religious. But, although in both his life and his work Joyce consistently rejected any organized church, I have concluded that *Ulysses* is a religious novel precisely as *Crime and Punishment* is a religious novel: explicitly and literally devout. Joyce's consistent antisectarian position can easily be reconciled with this thesis: the novel need only represent the fallen churches (as I believe that both it and *Finnegans Wake* do) as imperfect ways to a truth (God) which its author accepts and finds good. To demonstrate the validity of my doctrinaire, and in our day suspiciously modish, thesis is more difficult.

Ulysses asserts that Bloom's only salvation is in becoming a proper husband and father again, and provides not only personal and social but also explicitly religious grounds for the assertion; and Stephen quite simply must achieve a state of grace, in precisely those terms, through reverence for God. The essential problem of each has a religious aspect, and the resolution of that problem a religious value. If this were the only basis for my conclusion, it could be argued with respect to Bloom that the allusions to the prophet Malachi and the "pure in faith" are solely functional devices of exposition. Such an argument would not hold for Stephen even then. His story is too explicitly what it is. Indeed, the revelation in the action of the novel that enables him to escape his predicament (that Bloom is the deliverer promised him in his dream) is also a revelation in the strict religious sense. And, of course, the religious dimension of the characters' problems is not the only basis for my conclusion. In fact, it gains further support from the nature of the event that makes Stephen's revelation possible, the fulfilled dream-prophecy, as well as from an event of corresponding significance for Bloom. *Ulysses* presents, as an instrumental factor in the ultimate rescue of its protagonists, direct divine intervention in events—that is to say, miracle.

Stephen had a dream of rescue and escape just before the beginning of the novel, and Bloom had one of invitation and return. Both dreams are fulfilled in the action. The tone of the novel provides no basis for regarding that fulfilment as gratuitous or ironic accident. In fact, common sense dismisses even the possibility of so much coincidence, signifying such pointless irony, articulated in such climactic developments in the action. The conclusion seems to me inescapable: God announces, almost simultaneously, to each character the circumstances that shall attend his rescue and those circumstances promptly, almost simultaneously, occur.

Stephen's dream has so instrumental a role in the action of the novel that the ultimate fulfilment of its promise cannot be seen as merely signifying that dreams are sometimes prophetic; Bloom's dream, however, is not instrumental in the action. The event in his story that corresponds to Stephen's dream, the instrumental direct divine intervention that Joyce presents, is the concurrence of three events on the very day following the dream: the victory of Throwaway in the Gold Cup at Ascot, Molly's consummation of her affair with Boylan, and Bloom's meeting with Stephen. Throwaway's victory causes the revelation of Bloom's messianic power and is associated in the novel with that power, with his rescue of Stephen, and with his victory over Boylan. As are the dreams, the Throwaway-"throwaway" matter is external to the plot, in the strict sense, to the actions of the characters—it simply happens; as are the dreams, it is directly linked with the fortunate outcome of their predicaments; and as is Stephen's dream for him, it is instrumental in Bloom's story. There have been many ingenious and some absurd speculations about the reason for Joyce's choice of June 16, 1904, as the day for the action of the novel. The only reason for the date of Bloomsday that is in any way functional in the novel would seem to be the historical fact that a horse named Throwaway, a dark horse, in an upset that made the race a memorable one, won the coveted Gold Cup away from the famous Sceptre at Ascot on that day in that year. This alone of the public events of the day enters into the action of the novel. And because it does, its inclusion is not simply a matter of Joyce's historical realism. If an actual event which is not only unusual in kind but unique in nature (the name of the historical "dark horse" is vital) is instrumental in a fictional story, the implication is that the outcome of that story could have been what it was only as that event permitted. Bloom's story could have developed as it did only on the *very day* represented; and so, if the victory of Thowaway is not another absurdly ironic coincidence making all the action that depends from it pointless and crude, the hand of God guided the developments of Bloomsday that led to the hero's success and the deliverer's fulfilment of a young man's dreamed promise. Despite the rarity of such elements in literary works in recent centuries, two fundamental elements in the action of *Ulysses* are presented as miracles in the most literal sense.

WHEN *Ulysses* is seen to be a religious portrayal of the human condition, plausible conclusions about both the general philosophical affinity that Joyce expresses in it and the fundamental aesthetic out of which it was written suggest themselves. Like Odysseus, Bloom is 'Outis-Zeus, has within him the broadest potentiality; like Odysseus, his tribulation comes when he denies his God-like qualities; and much more explicit than does Homer, Joyce identifies the (eventual) heroic conduct of his Ulysses with an assertion of those qualities by the hero. What Joyce implies is a simple and familiar idea: man is an animal, yet he is created in the image of God; and each individual himself determines which of these antithetical facts about him dominates his existence. However, Joyce pushes the doctrine to its extreme, for he applies the pun on Odysseus' name to Bloom as literally as possible. When Bloom is his own villain instead of the hero, correspondent of Martha Clifford and follower of the bovine haunches of the neighbor's servant, he is the spiritually worthless Mister Nobody. On the other hand, the ascendancy of his heroic nature is neither more nor less than the realization of the divine in himself. Joyce neither claims divinity for Bloom nor denies it to Christ, but he asserts that Bloom's potentiality as a man is so great that when he fulfils it he is legitimately associated with Christ and Elijah.

The two philosophical assertions hitherto inferred from the novel are that a man must know the extent of his freedom to affect circumstances and must act accordingly, and that the world is ruled by God, actively, even to the extent that miracles occur in it. In the light of these, the former of which was anticipated by a humanist priest of the Renaissance, Joyce's assertion that man is potentially an exalted being indicates his general philosophical affinity in *Ulysses* with a familiar world view developed during the Renaissance, religious humanism. In a book called *The True Humanism*,[6] the French Catholic philosopher Jacques Maritain distinguishes between "theocentric" and "anthropocentric" humanism. Of course, he considers the former to be "the true humanism"; and although his judgment is controversial, Joyce seems to agree with it. Maritain's distinction is not between a religious creed and an explicitly

agnostic or atheistic one, but, as his terms suggest, between
a humanism that considers God the source and center of
all that man can achieve and one that does not accommo-
date God at all. The secular humanism, he says, causes
man to

> exalt his own proper movement as creature to the dignity
> of the first absolute movement and to attribute to his
> own created freedom the first initiative towards good-
> ness. Thus his movement of ascension has necessarily
> been separated from that of grace. . . .[7]

The similarity to the situation of Stephen as a young man
is striking.

Joyce himself, however, with his enthusiasm for life,
exaltation of the individual, intellectual avidity, also "recognizes that the center for man is God"—is a theocentric
humanist. He is more like the men described by M. Maritain
as closest to his conception of true humanism, men who
combined the qualities of the humanist with an intact
devoutness, maintained a tension between the limited
Christian world of the Middle Ages and their own essentially modern age—the men of the Renaissance[8]—than he
is like the men of what Maritain calls "our culture."

In comparing the two cultures and the two kinds of
humanist, Maritain is exploring the theological and historical aspects of a phenomenon whose aesthetic aspect has
been an important subject of modern literary criticism. The
intensity of our modern interest in this phenomenon and
in the age that presumably experienced its advent is itself
a prompting to caution; and generalizations about a highly
complex culture and its equally complex art are almost
destined to be partly specious in any case. In the following
paragraphs I quote some generalizations which seem to me
as sound as such things are likely to be, in order to make
some connections which seem to me meaningful.

T. S. Eliot's "dissociation of sensibility," the separation
of thought and feeling in poetry, is in some sense the
complement in art to Maritain's "our culture," the dissociation of reason and belief in metaphysics. And the men
who, prior to that dissociation, had the unified sensibility

of which Eliot writes were Maritain's theocentric humanists
of the Renaissance, who were able to reconcile humanism
and faith. The literary critic M. M. Mahood discusses Maritain's concept of two contrasted humanisms (adopting his
designations of "false" and "true") in a book called *Poetry
and Humanism*,[9] and then uses the idea of the "true humanist" as the rationale for a study of English Renaissance
poetry. Miss Mahood says:

> For over two centuries [the triumphant modern] false
> humanism ran parallel to a true humanism which, by in-
> tegrating all new achievements and discoveries with the
> central tenets of the medieval faith, led the greatest of
> sixteenth- and seventeenth-century artists to "the highest
> reaches of the human wit." . . .
> . . . The English religious poets of the seventeenth
> century . . . sought to restore the balance of a true form
> of humanism. They did not attempt to put the clock
> back, as the Tractarians were to do two centuries later.
> Instead, they enlarged the medieval notions of corre-
> spondence between the natural and spiritual worlds to
> accommodate every new discovery—the circulation of the
> blood, the motion of the earth, even the plurality of
> worlds.[10]

In discussing "Style in *Ulysses*," I presented specific
precedents and sources for the three kinds of special
stylistic devices in the novel and attempted to show that the
strategy of its style is an exceptional example of new
developments in fiction at, and immediately after, the turn
of the century. The fundamental aesthetic out of which it
was written, however, is suggested by neither of these
considerations. It is suggested by that essential characteristic of its style, elaboration. And it is suggested by a
quality of Joyce's character and work recalled by Miss
Mahood's statement "they enlarged the medieval notions of
correspondence": his almost compulsive respect for correspondences, discussed in "Joyce's Dublin and Dublin's
Joyce."

The relationship between this aesthetic and Joyce's philosophical affinity with the theocentric humanists of the
Renaissance seems to me as direct as that which Miss

Mahood draws between the art and the world view of certain of those men. His unremitting elaboration in the novel recalls a name borrowed by literary historians from the plastic arts for the writers she has in mind ("Donne and his followers") and others of the Renaissance: "baroque." One critic's conception of the "philosophy" and "aesthetic" of English baroque poetry and prose provides a good description (there may never be a definition) of the baroque quality:

> "Baroque" shall name such English poetry and prose antedating the neoclassical movement as would, by neo-classical standards, be judged "false wit." It subsumes the poetry of Quarles, Benlowes, Cleveland, Crashaw, and Donne; the prose of Andrewes, Browne, and Burton. Its philosophy is Christian and supernaturalist and in-carnational, a philosophy admissive of miracle and hence of surprise; its aesthetic, by appropriate consequence, indorses bold figures, verbal and imaginal—such figures as the pun, the oxymoron, the paradox, the metaphor which links events from seemingly alien, discontinuous spheres. It likes polar mixtures—the shepherds and the magi, the colloquial and the erudite. If it provides ecstasies, it allows also of ingenuities: anagrams and acrostics and poems shaped like obelisks or Easter wings.[11]

And a more extensive discussion of the style of baroque poetry in general by the same critic, Austin Warren, and René Wellek, is a discussion *mutatis mutandis* of the style of *Ulysses* as well:

> In the Baroque period, characteristic figures are . . . Christian, mystical, pluralist. . . . Truth is complex. . . . Some kinds of truths have to be stated by negation or calculated distortion. . . . The Neo-Classical mind likes clear distinctions and rational progressions. . . . But the Baroque mind invokes a universe at once of many worlds and of worlds all, in unpredictable ways, connected.[12]

Attempting to determine "the motives behind the Baroque practice," Mr. Wellek and Mr. Warren once again describe a literature of elaboration and correspondence:

. . . Its wider inclusiveness, its taste for richness over purity, polyphony over monophony. More specific motives are the appetite for surprise and shock; . . . pedagogic domestication of the remote by homely analogy.[13]

Finally, Warren explains of baroque poetry, the art of the Renaissance true humanists of unified sensibility about whom Maritain, Eliot, and Miss Mahood wrote:

a fully supernatural and sacramental conception of the world, a view which holds that miracles still occur in history, is the philosophy which best validates it.[14]

Ulysses seems to be a work of art whose aesthetic is manifest and is mated to its philosophy.

Bloom and Stephen turn from error to the right path. Although Stephen achieves "the serenity to accept the things [he] cannot change" and Bloom "the courage to change the things [he] can," the hand of God is manifestly instrumental in their salvation. Finally, Joyce's view of man and the world is that of the men who flourished in the Renaissance, whom Maritain calls true humanists; and his art is in the tradition of those men as we have come to know that tradition in Western literature, and as Miss Mahood, Eliot, Warren, and Wellek describe and explain it.

Harry Levin quotes Joyce as saying, "If there is any difficulty in what I write it is because of the material I use. The thought is always simple."[15] Joyce preaches the preservation of the family, acceptance of what must be accepted in life, right action where it is possible, the everyday existence of miracle, the goodness of God, and the great potentiality in man. His view of life is not only genial, it is sanguine. Life offers love spiritual and physical, food, learning, fun. Man can help himself. And God will take mercy on him and help him.

Ulysses is a comic novel in the sense that it depicts a reconciliation rather than an irrevocable rupture between man and life: Bloom and Stephen correct and adjust to

their situations. It is a religious novel as well. Joyce does
not leave implicit the force that effects the comic conclusion.
The world he portrays has a moral and religious foundation.
The path of virtue must be striven for by Bloom and
Stephen; and once reached, it leads directly to rescue; this
is moral statement in fictional terms. The hand of God is
explicitly represented as aiding Bloom and Stephen; this is
religious statement.

Ulysses is a comic novel and a religious novel, but it is
not a sentimental novel. There is no statement of facile
optimism. Purefoy is the only man "pure in faith" until
finally Bloom and Stephen are regenerated and so join him.
Their story has a "happy ending." But the world in which
they live is depicted as headed for the destruction prophesied
by Malachi at the end of an earlier civilization. It is a world
of ignorance, bigotry, sterility, chauvinism, cruelty, materialism. Bloom is superior to it, and Stephen finally succeeds in
escaping it, but essentially all of Dublin remains loyal to it.

I have saved for last the unavoidable question of autobiographical statement in *Ulysses* because of my awareness
that it is also in a sense unanswerable. The general conclusions presented above can be tested by reference to the
novel itself, a definite although difficult composition of
words; conclusions about an author's personal divulgings
in a work of fiction can never be proven, and Joyce is
subtle and elusive. Nevertheless, I believe that he is making
a statement about himself in *Ulysses,* and that it embellishes
both his novel and his life story.

It has been pointed out that the maudlin young man and
papier-mâché artist Stephen Dedalus is very different from
the "Sunny Jim" Joyce who spoke and wrote about literary
and cultural questions, and who was published and listened
to with respect. Although the same age as Stephen, Joyce
was a promising young *fin de siècle* man of letters on June
16, 1904. In addition to his Ibsen essay and other prose
pieces, he had written a number of delicate poems which
had been praised by Yeats and Arthur Symons and had
been appearing in print. The rejection of his lyrical essay
"A Portrait of the Artist" by the editors of *Dana* had

caused him to begin work four months before[16] on the novel he was to entitle *Stephen Hero,* and he had made good progress on it by that date. Nevertheless a significant similarity between character and creator does exist.

The young Joyce's work was much more consistent with his expressed attitudes toward society, the artist, and the relationship between the two than with his professed artistic principles, for it was solipsistic, escapist, and lovely. His assertion of the importance of faithfulness to reality in his essay on Mangan is professed principle, but the Paterian prose in which that is couched is artistic commitment. The poems that were to compose the volume *Chamber Music* and the equally elegant, elliptical, and euphonious autobiographical "portrait" of that period were precisely *fin de siècle:* they were the work of a young aesthete. Furthermore, as different as it is from the lovely lyrics and essay, and although in writing it Joyce professed the sound principle, especially for fiction, of "converting the bread of everyday life into something that has a permanent artistic life of its own,"[17] *Stephen Hero* is blighted by the self-centeredness of the aesthete who was its author.

The problem of "converting" material into art is different for the poem and the essay from what it is for fiction, and on the whole Joyce's literary and personal essays are interesting, if overripe, period pieces, his poems pretty if slight. However, through the completion of *Ulysses* in his fortieth year, his valuable work was in fiction; to judge from the fragment and from his opinion of the whole novel, *Stephen Hero* is not valuable fiction; and its failure is his own failure at that time to make a "dramatic" work (in his term), a work freed from the personality of the artist, autonomous in its form and its life. Stephen was a sterile aesthete before Bloomsday; although far from sterile, Joyce was also an aesthete. And when he began to write fiction, in which he was later to fulfil his genius, he proved to be precisely the way Stephen was, unable to deal with reality (at least as artist), to work like "the man with the hat" in Chapter IV of the *Portrait* and create "out of the . . . earth a . . . soaring . . . being."

He was first able to do this in the short stories of *Dubliners.* In them he did achieve his professed aim of "converting" (transubstantiating with the God-given hieratic power of the artist) the "bread" of the particular reality he knew into universal "dramatic" art; with them began the fulfilment of his genius as an artist of fiction. And the first of those stories, "The Sisters," his first successful work of fiction, was begun and promptly completed in July of 1904.[18] It was followed by two more, "Eveline" and "After the Race," in a series (of ten) projected in July.[19] On August 13, less than two months after Bloomsday, "The Sisters" was published in the *Irish Homestead* under the pseudonym "Stephen Daedalus."

Prior to the early summer of 1904, then, Joyce had written and published, but he had been unable to write in the way that realized his full powers as an artist. Furthermore, with even greater similarity to Stephen, he had been unable to return to the Continent since his mother's death in August, 1903, despite his belief that emigration was necessary for his development and his personal well-being. At the end of *Ulysses*, Stephen Dedalus no longer wishes to express hostility toward God's world and way through "Carnal Concupiscence"—he is freed from the nets within himself that had snared the would-be man and artist and is enabled to leave his family, his Church, and his country to pursue the artist's calling in that independent way of life. On October 8, 1904, between the appearance in the *Irish Homestead* of the second and third stories of his first major work, James Joyce left Ireland for the Continent with a young woman to spend the rest of his life there as a dedicated writer and devoted husband and father. The destiny promised for Stephen at the end of *Ulysses* is that which Joyce himself had realized immediately after the time of the novel.

That Joyce began to fulfil himself as man and artist in the ways and at the time his character had been freed to do so is historical fact. Of course, this fact does not of itself signify that he had been enabled to work and live in the world by an experience like that he created for Stephen in his novel, especially one which occurred precisely on the evening of June 16, 1904. But in my opinion, the statement he is making about himself in *Ulysses* is that he indeed did have such an experience, and furthermore that it began on that very evening.

Richard Ellmann's authoritative biography discloses that Joyce's first date (although not his first meeting) with his future wife, Nora Barnacle, occurred on the evening of June 16, 1904, and comments:

> To set *Ulysses* on this date was Joyce's most eloquent if indirect tribute to Nora, a recognition of the determining effect upon his life of his attachment to her. On June 16 he entered into relation with the world around him and left behind him the loneliness he had felt since his mother's death. He would tell her later, "You made me a man." June 16 was the sacred day that divided Stephen Dedalus, the insurgent youth, from Leopold Bloom, the complaisant husband.[20]

The suggestion that on June 16, 1904, Joyce changed from similarity to Stephen to similarity to Bloom may be set aside, for the novel discloses that Stephen himself changed. But this very fact—that "the insurgent youth" of *Ulysses* precisely "entered into relation with the world around him"—confirms the general point, which is that the correspondence between the fictional situation in which on a specific evening Stephen Dedalus' "youth" reached its "end" and the real situation in which on the same evening James Joyce began to be "made" "a man" is too close to be anything but significant. Joyce's tribute to his wife in his dating of *Ulysses* involves more than the mere arbitrary commemoration of the day their relationship began, which would have been a superficial, and in the fullest sense sentimental, imposition of autobiography on art. As his declaration to her that she "made me a man" suggests, he made the personal tribute because he regarded the date to have been significant for his own life in exactly the way he caused it to be significant for the life of his autobiographical projection. This could not be shown before the story of Stephen Dedalus on Bloomsday was clarified. By means of that story Joyce illuminates the known facts of his life at Stephen's age, and so adds a revealing chapter to his biography.

Therefore, while the day chosen for the novel is intrinsically functional, it also commemorates the hours when Nora began to show Joyce what Bloom showed Stephen and when she consequently began to rescue him as Bloom rescued Stephen. To have Bloom share Nora with Molly, who is conventionally compared to her in obvious ways, may seem shocking at first; but it is a less extreme adaptation of his human material than Joyce worked in other instances (the elements of himself in the despicable Mr. Deasy, for example), and speaks more for both his wit and his wisdom than the more apparent similarity between woman and woman.

In discussing the role of historical fact in the novel, I pointed out that when Stephen attributed to art "lyrical," "epical," and "dramatic" "forms" during his aesthetic discourse in the *Portrait,* he not only made a general statement about the stages of the process of artistic creation but, in addition, described the decade-long history of his creator's own autobiographical "portrait," from personal essay, through its intermediate "form," to fully realized work of art. Similarly, in making the day of *Ulysses* June 16, 1904, Joyce was able to combine a vital functional purpose with an autobiographical one. Indeed, his apparent "sacramental conception of the world" and his interest, in the light of that conception far more than just habit of mind, in correspondences both existing and created, suggest that his (historical) personal experience on that particular date motivated his constructing the story of the corresponding experience of Stephen Dedalus in such a way that the historical fact of the singular result of the Ascot Gold Cup horserace on that date *would* be a vital circumstantial element of that story.

The dazzling varieties of *Ulysses* are not merely contained in a harmonious and autonomous work but are transformed into the richest example of the art of fiction in history. The beauties of the unfolding of its story, the life it creates, and the achieved form of the whole are not themselves its end, for it embodies moral and philosophical high seriousness. Finally, Joyce extends his accomplishment with unfaltering finesse into the wholly separate dimension of autobiography.

The representation of the artist himself in his art, Stephen Dedalus is as specific a character as possible; but the young Joyce's nature makes Stephen also as general as possible— the model of the Western artist at the beginning of the modern era. Repelled by the reality around him, that artist tried for a time to escape from it to an exotic alternative: the age of belief, or a utopia of socialism and handicraft, or a pagan cosmology, or a private world of cultivated beauty. Finally, the *fin de siècle* ended; in the new century he faced that reality, dealt with it, and created one of the richest artistic periods in Western civilization. Proof of the ultimate achievement of the fledgling artist it calls "Stephen Dedalus," *Ulysses* also allegorizes the historical development in our culture of which *Ulysses* is a consummate example. The novel is a testament of both Joyce himself and the age.

1. Damon, in Givens, p. 227 ff.

2. Kenner, "The Portrait in Perspective," p. 172.

3. Blackmur, p. 102. Quoted from Cyril Connolly as from Baudelaire.

4. I am referring here to the fundamental opposition Dostoevsky presents in his novel between feeling and submission to the world, on the one hand, and thought and assertion of the self or ego, on the other. The extreme embodiment of the former is Marmeladov, who figuratively lives in the tavern, is a drunkard (without self-control, strength of ego), and finally allows the world to destroy him. The extreme embodiment of the latter is Svidrigailov, who cannot drink (will not relax his self-control—drink gives him a *head*-ache), and in his suicide commits the ultimate act of ego, self-destruction. Raskolnikov's "crime," his plotted murder of the pawnbroker, is an extreme assertion of the ego in despite of the divinely-created world. And such assertion, the cause of Svidrigailov's crimes, perversions, and suicide, is madness. This condition is opposed by Dostoevsky to the condition which he causes to express Marmeladov's equally reprehensible weak will: drunkeness. For example, while Marmeladov's place is the tavern, a public house, Raskolnikov's at this time is his tiny yellow-walled room; and on more than one occasion before he begins to liberate himself from his "disease" of egotism by kissing the created earth at a place which forms a cross and at which people congregate, Raskolnikov finds temporary relief from that extremity in beer or a visit to a tavern.

Joyce is not so simply theocentric as Dostoevsky, but the similarity between the story of Stephen and that of Raskolnikov is striking.

5. The prayer has been adopted by the organization Alcoholics Anonymous; the present wording is attributed to Reinhold Niebuhr.

6. M. R. Adamson (trans.), London, 1950.

7. Maritain, p. 19.

8. "The Renaissance sense of abounding life, that joy in the comprehension of the world and in freedom, the impetus towards scientific discovery, its creative rapture and delight in the beauty of sensible forms reveal an inextricable mingling of natural and christian sources"—*Ibid.*, p. 17.

9. New Haven, 1950.

10. Mahood, p. 20.

11. Austin Warren, *Rage for Order* (Chicago, 1948), p. 2.

12. René Wellek and Austin Warren, *Theory of Literature* (New York, 1949), p. 203.

13. *Ibid.*, p. 205.

14. Warren, p. 2.

15. Levin, p. 134.

16. At the beginning of February, 1904; see *James Joyce*, pp. 152–53.

17. *Ibid.*, p. 169.

18. *Ibid.* Ellmann dates the story on the bases of a letter from George Russell suggesting that Joyce try to write a short story for the *Irish Homestead* and a letter accepting "The Sisters" and enclosing payment from H. F. Norman, the editor, both of which are extant. No extant manuscript of a short story is dated earlier (see John J. Slocum and Herbert Cahoon, *A Bibliography of James Joyce [1882–1941]* [New Haven, 1953]), and there is no evidence that any was written before it.

19. *Ibid.;* see also *ibid.*, p. 774, n. 56.

20. *Ibid.*, pp. 162–63.

index

Characters (as distinguished from names merely mentioned) and certain other elements in Joyce's works are listed and marked by asterisks. References to other literary and operatic characters and all literary and musical works are listed under the names of the authors and composers.

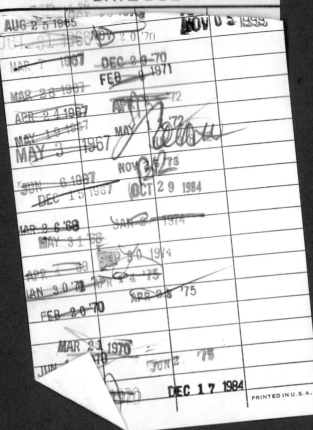

DATE DUE

AUG 2 5 1965		NOV 0 5 1999
OCT 31 1966	NOV 2 0 '70	
MAR 7 1967	DEC 2 9 '70	
	FEB 9 1971	
MAR 2 8 1967		
APR 2 4 1967	APR 72	
MAY 1 9 1967	MAY '72	
MAY 3 1967	NOV 5 73	
JUN 6 1967		
DEC 1 5 1967	OCT 2 9 1984	
MAR 2 6 '68	JAN 1974	
MAY 3 1 68		
APR 69	SEP 3 0 1974	
JAN 3 0 71	APR 1 4 75	
FEB 2 0 '70	APR 2 8 '75	
MAR 2 3 1970		
JUN 70	JUN 2 '75	
70	DEC 1 7 1984	

PRINTED IN U.S.A.